An Introduction to Critical Reading

THIRD EDITION

TOM BARNWELL
LEAH McCRANEY

University of Alabama at Birmingham

Harcourt Brace College Publishers

Fort Worth   Philadelphia   San Diego   New York   Orlando   Austin   San Antonio
Toronto   Montreal   London   Sydney   Tokyo

Publisher	Christopher P. Klein
Senior Acquisitions Editor	Carol Wada
Project Editor	Kathryn Stewart
Production Manager	Jane Tyndall Ponceti
Art Director	Jeanette Barber
Photo Researcher	Lili Weiner
Permissions Editor	Cristi Grider

Cover Image	Ralph Fasanell, *The Great Strike—Lawrence 1912*, 1978, 65 x 118, Oil on canvas

Some material in this work previously appeared in INTRODUCTION TO CRITICAL READING, Second Edition, copyright © 1994, 1990 by Holt, Rinehart and Winston, Inc. All rights reserved.

Supplements: Harcourt Brace & Company may provide complimentary instructional aids and supplements or supplement packages to those adopters qualified under our adoption policy. Please contact your sales representative for more information. If as an adopter or potential user you receive supplements you do not need, please return them to your sales representative or send them to: Attn: Returns Department, Troy Warehouse, 465 South Lincoln Drive, Troy, MO 63379.

Address for Editorial Correspondence: Harcourt Brace College Publishers, 301 Commerce Street, Suite 3700, Fort Worth, TX 76102

Address for Orders: Harcourt Brace College Publishers, 6277 Sea Harbor Drive, Orlando, FL 32887
1-800-782-4479, or 1-800-433-0001 (in Florida)

(Copyright Acknowledgments begin on page 329, which constitutes a continuation of this copyright page.)

ISBN: 0-15-503441-3

Library of Congress Catalog Card Number: 96-76291

Printed in the United States of America

6 7 8 9 0 1 2 3 4 5   0 6 6   9 8 7 6 5 4 3 2 1

An Introduction to Critical Reading

THIRD EDITION

For Traci, Dot, and Britt
and
In memory of Frank, Lindy, Linnie, and Tim

Preface

To the Instructor

An Introduction to Critical Reading is an anthology of poems, short stories, essays, and college textbook chapters. The instructor's manual that accompanies the anthology presents an approach to developmental reading that departs from the traditional, skills-based approach. The manual suggests ways of using the pieces in the anthology to improve reading skills and critical thinking. The anthology is different from other developmental reading texts in its rationale and in its content.

The pieces in the anthology were selected not on the basis of a "readability formula," but because they are representative of the materials college students are required to read and because they encourage critical thinking. The selections for each genre present a range of difficulties, permitting instructors to choose texts appropriate to the abilities of their specific classes. Texts containing extensive literary allusions or problems of style, such as stream of consciousness, are not included. Such pieces require more time than the primary purposes of a reading course allow.

The selections were also made with critical thinking and critical reading in mind. A detailed discussion of critical thinking, a term that has a variety of meanings, is included in the introductory essay of the instructor's manual. Suffice it to say that the heart of critical thinking is an active, personal involvement stemming from a desire "to know." Students who become actively involved in a text will eventually come to terms with it. This does not mean students will understand all of the information contained in a piece or make every possible inference. But most college students, regardless of their developmental status, can discern the essential message of a piece if they want "to know." The pieces in the anthology revolve around issues that are of interest to most readers: family, relationships, society, and so forth. The selections also reflect the cultural diversity of college readers. Roughly half of the selections are by women and nonwhite writers.

To eliminate some problems of comprehension and to provide the best possible opportunity for active involvement, the anthology provides the following aids:

1. Definitions of difficult words that are not defined in context
2. Explanatory notes on allusions to literature, history, art, and so on
3. A glossary that includes definitions and examples of common literary and rhetorical devices

The anthology does not include questions on the content of the pieces. The instructor's manual discusses the importance of encouraging student questions and student-generated criteria. Questions that come from editors invite a mechanical investigation of what the editors think to be important. Such an investigation limits the possibilities of a piece of writing and limits student thinking to those points addressed by the questions. There is a need, of course, for some teacher questions and teacher-generated criteria. The instructor's manual provides such criteria, not only for evaluating the content of a piece, but also for developing critical thinking. The suggestions in the manual are not meant to limit the teacher's approach, but to suggest typical questions that can accomplish specific goals.

The apparatus is in the instructor's manual. None is included in the anthology for the following reasons:

1. Students tend either to ignore explanatory material or to embrace it so completely that they do not go beyond it and think independently.
2. Students become better readers by reading—not by being told how to read.
3. Textbook generalizations about how an adult *should* read, how "good" readers read, and what a reader should glean from a piece of writing exclude consideration of the great variety of effective reading styles and of the possible differences in readers' interpretations.
4. An instructor's ideas about the reading process or about a "good" college reader are far more suitable for that teacher's actual audience than a textbook apparatus written for an implied audience.

The instructor's manual contains the following:

1. An introductory essay, providing teachers with the rationale for the anthology, explaining the nature of critical thinking, and providing general guidelines for helping students develop critical thinking
2. A discussion of each selection in the anthology, explicating contents and pointing out issues that teachers may want to explore in class discussions
3. Specific suggestions for each piece contained in the anthology. These suggestions are intended to involve students in the content of the piece and to encourage the development of critical thinking. Cross-genre studies are suggested frequently to assist those instructors who prefer such studies to the genre-by-genre approach.

The method recommended in the instructor's manual is practical. It not only results in measurable improvement, but it also encourages positive treatment of students whose egos may be fragile. The philosophy of the approach presented in this textbook corresponds to the motto of the Scripps Howard newspapers: "Give light and the people will find their own way." The light students need is the practice of critical thinking—a tool that is needed regardless of the direction they take.

Acknowledgments

We would like to thank Professor Mary Flowers Braswell, Department of English, University of Alabama at Birmingham. Her keen interest, astute observations, and thoughtful suggestions, as well as her unwavering friendship, have been invaluable to us, both professionally and personally. We also thank Carol Wada of Harcourt Brace. Her enthusiasm, insight and direction have greatly improved this edition, and her patience and flexibility have been sincerely appreciated.

For various types of assistance and kindness, we thank the following: Bert Andrews, Susan Blair, Henny and Milton Bordwin, Malka Bordwin, Judy Boyer, Tom Brown, Sid Burgess, Jason Burnett, John Coley, Stella Cocoris, Robby Cox, Keith Cullen, Tim Douglas, Betty Duff, Barbara Enlow, Paula Fulton, Delores Gallo, Al Gardener, Travis Gordon, John Haggerty, Barbara Hill, Helen

Jackson, Felicia Johnson, Tracey Kell, Marilyn Kurata, Susan Mitchell, Stephen Morris, Mark Myers, Rose Norman, Iris and Colm O'Dunlaing, Jane Patton, Bob Penny, Terry Proctor, Candace Ridington, Beebe Roberts, Dave Roberts, Penny Sanchez, Eluteria Torrez Sanchez, Richard Torrez Sanchez, John Schnorrenberg, Melissa Tate, Reuben Triplett, John Walker, Barbara Williams, and Traci Ziegler.

Thanks as well to following reviewers: Dorothy Hoffner, Union Community College; Patricia DeLessio, Dutchess Community College; Joyce Kammeraad, Inver Hills Community College; Anne Lehman, Milwaukee Area Technical College; Rose Wassman, De Anza College; and Janet Elder, Richland College.

Finally, we thank our students, who always remind us that meaningful learning involves reaching beyond what one can grasp.

To the Student

The readings in this book were selected for a number of reasons. First, they are all excellent pieces of writing. Second, they comprise a representative sample of four common types of writing: poetry, fiction, essays, and textbook chapters. Third, they are thought-provoking.

This third reason is of utmost importance to the purposes of this book. Meaningful learning occurs when one is actively involved in the learning process, when one finds something in the process that is of personal importance. The majority of readings in this book offer ideas that are likely to be important to most readers. Literature in particular offers a field of universal ideas—after all, the essence of literature is life—and this is one reason such a wide variety of literature has been included.

Reading allows one the opportunity to examine one's own principles and the principles of others. The Socratic position is that the unexamined life is not worth living. This position suggests that one must value one's own thinking and judgment. It is grounded in the belief that examining—questioning—is the foundation for being free.

Contents

PART III   ESSAYS   173

PART IV   TEXTBOOK CHAPTERS   251

1

Poetry

Lot's Wife

Kristine Batey

While Lot, the conscience of a nation,
struggles with the Lord,
she struggles with the housework.
The City of Sin is where
5   she raises the children.
Ba'al or Adonai—
Whoever is God—
the bread must still be made
and the doorsills swept.

10   The Lord may kill the children tomorrow,
but today they must be bathed and fed.
Well and good to condemn your neighbor's religion;
but weren't they there
when the baby was born,
15   and when the well collapsed?
While her husband communes with God,
she tucks the children into bed.
In the morning when he tells her of the judgment,
she puts down the lamp she is cleaning
20   and calmly begins to pack.
In between bundling up the children
and deciding what will go,
she runs for a moment
to say goodbye to the herd,
25   gently patting each soft head
with tears in her eyes for the animals that will not understand.
She smiles blindly to the woman
who held her hand at childbed.
It is easy for eyes that have always turned to heaven
30   not to look back;
those that have been—by necessity—drawn to earth
cannot forget that life is lived from day to day.
Good, to a God, and good in human terms
are two different things?
35   On the breast of the hill, she chooses to be human,
and turns, in farewell—
and never regrets
the sacrifice.

NOTES
Ba'al or Adonai (l. 6): Ba'al was the name for the Canaanite god of Lot's time;
Adonai is one of the names of the Hebrew god.
communes (l. 16): communicates
at childbed (l. 28): at childbirth

Genesis 19:12–26

1   The two angels said to Lot, "Have you anyone else here, sons-in-law, sons or daughters, or any who belong to you in the city? Get them out of this place, because we are going to destroy it. The outcry against it has been so great that the Lord has sent us to destroy it." So Lot went out and spoke to his intended sons-in-law. He said, "Be quick and leave this place; the Lord is going to destroy the city." But they did not take him seriously.

2   As soon as it was dawn, the angels urged Lot to go, saying, "Be quick, take your wife and your two daughters who are here, or you will be swept away when the city is punished." When he lingered, they took him by the hand, with his wife and his daughters, and, because the Lord had spared him, led him on until he was outside the city. When they had brought them out, they said, "Flee for your lives; do not look back and do not stop anywhere in the Plain. Flee to the hills or you will be swept away." Lot replied, "No, sirs. You have shown your servant favour and you have added to your unfailing care for me by saving my life, but I cannot escape to the hills; I shall be overtaken by the disaster, and die. Look, here is a town, only a small place, near enough for me to reach quickly. Let me escape to it—it is very small—and save my life." He said to him, "I grant your request: I will not overthrow this town you speak of. But flee there quickly, because I can do nothing until you are there." That is why the place is called Zoar. The sun had risen over the land as Lot entered Zoar; and then the Lord rained down fire and brimstone from the skies on Sodom and Gomorrah. He overthrew those cities and destroyed all the Plain, with everyone living there and everything growing in the ground. But Lot's wife, behind him, looked back, and she turned into a pillar of salt.

NOTES
two angels (par. 1): messengers sent by God
Zoar (par. 2): The word means "small."

Richard Cory

E. A. Robinson

Whenever Richard Cory went down town,
We people on the pavement looked at him;
He was a gentleman from sole to crown,
Clean favored, and imperially slim.

5   And he was always quietly arrayed,
And he was always human when he talked;
But still he fluttered pulses when he said,
"Good-morning," and he glittered when he walked.
And he was rich—yes, richer than a king—
10   And admirably schooled in every grace:
In fine, we thought that he was everything
To make us wish that we were in his place.

So on we worked, and waited for the light,
And went without the meat, and cursed the bread;
15   And Richard Cory, one calm summer night,
Went home and put a bullet through his head.

NOTES
imperially (l. 4): royally
arrayed (l. 5): finely dressed
In fine (l. 11): in short or in summary

The Road Not Taken

Robert Frost

Two roads diverged in a yellow wood,
And sorry I could not travel both
And be one traveler, long I stood
And looked down one as far as I could
5   To where it bent in the undergrowth;

Then took the other, as just as fair,
And having perhaps the better claim,
Because it was grassy and wanted wear;
Though as for that, the passing there
10   Had worn them really about the same,

And both that morning equally lay
In leaves no step had trodden black.
Oh, I kept the first for another day!
Yet knowing how way leads on to way,
15   I doubted if I should ever come back.

I shall be telling this with a sigh
Somewhere ages and ages hence:
Two roads diverged in a wood, and I—
I took the one less traveled by,
20   And that has made all the difference.

NOTES
Two roads diverged (l. 1): The road became two roads that went in different directions.
undergrowth (l. 5): plants or bushes growing beneath trees
wanted wear (l. 8): lacked or needed wear
trodden (l. 12): crushed
hence (l. 17): from this time

I, Too

Langston Hughes

I, too, sing America.

I am the darker brother.
They send me to eat in the kitchen
When company comes,
5   But I laugh,
And eat well,
And grow strong.

Tomorrow,
I'll sit at the table
10   When company comes.
Nobody'll dare
Say to me,
"Eat in the kitchen,"
Then.

15   Besides,
They'll see how beautiful I am
And be ashamed—

I, too, am America.

Harlem

Langston Hughes

What happens to a dream deferred?

Does it dry up
like a raisin in the sun?
Or fester like a sore—
5   And then run?
Does it stink like rotten meat?
Or crust and sugar over—
like a syrupy sweet?

Maybe it just sags
10   like a heavy load.

Or does it explode?

NOTES
Harlem (title): an area of New York City, predominantly African-American
deferred (l. 1): postponed or put off
fester (l. 4) and *run* (l. 5): "Fester" refers to the swelling of inflamed tissue; when the tissue opens, pus is released or "runs."
crust and sugar over. . . (ll. 7–8): After a period of time, a sugary crust will form on some syrupy sweets (such as jelly and honey).

Mother to Son

Langston Hughes

Well, son, I'll tell you:
Life for me ain't been no crystal stair.
It's had tacks in it,
And splinters,
5 And boards torn up,
And places with no carpet on the floor—
Bare.
But all the time
I'se been a-climbin' on,
10 And reachin' landin's
And turnin' corners,
And sometimes goin' in the dark
Where there ain't been no light.
So, boy, don't you turn back.
15 Don't you set down on the steps
'Cause you finds it kinder hard.
Don't you fall now—
For I'se still goin', honey,
I'se still climbin',
20 And life for me ain't been no crystal stair.

Those Winter Sundays

Robert Hayden

Sundays too my father got up early
and put his clothes on in the blueblack cold,
then with cracked hands that ached
from labor in the weekday weather made
5 banked fires blaze. No one ever thanked him.

I'd wake and hear the cold splintering, breaking.
When the rooms were warm, he'd call,
and slowly I would rise and dress,
fearing the chronic angers of that house,

10 Speaking indifferently to him,
who had driven out the cold
and polished my good shoes as well.
What did I know, what did I know
of love's austere and lonely offices?

NOTES
banked fires (l. 5): fires that have been smothered with ashes so that the coals will
remain hot and can be used later to start another fire
chronic (l. 9): frequently occurring
austere (l. 14): marked by self-denial or self-discipline

A Red Palm

Gary Soto

You're in this dream of cotton plants.
You raise a hoe, swing, and the first weeds
Fall with a sigh. You take another step,
Chop, and the sigh comes again,
5   Until you yourself are breathing that way
With each step, a sigh that will follow you into town.

That's hours later. The sun is a red blister
Coming up in your palm. Your back is strong,
Young, not yet the broken chair
10 In an abandoned school of dry spiders.
Dust settles on your forehead, dirt
Smiles under each fingernail.
You chop, step, and by the end of the first row,
You can buy one splendid fish for wife
15 And three sons. Another row, another fish,
Until you have enough and move on to milk,
Bread, meat. Ten hours and the cupboards creak.
You can rest in the back yard under a tree.
Your hands twitch on your lap,
20 Not unlike the fish on a pier or the bottom
Of a boat. You drink iced tea. The minutes jerk
Like flies.
        It's dusk, now night,
And the lights in your home are on.
25 That costs money, yellow light
In the kitchen. That's thirty steps,
You say to your hands,
Now shaped into binoculars.
You could raise them to your eyes:
30 You were a fool in school, now look at you.
You're a giant among cotton plants,
The lung-shaped leaves that run breathing for miles.

Now you see your oldest boy, also running.
Papa, he says, it's time to come in.
35 You pull him into your lap
And ask, What's forty times nine?
He knows as well as you, and you smile.
The wind makes peace with the trees,
The stars strike themselves in the dark.
40 You get up and walk with the sigh of cotton plants.
You go to sleep with a red sun on your palm,
The sore light you see when you first stir in bed.

Daystar

Rita Dove

She wanted a little room for thinking:
but she saw diapers steaming on the line,
a doll slumped behind the door.

So she lugged a chair behind the garage
5 to sit out the children's naps.
Sometimes there were things to watch—
the pinched armor of a vanished cricket,
a floating maple leaf. Other days
she stared until she was assured
10 when she closed her eyes
she'd see only her own vivid blood.

She had an hour, at best, before Liza appeared
pouting from the top of the stairs.
And just *what* was mother doing
15 out back with the field mice? Why,

building a palace. Later
that night when Thomas rolled over and
lurched into her, she would open her eyes
and think of the place that was hers
20 for an hour—where
she was nothing,
pure nothing, in the middle of the day.

Once a Lady Told Me

Nikki Giovanni

like my mother and her grandmother before
i paddle around the house
in soft-soled shoes
chasing ghosts from corners
5 with incense
they are such a disturbance my ghosts
they break my bric-a-brac and make
me forget to turn my heating stove

the children say you must come to live
10 with us all my life i told them i've lived
with you now i shall live with myself

the grandchildren say it's disgraceful
you in this dark house with the curtains
pulled snuff dripping from your chin
15 would they be happier if i smoked cigarettes

i was very exquisite once very small and well courted
some would say a beauty when my hair was plaited
and i was bustled up

my children wanted my life
20 and now they want my death

but i shall pad around my house
in my purple soft-soled shoes
i'm very happy now
it's not so very neat, you know, but it's my
25 life

Four Poems from
Spoon River Anthology

Edgar Lee Masters

MINERVA JONES

I AM Minerva, the village poetess,
Hooted at, jeered at by the Yahoos of the street
For my heavy body, cock-eye, and rolling walk,
And all the more when "Butch" Weldy
5 Captured me after a brutal hunt.
He left me to my fate with Doctor Meyers;
And I sank into death, growing numb from the feet up,
Like one stepping deeper and deeper into a stream of ice.
Will some one go to the village newspaper,
10 And gather into a book the verses I wrote?—
I thirsted so for love!
I hungered so for life!

NOTES
Spoon River Anthology: a collection of poems about the citizens of Spoon River, a
community invented by the poet; each poem is an epitaph, an inscription on the
tomb in memory of the person buried there
Yahoos (l. 2): coarse, rude persons

"INDIGNATION" JONES

YOU would not believe, would you,
That I came from good Welsh stock?
That I was purer blooded than the white trash here?
And of more direct lineage than the New Englanders
5 And Virginians of Spoon River?
You would not believe that I had been to school
And read some books.
You saw me only as a run-down man,
With matted hair and beard
10 And ragged clothes.
Sometimes a man's life turns into a cancer
From being bruised and continually bruised,

And swells into a purplish mass,
Like growths on stalks of corn.
15 Here was I, a carpenter, mired in a bog of life
Into which I walked, thinking it was a meadow,
With a slattern for a wife, and poor Minerva, my daughter,
Whom you tormented and drove to death.
So I crept, crept, like a snail through the days
20 Of my life.
No more you hear my footsteps in the morning,
Resounding on the hollow sidewalk,
Going to the grocery store for a little corn meal
And a nickel's worth of bacon.

NOTES

Welsh (l. 2): descended from a native of Wales, an area in southwest Great Britain
trash (l. 3): worthless people
lineage (l. 4): line of descent from ancestors
mired (l. 15): stuck
bog (l. 15): literally, a swamp-like area
slattern (l. 17): an untidy or immoral woman

DOCTOR MEYERS

NO other man, unless it was Doc Hill,
Did more for people in this town than I.
And all the weak, the halt, the improvident
And those who could not pay flocked to me.
5 I was good-hearted, easy Doctor Meyers.
I was healthy, happy, in comfortable fortune,
Blest with a congenial mate, my children raised,
All wedded, doing well in the world.
And then one night, Minerva, the poetess,
10 Came to me in her trouble, crying.
I tried to help her out—she died—
They indicted me, the newspapers disgraced me,
My wife perished of a broken heart.
And pneumonia finished me.

NOTES

halt (l. 3): crippled
improvident (l. 3): those who do not prepare for the future
congenial (l. 7): pleasant and harmonious
indicted (l. 12): to be charged with a crime by a jury

MRS. MEYERS

HE protested all his life long
The newspapers lied about him villainously;
That he was not at fault for Minerva's fall,
But only tried to help her.
5 Poor soul so sunk in sin he could not see

That even trying to help her, as he called it,
He had broken the law human and divine.
Passers by, an ancient admonition to you:
If your ways would be ways of pleasantness,

10   And all your pathways peace,
Love God and keep his commandments.

NOTES
villainously (l. 2): viciously
divine (l. 7): relating to God
admonition (l. 8): warning

The Chimney Sweeper
from *Songs of Innocence*

William Blake

When my mother died I was very young,
And my father sold me while yet my tongue
Could scarcely cry "'weep! 'weep! 'weep! 'weep!"
So your chimneys I sweep & in soot I sleep.

5   There's little Tom Dacre, who cried when his head,
That curl'd like a lamb's back, was shav'd, so I said,
"Hush, Tom! never mind it, for when your head's bare,
You know that the soot cannot spoil your white hair."

And so he was quiet, & that very night,
10   As Tom was a-sleeping he had such a sight!
That thousands of sweepers, Dick, Joe, Ned, & Jack,
Were all of them lock'd up in coffins of black;

And by came an Angel who had a bright key,
And he open'd the coffins & set them all free;
15   Then down a green plain, leaping, laughing they run,
And wash in a river and shine in the Sun.

Then naked & white, all their bags left behind,
They rise upon clouds, and sport in the wind.
And the Angel told Tom, if he'd be a good boy,
20   He'd have God for his father & never want joy.

And so Tom awoke; and we rose in the dark
And got with our bags & our brushes to work.
Tho' the morning was cold, Tom was happy & warm;
So if all do their duty, they need not fear harm.

NOTES
'weep (l. 3): sweep. Chimney sweepers would advertise their service by walking the streets and calling out "Sweep!" This child is so young that he cannot plainly pronounce the word.

The Chimney Sweeper
from *Songs of Experience*

William Blake

A little black thing among the snow
Crying "'weep, 'weep," in notes of woe!
"Where are thy father & mother? say?"
"They are both gone up to the church to pray.

5 "Because I was happy upon the heath,
And smil'd among the winter's snow;
They clothed me in the clothes of death,
And taught me to sing the notes of woe.

"And because I am happy, & dance & sing,
10 They think they have done me no injury,
And are gone to praise God & his Priest & King,
Who make up a heaven of our misery."

NOTES
'weep (l. 2): See note to preceding poem.
heath (l. 5): an area of land covered with small bushes

Channel Firing

Thomas Hardy

That night your great guns, unawares,
Shook all our coffins as we lay,
And broke the chancel window-squares,
We thought it was the Judgment-day

5 And sat upright. While drearisome
Arose the howl of wakened hounds:
The mouse let fall the altar-crumb,
The worms drew back into the mounds,

The glebe cow drooled. Till God called, "No;
10 It's gunnery practice out at sea
Just as before you went below;
The world is as it used to be:

"All nations striving strong to make
Red war yet redder. Mad as hatters
15 They do no more for Christés sake
Than you who are helpless in such matters.

"That it is not the judgment-hour
For some of them's a blessed thing,
For if it were they'd have to scour
20   Hell's floor for so much threatening. . . .

"Ha, ha. It will be warmer when
I blow the trumpet (if indeed
I ever do; for you are men,
And rest eternal sorely need)."

25   So down we lay again. "I wonder,
Will the world ever saner be,"
Said one, "than when He sent us under
In our indifferent century!"

And many a skeleton shook his head.
30   "Instead of preaching forty year,"
My neighbor Parson Thirdly said,
"I wish I had stuck to pipes and beer."

Again the guns disturbed the hour,
Roaring their readiness to avenge,
35   As far inland as Stourton Tower,
And Camelot, and starlit Stonehenge.

NOTES

Channel Firing (title): The channel referred to is the English Channel; the firing is the gunnery practice of British ships in preparation for war. World War I began four months after this poem was written.

unawares (l. 1): unexpectedly

chancel (l. 3): the part of a church containing the altar

Judgment-day (l. 4): the day of God's judgment of man. Another reference to Judgment day is "blow the trumpet" (l. 22), a signal that Judgment day has begun.

drearisome (l. 5): sadly

altar-crumb (l. 7): a crumb of bread left from communion

glebe (l. 9): a plot of land providing income for a parish church

Mad as hatters (l. 14): a phrase made popular by Lewis Carroll in *Alice in Wonderland.* The idea that hatters are mad or insane probably comes from the behavior of hatters who used the chemical mercurous nitrate in making hats; exposure to this chemical can cause a nervous disorder known as St. Vitus's Dance.

Christés (l. 15): Christ's

scour (l. 19): to clean by vigorous scrubbing

sorely (l. 24): desperately

avenge (l. 34): to get revenge

Stourton Tower (l. 35): a memorial erected to commemorate King Alfred's defeat of the Danes in 879 A.D.

Camelot (l. 36): the legendary location of King Arthur's court

Stonehenge (l. 36): located in Wiltshire, England, the remains of a circle formed with large stones, probably a place of worship for an ancient people

Dulce et Decorum Est

Wilfred Owen

Bent double, like old beggars under sacks,
Knock-kneed, coughing like hags, we cursed through sludge,
Till on the haunting flares we turned our backs,
And towards our distant rest began to trudge.
5 Men marched asleep. Many had lost their boots,
But limped on, blood-shod. All went lame, all blind;
Drunk with fatigue; deaf even to the hoots
Of Five-Nines dropping softly behind.

Gas! GAS! Quick, boys!— An ecstasy of fumbling,
10 Fitting the clumsy helmets just in time,
But someone still was yelling out and stumbling
And flound'ring like a man in fire or lime.—
Dim through the misty panes and thick green light,
As under a green sea, I saw him drowning.

15 In all my dreams before my helpless sight
He plunges at me, guttering, choking, drowning.

If in some smothering dreams, you too could pace
Behind the wagon that we flung him in,
And watch the white eyes writhing in his face,
20 His hanging face, like a devil's sick of sin,
If you could hear, at every jolt, the blood
Come gargling from the froth-corrupted lungs,
Obscene as cancer, bitter as the cud
Of vile, incurable sores on innocent tongues—
25 My friend, you would not tell with such high zest
To children ardent for some desperate glory,
The old lie: *Dulce et decorum est*
Pro patria mori.

NOTES

Dulce et Decorum Est (title): a quotation from Horace (Roman poet). The entire statement is given in the last two lines and means "It is sweet and fitting to die for one's country." The action referred to in the poem occurs in World War I, in which Wilfred Owen died a week before the fighting ended.
flares (l. 3): devices containing an explosive material that lights the sky
blood-shod (l. 6): "Shod" literally means wearing shoes.
Five-Nines (l. 8): exploding shells of poisonous gas
ecstasy (l. 9): furious activity
flound'ring (l. 12): floundering: struggling
lime (l. 12): an acid-like chemical
guttering (l. 16): harsh sounds made deep in the throat
writhing (l. 19): twisting in pain
froth-corrupted (l. 22): filled with foam
cud (l. 23): literally, something that is chewed; a wad
vile (l. 24): repulsive
zest (l. 25): great enthusiasm
ardent (l. 26): full of desire

Pieter Bruegel, the Elder, *Landscape with the Fall of Icarus.*

—Patrimoine Des Musées Royaux Des Beaux-Arts, Bruxelles.

Musée des Beaux Arts

W.H. Auden

About suffering they were never wrong,
The Old Masters: how well they understood
Its human position; how it takes place
While someone else is eating or opening a window or just walking dully along;
5 How, when the aged are reverently, passionately waiting
For the miraculous birth, there always must be
Children who did not specially want it to happen; skating
On a pond at the edge of the wood:
They never forgot
10 That even the dreadful martyrdom must run its course
Anyhow in a corner, some untidy spot
Where the dogs go on with their doggy life and the torturer's horse
Scratches its innocent behind on a tree.

In Brueghel's *Icarus*, for instance: how everything turns away
15 Quite leisurely from the disaster; the plowman may
Have heard the splash, the forsaken cry,
But for him it was not an important failure; the sun shone
As it had to on the white legs disappearing into the green
Water; and the expensive delicate ship that must have seen
20 Something amazing, a boy falling out of the sky,
Had somewhere to get to and sailed calmly on.

NOTES
Musée des Beaux Arts (title): Museum of Fine Arts. The **Old Masters** (l. 2) are the great painters of the Renaissance; one of the Old Masters was **Brueghel** (l. 14), whose painting, *Landscape with the Fall of Icarus*, is discussed in the last stanza of the poem and is reproduced on p. 16. The painting is based on a story from Greek Mythology. Icarus and his father made wings of wax and feathers in order to escape from the maze where they had been imprisoned by King Minos. Using their wings, they flew out of the maze, but Icarus, thrilled by his ability to fly like a bird, unwisely flew too close to the sun. The wax melted, his wings came apart, and he fell into the Aegean Sea and drowned.
reverently (l. 5): with great respect
miraculous birth (l. 6): afterlife
martyrdom (l. 10): suffering death for a worthwhile cause, especially a religious cause

The Accident

Willie Morris

    One afternoon in late August, as the summer's sun streamed into the car and made little jumping shadows on the windows, I sat gazing out at the tenement-dwellers, who were themselves looking out of their windows from the gray crumbling buildings along the tracks of upper Manhattan. As we crossed
5 into the Bronx, the train unexpectedly slowed down for a few miles. Suddenly

from out of my window I saw a large crowd near the tracks, held back by two policemen. Then, on the other side, from my window, I saw a sight I will never be able to forget: a little boy almost severed in halves, lying at an in-credible angle near the track. The ground was covered with blood, and the
10   boy's eyes were opened wide, strained and disbelieving in his sudden obliv-ion. A policeman stood next to him, his arms folded, staring straight ahead at the windows of our train. In the orange glow of late afternoon the police-men, the crowd, the corpse of the boy were for a brief moment immobile, mo-tionless, a small tableau to violence and death in the city. Behind me, in the
15   next row of seats, there was a game of bridge. I heard one of the four men say as he looked at the sight, "God, that's horrible." Another said, in a whisper, "Terrible, terrible." There was a momentary silence, punctuated only by the clicking of the wheels on the track. Then, after a pause, I heard the first man say: "Two hearts."

NOTES
tenement-dwellers: people who live in run-down, low-rent apartment buildings
Manhattan and the Bronx: areas of New York City
oblivion: loss of consciousness
tableau to: picture of
Two hearts: a bid in the game of bridge

To a Friend Whose Work Has Come to Triumph

Anne Sexton

Consider Icarus, pasting those sticky wings on,
testing that strange little tug at his shoulder blade,
and think of that first flawless moment over the lawn
of the labyrinth. Think of the difference it made!
5   There below are the trees, as awkward as camels;
and here are the shocked starlings pumping past
and think of innocent Icarus who is doing quite well:
larger than a sail, over the fog and the blast
of the plushy ocean, he goes. Admire his wings!
10   Feel the fire at his neck and see how casually
he glances up and is caught, wondrously tunneling
into that hot eye. Who cares that he fell back to the sea?
See him acclaiming the sun and come plunging down
while his sensible daddy goes straight into town.

NOTES
Icarus (l. 1): According to Greek mythology, King Minos was enraged that Daedalus, the father of Icarus, had helped Theseus escape from his *labyrinth* (l. 4), or maze. He imprisoned Daedalus and Icarus in the labyrinth. They escaped by making wings of wax and feathers and flying out of it. Icarus, thrilled by his ability to fly like a bird, unwisely flew too close to the sun. The wax melted, his wings came apart, and he fell into the Aegean Sea and drowned.
acclaiming (l. 13): praising

Barbie Doll

Marge Piercy

This girlchild was born as usual
and presented dolls that did pee-pee
and miniature GE stoves and irons
and wee lipsticks the color of cherry candy.
5   Then in the magic of puberty, a classmate said:
You have a great big nose and fat legs.

She was healthy, tested intelligent,
possessed strong arms and back,
abundant sexual drive and manual dexterity.
10   She went to and fro apologizing.
Everyone saw a fat nose on thick legs.

She was advised to play coy,
exhorted to come on hearty,
exercise, diet, smile and wheedle.
15   Her good nature wore out
like a fan belt.
So she cut off her nose and legs
and offered them up.

In the casket displayed on satin she lay
20   with the undertaker's cosmetics painted on,
a turned-up putty nose,
dressed in a pink and white nightie.
Doesn't she look pretty? everyone said.
Consummation at last.
25   To every woman a happy ending.

NOTES
dexterity (l. 9): skillfulness
coy (l. 12): pretended shyness or "cuteness"
exhorted (l. 13): strongly urged or advised
wheedle (l. 14): to influence by flattery
consummation (l. 24): completion or fulfillment of a goal

Mr. Z

M. Carl Holman

Taught early that his mother's skin was the sign of error,
He dressed and spoke the perfect part of honor;
Won scholarships, attended the best schools,
Disclaimed kinship with jazz and spirituals;
5   Chose prudent, raceless views for each situation,
Or when he could not cleanly skirt dissension,
Faced up to the dilemma, firmly seized
Whatever ground was Anglo-Saxonized.

In diet, too, his practice was exemplary:
10   Of pork in its profane forms he was wary;
Expert in vintage wines, sauces and salads,
His palate shrank from cornbread, yams and collards.

He was as careful whom he chose to kiss:
His bride had somewhere lost her Jewishness,
15   But kept her blue eyes; an Episcopalian
Prelate proclaimed them matched chameleon.
Choosing the right addresses, here, abroad,
They shunned those places where they might be barred;
Even less anxious to be asked to dine
20   Where hosts catered to kosher accent or exotic skin.
And so he climbed, unclogged by ethnic weights,
An airborne plant, flourishing without roots.
Not one false note was struck—until he died:
His subtly grieving widow could have flayed
25   The obit writers, ringing crude changes on a clumsy phrase:
"One of the most distinguished members of his race."

NOTES

disclaimed (l. 4): refused to claim
prudent (l. 5): wise, reasonable
skirt dissension (l. 6): avoid disagreement
dilemma (l. 7): a complex problem
Anglo-Saxonized (l. 8): dominated by Anglo-Saxon thinking, that is, "white" thinking
exemplary (l. 9): worth imitating
profane (l. 10): crude, coarse
wary (l. 10): cautious
vintage (l. 11): fine
palate (l. 12): taste buds
shrank from (l. 12): rejected
Prelate (l. 16): a high-ranking church official, such as a bishop
chameleon (l. 16): literally, a lizard with the ability to change its color
shunned (l. 18): avoided
barred (l. 18): not allowed to enter
catered to (l. 20): provided what was needed or desired
kosher (l. 20): literally, approved by Jewish law
exotic (l. 20): strange, different
unclogged (l. 21): freed from a difficulty
ethnic (l. 21): relating to a group of people that have certain characteristics in common, such as race, language, religion, etc.
subtly (l. 24): quietly, unobviously
flayed (l. 24): literally, to strip off the skin (as by lashing with a whip)
obit (l. 25): short for obituary, a notice of a person's death, usually with a short account of the person's life
ringing . . . changes (l. 25): running through the possible variations
distinguished (l. 26): outstanding

In a Prominent Bar in Secaucus One Day

X. J. Kennedy

To the tune of "The Old Orange Flute" or the tune of "Sweet Betsy from Pike"

In a prominent bar in Secaucus one day
Rose a lady in skunk with a topheavy sway,
Raised a knobby red finger—all turned from their beer—
While with eyes bright as snowcrust she sang high and clear:

5 "Now who of you'd think from an eyeload of me
That I once was a lady as proud as could be?
Oh I'd never sit down by a tumbledown drunk
If it wasn't, my dears, for the high cost of junk.

"All the gents used to swear that the white of my calf
10 Beat the down of a swan by a length and a half.
In the kerchief of linen I caught to my nose
Ah, there never fell snot, but a little gold rose.

"I had seven gold teeth and a toothpick of gold,
My Virginia cheroot was a leaf of it rolled
15 And I'd light it each time with a thousand in cash—
Why the bums used to fight if I flicked them an ash.

"Once the toast of the Biltmore, the belle of the Taft,
I would drink bottle beer at the Drake, never draft,
And dine at the Astor on Salisbury steak
20 With a clean tablecloth for each bite I did take.

"In a car like the Roxy I'd roll to the track,
A steel-guitar trio, a bar in the back,
And the wheels made no noise, they turned over so fast,
Still it took you ten minutes to see me go past.

25 "When the horses bowed down to me that I might choose,
I bet on them all, for I hated to lose.
Now I'm saddled each night for my butter and eggs
And the broken threads race down the backs of my legs.

"Let you hold in mind, girls, that your beauty must pass
30 Like a lovely white clover that rusts with its grass.
Keep your bottoms off barstools and marry you young
Or be left—an old barrel with many a bung.

"For when time takes you out for a spin in his car
You'll be hard-pressed to stop him from going too far
35 And be left by the roadside, for all your good deeds,
Two toadstools for tits and a face full of weeds."

All the house raised a cheer, but the man at the bar
Made a phonecall and up pulled a red patrol car
And she blew us a kiss as they copped her away
40 From that prominent bar in Secaucus, N.J.

NOTES
Prominent (title): well-known
junk (l. 8): narcotics
down (l. 10): soft feathers
length and a half (l. 10): literally, a term used in horse racing to indicate the distance between horses; "length" refers to the length of a horse
cheroot (l. 14): a cigar
Biltmore, Taft, Drake, Astor (ll. 17–19): expensive hotels in New York City
Roxy (l. 21): theatre in New York City
bung (l. 32): hole

Ozymandias

Percy Bysshe Shelley

I met a traveler from an antique land
Who said: Two vast and trunkless legs of stone
Stand in the desert . . . Near them, on the sand,
Half sunk, a shattered visage lies, whose frown,
5   And wrinkled lip, and sneer of cold command,
Tell that its sculptor well those passions read
Which yet survive, stamped on these lifeless things,
The hand that mocked them, and the heart that fed;
And on the pedestal these words appear:
10   "My name is Ozymandias, king of kings:
Look on my works, ye Mighty, and despair!"
Nothing beside remains. Round the decay
Of that colossal wreck, boundless and bare
The lone and level sands stretch far away.

NOTES
Ozymandias (title): the Greek name for Ramses II, who ruled Egypt from 1292–1225 B.C.
antique land (l. 1): ancient civilization
visage (l. 4): face
yet (l. 7): still
mocked (l. 8): recreated. The "hand" is the hand of the sculptor; the "heart" is the heart of Ozymandias.
pedestal (l. 9): the base of the statue
colossal (l. 13): referring to colossus, a gigantic statue

Mending Wall

Robert Frost

Something there is that doesn't love a wall,
That sends the frozen-ground-swell under it,
And spills the upper boulders in the sun;
And makes gaps even two can pass abreast.
5   The work of hunters is another thing:

Stone Wall, Concord, Massachusetts.

—Leah McCraney.

I have come after them and made repair
Where they have left not one stone on a stone,
But they would have the rabbit out of hiding,
To please the yelping dogs. The gaps I mean,
10 No one has seen them made or heard them made,
But at spring mending-time we find them there.
I let my neighbor know beyond the hill;
And on a day we meet to walk the line
And set the wall between us once again.
15 We keep the wall between us as we go.
To each the boulders that have fallen to each.
And some are loaves and some so nearly balls
We have to use a spell to make them balance:
"Stay where you are until our backs are turned!"
20 We wear our fingers rough with handling them.
Oh, just another kind of outdoor game,
One on a side. It comes to little more:
There where it is we do not need the wall:
He is all pine and I am apple orchard.
25 My apple trees will never get across
And eat the cones under his pines, I tell him.
He only says, "Good fences make good neighbors."
Spring is the mischief in me, and I wonder
If I could put a notion in his head:
30 "*Why* do they make good neighbors? Isn't it
Where there are cows? But here there are no cows.
Before I built a wall I'd ask to know
What I was walling in or walling out,
And to whom I was like to give offense.
35 Something there is that doesn't love a wall,
That wants it down." I could say "Elves" to him,
But it's not elves exactly, and I'd rather
He said it for himself. I see him there
Bringing a stone grasped firmly by the top
40 In each hand, like an old-stone savage armed.
He moves in darkness as it seems to me,
Not of woods only and the shade of trees.
He will not go behind his father's saying,
And he likes having thought of it so well
45 He says again, "Good fences make good neighbors."

NOTES

frozen-ground-swell (l. 2): When the earth freezes, it expands or "swells."
abreast (l. 4): side by side
boulders (l. 3): large stones
yelping (l. 9): barking
spell (l. 18): a magic phrase
Spring is the mischief in me (l. 28): Spring makes me mischievous.
old-stone savage (l. 40): suggesting the image of a stone-age man or "cave man"
go behind (l. 43): dispute, abandon

The Unknown Citizen

W.H. Auden

(To JS/07/M/378
This Marble Monument
Is Erected by the State)

He was found by the Bureau of Statistics to be
One against whom there was no official complaint,
And all the reports on his conduct agree
That, in the modern sense of an old-fashioned word, he was a saint,
5   For in everything he did he served the Greater Community.
Except for the War till the day he retired
He worked in a factory and never got fired,
But satisfied his employers, Fudge Motors Inc.
Yet he wasn't a scab or odd in his views,
10   For his union reports that he paid his dues,
(Our report on his Union shows it was sound)
And our Social Psychology workers found
That he was popular with his mates and liked a drink.
The Press are convinced that he bought a paper every day
15   And that his reactions to advertisements were normal in every way.
Policies taken out in his name prove that he was fully insured,
And his Health-card shows he was once in hospital but left it cured.
Both Producers Research and High-Grade Living declare
He was fully sensible to the advantages of the Installment Plan
20   And had everything necessary to the Modern Man,
A phonograph, a radio, a car and a frigidaire.
Our researchers into Public Opinion are content
That he held the proper opinions for the time of year;
When there was peace, he was for peace; when there was war, he went.
25   He was married and added five children to the population,
Which our Eugenist says was the right number for a parent of his generation.
And our teachers report that he never interfered with their education.

Was he free? Was he happy? The question is absurd:
Had anything been wrong, we should certainly have heard.

NOTES
scab (l. 9): a worker who will not join a labor union or who takes a striker's job
Installment Plan (l. 19): a plan in which goods are paid for over a period of time
frigidaire (l. 21): a refrigerator
Eugenist (l. 26): an expert on the production of healthy offspring
absurd (l. 28): ridiculous

Curiosity

Alastair Reid

may have killed the cat; more likely
the cat was just unlucky, or else curious
to see what death was like, having no cause
to go on licking paws, or fathering

5 litter on litter of kittens, predictably.
Nevertheless, to be curious
is dangerous enough. To distrust
what is always said, what seems,
to ask odd questions, interfere in dreams,

10 leave home, smell rats, have hunches
do not endear cats to those doggy circles
where well-smelt baskets, suitable wives, good lunches
are the order of things, and where prevails
much wagging of incurious heads and tails.

15 Face it. Curiosity
will not cause us to die—
only lack of it will.
Never to want to see
the other side of the hill

20 or that improbable country
where living is an idyll
(although a probable hell)
would kill us all.
Only the curious

25 have, if they live, a tale
worth telling at all.

Dogs say cats love too much, are irresponsible,
are changeable, marry too many wives,
desert their children, chill all dinner tables

30 with tales of their nine lives.
Well, they are lucky. Let them be
nine-lived and contradictory,
curious enough to change, prepared to pay
the cat price, which is to die

35 and die again and again,
each time with no less pain.
A cat minority of one
is all that can be counted on
to tell the truth. And what cats have to tell

40 on each return from hell
is this: that dying is what the living do,
that dying is what the loving do,
and that dead dogs are those who do not know
that dying is what, to live, each has to do.

NOTE
idyll (l. 21): a simple, peaceful, or carefree existence

Terence, This Is Stupid Stuff

A. E. Housman

"Terence, this is stupid stuff:
You eat your victuals fast enough;
There can't be much amiss, 'tis clear,
To see the rate you drink your beer.
5   But oh, good Lord, the verse you make,
It gives a chap the belly-ache.
The cow, the old cow, she is dead;
It sleeps well, the horned head:
We poor lads, 'tis our turn now
10   To hear such tunes as killed the cow.
Pretty friendship 'tis to rhyme
Your friends to death before their time
Moping melancholy mad:
Come, pipe a tune to dance to, lad."

15   Why, if 'tis dancing you would be,
There's brisker pipes than poetry.
Say, for what were hop-yards meant,
Or why was Burton built on Trent?
On many a peer of England brews
20   Livelier liquor than the Muse,
And malt does more than Milton can
To justify God's ways to man.
Ale, man, ale's the stuff to drink
For fellows whom it hurts to think:
25   Look into the pewter pot
To see the world as the world's not.
And faith, 'tis pleasant till 'tis past:
The mischief is that 'twill not last.
Oh I have been to Ludlow fair
30   And left my necktie god knows where,
And carried half-way home, or near,
Pints and quarts of Ludlow beer:
Then the world seemed none so bad,
And I myself a sterling lad;
35   And down in lovely muck I've lain,
Happy till I woke again.
Then I saw the morning sky:
Heigho, the tale was all a lie;
The world, it was the old world yet,
40   I was I, my things were wet,
And nothing now remained to do
But begin the game anew.

    Therefore, since the world has still
Much good, but much less good than ill,
45   And while the sun and moon endure
Luck's a chance, but trouble's sure,
I'd face it as a wise man would,
And train for ill and not for good.
'Tis true, the stuff I bring for sale

50   Is not so brisk a brew as ale:
      Out of a stem that scored the hand
      I wrung it in a weary land.
      But take it: if the smack is sour,
      The better for the embittered hour;
55   It should do good to heart and head
      When your soul is in my soul's stead;
      And I will friend you, if I may,
      In the dark and cloudy day.

        There was a king reigned in the East:
60   There, when kings will sit to feast,
      They get their fill before they think
      With poisoned meat and poisoned drink.
      He gathered all that springs to birth
      From the many-venomed earth;
65   First a little, thence to more,
      He sampled all her killing store;
      And easy, smiling, seasoned sound,
      Sate the king when healths went round.
      They put arsenic in his meat
70   And stared aghast to watch him eat;
      They poured strychnine in his cup
      And shook to see him drink it up:
      They shook, they stared as white's their shirt:
      Them it was their poison hurt.
75   —I tell the tale that I heard told.
      Mithridates, he died old.

NOTES

Terence, This Is Stupid Stuff (title): Terence is a poet; his poetry is "stupid stuff" according to one of his friends, the speaker in the first stanza. Beginning in stanza two, Terence responds to the statements made by his friend.

victuals (l. 2): food

amiss (l. 3): wrong

hop-yards (l. 17): fields of hops, a plant used in the brewing of beer and ale

Burton built on Trent (l. 18): Burton-on-Trent is an English town noted for its breweries.

peer (l. 19): nobleman

Muse (l. 20): from Greek mythology, the goddess of poetry

Milton (l. 21): John Milton (1608–1674), British poet. In the opening stanzas of *Paradise Lost*, Milton states that his purpose in writing the poem is to "justify the ways of God to man."

pewter pot (l. 25): a large mug

faith (l. 27): certainly

Ludlow (l. 29): an English town

sterling (l. 34): very good

Heigho (l. 38): an expression of disappointment

stem (l. 51): pen

scored (l. 51): marked, cut

wrung (l. 52): created through great effort

stead (l. 56): place

king (l. 59): Mithridates, who, over a period of time, took small doses of poison, thereby making himself immune to it

killing store (l. 66): poisons

seasoned sound (l. 67): conditioned thoroughly

sate (l. 68): drank

healths (l. 68): toasts

aghast (l. 70): shocked

2

Fiction

Birthday Party

Katharine Brush

1   They were a couple in their late thirties, and they looked unmistakably married. They sat on the banquette opposite us in a little narrow restaurant, having dinner. The man had a round, self-satisfied face, with glasses on it; the woman was fadingly pretty, in a big hat. There was nothing conspicuous about them, nothing particularly noticeable, until the end of their meal, when it suddenly became obvious that this was an Occasion—in fact, the husband's birthday, and the wife had planned a little surprise for him.

2   It arrived, in the form of a small but glossy birthday cake, with one pink candle burning in the center. The headwaiter brought it in and placed it before the husband, and meanwhile the violin-and-piano orchestra played "Happy Birthday to You," and the wife beamed with shy pride over her little surprise, and such few people as there were in the restaurant tried to help out with a pattering of applause. It became clear at once that help was needed, because the husband was not pleased. Instead he was hotly embarrassed, and indignant at his wife for embarrassing him.

3   You looked at him and saw this and you thought, "Oh, now don't *be* like that!" But he was like that, and as soon as the little cake had been deposited on the table, and the orchestra had finished the birthday piece, and the general attention had shifted from the man and woman, I saw him say something to her under his breath—some punishing thing, quick and curt and unkind. I couldn't bear to look at the woman then, so I stared at my plate and waited for quite a long time. Not long enough, though. She was still crying when I finally glanced over there again. Crying quietly and heartbrokenly and hopelessly, all to herself, under the gay big brim of her best hat.

NOTES
banquette (par. 1): an upholstered bench along a wall
indignant (par. 2): angry

The Lottery

Shirley Jackson

1   The morning of June 27th was clear and sunny, with the fresh warmth of a full-summer day; the flowers were blossoming profusely and the grass was richly green. The people of the village began to gather in the square, between

NOTE
profusely (par. 1): in great quantity

the post office and the bank, around ten o'clock; in some towns there were so many people that the lottery took two days and had to be started on June 26th, but in this village, where there were only about three hundred people, the whole lottery took less than two hours, so it could begin at ten o'clock in the morning and still be through in time to allow the villagers to get home for noon dinner.

2   The children assembled first, of course. School was recently over for the summer, and the feeling of liberty sat uneasily on most of them; they tended to gather together quietly for a while before they broke into boisterous play, and their talk was still of the classroom and the teacher, of books and reprimands. Bobby Martin had already stuffed his pockets full of stones, and the other boys soon followed his example, selecting the smoothest and roundest stones; Bobby and Harry Jones and Dickie Delacroix—the villagers pronounced this name "Dellacroy"—eventually made a great pile of stones in one corner of the square and guarded it against the raids of the other boys. The girls stood aside, talking among themselves, looking over their shoulders at the boys, and the very small children rolled in the dust or clung to the hands of their older brothers or sisters.

3   Soon the men began to gather, surveying their own children, speaking of planting and rain, tractors and taxes. They stood together, away from the pile of stones in the corner, and their jokes were quiet and they smiled rather than laughed. The women, wearing faded house dresses and sweaters, came shortly after their menfolk. They greeted one another and exchanged bits of gossip as they went to join their husbands. Soon the women, standing by their husbands, began to call to their children, and the children came reluctantly, having to be called four or five times. Bobby Martin ducked under his mother's grasping hand and ran, laughing, back to the pile of stones. His father spoke up sharply, and Bobby came quickly and took his place between his father and his oldest brother.

4   The lottery was conducted—as were the square dances, the teenage club, the Halloween program—by Mr. Summers, who had time and energy to devote to civic activities. He was a round-faced, jovial man and he ran the coal business, and people were sorry for him, because he had no children and his wife was a scold. When he arrived in the square, carrying the black wooden box, there was a murmur of conversation among the villagers, and he waved and called, "Little late today, folks." The postmaster, Mr. Graves, followed him, carrying a three-legged stool, and the stool was put in the center of the square and Mr. Summers set the black box down on it. The villagers kept their distance, leaving a space between themselves and the stool, and when Mr. Summers said, "Some of you fellows want to give me a hand?" there was a hesitation before two men, Mr. Martin and his oldest son, Baxter, came forward to hold the box steady on the stool while Mr. Summers stirred up the papers inside it.

5   The original paraphernalia for the lottery had been lost long ago, and the black box now resting on the stool had been put into use even before Old Man Warner, the oldest man in town, was born. Mr. Summers spoke frequently to the villagers about making a new box, but no one liked to upset even as much tradition as was represented by the black box. There was a story that the pre-

NOTES
boisterous (par. 2): noisy, rough
reprimands (par. 2): scoldings, criticisms
jovial (par. 4): jolly
paraphernalia (par. 5): the articles or equipment used in some activity

sent box had been made with some of the box that had preceded it, the one that had been constructed when the first people settled down to make a village here. Every year, after the lottery, Mr. Summers began talking again about a new box, but every year the subject was allowed to fade off without anything's being done. The black box grew shabbier each year; by now it was no longer completely black but splintered badly along one side to show the original wood color, and in some places faded or stained.

6   Mr. Martin and his oldest son, Baxter, held the black box securely on the stool until Mr. Summers had stirred the papers thoroughly with his hand. Because so much of the ritual had been forgotten or discarded, Mr. Summers had been successful in having slips of paper substituted for the chips of wood that had been used for generations. Chips of wood, Mr. Summers had argued, had been all very well when the village was tiny, but now that the population was more than three hundred and likely to keep on growing, it was necessary to use something that would fit more easily into the black box. The night before the lottery, Mr. Summers and Mr. Graves made up the slips of paper and put them in the box, and it was taken to the safe of Mr. Summers' coal company and locked up until Mr. Summers was ready to take it to the square next morning. The rest of the year, the box was put away, sometimes one place, sometimes another; it had spent one year in Mr. Graves's barn and another year underfoot in the post office, and sometimes it was set on a shelf in the Martin grocery and left there.

7   There was a great deal of fussing to be done before Mr. Summers declared the lottery open. There were the lists to make up—of heads of families, heads of households in each family, members of each household in each family. There was the proper swearing-in of Mr. Summers by the postmaster, as the official of the lottery; at one time, some people remembered, there had been a recital of some sort, performed by the official of the lottery, a perfunctory, tuneless chant that had been rattled off duly each year; some people believed that the official of the lottery used to stand just so when he said or sang it, others believed that he was supposed to walk among the people, but years and years ago this part of the ritual had been allowed to lapse. There had been, also, a ritual salute, which the official of the lottery had had to use in addressing each person who came up to draw from the box, but this also had changed with time, until now it was felt necessary only for the official to speak to each person approaching. Mr. Summers was very good at all this; in his clean white shirt and blue jeans, with one hand resting carelessly on the black box. He seemed very proper and important as he talked interminably to Mr. Graves and the Martins.

8   Just as Mr. Summers finally left off talking and turned to the assembled villagers, Mrs. Hutchinson came hurriedly along the path to the square, her sweater thrown over her shoulders, and slid into place in the back of the crowd. "Clean forgot what day it was," she said to Mrs. Delacroix, who stood next to her, and they both laughed softly. "Thought my old man was out back stacking wood," Mrs. Hutchinson went on, "and then I looked out the window and the kids were gone, and then I remembered it was the twenty-seventh and came a-running." She dried her hands on her apron, and Mrs. Delacroix said, "You're in time, though. They're still talking away up there."

9   Mrs. Hutchinson craned her neck to see through the crowd and found her husband and children standing near the front. She tapped Mrs. Delacroix on

NOTES

perfunctory (par. 7): done automatically or with little personal interest
interminably (par. 7): endlessly

the arm as a farewell and began to make her way through the crowd. The people separated good-humoredly to let her through; two or three people said, in voices just loud enough to be heard across the crowd, "Here comes your Missus, Hutchinson," and "Bill, she made it after all." Mrs. Hutchinson reached her husband, and Mr. Summers, who had been waiting, said cheerfully, "Thought we were going to have to get on without you, Tessie." Mrs. Hutchinson said, grinning, "Wouldn't have me leave m'dishes in the sink, now, would you, Joe?" and soft laughter ran through the crowd as the people stirred back into position after Mrs. Hutchinson's arrival. "Well, now," Mr. Summers said soberly, "guess we better get started, get this over with, so's we can go back to work. Anybody ain't here?"

10   "Dunbar," several people said. "Dunbar, Dunbar."

11   Mr. Summers consulted his list. "Clyde Dunbar," he said. "That's right. He's broke his leg, hasn't he? Who's drawing for him?"

12   "Me, I guess," a woman said, and Mr. Summers turned to look at her. "Wife draws for her husband," Mr. Summers said. "Don't you have a grown boy to do it for you, Janey?" Although Mr. Summers and everyone else in the village knew the answer perfectly well, it was the business of the official of the lottery to ask such questions formally. Mr. Summers waited with an expression of polite interest while Mrs. Dunbar answered.

13   "Horace's not but sixteen yet," Mrs. Dunbar said regretfully. "Guess I gotta fill in for the old man this year."

14   "Right," Mr. Summers said. He made a note on the list he was holding. Then he asked, "Watson boy drawing this year?"

15   A tall boy in the crowd raised his hand. "Here," he said. "I'm drawing for m'mother and me." He blinked his eyes nervously and ducked his head as several voices in the crowd said things like "Good fellow, Jack," and "Glad to see your mother's got a man to do it."

16   "Well," Mr. Summers said, "guess that's everyone. Old Man Warner make it?"

17   "Here," a voice said, and Mr. Summers nodded.

18   A sudden hush fell on the crowd as Mr. Summers cleared his throat and looked at the list. "All ready?" he said. "Now, I'll read the names—heads of families first—and the men come up and take a paper out of the box. Keep the paper folded in your hand without looking at it until everyone has had a turn. Everything clear?"

19   The people had done it so many times that they only half listened to the directions; most of them were quiet, wetting their lips, not looking around. Then Mr. Summers raised one hand high and said, "Adams." A man disengaged himself from the crowd and came forward. "Hi, Steve," Mr. Summers said, and Mr. Adams said, "Hi, Joe." They grinned at one another humorlessly and nervously. Then Mr. Adams reached into the black box and took out a folded paper. He held it firmly by one corner as he turned and went hastily back to his place in the crowd, where he stood a little apart from his family, not looking down at his hand.

20   "Allen," Mr. Summers said. "Anderson. . . . Bentham."

21   "Seems like there's no time at all between lotteries any more," Mrs. Delacroix said to Mrs. Graves in the back row. "Seems like we got through with the last one only last week."

22   "Time sure goes fast," Mrs. Graves said.

23   "Clark. . . . Delacroix."

24   "There goes my old man," Mrs. Delacroix said. She held her breath while her husband went forward.

25   "Dunbar," Mr. Summers said, and Mrs. Dunbar went steadily to the box while one of the women said, "Go on, Janey," and another said, "There she goes."

26   "We're next," Mrs. Graves said. She watched while Mr. Graves came around from the side of the box, greeted Mr. Summers gravely, and selected a slip of paper from the box. By now, all through the crowd there were men holding the small folded papers in their large hands, turning them over and over nervously. Mrs. Dunbar and her two sons stood together, Mrs. Dunbar holding the slip of paper.

27   "Harburt. . . . Hutchinson."

28   "Get up there, Bill," Mrs. Hutchinson said, and the people near her laughed.

29   "Jones."

30   "They do say," Mr. Adams said to Old Man Warner, who stood next to him, "that over in the north village they're talking of giving up the lottery."

31   Old Man Warner snorted. "Pack of crazy fools," he said. "Listening to the young folks, nothing's good enough for them. Next thing you know, they'll be wanting to go back to living in caves, nobody work any more, live *that* way for a while. Used to be a saying about 'Lottery in June, corn be heavy soon.' First thing you know, we'd all be eating stewed chickweed and acorns. There's *always* been a lottery," he added petulantly. "Bad enough to see young Joe Summers up there joking with everybody."

32   "Some places have already quit lotteries," Mrs. Adams said.

33   "Nothing but trouble in *that*," Old Man Warner said stoutly. "Pack of young fools."

34   "Martin." And Bobby Martin watched his father go forward. "Overdyke. . . . Percy."

35   "I wish they'd hurry," Mrs. Dunbar said to her older son. "I wish they'd hurry."

36   "They're almost through," her son said.

37   "You get ready to run tell Dad," Mrs. Dunbar said.

38   Mr. Summers called his own name and then stepped forward precisely and selected a slip from the box. Then he called, "Warner."

39   "Seventy-seventh year I been in the lottery," Old Man Warner said as he went through the crowd. "Seventy-seventh time."

40   "Watson." The tall boy came awkwardly through the crowd. Someone said, "Don't be nervous, Jack," and Mr. Summers said, "Take your time, son."

41   "Zanini."

42   After that, there was a long pause, a breathless pause, until Mr. Summers, holding his slip of paper in the air, said, "All right, fellows." For a minute, no one moved, and then all the slips of paper were opened. Suddenly, all the women began to speak at once, saying, "Who is it?," "Who's got it?," "Is it the Dunbars?," "Is it the Watsons?" Then the voices began to say, "It's Hutchinson. It's Bill," "Bill Hutchinson's got it."

43   "Go tell your father," Mrs. Dunbar said to her older son.

44   People began to look around to see the Hutchinsons. Bill Hutchinson was standing quiet, staring down at the paper in his hand. Suddenly, Tessie Hutchinson shouted to Mr. Summers, "You didn't give him time enough to take any paper he wanted. I saw you. It wasn't fair."

45   "Be a good sport, Tessie," Mrs. Delacroix called, and Mrs. Graves said, "All of us took the same chance."

46   "Shut up, Tessie," Bill Hutchinson said.

NOTE

petulantly (par. 31): with irritation

47   "Well, everyone," Mr. Summers said, "that was done pretty fast, and now we've got to be hurrying a little more to get done in time." He consulted his next list. "Bill," he said, "you draw for the Hutchinson family. You got any other households in the Hutchinsons?"

48   "There's Don and Eva," Mrs. Hutchinson yelled. "Make *them* take their chance!"

49   "Daughters draw with their husbands' families, Tessie," Mr. Summers said gently. "You know that as well as anyone else."

50   "It wasn't *fair*," Tessie said.

51   "I guess not, Joe," Bill Hutchinson said regretfully. "My daughter draws with her husband's family, that's only fair. And I've got no other family except the kids."

52   "Then, as far as drawing for families is concerned, it's you," Mr. Summers said in explanation, "and as far as drawing for households is concerned, that's you, too. Right?"

53   "Right," Bill Hutchinson said.

54   "How many kids, Bill?" Mr. Summers asked formally.

55   "Three," Bill Hutchinson said. "There's Bill, Jr., and Nancy, and little Dave. And Tessie and me."

56   "All right, then," Mr. Summers said. "Harry, you got their tickets back?"

57   Mr. Graves nodded and held up the slips of paper. "Put them in the box, then," Mr. Summers directed. "Take Bill's and put it in."

58   "I think we ought to start over," Mrs. Hutchinson said, as quietly as she could. "I tell you it wasn't *fair*. You didn't give him time enough to choose. *Every*body saw that."

59   Mr. Graves had selected the five slips and put them in the box, and he dropped all the papers but those onto the ground, where the breeze caught them and lifted them off.

60   "Listen, everybody," Mrs. Hutchinson was saying to the people around her.

61   "Ready, Bill?" Mr. Summers asked, and Bill Hutchinson, with one quick glance around at his wife and children, nodded.

62   "Remember," Mr. Summers said, "take the slips and keep them folded until each person has taken one. Harry, you help little Dave." Mr. Graves took the hand of the little boy, who came willingly with him up to the box. "Take a paper out of the box, Davy," Mr. Summers said. Davy put his hand into the box and laughed. "Take just *one* paper," Mr. Summers said. "Harry, you hold it for him." Mr. Graves took the child's hand and removed the folded paper from the tight fist and held it while little Dave stood next to him and looked up at him wonderingly.

63   "Nancy next," Mr. Summers said. Nancy was twelve, and her school friends breathed heavily as she went forward, switching her skirt, and took a slip daintily from the box. "Bill, Jr.," Mr. Summers said, and Billy, his face red and his feet overlarge, nearly knocked the box over as he got a paper out. "Tessie," Mr. Summers said. She hesitated for a minute, looking around defiantly, and then set her lips and went up to the box. She snatched a paper out and held it behind her.

64   "Bill," Mr. Summers said, and Bill Hutchinson reached into the box and felt around, bringing his hand out at last with the slip of paper in it.

65   The crowd was quiet. A girl whispered, "I hope it's not Nancy," and the sound of the whisper reached the edges of the crowd.

NOTE

defiantly (par. 63): with challenge or resistance

66   "It's not the way it used to be," Old Man Warner said clearly. "People ain't the way they used to be."

67   "All right," Mr. Summers said. "Open the papers. Harry, you open little Davy's."

68   Mr. Graves opened the slip of paper and there was a general sigh through the crowd as he held it up and everyone could see that it was blank. Nancy and Bill, Jr., opened theirs at the same time, and both beamed and laughed, turning around to the crowd and holding their slips of paper above their heads.

69   "Tessie," Mr. Summers said. There was a pause, and then Mr. Summers looked at Bill Hutchinson, and Bill unfolded his paper and showed it. It was blank.

70   "It's Tessie," Mr. Summers said, and his voice was hushed. "Show us her paper, Bill."

71   Bill Hutchinson went over to his wife and forced the slip of paper out of her hand. It had a black spot on it, the black spot Mr. Summers had made the night before with the heavy pencil in the coal-company office. Bill Hutchinson held it up, and there was a stir in the crowd.

72   "All right, folks," Mr. Summers said. "Let's finish quickly."

73   Although the villagers had forgotten the ritual and lost the original black box, they still remembered to use stones. The pile of stones the boys had made earlier was ready; there were stones on the ground with the blowing scraps of paper that had come out of the box. Mrs. Delacroix selected a stone so large she had to pick it up with both hands and turned to Mrs. Dunbar. "Come on," she said. "Hurry up."

74   Mrs. Dunbar had small stones in both hands, and she said, gasping for breath, "I can't run at all. You'll have to go ahead and I'll catch up with you."

75   The children had stones already, and someone gave little Davy Hutchinson a few pebbles.

76   Tessie Hutchinson was in the center of a cleared space by now, and she held her hands out desperately as the villagers moved in on her. "It isn't fair," she said. A stone hit her on the side of the head.

77   Old Man Warner was saying, "Come on, come on, everyone." Steve Adams was in the front of the crowd of villagers, with Mrs. Graves beside him.

78   "It isn't fair, it isn't right," Mrs. Hutchinson screamed, and then they were upon her.

The Catbird Seat

James Thurber

1   Mr. Martin bought the pack of Camels on Monday night in the most crowded cigar store on Broadway. It was theater time and seven or eight men were buying cigarettes. The clerk didn't even glance at Mr. Martin, who put the pack in his overcoat pocket and went out. If any of the staff at F & S had seen him buy the cigarettes, they would have been astonished, for it was generally known that Mr. Martin did not smoke, and never had. No one saw him.

2   It was just a week to the day since Mr. Martin had decided to rub out Mrs. Ulgine Barrows. The term "rub out" pleased him because it suggested nothing more than the correction of an error—in this case an error of Mr. Fitweiler. Mr. Martin had spent each night of the past week working out his plan and examining it. As he walked home now he went over it again. For the hundredth time he resented the element of imprecision, the margin of guesswork

that entered into the business. The project as he had worked it out was casual and bold, the risks were considerable. Something might go wrong anywhere along the line. And therein lay the cunning of his scheme. No one would ever see in it the cautious, painstaking hand of Erwin Martin, head of the filing department at F & S, of whom Mr. Fitweiler had once said, "Man is fallible but Martin isn't." No one would see his hand, that is, unless it were caught in the act.

3   Sitting in his apartment, drinking a glass of milk, Mr. Martin reviewed his case against Mrs. Ulgine Barrows, as he had every night for seven nights. He began at the beginning. Her quacking voice and braying laugh had first profaned the halls of F & S on March 7, 1941 (Mr. Martin had a head for dates). Old Roberts, the personnel chief, had introduced her as the newly appointed special advisor to the president of the firm, Mr. Fitweiler. The woman had appalled Mr. Martin instantly, but he hadn't shown it. He had given her his dry hand, a look of studious concentration, and a faint smile. "Well," she had said, looking at the paper on his desk, "are you lifting the oxcart out of the ditch?" As Mr. Martin recalled that moment, over his milk, he squirmed slightly. He must keep his mind on her crimes as a special adviser, not on her peccadillos as a personality. This he found difficult to do, in spite of entering an objection and sustaining it. The faults of the woman as a woman kept chattering on in his mind like an unruly witness. She had, for almost two years now, baited him. In the halls, in the elevator, even in his own office, into which she romped now and then like a circus horse, she was constantly shouting these silly questions at him. "Are you lifting the oxcart out of the ditch? Are you tearing up the pea patch? Are you hollering down the rain barrel? Are you scraping around the bottom of the pickle barrel? Are you sitting in the catbird seat?"

4   It was Joey Hart, one of Mr. Martin's two assistants, who had explained what the gibberish meant. "She must be a Dodger fan," he had said. "Red Barber announces the Dodger games over the radio and he uses those expressions—picked 'em up down South." Joey had gone on to explain one or two. "Tearing up the pea patch" meant going on a rampage; "Sitting in the catbird seat" meant sitting pretty, like a batter with three balls and no strikes on him. Mr. Martin dismissed all this with an effort. It had been annoying, it had driven him near to distraction, but he was too solid a man to be moved to murder by anything so childish. It was fortunate, he reflected as he passed on to the important charges against Mrs. Barrows, that he had stood up under it so well. He had maintained always an outward appearance of polite tolerance. "Why, I even believe you like the woman," Miss Paird, his other assistant, had once said to him. He had simply smiled.

5   A gavel rapped in Mr. Martin's mind and the case proper was resumed. Mrs. Ulgine Barrows stood charged with willful, blatant, and persistent attempts to destroy the efficiency and system of F & S. It was competent, ma-

NOTES
cunning (par. 2): cleverness
fallible (par. 2): capable of making mistakes
braying (par. 3): loud, harsh
profaned (par. 3): corrupted, spoiled
appalled (par. 3): shocked, horrified
peccadillos (par. 3): small faults
baited (par. 3): aggravated
gibberish (par. 4): nonsense
distraction (par. 4): great emotional disturbance
blatant (par. 5): obvious

terial, and relevant to review her advent and rise to power. Mr. Martin had got the story from Miss Paird, who seemed always able to find things out. According to her, Mrs. Barrows had met Mr. Fitweiler at a party, where she had rescued him from the embraces of a powerfully built drunken man who had mistaken the president of F & S for a famous retired Middle Western football coach. She had led him to a sofa and somehow worked upon him a monstrous magic. The aging gentleman had jumped to the conclusion there and then that this was a woman of singular attainments, equipped to bring out the best in him and in the firm. A week later he had introduced her into F & S as his special adviser. On that day confusion got its foot in the door. After Miss Tyson, Mr. Brundage, and Mr. Bartlett had been fired and Mr. Munson had taken his hat and stalked out, mailing in his resignation later, old Roberts had been emboldened to speak to Mr. Fitweiler. He mentioned that Mr. Munson's department had been "a little disrupted" and hadn't they perhaps better resume the old system there? Mr. Fitweiler had said certainly not. He had the greatest faith in Mrs. Barrows' ideas. "They require a little seasoning, a little seasoning, is all," he had added. Mr. Roberts had given it up. Mr. Martin reviewed in detail all the changes wrought by Mrs. Barrows. She had begun chipping at the cornices of the firm's edifice and now she was swinging at the foundation stones with a pickaxe.

6   Mr. Martin came now, in his summing up, to the afternoon of Monday, November 2, 1942—just one week ago. On that day, at 3 P.M., Mrs. Barrows had bounced into his office. "Boo!" she had yelled. "Are you scraping around the bottom of the pickle barrel?" Mr. Martin had looked at her from under his green eyeshade, saying nothing. She had begun to wander about the office, taking it in with her great, popping eyes. "Do you really need *all* these filing cabinets?" she had demanded suddenly. Mr. Martin's heart had jumped. "Each of these files," he had said, keeping his voice even, "plays an indispensable part in the system of F & S." She had brayed at him, "Well, don't tear up the pea patch!" and gone to the door. From there she had bawled, "But you sure have got a lot of fine scrap in here!" Mr. Martin could no longer doubt that the finger was on his beloved department. Her pickaxe was on the upswing, poised for the first blow. It had not come yet; he had received no blue memo from the enchanted Mr. Fitweiler bearing nonsensical instructions deriving from the obscene woman. But there was no doubt in Mr. Martin's mind that one would be forthcoming. He must act quickly. Already a precious week had gone by. Mr. Martin stood up in his living room, still holding his milk glass. "Gentlemen of the jury," he said to himself, "I demand the death penalty for this horrible person."

7   The next day Mr. Martin followed his routine, as usual. He polished his glasses more often and once sharpened an already sharp pencil, but not even Miss Paird noticed. Only once did he catch sight of his victim; she swept past him in the hall with a patronizing "Hi!" At five-thirty he walked home, as usual, and had a glass of milk, as usual. He had never drunk anything stronger in his life—unless you could count ginger ale. The late Sam Schlosser, the S

NOTES

advent (par. 5): arrival
attainments (par. 5): accomplishments
had been emboldened (par. 5): became brave enough
wrought (par. 5): brought about
cornices (par. 5): molding around the top of a building
edifice (par. 5): a large building
patronizing (par. 7): assuming a superior attitude

of F & S, had praised Mr. Martin at a staff meeting several years before for his temperate habits. "Our most efficient worker neither drinks nor smokes," he had said. "The results speak for themselves," Mr. Fitweiler had sat by, nodding approval.

8   Mr. Martin was still thinking about that red-letter day as he walked over to the Schrafft's on Fifth Avenue near Forty-sixth Street. He got there, as he always did, at eight o'clock. He finished his dinner and the financial page of the *Sun* at a quarter to nine, as he always did. It was his custom after dinner to take a walk. This time he walked down Fifth Avenue at a casual pace. His gloved hands felt moist and warm, his forehead cold. He transferred the Camels from his overcoat to a jacket pocket. He wondered, as he did so, if they did not represent an unnecessary note of strain. Mrs. Barrows smoked only Luckies. It was his idea to puff a few puffs on a Camel (after the rubbing-out), stub it out in the ashtray holding her lipstick-stained Luckies and thus drag a small red herring across the trail. Perhaps it was not a good idea. It would take time. He might even choke, too loudly.

9   Mr. Martin had never seen the house on West Twelfth Street where Mrs. Barrows lived, but he had a clear enough picture of it. Fortunately, she had bragged to everybody about her ducky first-floor apartment in the perfectly darling three-story red-brick. There would be no doorman or other attendants; just the tenants of the second and third floors. As he walked along, Mr. Martin realized that he would get there before nine-thirty. He had considered walking north on Fifth Avenue from Schrafft's to a point from which it would take him until ten o'clock to reach the house. At that hour people were less likely to be coming in or going out. But the procedure would have made an awkward loop in the straight thread of his casualness, and he had abandoned it. It was impossible to figure when people would be entering or leaving the house, anyway. There was a great risk at any hour. If he ran into anybody, he would simply have to place the rubbing-out of Ulgine Barrows in the inactive file forever. The same thing would hold true if there were someone in her apartment. In that case he would just say that he had been passing by, recognized her charming house and thought to drop in.

10   It was eighteen minutes after nine when Mr. Martin turned into Twelfth Street. A man passed him, and a man and a woman talking. There was no one within fifty paces when he came to the house, halfway down the block. He was up the steps and in the small vestibule in no time, pressing the bell under the card that said "Mrs. Ulgine Barrows." When the clicking in the lock started, he jumped forward against the door. He got inside fast, closing the door behind him. A bulb in a lantern hung from the hall ceiling on a chain seemed to give a monstrously bright light. There was nobody on the stair, which went up ahead of him along the left wall. A door opened down the hall in the wall on the right. He went toward it swiftly, on tiptoe.

11   "Well, for God's sake, look who's here!" bawled Mrs. Barrows, and her braying laugh rang out like the report of a shotgun. He rushed past her like a football tackle, bumping her. "Hey, quit shoving!" she said, closing the door behind him. They were in her living room, which seemed to Mr. Martin to be lighted by a hundred lamps. "What's after you?" she said. "You're as jumpy

NOTES

drag a small red herring across the trail (par. 8): Red herring (a fish) is dragged across the trail of hunted animals to overpower their scent and, thus, throw the dogs off course; "red herring" has become a common expression meaning something intended to confuse or distract.
vestibule (par. 10): entry hall
report (par. 11): sound

as a goat." He found he was unable to speak. His heart was wheezing in his throat. "I—yes," he finally brought out. She was jabbering and laughing as she started to help him off with his coat. "No, no," he said. "I'll put it here." He took it off and put it on a chair near the door. "Your hat and gloves, too," she said. "You're in a lady's house." He put his hat on top of the coat. Mrs. Barrows seemed larger than he had thought. He kept his gloves on. "I was passing by," he said. "I recognized—is there anyone here?" She laughed louder than ever. "No," she said, "we're all alone. You're as white as a sheet, you funny man. Whatever *has* come over you? I'll mix you a toddy." She started toward a door across the room. "Scotch-and-soda be all right? But say, you don't drink do you?" She turned and gave him her amused look. Mr. Martin pulled himself together. "Scotch-and-soda will be all right," he heard himself say. He could hear her laughing in the kitchen.

12   Mr. Martin looked quickly around the living room for the weapon. He had counted on finding one there. There were andirons and a poker and something in a corner that looked like an Indian club. None of them would do. It couldn't be that way. He began to pace around. He came to a desk. On it lay a metal paper knife with an ornate handle. Would it be sharp enough? He reached for it and knocked over a small brass jar. Stamps spilled out of it and it fell to the floor with a clatter. "Hey," Mrs. Barrows yelled from the kitchen, "are you tearing up the pea patch?" Mr. Martin gave a strange laugh. Picking up the knife, he tried its point against his left wrist. It was blunt. It wouldn't do.

13   When Mrs. Barrows reappeared, carrying two highballs, Mr. Martin standing there with his gloves on, became acutely conscious of the fantasy he had wrought. Cigarettes in his pocket, a drink prepared for him—it was all too grossly improbable. It was more than that; it was impossible. Somewhere in the back of his mind a vague idea stirred, sprouted. "For heaven's sake, take off those gloves," said Mrs. Barrows. "I always wear them in the house," said Mr. Martin. The idea began to bloom, strange and wonderful. She put the glasses on a coffee table in front of a sofa and sat on the sofa. "Come over here, you odd little man," she said. Mr. Martin went over and sat beside her. It was difficult getting a cigarette out of the pack of Camels, but he managed it. She held a match for him, laughing. "Well," she said, handing him his drink, "this is perfectly marvelous. You with a drink and a cigarette."

14   Mr. Martin puffed, not too awkwardly, and took a gulp of the highball. "I drink and smoke all the time," he said. He clinked his glass against hers. "Here's nuts to that old windbag, Fitweiler," he said, and gulped again. The stuff tasted awful, but he made no grimace. "Really, Mr. Martin," she said, her voice and posture changing, "you are insulting our employer." Mrs. Barrows was now all special adviser to the president. "I am preparing a bomb," said Mr. Martin, "which will blow the old goat higher than hell." He had only had a little of the drink, which was not strong. It couldn't be that. "Do you take dope or something?" Mrs. Barrows asked coldly. "Heroin," said Mr. Martin. "I'll be coked to the gills when I bump that old buzzard off." "Mr. Martin!" she shouted, getting to her feet. "That will be all of that. You must go at once." Mr. Martin took another swallow of his drink. He tapped his cigarette out in the ashtray and put the pack of Camels on the coffee table. Then he got up. She stood glaring at him. He walked over and put on his hat and coat. "Not a word about this," he said, and laid an index finger against his lips. All Mrs. Barrows could bring out was "Really!" Mr. Martin put his hand

NOTES
andirons (par. 12): metal supports that hold up logs in a fireplace
ornate (par. 12): highly decorated
grimace (par. 14): facial expression of disgust

on the doorknob. "I'm sitting in the catbird seat," he said. He stuck his tongue out at her and left. Nobody saw him go.

15   Mr. Martin got to his apartment, walking, well before eleven. No one saw him go in. He had two glasses of milk after brushing his teeth, and he felt elated. It wasn't tipsiness, because he hadn't been tipsy. Anyway, the walk had worked off all effects of the whisky. He got in bed and read a magazine for a while. He was asleep before midnight.

16   Mr. Martin got to the office at eight-thirty the next morning, as usual. At a quarter to nine, Ulgine Barrows, who had never before arrived at work before ten, swept into his office. "I'm reporting to Mr. Fitweiler now!" she shouted. "If he turns you over to the police, it's no more than you deserve!" Mr. Martin gave her a look of shocked surprise. "I beg your pardon?" he said. Mrs. Barrows snorted and bounced out of the room, leaving Miss Paird and Joey Hart staring after her. "What's the matter with that old devil now?" asked Miss Paird. "I have no idea," said Mr. Martin, resuming his work. The other two looked at him and then at each other. Miss Paird got up and went out. She walked slowly past the closed door of Mr. Fitweiler's office. Mrs. Barrows was yelling inside, but she was not braying. Miss Paird could not hear what the woman was saying. She went back to her desk.

17   Forty-five minutes later, Mrs. Barrows left the president's office and went into her own, shutting the door. It wasn't until half an hour later that Mr. Fitweiler sent for Mr. Martin. The head of the filing department, neat, quiet, attentive, stood in front of the old man's desk. Mr. Fitweiler was pale and nervous. He took his glasses off and twiddled them. He made a small, bruffing sound in his throat. "Martin," he said, "you have been with us more than twenty years." "Twenty-two, sir," said Mr. Martin. "In that time," pursued the president, "your work and your—uh—manner have been exemplary." "I trust so, sir," said Mr. Martin. "I have understood, Martin," said Mr. Fitweiler, "that you have never taken a drink or smoked." "That is correct, sir," said Mr. Martin. "Ah, yes." Mr. Fitweiler polished his glasses. "You may describe what you did after leaving the office yesterday, Martin," he said. Mr. Martin allowed less than a second for his bewildered pause. "Certainly, sir," he said. "I walked home. Then I went to Schrafft's for dinner. Afterward I walked home again. I went to bed early, sir, and read a magazine for a while. I was asleep before eleven." "Ah, yes," said Mr. Fitweiler again. He was silent for a moment, searching for the proper words to say to the head of the filing department. "Mrs. Barrows," he said finally, "Mrs. Barrows has worked hard, Martin, very hard. It grieves me to report that she has suffered a severe breakdown. It has taken the form of a persecution complex accompanied by distressing hallucinations." "I am very sorry, sir," said Mr. Martin. "Mrs. Barrows is under the delusion," continued Mr. Fitweiler, "that you visited her last evening and behaved yourself in an—uh—unseemly manner." He raised his hand to silence Mr. Martin's little pained outcry. "It is the nature of these psychological diseases," Mr. Fitweiler said, "to fix upon the least likely and most innocent party as the—uh—source of persecution. These matters are not for the lay mind to grasp, Martin. I've just had my psychiatrist, Dr. Fitch, on the phone. He would not, of course, commit himself, but he made enough

NOTES
elated (par. 15): in high spirits
persecution complex (par. 17): a feeling that one is being singled out for unjust treatment
delusion (par. 17): false belief
lay (par. 17): nonprofessional

generalizations to substantiate my suspicions. I suggested to Mrs. Barrows when she had completed her—uh—story to me this morning, that she visit Dr. Fitch, for I suspected a condition at once. She flew, I regret to say, into a rage, and demanded—uh—requested that I call you on the carpet. You may not know, Martin, but Mrs. Barrows had planned a reorganization of your department—subject to my approval, of course, subject to my approval. This brought you, rather than anyone else, to her mind—but again that is a phenomenon for Dr. Fitch and not for us. So, Martin, I am afraid Mrs. Barrows' usefulness here is at an end." "I am dreadfully sorry, sir," said Mr. Martin.

18   It was at this point that the door to the office blew open with the suddenness of a gas-main explosion and Mrs. Barrows catapulted through it. "Is the little rat denying it?" she screamed. "He can't get away with that!" Mr. Martin got up and moved discreetly to a point beside Mr. Fitweiler's chair. "You drank and smoked at my apartment," she bawled at Mr. Martin, "and you know it! You called Mr. Fitweiler an old windbag and said you were going to blow him up when you got coked to the gills on your heroin!" She stopped yelling to catch her breath and a new glint came into her popping eyes. "If you weren't such a drab, ordinary little man," she said, "I'd think you'd planned it all. Sticking your tongue out at me, saying you were sitting in the catbird seat, because you thought no one would believe me when I told it! My God, it's really too perfect!" She brayed loudly and hysterically, and the fury was on her again. She glared at Mr. Fitweiler. "Can't you see how he has tricked us, you old fool! Can't you see his little game?" But Mr. Fitweiler had been surreptitiously pressing all the buttons under the top of his desk and employees of F & S began pouring into the room. "Stockton," said Mr. Fitweiler, "you and Fishbein will take Mrs. Barrows to her home. Mrs. Powell, you will go with them." Stockton, who had played a little football in high school, blocked Mrs. Barrows as she made for Mr. Martin. It took him and Fishbein together to force her out of the door into the hall, crowded with stenographers and office boys. She was still screaming imprecations at Mr. Martin, tangled and contradictory imprecations. The hubbub finally died out down the corridor.

19   "I regret that this has happened," said Mr. Fitweiler. "I shall ask you to dismiss it from your mind, Martin." "Yes, sir," said Mr. Martin, anticipating his chief's "That will be all" by moving to the door. "I will dismiss it." He went out and shut the door, and his step was light and quick in the hall. When he entered his department he had slowed down to his customary gait, and he walked quietly across the room to the W20 file, wearing a look of studious concentration.

NOTES
call you on the carpet (par. 17): sharply criticize you
phenomenon (par. 17): unusual occurrence
catapulted (par. 18): flew
surreptitiously (par. 18): secretly
stenographers (par. 18): someone skilled in shorthand
imprecations (par. 18): curses
gait (par. 19): manner of walking

The Gilded Six-Bits

Zora Neale Hurston

1   It was a Negro yard around a Negro house in a Negro settlement that looked to the payroll of the G and G Fertilizer works for its support.

2   But there was something happy about the place. The front yard was parted in the middle by a sidewalk from gate to doorstep, a sidewalk edged on either side by quart bottles driven neck down to the ground on a slant. A mess of homey flowers planted without a plan but blooming cheerily from their helter-skelter places. The fence and house were whitewashed. The porch and steps scrubbed white.

3   The front door stood open to the sunshine so that the floor of the front room could finish drying after its weekly scouring. It was Saturday. Everything clean from the front gate to the privy house. Yard raked so that the strokes of the rake would make a pattern. Fresh newspaper cut in fancy-edge on the kitchen shelves.

4   Missie May was bathing herself in the galvanized washtub in the bedroom. Her dark-brown skin glistened under the soapsuds that skittered down from her wash rag. Her stiff young breasts thrust forward aggressively like broad-based cones with the tips lacquered in black.

5   She heard men's voices in the distance and glanced at the dollar clock on the dresser.

6   "Humph! Ah'm way behind time t'day! Joe gointer be heah 'fore Ah git mah clothes on if Ah don't make haste."

7   She grabbed the clean meal sack at hand and dried herself hurriedly and began to dress. But before she could tie her slippers, there came the ring of singing metal on wood. Nine times.

8   Missie May grinned with delight. She had not seen the big tall man come stealing in the gate and creep up the walk grinning happily at the joyful mischief he was about to commit. But she knew that it was her husband throwing silver dollars in the door for her to pick up and pile beside her plate at dinner. It was this way every Saturday afternoon. The nine dollars hurled into the open door, he scurried to a hiding place behind the cape jasmine bush and waited.

9   Missie May promptly appeared at the door in mock alarm.

10   "Who dat chunkin' money in mah do'way?" she demanded. No answer from the yard. She leaped off the porch and began to search the shrubbery. She peeped under the porch and hung over the gate to look up and down the

NOTES

In this story, the dialogue is written in dialect. This mean that words are spelled the way they would be pronounced by the characters. For example, "I" would be pronounced "Ah," so it is spelled "Ah"; the "r" in "here" would not be pronounced, so it is spelled "heah"; and the "th" in "the" and "that" would be pronounced as a "d," so "the" is spelled "de" and "that" is spelled "dat."

Gilded (title): gold plated, covered with a thin layer of gold

Bits (title): an American slang term for the amount of $12 \frac{1}{2}$ cents, used only with even numbers (2 bits = 25 cents; 4 bits = 50 cents; 6 bits = 75 cents; and so forth)

helter-skelter (par. 2): random

privy house (par. 3): outdoor toilet

lacquered (par. 4): varnished

singing (par. 7): ringing

in mock alarm (par. 9): pretending to be concerned

road. While she did this, the man behind the jasmine darted to the chinaberry tree. She spied him and gave chase.

11   "Nobody ain't gointer be chunkin' money at me and Ah not do'em nothin'," she shouted in mock anger. He ran around the house with Missie May at his heels. She overtook him at the kitchen door. He ran inside but could not close it after him before she crowded in and locked with him in a rough and tumble. For several minutes the two were a furious mass of male and female energy. Shouting, laughing, twisting, turning, and Joe trying, but not too hard, to get away.

12   "Missie May, take yo' hand out mah pocket!" Joe shouted out between laughs.

13   "Ah ain't, Joe, not lessen you gwine gimme whateve' it is good you got in yo' pocket. Turn it go Joe, do Ah'll tear yo' clothes."

14   "Go on tear 'em. You de one dat pushes de needles round heah. Move yo' hand Missie May."

15   "Lemme git dat paper sack out yo' pocket. Ah bet its candy kisses."

16   "Tain't. Move yo' hand. Woman ain't got no business in a man's clothes nohow. Go 'way."

17   Missie May gouged way down and gave an upward jerk and triumphed.

18   "Unhhunh! Ah got it. It 'tis so candy kisses. Ah knowed you had somethin' for me in yo' clothes. Now Ah got to see whut's in every pocket you got."

19   Joe smiled indulgently and let his wife go through all of his pockets and take out the things that he had hidden there for her to find. She bore off the chewing gum, the cake of sweet soap, the pocket handkerchief as if she had wrested them from him, as if they had not been bought for the sake of this friendly battle.

20   "Whew! dat play-fight done got me all warmed up," Joe exclaimed. "Got me some water in de kittle?"

21   "Yo' water is on de fire and yo' clean things is cross de bed. Hurry up and wash yo'self and git changed so we kin eat. Ah'm hongry." As Missie said this, she bore the steaming kettle into the bedroom.

22   "You ain't hongry, sugar," Joe contradicted her. "Youse jes's little empty. Ah'm de one whut's hongry. Ah could eat up camp meetin', back off'ssociation, and drink Jurdan dry. Have it on de table when Ah git out de tub."

23   "Don't you mess wid mah business, man. You git in yo' clothes. Ah'm a real wife, not no dress and breath. Ah might not look lak one, but if you burn me, you won't git a thing but wife ashes."

24   Joe splashed in the bedroom and Missie May fanned around in the kitchen. A fresh red and white checked cloth on the table. Big pitcher of buttermilk beaded with pale drops of butter from the churn. Hot fried mullet, crackling bread, ham hocks atop a mound of string beans and new potatoes, and perched on the window-sill a pone of spicy potato pudding.

25   Very little talk during the meal but that little consisted of banter that pretended to deny affection but in reality flaunted it. Like when Missie May reached for a second helping of the tater pone. Joe snatched it out of her reach. After Missie May had made two of three unsuccessful grabs at the pan, she begged, "Aw, Joe gimme some mo' dat tater pone."

NOTES

gouged (par. 17): dug

wrested (par. 19): forced

camp meetin' (par. 22): an outdoor religious gathering, usually lasting several days

pone (par. 24): oval shaped cornbread

banter (par. 25): teasing comments

26   "Nope, sweetenin' is for us men-folks. Y'all pritty li'l frail eels don't need nothin' lak dis. You too sweet already."

27   "Please, Joe."

28   "Naw, naw. Ah don't want you to git no sweeter than whut you is already. We goin' down de road al li'l piece t'night so you go put on yo' Sunday-go-to-meetin' things."

29   Missie May looked at her husband to see if he was playing some prank. "Sho 'nuff, Joe?"

30   "Yeah. We goin' to de ice cream parlor."

31   "Where de ice cream parlor at, Joe?"

32   "A new man done come heah from Chicago and he done got a place and took and opened it up for a ice cream parlor, and bein' as it's real swell, Ah wants you to be one de first ladies to walk in dere and have some set down."

33   "Do Jesus, Ah ain't knowed nothin' 'bout it. Who de man done it?"

34   "Mister Otis D. Slemmons, of spots and places—Memphis, Chicago, Jacksonville, Philadelphia and so on."

35   "Dat heavy-set man wid his mouth full of gold teethes?"

36   "Yeah. Where did you see 'im at?"

37   "Ah went down to de sto' tuh git a box of lye and Ah seen 'im standin' on de corner talkin' to some of de mens, and Ah come on back and went to scrubbin' de floor, and he passed and tipped his hat whilst Ah was scourin' de steps. Ah thought never Ah seen *him* befo'."

38   Joe smiled pleasantly. "Yeah, he's up to date. He got de finest clothes Ah ever seen on a colored man's back."

39   "Aw, he don't look no better in his clothes than you do in yourn. He got a puzzlegut on 'im and he so chuckle-headed, he got a pone behind his neck."

40   Joe looked down at his own abdomen and said wistfully, "Wisht Ah had a build on me lak he got. He ain't puzzlegutted, honey. He jes' got a corperation. Dat make 'm look lak a rich white man. All rich mens is got some belly on 'em."

41   "Ah seen de pitchers of Henry Ford and he's a spare-built man and Rockefeller look lak he ain't got but one gut. But Ford and Rockefeller and dis Slemmons and all de rest kin be as many-gutted as dey please, ah'm satisfied wid you jes' lak you is, baby. God took pattern after a pine tree and built you noble. Youse a pritty still man, and if Ah knowed any way to make you mo' pritty still Ah'd take and do it."

42   Joe reached over gently and toyed with Missie May's ear. "You jes' say dat cause you love me, but Ah know Ah can't hold no light to Otis D. Slemmons. Ah ain't never been nowhere and Ah ain't got nothin' but you."

43   "How you know dat, Joe."

44   "He tole us hisself."

45   "Dat don't make it so. His mouf is cut cross-ways, ain't it? Well, he kin lie jes' lak anybody els."

46   "Good Lawd, Missie! You womens sho' is hard to sense into things. He's got a five-dollar gold piece for a stick-pin and he got a ten-dollar gold piece on his watch chain and his mouf is jes' crammed full of gold teethes. Sho' wisht it wuz mine. And whut make it so cool, he got money 'cumulated. And womens give it all to 'im."

47   "Ah don't see whut de womens see on 'im. Ah wouldn't give 'im a wind if de sherff wuz after 'im."

NOTES

Sunday-go-to-meetin' (par. 28): church
lye (par. 37): an acid-like substance used in making soap
His mouf is cut cross-ways (par. 45): his mouth goes from side to side

48   "Well, he tole us how de white womens in Chicago give 'im all dat gold money. So he don't 'low nobody to touch it at all. Not even put dey finger on it. Dey tole 'im not to. You kin make 'miration at it, but don't tetch it."

49   "Whyn't he stay up dere where dey so crazy 'bout im?"

50   "Ah reckon dey done made 'im vast-rich and he wants to travel some. He say dey wouldn't leave 'im hit a lick of work. He got mo' lady people crazy 'bout him than he kin shake a stick at."

51   "Joe, Ah hates to see you so dumb. Dat stray nigger jes' tell y'all anything and y'all b'lieve it."

52   "Go 'head on now, honey and put on yo' clothes. He talkin' 'bout his pritty womens—Ah want 'im to see *mine.*"

53   Missie May went off to dress and Joe spent the time trying to make his stomach punch out like Slemmons' middle. He tried the rolling swagger of the stranger, but found that his tall bone-and-muscle stride fitted ill with it. He just had time to drop back into his seat before Missie May came in dressed to go.

54   On the way home that night Joe was exultant. "Didn't Ah say ole Otis was swell? Can't he talk Chicago talk? Wuzn't dat funny whut he said when great big fat ole Ida Armstrong come in? He asted me, 'Who is dat broad wid de forty shake?' Dat's a new word. Us always thought forty was a set of figgers but he showed us where it means a whole heap of things. Sometimes he don't say forty, he jes' say thirty-eight and two and dat mean de same thing. Know whut he tole me when Ah was payin' for our ice cream? He say, 'Ah have to hand it to you, Joe. Dat wife of yours is jes' thirty-eight and two. Yessuh, she's forty!' Ain't he killin'?"

55   "He'll do in case of a rush. But he sho' is got uh heap uh gold on 'im. Dat's de first time Ah ever seed gold money. It lookted good on him sho' nuff, but it'd look a whole heap better on you."

56   "Who, me? Missie May was youse crazy! Where would a po' man lak me git gold money from?"

57   Missie May was silent for a minute, then she said, "Us might find some goin' long de road some time. Us could."

58   "Who would be losin' gold money 'round heah? We ain't even seen none dese white folks wearin' no gold money on dey watch chain. You must be figgeren' Mister Packard or Mister Cadillac goin' pass through heah . . . "

59   "You don't know whut been lost 'round heah. Maybe somebody way back in memorial times lost they gold money and went on off and it ain't never been found. And then if we wuz to find it, you could wear some 'thout havin' no gang of womens lak dat Slemmons say he got."

60   Joe laughed and hugged her. "Don't be so wishful 'bout me. Ah'm satisfied de way Ah is. So long as Ah be yo' husband, ah don't keer 'bout nothin' else. Ah'd ruther all de other womens in de world to be dead than for you to have de toothache. Less we go to bed and git our night rest."

61   It was Saturday night once more before Joe could parade his wife in Slemmons' ice cream parlor again. He worked the night shift and Saturday was his only night off. Every other evening around six o'clock he left home, and dying dawn saw him hustling home around the lake where the challenging sun flung a flaming sword from east to west across the trembling water.

62   That was the best part of life—going home to Missie May. Their whitewashed house, the mock battle on Saturday, the dinner and ice cream parlor

NOTE
exultant (par. 54): joyous

afterwards, church on Sunday nights when Missie outdressed any woman in town—all, everything was right.

63   One night around eleven the acid ran out at the G and G. The foreman knocked off the crew and let the steam die down. As Joe rounded the lake on his way home, a lean moon rode the lake in a silver boat. If anybody had asked Joe about the moon on the lake, he would have said he hadn't paid it any attention. But he saw it with his feelings. It made him yearn painfully for Missie. Creation obsessed him. He thought about children. They had been married for more than a year now. They had money put away. They ought to be making little feet for shoes. A little boy child would be about right.

64   He saw a dim light in the bedroom and decided to come in through the kitchen door. He could wash the fertilizer dust off himself before presenting himself to Missie May. It would be nice for her not to know that he was there until he slipped into his place in bed and hugged her back. She always liked that.

65   He eased the kitchen door open slowly and silently, but when he went to set his dinner bucket on the table he bumped it into a pile of dishes, and something crashed to the floor. He heared his wife gasp in fright and hurried to reassure her.

66   "Iss me, honey. Don't get skeered."

67   There was a quick, large movement in the bedroom. A rustle, a thud, and a stealthy silence. The light went out.

68   What? Robbers? Murderers? Some varmint attacking his helpless wife, perhaps. He struck a match, threw himself on guard and stepped over the doorsill into the bedroom.

69   The great belt on the wheel of Time slipped and eternity stood still. By the match light he could see the man's legs fighting with his breeches in his frantic desire to get them on. He had both chance and time to kill the intruder in his helpless condition—half-in and half-out of his pants—but he was too weak to take action. The shapeless enemies of humanity that live in the hours of Time had waylaid Joe. He was assaulted in his weakness. Like Samson awakening after his haircut. So he just opened his mouth and laughed.

70   The match went out and he struck another and lit the lamp. A howling wind raced across his heart, but underneath its fury he heard his wife sobbing and Slemmons pleading for his life. Offering to buy it with all that he had. "Please, suh, don't kill me. Sixty-two dollars at de sto' gold money."

71   Joe just stood. Slemmons looked at the window, but it was screened. Joe stood out like a rough-backed mountain between him and the door. Barring him from escape, from sunrise, from life.

72   He considered a surprise attack upon the big clown that stood there laughing like a chessy cat. But before his fist could travel an inch, Joe's own rushed out to crush him like a battering ram. Then Joe stood over him.

73   "Git into yo' damn rags, Slemmons, and dat quick."

74   Slemmons scrambled to his feet and into his vest and coat. As he grabbed his hat, Joe's fury overrode his intentions and he grabbed at Slemmons with his left hand and struck at him with his right. The right landed. The left grazed the front of his vest. Slemmons was knocked a somersault into the kitchen and fled through the open door. Joe found himself alone with Missie May, with the golden watch charm clutched in his left fist. A short bit of broken chain dangled between his fingers.

NOTES

waylaid (par. 69): ambushed

a chessy cat (par. 72): a Cheshire cat: a cat that grins broadly and continuously, popularized by Lewis Carroll in *Alice's Adventures in Wonderland*

75   Missie May was sobbing. Wails of weeping without words. Joe stood, and after awhile she found out that he had something in his hand. And then he stood and felt without thinking and without seeing with his natural eyes. Missie May kept on crying and Joe kept on feeling so much and not knowing what to do with all his feelings, he put Slemmons' watch charm in his pants pocket and took a good laugh and went to bed.

76   "Missie May, whut you crying for?"

77   "Cause Ah love you so hard and Ah know you don't love *me* no mo'."

78   Joe sank his face into the pillow for a spell then he said huskily, "You don't know de feelings of dat yet, Missie May."

79   "Oh Joe, honey, he said he wuz gointer gimme dat gold money and he jes' kept on after me—"

80   Joe was very still and silent for a long time. Then he said, "Well, don't cry no mo', Missie May. Ah got yo' gold piece for you."

81   The hours went past on their rusty ankles. Joe still and quiet on one bedrail and Missie May wrung dry of sobs on the other. Finally the sun's tide crept upon the shore of night and drowned all its hours. Missie May with her face stiff and streaked towards the window saw the dawn come into her yard. It was day. Nothing more. Joe wouldn't be coming home as usual. No need to fling open the front door and sweep off the porch, making it nice for Joe. Never no more breakfast to cook; no more washing and starching of Joe's jumper-jackets and pants. No more nothing. So why get up?

82   With this strange man in her bed, she felt embarrassed to get up and dress. She decided to wait till he had dressed and gone. Then she would get up, dress quickly and be gone forever beyond reach of Joe's looks and laughs. But he never moved. Red light turned to yellow, then white.

83   From beyond the no-man's land between them came a voice. A strange voice that yesterday had been Joe's.

84   "Missie May, ain't you gonna fix me no breakfus'?"

85   She sprang out of bed. "Yeah, Joe. Ah didn't reckon you wuz hongry."

86   No need to die today. Joe needed her for a few more minutes anyhow.

87   Soon there was a roaring fire in the cook stove. Water bucket full and two chickens killed. Joe loved fried chicken and rice. She didn't deserve a thing and good Joe was letting her cook him some breakfast. She rushed hot biscuits to the table as Joe took his seat.

88   He ate with his eyes on his plate. No laughter, no banter.

89   "Missie May, you ain't eatin' yo' breakfus'."

90   "Ah don't choose none, Ah thank yuh."

91   His coffee cup was empty. She sprang to refill it. When she turned from the stove and bent to set the cup beside Joe's plate, she saw the yellow coin on the table between them.

92   She slumped into her seat and wept into her arms.

93   Presently Joe said calmly, "Missie May, you cry too much. Don't look back lak Lot's wife and turn to salt."

94   The sun, the hero of every day, the impersonal old man that beams as brightly on death as on birth, came up every morning and raced across the blue dome and dipped into the sea of fire every evening. Water ran down hill and birds nested.

NOTE

lak Lot's wife and turn to salt (par. 93): According to the Bible, Lot was told by God's angels to flee with his family to the hills in order to escape the destruction of Sodom and Gomorrah and not to look back. Lot's wife looked back and was turned into a pillar of salt (Genesis 19:12–26).

95   Missie knew why she didn't leave Joe. She couldn't. She loved him too much. But she couldn't understand why Joe didn't leave her. He was polite, even kind at times, but aloof.

96   There were no more Saturday romps. No ringing silver dollars to stack beside her plate. No pockets to rifle. In fact the yellow coin in his trousers was like a monster hiding in the cave of his pockets to destroy her.

97   She often wondered if he still had it, but nothing could have induced her to ask nor yet to explore his pockets to see for herself. Its shadow was in the house whether or no.

98   One night Joe came home around midnight and complained of pains in the back. He asked Missie to rub him down with liniment. It had been three months since Missie had touched his body and it all seemed strange. But she rubbed him. Grateful for the chance. Before morning, youth triumphed and Missie exulted. But the next day, as she joyfully made up their bed, beneath her pillow she found the piece of money with the bit of chain attached.

99   Alone to herself, she looked at the thing with loathing, but look she must. She took it into the hands with trembling and saw first thing that it was no gold piece. It was a gilded half-dollar. Then she knew why Slemmons had forbidden anyone to touch his gold. He trusted village eyes at a distance not to recognize his stick-pin as a gilded quarter, and his watch charm as a four-bit piece.

100   She was glad at first that Joe had left it there. Perhaps he was through with her punishment. They were man and wife again. Then another thought came clawing at her. He had come home to buy from her as if she were any woman in the long house. Fifty cents for her love. As if to say that he could pay as well as Slemmons. She slid the coin into his Sunday pants pocket and dressed herself and left his house.

101   Halfway between her house and the quarters she met her husband's mother, and after a short talk she turned and went back home. If she had not the substance of marriage, she had the outside show. Joe must leave *her*. She let him see she didn't want his old gold four-bits too.

102   She saw no more of the coin for some time though she knew that Joe could not help finding it in his pocket. But his health kept poor, and he came home at least every ten days to be rubbed.

103   The sun swept around the horizon, trailing its robes of weeks and days. One morning as Joe came in from work, he found Missie May chopping wood. Without a word he took the ax and chopped a huge pile before he stopped.

104   "You ain't got no business choppin' wood, and you know it."

105   "How come? Ah been choppin' it for de last longest."

106   "Ah ain't blind. You makin' feet for shoes."

107   "Won't you be glad to have a li'l baby chile, Joe?"

108   "You know dat 'thout astin' me."

109   "Iss gointer be a boy chile and de very spit of you."

110   "You reckon, Missie May?"

111   "Who else could it look lak?"

112   Joe said nothing, but he thrust his hand deep into his pocket and fingered something there.

113   It was almost six months later Missie May took to bed and Joe went and got his mother to come wait on the house.

114   Missie May delivered a fine boy. Her travail was over when Joe came in

NOTES

aloof (par. 95): distant
de very spit of you (par. 109): the very spitting image of you: look just like you
travail (par. 114): labor (of childbirth)

from work one morning. His mother and the old women were drinking great bowls of coffee around the fire in the kitchen.

115   The minute Joe came into the room his mother called him aside.

116   "How did Missie May make out?" he asked quickly.

117   "Who, dat gal? She strong as a ox. She gointer have plenty mo'. We done fixed her wid de sugar and lard to sweeten her for de nex' one."

118   Joe stood silent awhile.

119   "You ain't ast 'bout de baby, Joe. You oughter be mighty proud cause he sho' is de spittin' image of yuh, son. Dat's yourn all right, if you never git another on, dat un is yourn. And you know Ah'm mighty proud too, son, cause Ah never thought well of you marryin' Missie May cause her make used tuh fan her foot 'round right smart and Ah been mighty skeered dat Missie May wuz gointer git misput on her road."

120   Joe said nothing. He fooled around the house till late in the day then just before he went to work, he went and stood at the foot of the bed and asked his wife how she felt. He did this every day during the week.

121   On Saturday he went to Orlando to make his market. It had been a long time since he had done that.

122   Meat and lard, meal and flour, soap and starch. Cans of corn and tomatoes. All the staples. He fooled around town for a while and bought bananas and apples. Way after while he went around to the candy store.

123   "Hellow, Joe," the clerk greeted him. "Ain't seen you in a long time."

124   "Nope, Ah ain't been heah. Been 'round spots and places."

125   "Want some of them molasses kisses you always buy?"

126   "Yessuh." He threw the gilded half-dollar on the counter. "Will dat spend?"

127   "Whut is it, Joe? Well, I'll be doggone! A gold-plated four-bit piece. Where'd you git it, Joe?"

128   "Offen a stray nigger dat come through Eatonville. He had it on his watch chain for a charm—goin' 'round making out iss gold money. Ha ha! He had a quarter on his tie pin and it wuz all golded up too. Tryin' to fool people. Makin' out he is rich and everything. Ha! Ha! Tryin' to tole off folkses wives from home."

129   "How did you git it, Joe? Did he fool you, too?"

130   "Who, me? Naw suh! He ain't fooled me none. Know whut Ah done? He come 'round me wid his smart talk. Ah hauled off and knocked 'im down and took his old four-bits 'way from 'im. Gointer buy my wife some good ole 'lasses kisses wid it. Gimme fifty cents worth of dem candy kisses."

131   "Fifty cents buys a mighty lot of candy kisses, Joe. Why don't you split it up and take some chocolate bars, too. They eat good, too."

132   "Yessuh, dey do, but Ah wants all dat in kisses. Ah got a li'l boy chile home now. Tain't a week old yet, but he kin suck a sugar tit and maybe eat one them kisses hisself."

133   Joe got his candy and left the store. The clerk turned to the next customer. "Wisht I could be like these darkies. Laughin' all the time. Nothin' worries 'em."

134   Back in Eatonville, Joe reached his own front door. There was the ring of singing metal on wood. Fifteen times. Missie May couldn't run to the door, but she crept there as quickly as she could.

135   "Joe Banks, Ah hear you chunkin' money in mah do'way. You wait till Ah got mah strength back and Ah'm gointer fix you for dat."

The Veldt

Ray Bradbury

1   "George, I wish you'd look at the nursery."

2   "What's wrong with it?"

3   "I don't know."

4   "Well, then."

5   "I just want you to look at it, is all, or call a psychologist in to look at it."

6   "What would a psychologist want with a nursery?"

7   "You know very well what he'd want." His wife paused in the middle of the kitchen and watched the stove busy humming to itself, making supper for four.

8   "It's just that the nursery is different now than it was."

9   "All right, let's have a look."

10   They walked down the hall of their soundproofed, Happylife Home, which had cost them thirty thousand dollars installed, this house which clothed and fed and rocked them to sleep and played and sang and was good to them. Their approach sensitized a switch somewhere and the nursery light flicked on when they came within ten feet of it. Similarly, behind them, in the halls, lights went on and off as they left them behind, with a soft automaticity.

11   "Well," said George Hadley.

12   They stood on the thatched floor of the nursery. It was forty feet across by forty feet long and thirty feet high; it had cost half again as much as the rest of the house. "But nothing's too good for our children," George had said.

13   The nursery was silent. It was empty as a jungle glade at hot high noon. The walls were blank and two dimensional. Now, as George and Lydia Hadley stood in the center of the room, the walls began to purr and recede into crystalline distance, it seemed, and presently an African veldt appeared, in three dimensions; on all sides, in colors reproduced to the final pebble and bit of straw. The ceiling above them became a deep sky with a hot yellow sun.

14   George Hadley felt the perspiration start on his brow.

15   "Let's get out of the sun," he said. "This is a little too real. But I don't see anything wrong."

16   "Wait a moment, you'll see," said his wife.

17   Now the hidden odorophonics were beginning to blow a wind of odor at the two people in the middle of the baked veldtland. The hot straw smell of lion grass, the cool green smell of the hidden water hole, the great rusty smell of animals, the smell of dust like a red paprika in the hot air. And now the sounds: the thump of distant antelope feet on grassy sod, the papery rustling of vultures. A shadow passed through the sky. The shadow flickered on George Hadley's upturned, sweating face.

18   "Filthy creatures," he heard his wife say.

19   "The vultures."

NOTES

Veldt (title): grassland

thatched (par. 12): straw covered

glade (par. 13): an open space in the middle of a forest

two dimensional (par. 13): having height and width

recede into crystalline distance (par. 13): become transparent

three dimensional (par. 13): having height, width, and depth

20   "You see, there are the lions, far over, that way. Now they're on their way to the water hole. They've just been eating," said Lydia. "I don't know what."

21   "Some animal." George Hadley put his hand up to shield off the burning light from his squinted eyes. "A zebra or a baby giraffe, maybe."

22   "Are you sure?" His wife sounded peculiarly tense.

23   "No, it's a little late to be sure," he said, amused. "Nothing over there I can see but cleaned bone, and the vultures dropping for what's left."

24   "Did you hear that scream?" she asked.

25   "No."

26   "About a minute ago?"

27   "Sorry, no."

28   The lions were coming. And again George Hadley was filled with admiration for the mechanical genius who had conceived this room. A miracle of efficiency selling for an absurdly low price. Every home should have one. Oh, occasionally they frightened you with their clinical accuracy, they startled you, gave you a twinge, but most of the time what fun for everyone, not only your own son and daughter, but for yourself when you felt like a quick jaunt to a foreign land, a quick change of scenery. Well, here it was!

29   And here were the lions now, fifteen feet away, so real, so feverishly and startlingly real that you could feel the prickling fur on your hand, and your mouth was stuffed with the dusty upholstery smell of their heated pelts, and the yellow of them was in your eyes like the yellow of an exquisite French tapestry, the yellows of lions and summer grass, and the sound of the matted lion lungs exhaling on the silent noontide, and the smell of meat from the panting, dripping mouths.

30   The lions stood looking at George and Lydia Hadley with terrible green-yellow eyes.

31   "Watch out!" screamed Lydia.

32   The lions came running at them.

33   Lydia bolted and ran. Instinctively, George sprang after her. Outside, in the hall, with the door slammed, he was laughing and she was crying, and they both stood appalled at the other's reaction.

34   "George!"

35   "Lydia! Oh, my dear poor sweet Lydia!"

36   "They almost got us!"

37   "Walls, Lydia, remember; crystal walls, that's all they are. Oh, they look real, I must admit—Africa in your parlor—but it's all dimensional superreactionary, supersensitive color film and mental tape film behind glass screens. It's all odorophonics and sonics, Lydia. Here's my handkerchief."

38   "I'm afraid." She came to him and put her body against him and cried steadily. "Did you see? Did you *feel?* It's too real."

39   "Now, Lydia . . . "

40   "You've got to tell Wendy and Peter not to read any more on Africa."

41   "Of course—of course." He patted her.

42   "Promise?"

43   "Sure."

44   "And lock the nursery for a few days until I get my nerves settled."

NOTES

jaunt (par. 28): pleasure trip

tapestry (par. 29): a heavy cloth woven with designs, frequently used as a wall-hanging

bolted (par. 33): jerked, moved suddenly

appalled (par. 33): shocked

45   "You know how difficult Peter is about that. When I punished him a month ago by locking the nursery for even a few hours—the tantrum he threw! And Wendy too. They *live* for the nursery."

46   "It's got to be locked, that's all there is to it."

47   "All right." Reluctantly he locked the huge door. "You've been working too hard. You need a rest."

48   "I don't know—I don't know," she said, blowing her nose, sitting down in a chair that immediately began to rock and comfort her. "Maybe I don't have enough to do. Maybe I have time to think too much. Why don't we shut the whole house off for a few days and take a vacation?"

49   "You mean you want to fry my eggs for me?"

50   "Yes." She nodded.

51   "And darn my socks?"

52   "Yes." A frantic, watery-eyed nodding.

53   "And sweep the house?"

54   "Yes, yes—oh, yes!"

55   "But I thought that's why we bought this house, so we wouldn't have to do anything?"

56   "That's just it. I feel like I don't belong here. The house is wife and mother now and nursemaid. Can I compete with an African veldt? Can I give a bath and scrub the children as efficiently or quickly as the automatic scrub bath can? I can not. And it isn't just me. It's you. You've been awfully nervous lately."

57   "I suppose I have been smoking too much."

58   "You look as if you didn't know what to do with yourself in this house, either. You smoke a little more every morning and drink a little more every afternoon and need a little more sedative every night. You're beginning to feel unnecessary too."

59   "Am I?" He paused and tried to feel into himself to see what was really there.

60   "Oh, George!" She looked beyond him, at the nursery door: "Those lions can't get out of there, can they?"

61   He looked at the door and saw it tremble as if something had jumped against it from the other side.

62   "Of course not," he said.

63   At dinner they ate alone, for Wendy and Peter were at a special plastic carnival across town and had televised home to say they'd be late, to go ahead eating. So George Hadley, bemused, sat watching the dining-room table produce warm dishes of food from its mechanical interior.

64   "We forgot the ketchup," he said.

65   "Sorry," said a small voice within the table, and ketchup appeared.

66   As for the nursery, thought George Hadley, it won't hurt for the children to be locked out of it awhile. Too much of anything isn't good for anyone. And it was clearly indicated that the children had been spending a little too much time on Africa. That sun. He could feel it on his neck, still, like a hot paw. And the lions. And the smell of blood. Remarkable how the nursery caught the telepathic emanations of the children's minds and created life to fill their every desire. The children thought lions, and there were lions. The children thought zebras, and there were zebras. Sun—sun. Giraffes—giraffes. Death and death.

NOTES

bemused (par. 63): lost in thought
telepathic emanations (par. 66): thoughts

67   That last. He chewed tastelessly on the meat that the table had cut for him. Death thoughts. They were awfully young, Wendy and Peter, for death thoughts. Or, no, you were never too young, really. Long before you knew what death was you were wishing it on someone else. When you were two years old you were shooting people with cap pistols.

68   But this—the long, hot African veldt—the awful death in the jaws of a lion. And repeated again and again.

69   "Where are you going?"

70   He didn't answer Lydia. Preoccupied, he let the lights glow softly on ahead of him, extinguished behind him as he padded to the nursery door. He listened against it. Far away, a lion roared.

71   He unlocked the door and opened it. Just before he stepped inside, he heard a faraway scream. And then another roar from the lions, which subsided quickly.

72   He stepped into Africa. How many times in the last year had he opened this door and found Wonderland, Alice, the Mock Turtle, or Aladdin and his Magical Lamp, or Jack Pumpkinhead of Oz, or Dr. Doolittle, or the cow jumping over a very real-appearing moon—all the delightful contraptions of a make-believe world. How often had he seen Pegasus flying in the sky ceiling, or seen fountains of red fireworks, or heard angel voices singing. But now, this yellow hot Africa, this bake oven with murder in the heat. Perhaps Lydia was right. Perhaps they needed a little vacation from the fantasy which was growing a bit too real for ten-year-old children. It was all right to exercise one's mind with gymnastic fantasies, but when the lively child mind settled on *one* pattern . . . ? It seemed that, at a distance, for the past month, he had heard lions roaring, and smelled their strong odor seeping as far away as his study door. But, being busy, he had paid it no attention.

73   George Hadley stood on the African grassland alone. The lions looked up from their feeding, watching him. The only flaw to the illusion was the open door through which he could see his wife, far down the dark hall, like a framed picture, eating her dinner abstractedly.

74   "Go away," he said to the lions.

75   They did not go.

76   He knew the principle of the room exactly. You sent out your thoughts. Whatever you thought would appear.

77   "Let's have Aladdin and his lamp," he snapped.

78   The veldtland remained; the lions remained.

79   "Come on, room! I demand Aladdin!" he said.

80   Nothing happened. The lions mumbled in their baked pelts.

81   "Aladdin!"

82   He went back to dinner. "The fool room's out of order," he said. "It won't respond."

83   "Or—"

84   "Or what?"

85   "Or it *can't* respond," said Lydia, "because the children have thought about Africa and lions and killing so many days that the room's in a rut."

86   "Could be."

87   "Or Peter's set it to remain that way."

88   "*Set* it?"

89   "He may have got into the machinery and fixed something."

NOTES

subsided (par. 71): stopped

Wonderland, Alice . . . moon (par. 72): places and characters from children's stories

contraptions (par. 72): inventions

Pegasus (par. 72): a winged horse in Greek mythology

90   "Peter doesn't know machinery."

91   "He's a wise one for ten. That I.Q. of his—"

92   "Nevertheless—"

93   "Hello, Mom. Hello, Dad."

94   The Hadleys turned. Wendy and Peter were coming in the front door, cheeks like peppermint candy, eyes like bright blue agate marbles, a smell of ozone on their jumpers from their trip in the helicopter.

95   "You're just in time for supper," said both parents.

96   "We're full of strawberry ice cream and hot dogs," said the children, holding hands. "But we'll sit and watch."

97   "Yes, come tell us about the nursery," said George Hadley.

98   The brother and sister blinked at him and then at each other. "Nursery?"

99   "All about Africa and everything," said the father with false joviality.

100   "I don't understand," said Peter.

101   "Your mother and I were just traveling through Africa with rod and reel; Tom Swift and his Electric Lion," said George Hadley.

102   "There's no Africa in the nursery," said Peter simply.

103   "Oh, come now, Peter. We know better."

104   "I don't remember any Africa," said Peter to Wendy. "Do you?"

105   "No."

106   "Run see and come tell."

107   She obeyed.

108   "Wendy, come back here!" said George Hadley, but she was gone.

109   The house lights followed her like a flock of fireflies. Too late, he realized he had forgotten to lock the nursery door after his last inspection.

110   "Wendy'll look and come tell us," said Peter.

111   "She doesn't have to tell *me*. I've seen it."

112   "I'm sure you're mistaken, Father."

113   "I'm not, Peter. Come along now."

114   But Wendy was back. "It's not Africa," she said breathlessly.

115   "We'll see about this," said George Hadley, and they all walked down the hall together and opened the nursery door.

116   There was a green, lovely forest, a lovely river, a purple mountain, high voices singing, and Rima, lovely and mysterious, lurking in the trees with colorful flights of butterflies, like animated bouquets, lingering on her long hair. The African veldtland was gone. The lions were gone. Only Rima was here now, singing a song so beautiful that it brought tears to your eyes.

117   George Hadley looked in at the changed scene. "Go to bed," he said to the children.

118   They opened their mouths.

119   "You heard me," he said.

120   They went off to the air closet, where a wind sucked them like brown leaves up the flue to their slumber rooms.

NOTES

agate (par. 94): quartz

ozone (par. 94): a gaseous substance with a strong, irritating odor; high concentrations of ozone are found in the upper atmosphere.

joviality (par. 99): jolliness

Tom Swift (par. 101): a character in the novels of Victor Appleton (1892–1965)

Rima (par. 116): a character in the novel *Green Mansions* by William H. Hudson (1841–1922)

lurking (par. 116): hiding

animated (par. 116): moving, living

flue (par. 120): passageway

121   George Hadley walked through the singing glade and picked up something that lay in the corner near where the lions had been. He walked slowly back to his wife.

122   "What is that?" she asked.

123   "An old wallet of mine," he said.

124   He showed it to her. The smell of hot grass was on it and the smell of a lion. There were drops of saliva on it, it had been chewed, and there were blood smears on both sides.

125   He closed the nursery door and locked it, tight.

126   In the middle of the night he was still awake and he knew his wife was awake. "Do you think Wendy changed it?" she said at last, in the dark room.

127   "Of course."

128   "Made it from a veldt into a forest and put Rima there instead of lions?"

129   "Yes."

130   "Why?"

131   "I don't know. But it's staying locked until I find out."

132   "How did your wallet get there?"

133   "I don't know anything," he said, "except that I'm beginning to be sorry we bought that room for the children. If children are neurotic at all, a room like that—"

134   "It's supposed to help them work off their neuroses in a healthful way."

135   "I'm starting to wonder." He stared at the ceiling.

136   "We've given the children everything they ever wanted. Is this our reward—secrecy, disobedience?"

137   "Who was it said, 'Children are carpets, they should be stepped on occasionally'? We've never lifted a hand. They're insufferable—let's admit it. They come and go when they like; they treat us as if *we* were offspring. They're spoiled and we're spoiled."

138   "They've been acting funny ever since you forbade them to take the rocket to New York a few months ago."

139   "They're not old enough to do that alone, I explained."

140   "Nevertheless, I've noticed they've been decidedly cool toward us since."

141   "I think I'll have David McClean come tomorrow morning to have a look at Africa."

142   "But it's not Africa now, it's Green Mansions country and Rima."

143   "I have a feeling it'll be Africa again before then."

144   A moment later they heard the screams.

145   Two screams. Two people screaming from downstairs. And then a roar of lions.

146   "Wendy and Peter aren't in their rooms," said his wife.

147   He lay in his bed with his beating heart. "No," he said. "They've broken into the nursery."

148   "Those screams—they sound familiar."

149   "Do they?"

150   "Yes, awfully."

151   And although their beds tried very hard, the two adults couldn't be rocked to sleep for another hour. A smell of cats was in the night air.

NOTES

neurotic (par. 133): mentally unstable

insufferable (par. 137): intolerable

152   "Father?" said Peter.

153   "Yes."

154   Peter looked at his shoes. He never looked at his father any more, nor at his mother. "You aren't going to lock up the nursery for good, are you?"

155   "That all depends."

156   "On what?" snapped Peter.

157   "On you and your sister. If you intersperse this Africa with a little variety—oh, Sweden perhaps, or Denmark or China—"

158   "I thought we were free to play as we wished."

159   "You are, within reasonable bounds."

160   "What's wrong with Africa, Father?"

161   "Oh, so now you admit you have been conjuring up Africa, do you?"

162   "I wouldn't want the nursery locked up," said Peter coldly. "Ever."

163   "Matter of fact, we're thinking of turning the whole house off for about a month. Live sort of a carefree one-for-all existence."

164   "That sounds dreadful! Would I have to tie my own shoes instead of letting the shoe tier do it? And brush my own teeth and comb my hair and give myself a bath?"

165   "It would be fun for a change, don't you think?"

166   "No, it would be horrid. I didn't like it when you took out the picture painter last month."

167   "That's because I wanted you to learn to paint all by yourself, son."

168   "I don't want to do anything but look and listen and smell; what else *is* there to do?"

169   "All right, go play in Africa."

170   "Will you shut off the house sometime soon?"

171   "We're considering it."

172   "I don't think you'd better consider it any more, Father."

173   "I won't have any threats from my son!"

174   "Very well." And Peter strolled off to the nursery.

175   "Am I on time?" said David McClean.

176   "Breakfast?" asked George Hadley.

177   "Thanks, had some. What's the trouble?"

178   "David, you're a psychologist."

179   "I should hope so."

180   "Well, then, have a look at our nursery. You saw it a year ago when you dropped by; did you notice anything peculiar about it then?"

181   "Can't say I did; the usual violences, a tendency toward a slight paranoia here or there, usual in children because they feel persecuted by parents constantly, but, oh, really nothing."

182   They walked down the hall. "I locked the nursery up," explained the father, "and the children broke back into it during the night. I let them stay so they could form the patterns for you to see."

183   There was a terrible screaming from the nursery.

184   "There it is," said George Hadley. "See what you make of it."

185   They walked in on the children without rapping.

186   The screams had faded. The lions were feeding.

NOTES

intersperse (par. 157): mix
paranoia (par. 181): unreasonable suspicion or distrust
rapping (par. 185): knocking

187   "Run outside a moment, children," said George Hadley. "No, don't change the mental combination. Leave the walls as they are. Get!"

188   With the children gone, the two men stood studying the lions clustered at a distance, eating with great relish whatever it was they had caught.

189   "I wish I knew what it was," said George Hadley. "Sometimes I can almost see. Do you think if I brought high-powered binoculars here and—"

190   David McClean laughed dryly. "Hardly." He turned to study all four walls. "How long has this been going on?"

191   "A little over a month."

192   "It certainly doesn't *feel* good."

193   "I want facts, not feelings."

194   "My dear George, a psychologist never saw a fact in his life. He only hears about feelings; vague things. This doesn't feel good, I tell you. Trust my hunches and my instincts. I have a nose for something bad. This is very bad. My advice to you is to have the whole damn room torn down and your children brought to me every day during the next year for treatment."

195   "Is it that bad?"

196   "I'm afraid so. One of the original uses of these nurseries was so that we could study the patterns left on the walls by the child's mind, study at our leisure, and help the child. In this case, however, the room has become a channel toward—destructive thoughts, instead of a release away from them."

197   "Didn't you sense this before?"

198   "I sensed only that you had spoiled your children more than most. And now you're letting them down in some way. What way?"

199   "I wouldn't let them go to New York."

200   "What else?"

201   "I've taken a few machines from the house and threatened them, a month ago, with closing up the nursery unless they did their homework. I did close it for a few days to show I meant business."

202   "Ah, ha!"

203   "Does that mean anything?"

204   "Everything. Where before they had a Santa Claus now they have a Scrooge. Children prefer Santas. You've let this room and this house replace you and your wife in your children's affections. This room is their mother and father, far more important in their lives than their real parents. And now you come along and want to shut it off. No wonder there's hatred here. You can feel it coming out of the sky. Feel that sun. George, you'll have to change your life. Like too many others, you've built it around creature comforts. Why, you'd starve tomorrow if something went wrong in your kitchen. You wouldn't know how to tap an egg. Nevertheless, turn everything off. Start new. It'll take time. But we'll make good children out of bad in a year, wait and see."

205   "But won't the shock be too much for the children, shutting the room up abruptly, for good?"

206   "I don't want them going any deeper into this, that's all."

207   The lions were finished with their red feast.

208   The lions were standing on the edge of the clearing watching the two men.

209   "Now *I'm* feeling persecuted," said McClean. "Let's get out of here. I never have cared for these damned rooms. Make me nervous."

210   "The lions look real, don't they?" said George Hadley. "I don't suppose there's any way—"

211   "What?"

212   "—that they could *become* real?"

213   "Not that I know."

214   "Some flaw in the machinery, a tampering or something?"

215   "No."

216   They went to the door.

217   "I don't imagine the room will like being turned off," said the father.

218   "Nothing ever likes to die—even a room."

219   "I wonder if it hates me for wanting to switch it off?"

220   "Paranoia is thick around here today," said David McClean. "You can follow it like a spoor. Hello." He bent and picked up a bloody scarf. "This yours?"

221   "No." George Hadley's face was rigid. "It belongs to Lydia."

222   They went to the fuse box together and threw the switch that killed the nursery.

223   The two children were in hysterics. They screamed and pranced and threw things. They yelled and sobbed and swore and jumped at the furniture.

224   "You can't do that to the nursery, you can't!"

225   "Now, children."

226   The children flung themselves onto a couch, weeping.

227   "George," said Lydia Hadley, "turn on the nursery, just for a few moments. You can't be so abrupt."

228   "No."

229   "You can't be so cruel."

230   "Lydia, it's off, and it stays off. And the whole damn house dies as of here and now. The more I see of the mess we've put ourselves in, the more it sickens me. We've been contemplating our mechanical, electronic navels for too long. My God, how we need a breath of honest air!"

231   And he marched about the house turning off the voice clocks, the stoves, the heaters, the shoe shiners, the shoe lacers, the body scrubbers and swabbers and massagers, and every other machine he could put his hand to.

232   The house was full of dead bodies, it seemed. It felt like a mechanical cemetery. So silent. None of the humming hidden energy of machines waiting to function at the tap of a button.

233   "Don't let them do it!" wailed Peter at the ceiling, as if he was talking to the house, the nursery. "Don't let Father kill everything." He turned to his father. "Oh, I hate you!"

234   "Insults won't get you anywhere."

235   "I wish you were dead!"

236   "We were, for a long while. Now we're going to really start living. Instead of being handled and massaged, we're going to *live*."

237   Wendy was still crying and Peter joined her again. "Just a moment, just one moment, just another moment of nursery," they wailed.

238   "Oh, George," said the wife, "It can't hurt."

239   "All right—all right, if they'll only just shut up. One minute, mind you, and then off forever."

240   "Daddy, Daddy, Daddy!" sang the children, smiling with wet faces.

241   "And then we're going on a vacation. David McClean is coming back in half an hour to help us move out and get to the airport. I'm going to dress. You turn the nursery on for a minute, Lydia, just a minute, mind you."

242   And the three of them went babbling off while he let himself be vacuumed upstairs through the air flue and set about dressing himself. A minute later Lydia appeared.

243   "I'll be glad when we get away," she sighed.

244   "Did you leave them in the nursery?"

NOTES

spoor (par. 220): trail or droppings of a wild animal
wailed (par. 233): cried

245   "I wanted to dress too. Oh, that horrid Africa. What can they see in it?"

246   "Well, in five minutes we'll be on our way to Iowa. Lord, how did we ever get in this house? What prompted us to buy a nightmare?"

247   "Pride, money, foolishness."

248   "I think we'd better get downstairs before those kids get engrossed with those damned beasts again."

249   Just then they heard the children calling, "Daddy, Mommy, come quick—quick!"

250   They went downstairs in the air flue and ran down the hall. The children were nowhere in sight. "Wendy? Peter!"

251   They ran into the nursery. The veldtland was empty save for the lions waiting, looking at them. "Peter, Wendy?"

252   The door slammed.

253   "Wendy, Peter!"

254   George Hadley and his wife whirled and ran back to the door.

255   "Open the door!" cried George Hadley, trying the knob. "Why, they've locked it from the outside! Peter!" He beat at the door. "Open up!"

256   He heard Peter's voice outside, against the door.

257   "Don't let them switch off the nursery and the house," he was saying.

258   Mr. and Mrs. George Hadley beat at the door. "Now, don't be ridiculous, children. It's time to go. Mr. McClean'll be here in a minute and . . . "

259   And then they heard the sounds.

260   The lions on three sides of them, in the yellow veldt grass, padding through the dry straw, rumbling and roaring in their throats.

261   The lions.

262   Mr. Hadley looked at his wife and they turned and looked back at the beasts edging slowly forward, crouching, tails stiff.

263   Mr. and Mrs. Hadley screamed.

264   And suddenly they realized why those other screams had sounded familiar.

265   "Well, here I am," said David McClean in the nursery doorway. "Oh, hello." He stared at the two children seated in the center of the open glade eating a little picnic lunch. Beyond them was the water hole and the yellow veldtland; above was the hot sun. He began to perspire. "Where are your father and mother?"

266   The children looked up and smiled. "Oh, they'll be here directly."

267   "Good, we must get going." At a distance Mr. McClean saw the lions fighting and clawing and then quieting down to feed in silence under the shady trees.

268   He squinted at the lions with his hand up to his eyes.

269   Now the lions were done feeding. They moved to the water hole to drink.

270   A shadow flickered over Mr. McClean's hot face. Many shadows flickered. The vultures were dropping down the blazing sky.

271   "A cup of tea?" asked Wendy in the silence.

NOTE

engrossed with (par. 248): deeping involved with, totally occupied by

The Kugelmass Episode

Woody Allen

1   Kugelmass, a professor of humanities at City College, was unhappily married for the second time. Daphne Kugelmass was an oaf. He also had two dull sons by his first wife, Flo, and was up to his neck in alimony and child support.

2   "Did I know it would turn out so badly?" Kugelmass whined to his analyst one day. "Daphne had promise. Who suspected she'd let herself go and swell up like a beach ball? Plus she had a few bucks, which is not in itself a healthy reason to marry a person, but it doesn't hurt, with the kind of operating nut I have. You see my point?"

3   Kugelmass was bald and as hairy as a bear, but he had soul.

4   "I need to meet a new woman," he went on. "I need to have an affair. I may not look the part, but I'm a man who needs romance. I need softness, I need flirtation. I'm not getting younger, so before it's too late I want to make love in Venice, trade quips at '21,' and exchange coy glances over red wine and candlelight. You see what I'm saying?"

5   Dr. Mandel shifted in his chair and said, "An affair will solve nothing. You're so unrealistic. Your problems run much deeper."

6   "And also this affair must be discreet," Kugelmass continued. "I can't afford a second divorce. Daphne would really sock it to me."

7   "Mr. Kugelmass—"

8   "But it can't be anyone at City College, because Daphne also works there. Not that anyone on the faculty at C.C.N.Y. is any great shakes, but some of those coeds . . . "

9   "Mr. Kugelmass—"

10   "Help me. I had a dream last night. I was skipping through a meadow holding a picnic basket and the basket was marked 'Options.' And then I saw there was a hole in the basket."

11   "Mr. Kugelmass, the worst thing you could do is act out. You must simply express your feelings here, and together we'll analyze them. You have been in treatment long enough to know there is no overnight cure. After all, I'm an analyst, not a magician."

12   "Then perhaps what I need is a magician," Kugelmass said, rising from his chair. And with that he terminated his therapy.

13   A couple of weeks later, while Kugelmass and Daphne were moping around in their apartment one night like two pieces of old furniture, the phone rang.

14   "I'll get it," Kugelmass said. "Hello."

NOTES

Kugelmass (title): In Yiddish, a "kugel" is a noodle pudding. Yiddish is a combination of Hebrew, German, and Eastern European languages.
oaf (par. 1): a stupid person
analyst (par. 2): a psychiatrist or psychologist
operating nut (par. 2): expenses
quips (par. 4): clever remarks
"21" (par. 4): nightclub in New York City
coy (par. 4): teasing
discreet (par. 6): secret
C.C.N.Y. (par. 8): City College of New York
act out (par. 11): that is, to carry out
terminated (par. 12): ended

15   "Kugelmass?" a voice said. "Kugelmass, this is Persky."

16   "Who?"

17   "Persky. Or should I say The Great Persky?"

18   "Pardon me?"

19   "I hear you're looking all over town for a magician to bring a little exotica into your life? Yes or no?"

20   "Sh-h-h," Kugelmass whispered. "Don't hang up. Where are you calling from, Persky?"

21   Early the following afternoon, Kugelmass climbed three flights of stairs in a broken-down apartment house in the Bushwick section of Brooklyn. Peering through the darkness of the hall, he found the door he was looking for and pressed the bell. I'm going to regret this, he thought to himself.

22   Seconds later, he was greeted by a short, thin, waxy-looking man.

23   "*You're* Persky the Great?" Kugelmass said.

24   "The Great Persky. You want a tea?"

25   "No, I want romance. I want music. I want love and beauty."

26   "But not tea, eh? Amazing. O.K., sit down."

27   Persky went to the back room, and Kugelmass heard the sounds of boxes and furniture being moved around. Persky reappeared, pushing before him a large object on squeaky roller-skate wheels. He removed some old silk handkerchiefs that were lying on its top and blew away a bit of dust. It was a cheap-looking Chinese cabinet, badly lacquered.

28   "Persky," Kugelmass said, "what's your scam?"

29   "Pay attention," Persky said. "This is some beautiful effect. I developed it for a Knights of Pythias date last year, but the booking fell through. Get into the cabinet."

30   "Why, so you can stick it full of swords or something?"

31   "You see any swords?"

32   Kugelmass made a face and, grunting, climbed into the cabinet. He couldn't help noticing a couple of ugly rhinestones glued onto the raw plywood just in front of his face. "If this is a joke," he said.

33   "Some joke. Now, here's the point. If I throw any novel into this cabinet with you, shut the doors, and tap it three times, you will find yourself projected into that book."

34   Kugelmass made a grimace of disbelief.

35   "It's the emess," Persky said. "My hand to God. Not just a novel, either. A short story, a play, a poem. You can meet any of the women created by the world's best writers. Whoever you dreamed of. You could carry on all you like with a real winner. Then when you've had enough you give a yell, and I'll see you're back there in a split second."

36   "Persky, are you some kind of outpatient?"

37   "I'm telling you it's on the level," Persky said.

38   Kugelmass remained skeptical. "What are you telling me—that this cheesy homemade box can take me on a ride like you're describing?"

39   "For a double sawbuck."

NOTES

exotica (par. 19): something exciting and different
Brooklyn (par. 21): a section of New York City
lacquered (par. 27): covered with a high-gloss coating (lacquer)
scam (par. 28): a "con" game
Knights of Pythias (par. 29): a men's charitable organization
grimace (par. 34): a facial expression
emess (par. 35): Yiddish for "truth"
skeptical (par. 38): doubtful
double sawbuck (par. 39): twenty dollars

40   Kugelmass reached for his wallet. "I'll believe this when I see it," he said.

41   Persky tucked the bills in his pants pocket and turned toward his bookcase. "So who do you want to meet? Sister Carrie? Hester Prynne? Ophelia? Maybe someone by Saul Bellow? Hey, what about Temple Drake? Although for a man your age she'd be a workout."

42   "French. I want to have an affair with a French lover."

43   "Nana?"

44   "I don't want to have to pay for it."

45   "What about Natasha in *War and Peace*?"

46   "I said French. I know! What about Emma Bovary? That sounds to me perfect."

47   "You got it, Kugelmass. Give me a holler when you've had enough." Persky tossed in a paperback copy of Flaubert's novel.

48   "You sure this is safe?" Kugelmass asked as Persky began shutting the cabinet doors.

49   "Safe. Is anything safe in this crazy world?" Persky rapped three times on the cabinet and flung open the doors.

50   Kugelmass was gone. At the same moment, he appeared in the bedroom of Charles and Emma Bovary's house at Yonville. Before him was a beautiful woman, standing alone with her back turned to him as she folded some linen. I can't believe this, thought Kugelmass, staring at the doctor's ravishing wife. This is uncanny. I'm here. It's her.

51   Emma turned in surprise. "Goodness, you startled me," she said.

52   "Who are you?" She spoke in the same fine English translation as the paperback.

53   It's simply devastating, he thought. Then, realizing that it was he whom she had addressed, he said, "Excuse me. I'm Sidney Kugelmass. I'm from City College. A professor of humanities. C.C.N.Y.? Uptown. I—oh, boy!"

54   Emma Bovary smiled flirtatiously and said, "Would you like a drink? A glass of wine, perhaps?"

55   She is beautiful, Kugelmass thought. What a contrast with the troglodyte who shared his bed! He felt a sudden impulse to take this vision into his arms and tell her she was the kind of woman he had dreamed of all his life.

56   "Yes, some wine," he said hoarsely. "White. No, red. No, white. Make it white."

57   "Charles is out for the day," Emma said, her voice full of playful implication.

NOTES

Sister Carrie (par. 41): a character in the novel *Sister Carrie* by Theodore Dreiser (1871–1945)
Hester Prynne (par. 41): a character in the novel *The Scarlet Letter* by Nathaniel Hawthorne (1804–1864)
Ophelia (par. 41): a character in the play *Hamlet* by Shakespeare (1564–1616)
Saul Bellow (par. 41): an American novelist (b. 1925)
Temple Drake (par. 41): a character in the novel *Sanctuary* by William Faulkner (1897–1962)
Nana (par. 43): a character in the novel *Nana* by Emile Zola (1840–1902)
War and Peace (par. 45): a novel by Leo Tolstoy (1828–1910)
Emma Bovary (par. 46): the main character in *Madame Bovary* by Gustave Flaubert (1821–1880); Emma's husband, Charles, is a doctor (par. 50), and they live in Yonville, France (par. 50). She has two lovers, Rodolphe (par. 71) and Leon (par. 78). Abbe Bournisien (par. 80) is her priest. Binet (par. 94) is the tax collector.
ravishing (par. 50): gorgeous, sexy
uncanny (par. 50): unbelievable
devastating (par. 53): amazing
troglodyte (par. 55): literally, a cave dweller
implication (par. 57): suggestion

58   After the wine, they went for a stroll in the lovely French countryside. "I've always dreamed that some mysterious stranger would appear and rescue me from the monotony of this crass rural existence," Emma said, clasping his hand. They passed a small church. "I love what you have on," she murmured. "I've never seen anything like it around here. It's so . . . so modern."

59   "It's called a leisure suit," he said romantically. "It was marked down." Suddenly he kissed her. For the next hour they reclined under a tree and whispered together and told each other deeply meaningful things with their eyes. Then Kugelmass sat up. He had just remembered he had to meet Daphne at Bloomingdale's. "I must go," he told her. "But don't worry, I'll be back."

60   "I hope so," Emma said.

61   He embraced her passionately, and the two walked back to the house. He held Emma's face cupped in his palms, kissed her again, and yelled, "O.K., Persky! I got to be at Bloomingdale's by three-thirty."

62   There was an audible pop, and Kugelmass was back in Brooklyn.

63   "So? Did I lie?" Persky asked triumphantly.

64   "Look, Persky, I'm right now late to meet the ball and chain at Lexington Avenue, but when can I go again? Tomorrow?"

65   "My pleasure. Just bring a twenty. And don't mention this to anybody."

66   "Yeah. I'm going to call Rupert Murdoch."

67   Kugelmass hailed a cab and sped off to the city. His heart danced on point. I am in love, he thought. I am the possessor of a wonderful secret. What he didn't realize was that at this very moment students in various classrooms across the country were saying to their teachers, "Who is this character on page 100? A bald Jew is kissing Madame Bovary?" A teacher in Sioux Falls, South Dakota, sighed and thought, Jesus, these kids, with their pot and acid. What goes through their minds!

68   Daphne Kugelmass was in the bathroom-accessories department at Bloomingdale's when Kugelmass arrived breathlessly. "Where've you been?" she snapped. "It's four-thirty."

69   "I got held up in traffic," Kugelmass said.

70   Kugelmass visited Persky the next day, and in a few minutes was again passed magically to Yonville. Emma couldn't hide her excitement at seeing him. The two spent hours together, laughing and talking about their different backgrounds. Before Kugelmass left, they made love. "My God, I'm doing it with Madame Bovary! Kugelmass whispered to himself. "Me, who failed freshman English."

71   As the months passed, Kugelmass saw Persky many times and developed a close and passionate relationship with Emma Bovary. "Make sure and always get me into the book before page 120," Kugelmass said to the magician one day. "I always have to meet her before she hooks up with this Rodolphe character."

72   "Why?" Persky asked. "You can't beat his time?"

73   "Beat his time. He's landed gentry. Those guys have nothing better to do than flirt and ride horses. To me, he's one of those faces you see in the pages

NOTES

monotony (par. 58): boredom

crass (par. 58): common, lacking "class"

Bloomingdale's (par. 59): department store in New York City located on Lexington Avenue (par. 64)

audible (par. 62): loud enough to be heard

the ball and chain (par. 64): that is, his wife, Daphne; A ball and chain were once attached to prisoners to prevent them from escaping.

Rupert Murdoch (par. 66): a newspaper publisher

landed gentry (par. 73): a landowner of high social position

of *Women's Wear Daily*. With the Helmut Berger hairdo. But to her he's hot stuff."

74   "And her husband suspects nothing?"

75   "He's out of his depth. He's a lackluster little paramedic who's thrown in his lot with a jitterbug. He's ready to go to sleep by ten, and she's putting on her dancing shoes. Oh, well . . . See you later."

76   And once again Kugelmass entered the cabinet and passed instantly to the Bovary estate at Yonville. "How you doing, cupcake?" he said to Emma.

77   "Oh, Kugelmass," Emma sighed. "What I have to put up with. Last night at dinner, Mr. Personality dropped off to sleep in the middle of the dessert course. I'm pouring my heart out about Maxim's and the ballet, and out of the blue I hear snoring."

78   "It's O.K., darling. I'm here now," Kugelmass said, embracing her. I've earned this, he thought, smelling Emma's French perfume and burying his nose in her hair. I've suffered enough. I've paid enough analysts. I've searched till I'm weary. She's young and nubile, and I'm here a few pages after Leon and just before Rodolphe. By showing up during the correct chapters, I've got the situation knocked.

79   Emma, to be sure, was just as happy as Kugelmass. She had been starved for excitement, and his tales of Broadway night life, of fast cars and Hollywood and TV stars, enthralled the young French beauty.

80   "Tell me again about O. J. Simpson," she implored that evening, as she and Kugelmass strolled past Abbe Bournisien's church.

81   "What can I say? The man is great. He sets all kinds of rushing records. Such moves. They can't touch him."

82   "And the Academy Awards?" Emma said wistfully. "I'd give anything to win one."

83   "First you've got to be nominated."

84   "I know. You explained it. But I'm convinced I can act. Of course, I'd want to take a class or two. With Strasberg maybe. Then, if I had the right agent—"

85   "We'll see, we'll see. I'll speak to Persky."

86   That night, safely returned to Persky's flat, Kugelmass brought up the idea of having Emma visit him in the big city.

87   "Let me think about it," Persky said. "Maybe I could work it. Stranger things have happened." Of course, neither of them could think of one.

88   "Where the hell do you go all the time?" Daphne Kugelmass barked at her husband as he returned home late that evening. "You got a chippie stashed somewhere?"

89   "Yeah, sure, I'm just the type," Kugelmass said wearily. "I was with Leonard Popkin. We were discussing Socialist agriculture in Poland. You know Popkin. He's a freak on the subject."

NOTES

Women's Wear Daily (par. 73): a fashion magazine
lackluster (par. 75): dull
thrown in his lot (par. 75): joined in
jitterbug (par. 75): Literally, the jitterbug is a dance done to fast music such as jazz.
Maxim's (par. 77): a restaurant in Paris
nubile (par. 78): ready for sex
Broadway (par. 79): theatre district in New York City
O. J. Simpson (par. 80): At the time this story was published, Simpson played football for the Buffalo Bills and had led the National Football League in rushing in 1972, 1973, 1975, and 1976.
Strasberg (par. 84): Lee Strasberg (1901–1982) was a famous actor, acting teacher, and director.
chippie (par. 88): prostitute

90   "Well, you've been very odd lately," Daphne said. "Distant. Just don't forget about my father's birthday. On Saturday?"

91   "Oh, sure, sure," Kugelmass said, heading for the bathroom.

92   "My whole family will be there. We can see the twins. And Cousin Hamish. You should be more polite to Cousin Hamish—he likes you."

93   "Right, the twins," Kugelmass said, closing the bathroom door and shutting out the sound of his wife's voice. He leaned against it and took a deep breath. In a few hours he told himself, he would be back in Yonville again, back with his beloved. And this time, if all went well, he would bring Emma back with him.

94   At three-fifteen the following afternoon, Persky worked his wizardry again. Kugelmass appeared before Emma, smiling and eager. The two spent a few hours at Yonville with Binet and then remounted the Bovary carriage. Following Persky's instructions, they held each other tightly, closed their eyes, and counted to ten. When they opened them, the carriage was just drawing up at the side door of the Plaza Hotel, where Kugelmass had optimistically reserved a suite earlier in the day.

95   "I love it! It's everything I dreamed it would be," Emma said as she swirled joyously around the bedroom, surveying the city from their window. "There's F. A. O. Schwarz. And there's Central Park, and the Sherry is which one? Oh, there—I see. It's too divine."

96   On the bed there were boxes from Halston and Saint Laurent. Emma unwrapped a package and held up a pair of black velvet pants against her perfect body.

97   "The slacks suit is by Ralph Lauren," Kugelmass said. "You'll look like a million bucks in it. Come on, sugar, give us a kiss."

98   "I've never been so happy!" Emma squealed as she stood before the mirror. "Let's go out on the town. I want to see 'Chorus Line' and the Guggenheim and this Jack Nicholson character you always talk about. Are any of his flicks showing?"

99   "I cannot get my mind around this," a Stanford professor said. "First a strange character named Kugelmass, and now she's gone from the book. Well, I guess the mark of a classic is that you can reread it a thousand times and always find something new."

100   The lovers passed a blissful weekend. Kugelmass had told Daphne he would be away at a symposium in Boston and would return Monday. Savoring each moment, he and Emma went to the movies, had dinner in Chinatown, passed two hours at a discotheque, and went to bed with a TV movie. They slept till noon Sunday, visited SoHo, and ogled celebrities at Elaine's. They had caviar and champagne in their suite on Sunday night and talked until dawn. That morning, in the cab taking them to Persky's apartment,

NOTES

optimistically (par. 94): hopefully

F. A. O. Schwarz (par. 95): a toy store in New York City

the Sherry (par. 95): a hotel in New York City

Halston and Saint Laurent (par. 96): fashion designers

'Chorus Line' (par. 98): a Broadway musical

the Guggenheim (par. 98): an art museum

Jack Nicholson (par. 98): an actor

flicks (par. 98): movies

symposium (par. 100): conference

savoring (par. 100): enjoying

SoHo (par. 100): a popular district of New York City

ogled (par. 100): stared at

Elaine's (par. 100): a restaurant in New York City

Kugelmass thought, It was hectic, but worth it. I can't bring her here too often, but now and then it will be a charming contrast with Yonville.

101   At Persky's, Emma climbed into the cabinet, arranged her new boxes of clothes neatly around her, and kissed Kugelmass fondly. "My place next time," she said with a wink. Persky rapped three times on the cabinet. Nothing happened.

102   "Hmm." Persky said, scratching his head. He rapped again, but still no magic. "Something must be wrong," he mumbled.

103   "Persky you're joking!" Kugelmass cried. "How can it not work?"

104   "Relax, relax. Are you still in the box, Emma?"

105   "Yes."

106   Persky rapped again—harder this time.

107   "I'm still here, Persky."

108   "I know, darling. Sit tight."

109   "Persky, we *have* to get her back," Kugelmass whispered. "I'm a married man, and I have a class in three hours. I'm not prepared for anything more than a cautious affair at this point."

110   "I can't understand it," Persky muttered. "It's such a reliable little trick."

111   But he could do nothing. "It's going to take a little while," he said to Kugelmass. "I'm going to have to strip it down. I'll call you later."

112   Kugelmass bundled Emma into a cab and took her back to the Plaza. He barely made it to his class on time. He was on the phone all day, to Persky and to his mistress. The magician told him it might be several days before he got to the bottom of the trouble.

113   "How was the symposium?" Daphne asked him that night.

114   "Fine, fine," he said, lighting the filter end of a cigarette.

115   "What's wrong? You're as tense as a cat."

116   "Me? Ha, that's a laugh. I'm as calm as a summer night. I'm just going to take a walk." He eased out the door, hailed a cab, and flew to the Plaza.

117   "This is no good," Emma said. "Charles will miss me."

118   "Bear with me, sugar," Kugelmass said. He was pale and sweaty. He kissed her again, raced to the elevators, yelled at Persky over a pay phone in the Plaza lobby, and just made it home before midnight.

119   "According to Popkin, barley prices in Krakow have not been this stable since 1971," he said to Daphne, and smiled wanly as he climbed into bed.

120   The whole week went by like that. On Friday night, Kugelmass told Daphne there was another symposium he had to catch, this one in Syracuse. He hurried back to the Plaza, but the second weekend there was nothing like the first. "Get me back into the novel or marry me," Emma told Kugelmass. "Meanwhile, I want to get a job or go to class, because watching TV all day is the pits."

121   "Fine. We can use the money," Kugelmass said. "You consume twice your weight in room service."

122   "I met an Off Broadway producer in Central Park yesterday, and he said I might be right for a project he's doing," Emma said.

123   "Who is this clown?" Kugelmass asked.

124   "He not a clown. He's sensitive and kind and cute. His name's Jeff Something-or-Other, and he's up for a Tony."

125   Later that afternoon, Kugelmass showed up at Persky's drunk.

NOTES

Krakow (par. 119): city in Poland

wanly (par. 119): weakly

Syracuse (par. 120): city in New York

Tony (par. 124): award given for excellence in theatre

126 "Relax," Persky told him. "You'll get a coronary."

127 "Relax. The man says relax. I've got a fictional character stashed in a hotel room, and I think my wife is having me tailed by a private shamus."

128 "O.K., O.K. We know there's a problem." Persky crawled under the cabinet and started banging on something with a wrench.

129 "I'm like a wild animal," Kugelmass went on. "I'm sneaking around town, and Emma and I have had it up to here with each other. Not to mention a hotel tab that reads like the defense budget."

130 "So what should I do? This is the world of magic," Persky said. "It's all nuance."

131 "Nuance, my foot. I'm pouring Dom Perignon and black eggs into this little mouse, plus her wardrobe, plus she's enrolled at the Neighborhood Playhouse and suddenly needs professional photos. Also, Persky, Professor Fivish Kopkind, who teaches Comp Lit and who has always been jealous of me, has identified me as the sporadically appearing character in the Flaubert book. He's threatened to go to Daphne. I see ruin and alimony jail. For adultery with Madame Bovary, my wife will reduce me to beggary."

132 "What do you want me to say? I'm working on it night and day. As far as your personal anxiety goes, that I can't help you with. I'm a magician, not an analyst."

133 By Sunday afternoon, Emma had locked herself in the bathroom and refused to respond to Kugelmass's entreaties. Kugelmass stared out the window at the Wollman Rink and contemplated suicide. Too bad this is a low floor, he thought, or I'd do it right now. Maybe if I ran away to Europe and started life over . . . Maybe I could sell the *International Herald Tribune*, like those young girls used to.

134 The phone rang. Kugelmass lifted it to his ear mechanically.

135 "Bring her over," Persky said. "I think I got the bugs out of it."

136 Kugelmass's heart leaped. "You're serious?" he said. "You got it licked?"

137 "It was something in the transmission. Go figure."

138 "Persky, you're a genius. We'll be there in a minute. Less than a minute."

139 Again the lovers hurried to the magician's apartment, and again Emma Bovary climbed into the cabinet with her boxes. This time there was no kiss. Persky shut the doors, took a deep breath, and tapped the box three times. There was the reassuring popping noise, and when Persky peered inside, the box was empty. Madame Bovary was back in her novel. Kugelmass heaved a great sigh of relief and pumped the magician's hand.

140 "It's over," he said. "I learned my lesson. I'll never cheat again, I swear it." He pumped Persky's hand again and made a mental note to send him a necktie.

141 Three weeks later, at the end of a beautiful spring afternoon, Persky answered his doorbell. It was Kugelmass, with a sheepish expression on his face.

NOTES

shamus (par. 127): detective
nuance (par. 130): literally, a slight difference
Dom Perignon (par. 131): a brand of expensive champagne
black eggs (par. 131): caviar
Neighborhood Playhouse (par. 131): theatre in New York City
sporadically (par. 131): occasionally
entreaties (par. 133): pleas
Wollman Rink (par. 133): ice-skating rink in Central Park
International Herald Tribune (par. 133): an American newspaper published in France
sheepish (par. 141): timid, embarrassed

142   "O.K., Kugelmass," the magician said. "Where to this time?"

143   "It's just this once," Kugelmass said. "The weather is so lovely, and I'm not getting any younger. Listen, you've read *Portnoy's Complaint*? Remember The Monkey?"

144   "The price is now twenty-five dollars, because the cost of living is up, but I'll start you off with one freebie, due to all the trouble I caused you."

145   "You're good people," Kugelmass said, combing his few remaining hairs as he climbed into the cabinet again. "This'll work all right?"

146   "I hope. But I haven't tried it much since all that unpleasantness."

147   "Sex and romance," Kugelmass said from inside the box. "What we go through for a pretty face."

148   Persky tossed in a copy of *Portnoy's Complaint* and rapped three times on the box. This time, instead of a popping noise there was a dull explosion, followed by a series of crackling noises and a shower of sparks. Persky leaped back, was seized by a heart attack, and dropped dead. The cabinet burst into flames, and eventually the entire house burned down.

149   Kugelmass, unaware of this catastrophe, had his own problems. He had not been thrust into *Portnoy's Complaint*, or into any other novel, for that matter. He had been projected into an old textbook, *Remedial Spanish*, and was running for his life over a barren, rocky terrain as the word *"tener"* ("to have")—a large and hairy irregular verb—raced after him on its spindly legs.

NOTES

Portnoy's Complaint (par. 143): a novel by Philip Roth (b. 1933)
terrain (par. 149): ground
spindly (par. 149): long and skinny

A Worn Path

Eudora Welty

1   It was December—a bright frozen day in the early morning. Far out in the country there was an old Negro woman with her head tied in a red rag, coming along a path through the pinewoods. Her name was Phoenix Jackson. She was very old and small and she walked slowly in the dark pine shadows, moving a little from side to side in her steps, with the balanced heaviness and lightness of a pendulum in a grandfather clock. She carried a thin, small cane made from an umbrella, and with this she kept tapping the frozen earth in front of her. This made a grave and persistent noise in the still air, that seemed meditative like the chirping of a solitary little bird.

2   She wore a dark striped dress reaching down to her shoe tops, and an equally long apron of bleached sugar sacks, with a full pocket: all neat and tidy, but every time she took a step she might have fallen over her shoelaces, which dragged from her unlaced shoes. She looked straight ahead. Her eyes

NOTES

Phoenix (par. 1): The phoenix is an Egyptian mythological bird that lived in the desert for 500 years and then flew to Heliopolis to the temple of Re, the god of the sun. In the temple, the phoenix flew into the altar fire, was consumed by it, and arose from the ashes renewed.
meditative (par. 1): religiously or philosophically thoughtful

were blue with age. Her skin had a pattern all its own of numberless branching wrinkles and as though a whole little tree stood in the middle of her forehead, but a golden color ran underneath, and the two knobs of her cheeks were illuminated by a yellow burning under the dark. Under the red rag her hair came down on her neck in the frailest of ringlets, still black, and with an odor like copper.

3   Now and then there was a quivering in the thicket. Old Phoenix said, "Out of my way, all you foxes, owls, beetles, jack rabbits, coons and wild animals! . . . Keep out from under these feet, little bob-whites. . . . Keep the big wild hogs out of my path. Don't let none of those come running my direction. I got a long way." Under her small black-freckled hand her cane, limber as a buggy whip, would switch at the brush as if to rouse up any hiding things.

4   On she went. The woods were deep and still. The sun made the pine needles almost too bright to look at, up where the wind rocked. The cones dropped as light as feathers. Down in the hollow was the mourning dove—it was not too late for him.

5   The path ran up a hill. "Seem like there is chains about my feet, time I get this far," she said, in the voice of argument old people keep to use with themselves. "Something always take a hold of me on this hill—pleads I should stay."

6   After she got to the top she turned and gave a full, severe look behind her where she had come. "Up through pines," she said at length. "Now down through oaks."

7   Her eyes opened their widest, and she started down gently. But before she got to the bottom of the hill a bush caught her dress.

8   Her fingers were busy and intent, but her skirts were full and long, so that before she could pull them free in one place they were caught in another. It was not possible to allow the dress to tear. "I in the thorny bush," she said. "Thorns, you doing your appointed work. Never want to let folks pass, no sir. Old eyes thought you was a pretty little *green* bush."

9   Finally, trembling all over, she stood free, and after a moment dared to stoop for her cane.

10   "Sun so high!" she cried, leaning back and looking, while the thick tears went over her eyes. "The time getting all gone here."

11   At the foot of this hill was a place where a log was laid across the creek.

12   "Now comes the trial," said Phoenix.

13   Putting her right foot out, she mounted the log and shut her eyes. Lifting her skirt, leveling her cane fiercely before her, like a festival figure in some parade, she began to march across. Then she opened her eyes and she was safe on the other side.

14   "I wasn't as old as I thought," she said.

15   But she sat down to rest. She spread her skirts on the bank around her and folded her hands over her knees. Up above her was a tree in a pearly cloud of mistletoe. She did not dare to close her eyes, and when a little boy brought her a plate with a slice of marble-cake on it she spoke to him. "That would be acceptable," she said. But when she went to take it there was just her own hand in the air.

16   So she left that tree, and had to go through a barbed-wire fence. There she had to creep and crawl, spreading her knees and stretching her fingers like a baby trying to climb the steps. But she talked loudly to herself: she could not let her dress be torn now, so late in the day, and she could not pay for

NOTE
rouse up (par. 3): startle

having her arm or her leg sawed off if she got caught fast where she was.

17   At last she was safe through the fence and risen up out in the clearing. Big dead trees, like black men with one arm, were standing in the purple stalks of the withered cotton field. There sat a buzzard.

18   "Who you watching?"

19   In the furrow she made her way along.

20   "Glad this not the season for bulls," she said, looking sideways, "and the good Lord made his snakes to curl up and sleep in the winter. A pleasure I don't see no two-headed snake coming around that tree, where it come once. It took a while to get by him, back in the summer."

21   She passed through the old cotton and went into a field of dead corn. It whispered and shook and was taller than her head. "Through the maze now," she said, for there was no path.

22   Then there was something tall, black, and skinny there, moving before her.

23   At first she took it for a man. It could have been a man dancing in the field. But she stood still and listened, and it did not make a sound. It was as silent as a ghost.

24   "Ghost," she said sharply, "who be you the ghost of? For I have heard of nary death close by."

25   But there was no answer—only the ragged dancing in the wind.

26   She shut her eyes, reached out her hand, and touched a sleeve. She found a coat and inside that an emptiness, cold as ice.

27   "You scarecrow," she said. Her face lighted. "I ought to be shut up for good," she said with laughter. "My senses is gone. I too old. I the oldest people I ever know. Dance, old scarecrow," she said, "while I dancing with you."

28   She kicked her foot over the furrow, and with mouth drawn down, shook her head once or twice in a little strutting way. Some husks blew down and whirled in streamers about her skirts.

29   Then she went on, parting her way from side to side with the cane, through the whispering field. At last she came to the end, to a wagon track where the silver grass blew between the red ruts. The quail were walking around like pullets, seeming all dainty and unseen.

30   "Walk pretty," she said. "This the easy place. This the easy going."

31   She followed the track, swaying through the quiet bare fields, through the little strings of trees silver in their dead leaves, past cabins silver from weather, with the doors and windows boarded shut, all like old women under a spell sitting there. "I walking in their sleep," she said, nodding her head vigorously.

32   In a ravine she went where a spring was silent flowing through a hollow log. Old Phoenix bent and drank. "Sweet-gum makes the water sweet," she said, and drank more. "Nobody know who made this well, for it was here when I was born."

33   The track crossed a swampy part where the moss hung as white as lace from every limb. "Sleep on, alligators, and blow your bubbles." Then the track went into the road.

34   Deep, deep the road went down between the high green-colored banks. Overhead the live-oaks met, and it was as dark as a cave.

35   A black dog with a lolling tongue came up out of the weeds by the ditch. She was meditating, and not ready, and when he came at her she only hit him

NOTES

furrow (par. 19): plowed row

ravine (par. 32): a deep narrow valley

a lolling tongue (par. 35): its tongue hanging out

a little with her cane. Over she went in the ditch, like a little puff of milk-weed.

36   Down there, her senses drifted away. A dream visited her, and she reached her hand up, but nothing reached down and gave her a pull. So she lay there and presently went to talking. "Old woman," she said to herself, "that black dog come up out of the weeds to stall you off, and now there he sitting on his fine tail, smiling at you."

37   A white man finally came along and found her—a hunter, a young man, with his dog on a chain.

38   "Well, Granny!" he laughed. "What are you doing there?"

39   "Lying on my back like a June-bug waiting to be turned over, mister," she said, reaching up her hand.

40   He lifted her up, gave her a swing in the air, and set her down. "Anything broken, Granny?"

41   "No, sir, them old dead weeds is springy enough," said Phoenix, when she had got her breath. "I thank you for your trouble."

42   "Where do you live, Granny?" he asked, while the two dogs were growl-ing at each other.

43   "Away back yonder, sir, behind the ridge. You can't even see it from here."

44   "On your way home?"

45   "No sir, I going to town."

46   "Why, that's too far! That's as far as I walk when I come out myself, and I get something for my trouble." He patted the stuffed bag he carried, and there hung down a little closed claw. It was one of the bob-whites, and its beak hooked bitterly to show it was dead. "Now you go home, Granny!"

47   "I bound to go to town, mister," said Phoenix. "The time come around."

48   He gave another laugh, filling the whole landscape. "I know you old col-ored people! Wouldn't miss going to town to see Santa Claus!"

49   But something held old Phoenix very still. The deep lines in her face went into a fierce and different radiation. Without warning, she had seen with her own eyes a flashing nickel fall out of the man's pocket onto the ground.

50   "How old are you, Granny?" he was saying.

51   "There is no telling, mister," she said, "no telling."

52   Then she gave a little cry and clapped her hands and said, "Git on away from here, dog! Look! Look at that dog!" She laughed as if in admiration. "He ain't scared of nobody. He a big black dog." She whispered, "Sic him!"

53   "Watch me get rid of that cur," said the man. "Sic him, Pete! Sic him!"

54   Phoenix heard the dogs fighting, and heard the man running and throw-ing sticks. She even heard a gunshot. But she was slowly bending forward by that time, further and further forward, the lids stretched down over her eyes, as if she were doing this in her sleep. Her chin was lowered almost to her knees. The yellow palm of her hand came out from the fold of her apron. Her fingers slid down and along the ground under the piece of money with the grace and care they would have in lifting an egg from under a setting hen. Then she slowly straightened up, she stood erect, and the nickel was in her apron pocket. A bird flew by. Her lips moved. "God watching me the whole time. I come to stealing."

55   The man came back, and his own dog panted about them. "Well, I scared him off that time," he said, and then he laughed and lifted his gun and pointed it at Phoenix.

56   She stood straight and faced him.

NOTE

cur (par. 53): mutt

57   "Doesn't the gun scare you?" he said, still pointing it.

58   "No, sir, I seen plenty go off closer by, in my day, and for less than what I done," she said, holding utterly still.

59   He smiled, and shouldered the gun. "Well, Granny," he said, "you must be a hundred years old, and scared of nothing. I'd give you a dime if I had any money with me. But you take my advice and stay home, and nothing will happen to you."

60   "I bound to go on my way, mister," said Phoenix. She inclined her head in the red rag. Then they went in different directions, but she could hear the gun shooting again and again over the hill.

61   She walked on. The shadows hung from the oak trees to the road like curtains. Then she smelled wood-smoke, and smelled the river, and she saw a steeple and the cabins on their steep steps. Dozens of little black children whirled around her. There ahead was Natchez shining. Bells were ringing. She walked on.

62   In the paved city it was Christmas time. There were red and green electric lights strung and criss-crossed everywhere, and all turned on in the daytime. Old Phoenix would have been lost if she had not distrusted her eyesight and depended on her feet to know where to take her.

63   She paused quietly on the sidewalk where people were passing by. A lady came along in the crowd, carrying an armful of red-, green- and silver-wrapped presents; she gave off perfume like the red roses in hot summer, and Phoenix stopped her.

64   "Please, missy, will you lace up my shoe?" She held up her foot.

65   "What do you want, Grandma?"

66   "See my shoe," said Phoenix. "Do all right for out in the country, but wouldn't look right to go in a big building."

67   "Stand still then, Grandma," said the lady. She put her packages down on the sidewalk beside her and laced and tied both shoes tightly.

68   "Can't lace 'em with a cane," said Phoenix. "Thank you, missy. I doesn't mind asking a nice lady to tie up my shoe, when I gets out on the street."

69   Moving slowly and from side to side, she went into the big building, and into a tower of steps, where she walked up and around and around until her feet knew to stop.

70   She entered a door, and there she saw nailed up on the wall the document that had been stamped with the gold seal and framed in the gold frame, which matched the dream that was hung up in her head.

71   "Here I be," she said. There was a fixed and ceremonial stiffness over her body.

72   "A charity case, I suppose," said an attendant who sat at the desk before her.

73   But Phoenix only looked above her head. There was sweat on her face, the wrinkles in her skin shone like a bright net.

74   "Speak up, Grandma," the woman said. "What's your name? We must have your history, you know. Have you been here before? What seems to be the trouble with you?"

75   Old Phoenix only gave a twitch to her face as if a fly were bothering her.

76   "Are you deaf?" cried the attendant.

77   But then the nurse came in.

78   "Oh, that's just old Aunt Phoenix," she said. "She doesn't come for herself—she has a little grandson. She makes these trips just as regular as clock-

NOTE

Natchez (par. 61): a port city in Mississippi on the banks of the Mississippi river

work. She lives away back off the Old Natchez Trace." She bent down. "Well, Aunt Phoenix, why don't you just take a seat? We won't keep you standing after your long trip." She pointed.

79   The old woman sat down, bolt upright in the chair.

80   "Now, how is the boy?" asked the nurse.

81   Old Phoenix did not speak.

82   "I said, how is the boy?"

83   But Phoenix only waited and stared straight ahead, her face very solemn and withdrawn into rigidity.

84   "Is his throat any better?" asked the nurse. "Aunt Phoenix, don't you hear me? Is your grandson's throat any better since the last time you came for the medicine?"

85   With her hands on her knees, the old woman waited, silent, erect and motionless, just as if she were in armor.

86   "You mustn't take up our time this way, Aunt Phoenix," the nurse said. "Tell us quickly about your grandson, and get it over. He isn't dead, is he?"

87   At last there came a flicker and then a flame of comprehension across her face, and she spoke.

88   "My grandson. It was my memory had left me. There I sat and forgot why I made my long trip."

89   "Forgot?" The nurse frowned. "After you came so far?"

90   Then Phoenix was like an old woman begging a dignified forgiveness for waking up frightened in the night. "I never did go to school, I was too old at the Surrender," she said in a soft voice. "I'm an old woman without an education. It was my memory fail me. My little grandson, he is just the same, and I forgot it in the coming."

91   "Throat never heals, does it?" said the nurse, speaking in a loud, sure voice to old Phoenix. By now she had a card with something written on it, a little list. "Yes. Swallowed lye. When was it?—January—two-three years ago—"

92   Phoenix spoke unasked now. "No, missy, he not dead, he just the same. Every little while his throat begin to close up again, and he not able to swallow. He not get his breath. He not able to help himself. So the time come around, and I go on another trip for the soothing medicine."

93   "All right. The doctor said as long as you came to get it, you could have it," said the nurse. "But it's an obstinate case."

94   "My little grandson, he sit up there in the house all wrapped up, waiting by himself," Phoenix went on. "We is the only two left in the world. He suffer and it don't seem to put him back at all. He got a sweet look. He going to last. He wear a little patch quilt and peep out holding his mouth open like a little bird. I remembers so plain now. I not going to forget him again, no, the whole enduring time. I could tell him from all the others in creation."

95   "All right." The nurse was trying to hush her now. She brought her a bottle of medicine. "Charity," she said, making a check mark in a book.

96   Old Phoenix held the bottle close to her eyes, and then carefully put it into her pocket.

97   "I thank you," she said.

98   "It's Christmas time, Grandma," said the attendant. "Could I give you a few pennies out of my purse?"

NOTES
the Surrender (par. 90): the April 9, 1865 surrender of the South to the North; The act officially ended the Civil War in the United States.
lye (par. 91): an acid-like substance used in making soap
obstinate (par. 93): stubborn

99   "Five pennies is a nickel," said Phoenix stiffly.

100   "Here's a nickel," said the attendant.

101   Phoenix rose carefully and held out her hand. She received the nickel and then fished the other nickel out of her pocket and laid it beside the new one. She stared at her palm closely, with her head on one side.

102   Then she gave a tap with her cane on the floor.

103   "This is what come to me to do," she said. "I going to the store and buy my child a little windmill they sells, made out of paper. He going to find it hard to believe there such a thing in the world. I'll march myself back where he waiting, holding it straight up in this hand."

104   She lifted her free hand, gave a little nod, turned around, and walked out of the doctor's office. Then her slow step began on the stairs, going down.

He

Katherine Anne Porter

1   Life was very hard for the Whipples. It was hard to feed all the hungry mouths, it was hard to keep the children in flannels during the winter, short as it was: "God knows what would become of us if we lived north," they would say: keeping them decently clean was hard. "It looks like our luck won't never let up on us," said Mr. Whipple, but Mrs. Whipple was all for taking what was sent and calling it good, anyhow when the neighbors were in earshot. "Don't ever let a soul hear us complain," she kept saying to her husband. She couldn't stand to be pitied. "No, not if it comes to it that we have to live in a wagon and pick cotton around the country," she said, "nobody's going to get a chance to look down on us."

2   Mrs. Whipple loved her second son, the simple-minded one, better than she loved the other two children put together. She was forever saying so, and when she talked with certain of her neighbors, she would even throw in her husband and her mother for good measure.

3   "You needn't keep on saying it around," said Mr. Whipple, "you'll make people think nobody else has any feelings about Him but you."

4   "It's natural for a mother," Mrs. Whipple would remind him. "You know yourself it's more natural for a mother to be that way. People don't expect so much of fathers, some way."

5   This didn't keep the neighbors from talking plainly among themselves. "A Lord's pure mercy if He should die," they said. "It's the sins of the fathers," they agreed among themselves. "There's bad blood and bad doings somewhere, you can bet on that." This behind the Whipples' backs. To their faces everybody said, "He's not so bad off. He'll be all right yet. Look how He grows!"

6   Mrs. Whipple hated to talk about it, she tried to keep her mind off it, but every time anybody set foot in the house, the subject always came up, and she had to talk about Him first before she could get on to anything else. It seemed to ease her mind. "I wouldn't have anything happen to Him for all the world, but it just looks like I can't keep Him out of mischief. He's so strong and active, He's always into everything; He was like that since He could

NOTE

flannels (par. 1): underwear

walk. It's actually funny sometimes, the way He can do anything; it's laughable to see Him up to His tricks. Emly has more accidents; I'm forever tying up her bruises, and Adna can't fall a foot without cracking a bone. But He can do anything and not get a scratch. The preacher said such a nice thing once when he was here. He said, and I'll remember it to my dying day, 'The innocent walk with God—that's why He don't get hurt.'" Whenever Mrs. Whipple repeated these words, she always felt a warm pool spread in her breast, and the tears would fill her eyes, and then she could talk about something else.

7   He did grow and He never got hurt. A plank blew off the chicken house and struck Him on the head and He never seemed to know it. He had learned a few words, and after this He forgot them. He didn't whine for food as the other children did, but waited until it was given Him; He ate squatting in the corner, smacking and mumbling. Rolls of fat covered Him like an overcoat, and He could carry twice as much wood and water as Adna. Emly had a cold in the head most of the time—"she takes that after me," said Mrs. Whipple—so in bad weather they gave her the extra blanket off His cot. He never seemed to mind the cold.

8   Just the same, Mrs. Whipple's life was a torment for fear something might happen to Him. He climbed the peach trees much better than Adna and went skittering along the branches like a monkey, just a regular monkey. "Oh, Mrs. Whipple, you hadn't ought to let Him do that. He'll lose His balance sometime. He can't rightly know what He's doing."

9   Mrs. Whipple almost screamed out at the neighbor. "He *does* know what He's doing! He's as able as any other child! Come down out of there, you!" When He finally reached the ground she could hardly keep her hands off Him for acting like that before people, a grin all over His face and her worried sick about Him all the time.

10   "It's the neighbors," said Mrs. Whipple to her husband. "Oh, I do mortally wish they would keep out of our business. I can't afford to let Him do anything for fear they'll come nosing around about it. Look at the bees, now. Adna can't handle them, they sting him up so; I haven't got time to do everything, and now I don't dare let Him. But if He gets a sting He don't really mind."

11   "It's just because He ain't got sense enough to be scared of anything," said Mr. Whipple.

12   "You ought to be ashamed of yourself," said Mrs. Whipple, "talking that way about your own child. Who's to take up for Him if we don't, I'd like to know? He sees a lot that goes on, He listens to things all the time. And anything I tell Him to do He does it. Don't never let anybody hear you say such things. They'd think you favored the other children over Him."

13   "Well, now I don't, and you know it, and what's the use of getting all worked up about it? You always think the worst of everything. Just let Him alone, He'll get along somehow. He gets plenty to eat and wear, don't He?" Mr. Whipple suddenly felt tired out. "Anyhow, it can't be helped now."

14   Mrs. Whipple felt tired too, she complained in a tired voice. "What's done can't never be undone, I know that as good as anybody; but He's my child, and I'm not going to have people say anything. I get sick of people coming around saying things all the time."

NOTES

tying up (par. 6): bandaging
skittering (par. 8): moving lightly
mortally (par. 10): seriously

15   In the early fall Mrs. Whipple got a letter from her brother saying he and his wife and two children were coming over for a little visit next Sunday week. "Put the big pot in the little one," he wrote at the end. Mrs. Whipple read this part out loud twice, she was so pleased. Her brother was a great one for saying funny things. "We'll just show him that's no joke," she said, "we'll just butcher one of the sucking pigs."

16   "It's a waste and I don't hold with waste the way we are now," said Mr. Whipple. "That pig'll be worth money by Christmas."

17   "It's a shame and a pity we can't have a decent meal's vittles once in a while when my own family comes to see us," said Mrs. Whipple. "I'd hate for his wife to go back and say there wasn't a thing in the house to eat. My God, it's better than buying up a great chance of meat in town. There's where you'd spend the money!"

18   "All right, do it yourself then," said Mr. Whipple. "Christamighty, no wonder we can't get ahead!"

19   The question was how to get the little pig away from his ma, a great fighter, worse than a Jersey cow. Adna wouldn't try it: "That sow'd rip my insides out all over the pen." "All right, old fraidy," said Mrs. Whipple, "*He's* not scared. Watch *Him* do it." And she laughed as though it was all a good joke and gave Him a little push towards the pen. He sneaked up and snatched the pig right away from the teat and galloped back and was over the fence with the sow raging at His heels. The little black squirming thing was screeching like a baby in a tantrum, stiffening its back and stretching its mouth to the ears. Mrs. Whipple took the pig with her face stiff and sliced its throat with one stroke. When He saw the blood He gave a great jolting breath and ran away. "But He'll forget and eat plenty, just the same," thought Mrs. Whipple. Whenever she was thinking, her lips moved making words. "He'd eat it all if I didn't stop Him. He'd eat up every mouthful from the other two if I'd let Him."

20   She felt badly about it. He was ten years old now and a third again as large as Adna, who was going on fourteen. "It's a shame, a shame," she kept saying under her breath, "and Adna with so much brains!"

21   She kept on feeling badly about all sorts of things. In the first place it was the man's work to butcher; the sight of the pig scraped pink and naked made her sick. He was too fat and soft and pitiful-looking. It was simply a shame the way things had to happen. By the time she had finished it up, she almost wished her brother would stay at home.

21   Early Sunday morning Mrs. Whipple dropped everything to get Him all cleaned up. In an hour He was dirty again, with crawling under fences after a possum, and straddling along the rafters of the barn looking for eggs in the hayloft. "My Lord, look at you now after all my trying! And here's Adna and Emly staying so quiet. I get tired trying to keep you decent. Get off that shirt and put on another, people will say I don't half dress you!" And she boxed Him on the ears, hard. He blinked and blinked and rubbed His head, and His face hurt Mrs. Whipple's feelings. Her knees began to tremble, she had to sit down while she buttoned His shirt. "I'm just all gone before the days starts."

23   The brother came with his plump healthy wife and two great roaring hun-

NOTES

vittles (par. 17): food

chance of meat (par. 17): an amount of meat

sow (par. 19): female pig

teat (par. 19): tit

tantrum (par. 19): fit of anger

gry boys. They had a grand dinner, with the pig roasted to a crackling in the middle of the table, full of dressing, a pickled peach in his mouth and plenty of gravy for the sweet potatoes.

24   "This looks like prosperity all right," said the brother, "you're going to have to roll me home like I was a barrel when I'm done."

25   Everybody laughed out loud; it was fine to hear them laughing all at once around the table. Mrs. Whipple felt warm and good about it. "Oh, we've got six more of these; I say it's as little as we can do when you come to see us so seldom."

26   He wouldn't come into the dining room, and Mrs. Whipple passed it off very well. "He's timider than my other two," she said, "He'll just have to get used to you. There isn't everybody He'll make up with, you know how it is with children, even cousins." Nobody said anything out of the way.

27   "Just like my Alfy here," said the brother's wife. "I sometimes got to lick him to make him shake hands with his own grandmammy."

28   So that was over, and Mrs. Whipple loaded up a big plate for Him first, before everybody. "I always say He ain't to be slighted, no matter who else goes without," she said, and carried it to Him herself.

29   "He can chin Himself on the top of the door," said Emly, helping along.

30   "That's fine. He's getting along fine," said the brother.

31   They went away after supper. Mrs. Whipple rounded up the dishes, and sent the children to bed and sat down and unlaced her shoes. "You see?" she said to Mr. Whipple. "That's the way my whole family is. Nice and considerate about everything. No out-of-the-way remarks—they *have* got refinement. I get awfully sick of people's remarks. Wasn't that pig good?"

32   Mr. Whipple said, "Yes, we're out three hundred pounds of pork, that's all. It's easy to be polite when you come to eat. Who knows what they had in their minds all along?"

33   "Yes, that's like you," said Mrs. Whipple. "I don't expect anything else from you. You'll be telling me next that my own brother will be saying around that we made Him eat in the kitchen! Oh, my God!" She rocked her head in her hands, a hard pain started in the very middle of her forehead. "Now it's all spoiled, and everything was so nice and easy. All right, you don't like them and you never did—all right, they'll not come here again soon, never you mind! But they *can't* say He wasn't dressed every lick as good as Adna—oh, honest, sometimes I wish I was dead!"

34   "I wish you'd let up," said Mr. Whipple. "It's bad enough as it is."

35   It was a hard winter. It seemed to Mrs. Whipple that they hadn't ever known anything but hard times, and now to cap it all a winter like this. The crops were about half of what they had a right to expect; after the cotton was in it didn't do much more than cover the grocery bill. They swapped off one of the plow horses, and got cheated, for the new one died of the heaves. Mrs. Whipple kept thinking all the time it was terrible to have a man you couldn't depend on not to get cheated. They cut down on everything, but Mrs. Whipple kept saying there are things you can't cut down on, and they cost money. It took a lot of warm clothes for Adna and Emly, who walked four miles to

NOTES
crackling (par. 23): crisp
dressing (par. 23): stuffing
prosperity (par. 24): financial success
lick (par. 27): whip
slighted (par. 28): uncared for
refinement (par. 31): good manners

school during the three-months session. "He sets around the fire a lot, He won't need so much," said Mr. Whipple. "That's so," said Mrs. Whipple, "and when He does the outdoor chores He can wear your tarpaullion coat. I can't do no better, that's all."

36   In February He was taken sick, and lay curled up under His blanket looking very blue in the face and acting as if He would choke. Mr. and Mrs. Whipple did everything they could for Him for two days, and then they were scared and sent for the doctor. The doctor told them they must keep Him warm and give Him plenty of milk and eggs. "He isn't as stout as He looks, I'm afraid," said the doctor. "You've got to watch them when they're like that. You must put more cover onto Him, too."

37   "I just took off His big blanket to wash," said Mrs. Whipple, ashamed. "I can't stand dirt."

38   "Well, you'd better put it back on the minute it's dry," said the doctor, "or He'll have pneumonia."

39   Mr. and Mrs. Whipple took a blanket off their own bed and put His cot in by the fire. "They can't say we didn't do everything for Him," she said, "even to sleeping cold ourselves on His account."

40   When the winter broke He seemed to be well again, but He walked as if His feet hurt Him. He was able to run a cotton planter during the season.

41   "I got it all fixed up with Jim Ferguson about breeding the cow next time," said Mr. Whipple. "I'll pasture the bull this summer and give Jim some fodder in the fall. That's better than paying out money when you haven't got it."

42   "I hope you didn't say such a thing before Jim Ferguson," said Mrs. Whipple. "You oughtn't to let him know we're so down as all that."

43   "Godamighty, that ain't saying we're down. A man is got to look ahead sometimes. He can lead the bull over today. I need Adna on the place."

44   At first Mrs. Whipple felt easy in her mind about sending Him for the bull. Adna was too jumpy and couldn't be trusted. You've got to be steady around animals. After He was gone she started thinking, and after a while she could hardly bear it any longer. She stood in the lane and watched for Him. It was nearly three miles to go and a hot day, but He oughtn't to be so long about it. She shaded her eyes and stared until colored bubbles floated in her eyeballs. It was just like everything else in life, she must always worry and never know a moment's peace about anything. After a long time she saw Him turn into the side lane, limping. He came on very slowly, leading the big bulk of an animal by a ring in the nose, twirling a little stick in His hand, never looking back or sideways, but coming on like a sleepwalker with His eyes half shut.

45   Mrs. Whipple was scared sick of bulls; she had heard awful stories about how they followed on quietly enough, and then suddenly pitched on with a bellow and pawed and gored a body to pieces. Any second now that black monster would come down on Him, my God, He'd never have sense enough to run.

46   She mustn't make a sound nor a move; she mustn't get the bull started. The bull heaved his head aside and horned the air at a fly. Her voice burst out

NOTES

tarpaullion coat (par. 35): a waterproof overcoat
stout (par. 36): strong, healthy
fodder (par. 41): the stalks of corn, wheat, etc., used to feed farm animals
ring in the nose (par. 44): a ring placed through the nose of a farm animal as a means of controlling it
pitched (par. 45): dived, plunged
bellow (par. 45): roar

of her in a shriek, and she screamed at Him to come on, for God's sake. He didn't seem to hear her clamor, but kept on twirling His switch and limping on, and the bull lumbered along behind him as gently as a calf. Mrs. Whipple stopped calling and ran towards the house, praying under her breath: "Lord, don't let anything happen to Him. Lord, you *know* people will say we oughtn't to have sent Him. You *know* they'll say we didn't take care of Him. Oh, get Him home, safe home, safe home, and I'll look out for Him better! Amen."

47   She watched from the window while He led the beast in, and tied him up in the barn. It was no use trying to keep up, Mrs. Whipple couldn't bear another thing. She sat down and rocked and cried with her apron over her head.

48   From year to year the Whipples were growing poorer and poorer. The place just seemed to run down of itself, no matter how hard they worked. "We're losing our hold," said Mrs. Whipple. "Why can't we do like other people and watch for our best chances? They'll be calling us poor white trash next."

49   "When I get to be sixteen I'm going to leave," said Adna. "I'm going to get a job in Powell's grocery store. There's money in that. No more farm for me."

50   "I'm going to be a schoolteacher," said Emly. "But I've got to finish the eighth grade, anyhow. Then I can live in town. I don't see any chances here."

51   "Emly takes after my family," said Mrs. Whipple. "Ambitious every last one of them, and they don't take second place for anybody."

52   When fall came Emly got a chance to wait on tables in the railroad eating-house in the town near by, and it seemed such a shame not to take it when the wages were good and she could get her food too, that Mrs. Whipple decided to let her take it, and not bother with school until the next session. "You've got plenty of time," she said. "You're young and smart as a whip."

53   With Adna gone too, Mr. Whipple tried to run the farm with just Him to help. He seemed to get along fine, doing His work and part of Adna's without noticing it. They did well enough until Christmas time, when one morning He slipped on the ice coming up from the barn. Instead of getting up He thrashed round and round, and when Mr. Whipple got to Him, He was having some sort of fit.

54   They brought Him inside and tried to make Him sit up, but He blubbered and rolled, so they put Him to bed and Mr. Whipple rode to town for the doctor. All the way there and back he worried about where the money was to come from: it sure did look like he had about all the troubles he could carry.

55   From then on He stayed in bed. His legs swelled up double their size, and the fits kept coming back. After four months the doctor said, "It's no use, I think you'd better put Him in the County Home for treatment right away. I'll see about it for you. He'll have good care there and be off your hands."

56   "We don't begrudge Him any care, and I won't let Him out of my sight," said Mrs. Whipple. "I won't have it said I sent my sick child off among strangers."

57   "I know how you feel," said the doctor. "You can't tell me anything about that, Mrs. Whipple. I've got a boy of my own. But you'd better listen to me. I can't do anything more for Him, that's the truth."

58   Mr. and Mrs. Whipple talked it over a long time that night after they went to bed. "It's just charity," said Mrs. Whipple, "that's what we've come to, charity! I certainly never looked for this."

NOTES

clamor (par. 46): loud outcry
trash (par. 48): worthless people
begrudge (par. 56): resent giving

59   "We pay taxes to help support the place just like everybody else," said Mr. Whipple, "and I don't call that taking charity. I think it would be fine to have Him where He'd get the best of everything . . . and besides, I can't keep up with these doctor bills any longer."

60   "Maybe that's why the doctor wants us to send Him—he's scared he won't get his money," said Mrs. Whipple.

61   "Don't talk like that," said Mr. Whipple, feeling pretty sick, "or we won't be able to send Him."

62   "Oh, but we won't keep Him there long," said Mrs. Whipple. "Soon's He's better, we'll bring Him right back home."

63   "The doctor has told you and told you time and again He can't ever get better, and you might as well stop talking," said Mr. Whipple.

64   "Doctors don't know everything," said Mrs. Whipple, feeling almost happy. "But anyhow in the summer Emly can come home for a vacation, and Adna can get down for Sundays: we'll all work together and get on our feet again, and the children will feel they've got a place to come to."

65   All at once she saw it full summer again, with the garden going fine, and new white roller shades up all over the house, and Adna and Emly home, so full of life, all of them happy together. Oh, it could happen, things would ease up on them.

66   They didn't talk before Him much, but they never knew just how much He understood. Finally the doctor set the day and a neighbor who owned a double-seated carryall offered to drive them over. The hospital would have sent an ambulance, but Mrs. Whipple couldn't stand to see Him going away looking so sick as all that. They wrapped Him in blankets, and the neighbor and Mr. Whipple lifted Him into the back seat of the carryall beside Mrs. Whipple, who had on her black shirt waist. She couldn't stand to go looking like charity.

67   "You'll be all right, I guess I'll stay behind," said Mr. Whipple. "It don't look like everybody ought to leave the place at once."

68   "Besides, it ain't as if He was going to stay forever," said Mrs. Whipple to the neighbor. "This is only for a little while."

69   They started away, Mrs. Whipple holding to the edges of the blankets to keep Him from sagging sideways. He sat there blinking and blinking. He worked His hands out and began rubbing His nose with His knuckles, and then with the end of the blanket. Mrs. Whipple couldn't believe what she saw; He was scrubbing away big tears that rolled out of the corners of His eyes. He sniveled and made a gulping noise. Mrs. Whipple kept saying, "Oh, honey, you don't feel so bad, do you? You don't feel so bad, do you?" for He seemed to be accusing her of something. Maybe He remembered that time she boxed His ears, maybe He had been scared that day with the bull, maybe He had slept cold and couldn't tell her about it; maybe He knew they were sending Him away for good and all because they were too poor to keep Him. Whatever it was, Mrs. Whipple couldn't bear to think of it. She began to cry, frightfully, and wrapped her arms tight around Him. His head rolled on her shoulder: she had loved Him as much as she possibly could, there were Adna and Emly who had to be thought of too, there was nothing she could do to make up to Him for His life. Oh what a mortal pity He was ever born.

70   They came in sight of the hospital, with the neighbor driving very fast, not daring to look behind him.

NOTES

carryall (par. 66): a covered, four wheeled, one-horse carriage with two seats
shirt waist (par. 66): dress

I Stand Here Ironing

Tillie Olsen

1   I stand here ironing, and what you asked me moves tormented back and forth with the iron.

2   "I wish you would manage the time to come in and talk with me about your daughter. I'm sure you can help me understand her. She's a youngster who needs help and whom I'm deeply interested in helping."

3   "Who needs help. . . . " Even if I came, what good would it do? You think because I am her mother I have a key, or that in some way you could use me as a key? She has lived for nineteen years. There is all that life that has happened outside of me, beyond me.

4   And when is there time to remember, to sift, to weigh, to estimate, to total? I will start and there will be an interruption and I will have to gather it all together again. Or I will become engulfed with all I did or did not do, with what should have been and what cannot be helped.

5   She was a beautiful baby. The first and only one of our five that was beautiful at birth. You do not guess how new and uneasy her tenancy in her now-loveliness. You did not know her all those years she was thought homely, or see her poring over her baby pictures, making me tell her over and over how beautiful she had been—and would be, I would tell her—and was now, to the seeing eye. But the seeing eyes were few or non-existent. Including mine.

6   I nursed her. They feel that's important nowadays. I nursed all the children, but with her, with all the fierce rigidity of first motherhood, I did like the books then said. Though her cries battered me to trembling and my breasts ached with swollenness, I waited till the clock decreed.

7   Why do I put that first? I do not even know if it matters, or if it explains anything.

8   She was a beautiful baby. She blew shining bubbles of sound. She loved motion, loved light, loved color and music and textures. She would lie on the floor in her blue overalls patting the surface so hard in ecstasy her hands and feet would blur. She was a miracle to me, but when she was eight months old I had to leave her daytimes with the woman downstairs to whom she was no miracle at all, for I worked or looked for work and for Emily's father, who "could no longer endure" (he wrote in his good-bye note) "sharing want with us."

9   I was nineteen. It was the pre-relief, pre-WPA world of the depression. I would start running as soon as I got off the streetcar, running up the stairs, the place smelling sour, and awake or asleep to startle awake, when she saw me she would break into a clogged weeping that could not be comforted, a weeping I can hear yet.

10   After a while I found a job hashing at night so I could be with her days, and it was better. But it came to where I had to bring her to his family and leave her.

NOTES
engulfed (par. 4): overwhelmed
tenancy (par. 5): occupancy
ecstasy (par. 8): great joy
pre-relief (par. 9): before welfare
pre-WPA (par. 9): before Work Projects Administration, a government program that provided jobs during the 1930s
the depression (par. 9): a time of terrible economic conditions, beginning with the great Stock Market crash in 1929 and lasting until about 1940
hashing (par. 10): cooking

11   It took a long time to raise the money for her fare back. Then she got chicken pox and I had to wait longer. When she finally came, I hardly knew her, walking quick and nervous like her father, looking like her father, thin, and dressed in a shoddy red that yellowed her skin and glared at the pockmarks. All the baby loveliness gone.

12   She was two. Old enough for nursery school they said, and I did not know then what I know now—the fatigue of the long day, and the lacerations of group life in the kinds of nurseries that are only parking places for children.

13   Except that it would have made no difference if I had known. It was the only place there was. It was the only way we could be together, the only way I could hold a job.

14   And even without knowing, I knew. I knew the teacher that was evil because all these years it has curdled into my memory, the little boy hunched in the corner, her rasp, "why aren't you outside, because Alvin hits you? that's no reason, go out, scaredy." I knew Emily hated it even if she did not clutch and implore "don't go Mommy" like the other children, mornings.

15   She always had a reason why we should stay home. Momma, you look sick, Momma. I feel sick. Momma, the teachers aren't there today, they're sick. Momma, we can't go, there was a fire there last night. Momma, it's a holiday today, no school, they told me.

16   But never a direct protest, never rebellion. I think of our others in their three-, four-year-oldness—the explosions, the tempers, the denunciations, the demands—and I feel suddenly ill. I put the iron down. What in me demanded that goodness in her? And what was the cost, the cost to her of such goodness?

17   The old man living in the back once said in his gentle way: "You should smile at Emily more when you look at her." What *was* in my face when I looked at her? I loved her. There were all the acts of love.

18   It was only with others I remembered what he said, and it was the face of joy, and not of care or tightness or worry I turned to them—too late for Emily. She does not smile easily, let alone almost always as her brothers and sisters do. Her face is closed and sombre, but when she wants, how fluid. You must have seen it in her pantomimes, you spoke of her rare gift for comedy on the stage that rouses a laughter out of the audience so dear they applaud and applaud and do not want to let her go.

19   Where does it come from, that comedy? There was none of it in her when she came back to me that second time, after I had had to send her away again. She had a new daddy now to learn to love, and I think perhaps it was a better time.

20   Except when we left her alone nights, telling ourselves she was old enough.

21   "Can't you go some other time, Mommy, like tomorrow?" she would ask. "Will it be just a little while you'll be gone? Do you promise?"

NOTES

shoddy (par. 11): cheap
lacerations (par. 12): literally, wounds
curdled (par. 14): literally, thickened and soured
rasp (par. 14): harsh voice
denunciations (par. 16): accusations
sombre (par. 18): serious
fluid (par. 18): full of expression
pantomimes (par. 18): acting in which the performer communicates by movements rather than by speech
rouses a laughter out of the audience (par. 18): excites from the audience

22   The time we came back, the front door open, the clock on the floor in the hall. She rigid awake. "It wasn't just a little while. I didn't cry. Three times I called you, just three times, and then I ran downstairs to open the door so you could come faster. The clock talked loud. I threw it away, it scared me what it talked."

23   She said the clock talked loud again that night I went to the hospital to have Susan. She was delirious with the fever that comes before red measles, but she was fully conscious all the week I was gone and the week after we were home when she could not come near the new baby or me.

24   She did not get well. She stayed skeleton thin, not wanting to eat, and night after night she had nightmares. She would call for me, and I would rouse from exhaustion to sleepily call back: "You're all right, darling, go to sleep, it's just a dream," and if she still called, in a sterner voice, "now go to sleep, Emily, there's nothing to hurt you." Twice, only twice, when I had to get up for Susan anyhow, I went in to sit with her.

25   Now when it is too late (as if she would let me hold and comfort her like I do the others) I get up and go to her at once at her moan or restless stirring. "Are you awake, Emily? Can I get you something?" And the answer is always the same: "No, I'm all right, go back to sleep, Mother."

26   They persuaded me at the clinic to send her away to a convalescent home in the country where "she can have the kind of food and care you can't manage for her, and you'll be free to concentrate on the new baby." They still send children to that place. I see pictures on the society page of sleek young women planning affairs to raise money for it, or dancing at the affairs, or decorating Easter eggs or filling Christmas stockings for the children.

27   They never have a picture of the children so I do not know if the girls still wear those gigantic red bows and the ravaged looks on the every other Sunday when parents can come to visit "unless otherwise notified"—as we were notified the first six weeks.

28   Oh it is a handsome place, green lawns and tall trees and fluted flower beds. High up on the balconies of each cottage the children stand, the girls in their red bows and the white dresses, the boys in white suits and giant red ties. The parents stand below shrieking up to be heard and the children shriek down to be heard, and between them the invisible wall "Not To Be Contaminated by Parental Germs or Physical Affection."

29   There was a tiny girl who always stood hand in hand with Emily. Her parents never came. One visit she was gone. "They moved her to Rose Cottage," Emily shouted in explanation. "They don't like you to love anybody here."

30   She wrote once a week, the labored writing of a seven-year-old. "I am fine. How is the baby. If I write my letter nicly I will have a star. Love." There never was a star. We wrote every other day, letters she could never hold or keep but only hear read—once. "We simply do not have room for children to keep any personal possessions," they patiently explained when we pieced one Sunday's shrieking together to plead how much it would mean to Emily, who loved so to keep things, to be allowed to keep her letters and cards.

NOTES

delirious (par. 23): mentally confused
rouse (par. 24): wake up
convalescent home (par. 26): an institution where people go to rest and recover from an illness
sleek (par. 26): slender and graceful
ravaged (par. 27): defeated
labored (par. 30): showing much effort

31   Each visit she looked frailer. "She isn't eating," they told us.

32   (They had runny eggs for breakfast or mush with lumps, Emily said later, I'd hold it in my mouth and not swallow. Nothing ever tasted good, just when they had chicken.)

33   It took us eight months to get her released home, and only the fact that she gained back so little of her seven lost pounds convinced the social worker.

34   I used to try to hold and love her after she came back, but her body would stay stiff, and after a while she'd push away. She ate little. Food sickened her, and I think much of life too. Oh she had physical lightness and brightness, twinkling by on skates, bouncing like a ball up and down up and down over the jump rope, skimming over the hill; but these were momentary.

35   She fretted about her appearance, thin and dark and foreign-looking at a time when every little girl was supposed to look or thought she should look a chubby blonde replica of Shirley Temple. The doorbell sometimes rang for her, but no one seemed to come and play in the house or be a best friend. Maybe because we moved so much.

36   There was a boy she loved painfully through two school semesters. Months later she told me how she had taken pennies from my purse to buy him candy. "Licorice was his favorite and I brought him some every day, but he still liked Jennifer better'n me. Why, Mommy?" The kind of question for which there is no answer.

37   School was a worry to her. She was not glib or quick in a world where glibness and quickness were easily confused with ability to learn. To her overworked and exasperated teachers she was an overconscientious "slow learner" who kept trying to catch up and was absent entirely too often.

38   I let her be absent, though sometimes the illness was imaginary. How different from my now-strictness about attendance with the others. I wasn't working. We had a new baby, I was home anyhow. Sometimes, after Susan grew old enough, I would keep her home from school, too, to have them all together.

39   Mostly Emily had asthma, and her breathing, harsh and labored, would fill the house with a curiously tranquil sound. I would bring the two old dresser mirrors and her boxes of collections to her bed. She would select beads and single earrings, bottle tops and shells, dried flowers and pebbles, old postcards and scraps, all sorts of oddments; then she and Susan would play Kingdom, setting up landscapes and furniture, peopling them with action.

40   Those were the only times of peaceful companionship between her and Susan. I have edged away from it, that poisonous feeling between them, that terrible balancing of hurts and needs I had to do between the two, and did so badly, those earlier years.

41   Oh there are conflicts between the others too, each one human, needing, demanding, hurting, taking—but only between Emily and Susan, no Emily toward Susan that corroding resentment. It seems so obvious on the surface, yet it is not obvious. Susan, the second child, Susan, golden- and curly-haired and

NOTES

mush (par. 32): boiled cornmeal
fretted (par. 35): worried
replica (par. 35): copy
glib (par. 37): quick with words
exasperated (par. 37): frustrated
overconscientious (par. 37): overly dedicated
tranquil (par. 39): peaceful
corroding (par. 41): destructive

chubby, quick and articulate and assured, everything in appearance and manner Emily was not; Susan, not able to resist Emily's precious things, losing or sometimes clumsily breaking them: Susan telling jokes and riddles to company for applause while Emily sat silent (to say to me later: that was *my* riddle, Mother. I told it to Susan); Susan, who for all the five years' difference in age was just a year behind Emily in developing physically.

42   I am glad for that slow physical development that widened the difference between her and her contemporaries, though she suffered over it. She was too vulnerable for that terrible world of youthful competition, of preening and parading, of constant measuring of yourself against every other, of envy, "If I had that copper hair," "If I had that skin. . . . " She tormented herself enough about not looking like the others, there was enough of the unsureness, the having to be conscious of words before you speak, the constant caring—what are they thinking of me? without having it all magnified by the merciless physical drives.

43   Ronnie is calling. He is wet and I change him. It is rare there is such a cry now. That time of motherhood is almost behind me when the ear is not one's own but must always be racked and listening for the child cry, the child call. We sit for a while and I hold him, looking out over the city spread in charcoal with its soft aisles of light. "*Shoogily,*" he breathes and curls closer. I carry him back to bed, asleep. *Shoogily.* A funny word, a family word, inherited from Emily, invented by her to say: *comfort.*

44   In this and other ways she leaves her seal, I say aloud. And startle at my saying it. What do I mean? What did I start to gather together, to try and make coherent? I was at the terrible, growing years. War years. I do not remember them well. I was working, there were four smaller ones now, there was not time for her. She had to help be a mother, and housekeeper, and shopper. She had to set her seal. Mornings of crisis and near hysteria trying to get lunches packed, hair combed, coats and shoes found, everyone to school or Child Care on time, the baby ready for transportation. And always the paper scribbled on by a smaller one, the book looked at by Susan then mislaid, the homework not done. Running out to that huge school where she was one, she was lost, she was a drop; suffering over the unpreparedness, stammering and unsure in her classes.

45   There was so little time left at night after the kids were bedded down. She would struggle over books, always eating (it was those years she developed her enormous appetite that is legendary in our family) and I would be ironing, or preparing food for the next day, or writing V-mail to Bill, or tending the baby. Sometimes, to make me laugh, or out of her despair, she would imitate happenings or types at school.

46   I think I said once: "Why don't you do something like this in the school amateur show?" One morning she phoned me at work, hardly understandable through the weeping: "Mother, I did it. I won, I won; they gave me first prize; they clapped and clapped and wouldn't let me go."

NOTES
articulate (par. 41): good with words
vulnerable (par. 42): defenseless
preening (par. 42): primping
racked (par. 43): strained
coherent (par. 44): understandable
hysteria (par. 44): panic
V-mail (par. 45): Victory mail—the name given to mail sent to soldiers during World War II

47   Now suddenly she was Somebody, and as imprisoned in her difference as she had been in anonymity.

48   She began to be asked to perform at other high schools, even in colleges, then at city and statewide affairs. The first one we went to, I only recognized her that first moment when thin, shy, she almost drowned herself into the curtains. Then: Was this Emily? The control, the command, the convulsing and deadly clowning, the spell, then the roaring, stamping audience, unwilling to let this rare and precious laughter out of their lives.

49   Afterwards: You ought to do something about her with a gift like that—but without money or knowing how, what does one do? We have left it all to her, and the gift has as often eddied inside, clogged and clotted, as been used and growing.

50   She is coming. She runs up the stairs two at a time with her light graceful step, and I know she is happy tonight. Whatever it was that occasioned your call did not happen today.

51   "Aren't you ever going to finish the ironing, Mother? Whistler painted his mother in a rocker. I'd have to paint mine standing over an ironing board." This is one of her communicative nights and she tells me everything and nothing as she fixes herself a plate of food out of the icebox.

52   She is so lovely. Why did you want me to come in at all? Why were you concerned? She will find her way.

53   She starts up the stairs to bed. "Don't get me up with the rest in the morning." "But I thought you were having midterms." "Oh, those," she comes back in, kisses me, and says lightly, "in a couple of years when we'll all be atom-dead they won't matter a bit."

54   She has said it before. She *believes* it. But because I have been dredging the past, and all that compounds a human being is so heavy and meaningful in me, I cannot endure it tonight.

55   I will never total it all. I will never come in to say: She was a child seldom smiled at. Her father left me before she was a year old. I had to work her first six years when there was work, or I sent her home and to his relatives. There were years she had care she hated. She was dark and thin and foreign-looking in a world where the prestige went to blondeness and curly hair and dimples, she was slow where glibness was prized. She was a child of anxious, not proud, love. We were poor and could not afford for her the soil of easy growth. I was a young mother, I was a distracted mother. There were the other children pushing up, demanding. Her younger sister seemed all that she was not. There were years she did not want me to touch her. She kept too much in herself, her life was such she had to keep too much in herself. My wisdom came too late. She has much to her and probably little will come of it. She is a child of her age, of depression, of war, of fear.

56   Let her be. So all that is in her will not bloom—but in how many does it? There is still enough left to live by. Only help her to know—help make it so there is cause for her to know—that she is more than this dress on the ironing board, helpless before the iron.

NOTES

anonymity (par. 47): state of being unknown
convulsing (par. 48): laughable
occasioned (par. 50): caused
Whistler (par. 51): James Abbot Whistler (1834–1903), American painter
icebox (par. 51): refrigerator
dredging (par. 54): digging up
anxious (par. 55): nervous, worried
distracted (par. 55): distressed

The Kind of Light That Shines on Texas

Reginald McKnight

1   I never liked Marvin Pruitt. Never liked him, never knew him, even though there were only three of us in the class. Three black kids. In our school there were fourteen classrooms of thirty-odd white kids (in '66, they considered Chicanos provisionally white) and three or four black kids. Primary school in primary colors. Neat division. Alphabetized. They didn't stick us in the back, or arrange us by degrees of hue, aparteidlike. This was real integration, a ten-to-one ratio as tidy as upper-class landscaping. If it all worked, you could have ten white kids all to yourself. They could talk to you, get the feel of you, scrutinize you bone deep if they wanted to. They seldom wanted to, and that was fine with me for two reasons. The first was that their scrutiny was irritating. How do you comb your hair—why do you comb your hair—may I please touch your hair—were the kinds of questions they asked. This is no way to feel at home. The second reason was Marvin. He embarrassed me. He smelled bad, was at least two grades behind, was hostile, dark skinned, homely, close-mouthed. I feared him for his size, pitied him for his dress, watched him all the time. Marveled at him, mystified, astonished, uneasy.

2   He had the habit of spitting on his right arm, juicing it down till it would glisten. He would start in immediately after taking his seat when we'd finished with the Pledge of Allegiance, "The Yellow Rose of Texas," "The Eyes of Texas Are upon You," and "Mistress Shady." Marvin would rub his spit-flecked arm with his left hand, rub and roll as if polishing an ebony pool cue. Then he would rest his head in the crook of his arm, sniffing, huffing deep like blackjacket boys huff bagsful of acrylics. After ten minutes or so, his eyes would close, heavy. He would sleep till recess. Mrs. Wickham would let him.

3   There was one other black kid in our class, a girl they called Ah-so. I never learned what she did to earn this name. There was nothing Asian about this big-shouldered girl. She was the tallest, heaviest kid in school. She was quiet, but I don't think any one of us was subtle or sophisticated enough to nickname our classmates according to any but physical attributes. Fat kids were called Porky or Butterball; skinny ones were called Stick or Ichabod. Ah-so was big, thick, and African. She would impassively sit, sullen, silent as Marvin. She wore the same dark blue pleated skirt every day, the same ruffled white blouse every day. Her skin always shone as if worked by Marvin's palms and fingers. I never spoke one word to her, nor she to me.

4   Of the three of us, Mrs. Wickham called only on Ah-so and me. Ah-so never answered one question, correctly or incorrectly, so far as I can recall. She wasn't stupid. When asked to read aloud she read well, seldom stumbling over long words, reading with humor and expression. But when Wickham asked her about Farmer Brown and how many cows, or the capital of Vermont, or the date of this war or that, Ah-so never spoke. Not one word. But you always felt she could have answered those questions if she'd wanted to. I sensed no tension, embarrassment, or anger in Ah-so's reticence. She

NOTES
hue (par. 1): color
apartheidlike (par. 1): segregated, separated by race
integration (par. 1): bringing together children of different races to attend school

simply refused to speak. There was something unshakable about her, some core so impenetrably solid, you got the feeling that if you stood too close to her she could eat your thoughts like a black star eats light. I didn't despise Ah-so as I despised Marvin. There was nothing malevolent about her. She sat like a great icon in the back of the classroom, tranquil, guarded, sealed up, watchful. She was close to sixteen, and it was my guess she'd given up on school. Perhaps she was just obliging the wishes of her family, sticking it out till the law could no longer reach her.

5   There were at least half a dozen older kids in our class. Besides Marvin and Ah-so there was Oakley, who sat behind me, whispering threats into my ear; Varna Willard with the large breasts; Eddie Limon, who played bass for a high school rock band; and Lawrence Ridderbeck, whom everyone said had a kid and a wife. You couldn't expect me to know anything about Texan educational practices of the 1960s, so I never knew why there were so many older kids in my sixth grade class. After all, I was just a boy and had transferred into the school around midyear. My father, an air force sergeant, had been sent to Viet Nam. The air force sent my mother, my sister Claire, and me to Connolly Air Force Base, which during the war housed "unaccompanied wives." I'd been to so many different schools in my short life that I ceased wondering about their differences. All I knew about the Texas schools is that they weren't afraid to flunk you.

6   Yet though I was only twelve then, I had a good idea why Wickham never once called on Marvin, why she let him snooze in the crook of his polished arm. I knew why she would press her lips together, and narrow her eyes at me whenever I correctly answered a question, rare as that was. I knew why she badgered Ah-so with questions everyone knew Ah-so would never even consider answering. Wickham didn't like us. She wasn't gross about it, but it was clear she didn't want us around. She would prove her dislike day after day with little stories and jokes. "I just want to share with you all," she would say, "a little riddle my daughter told me at the supper table th'other day. Now, where do you go when you injure your knee?" Then one, two, or all three of her pets would say for the rest of us, "We don't know, Miz Wickham," in that skin-chilling way suckasses speak, "where?" "Why, to Africa," Wickham would say, "where the knee grows."

7   The thirty-odd white kids would laugh, and I would look across the room at Marvin. He'd be asleep. I would glance back at Ah-so. She'd be sitting still as a projected image, staring down at her desk. I, myself, would smile at Wickham's stupid jokes, sometimes fake a laugh. I tried to show her that at least one of us was alive and alert, even though her jokes hurt. I sucked ass, too, I suppose. But I wanted her to understand more than anything that I was not like her other nigra children, that I was worthy of more than the nonattention and the negative attention she paid Marvin and Ah-so. I hated her, but never showed it. No one could safely contradict that woman. She knew all kinds of tricks to demean, control, and punish you. And she could swing her two-foot paddle as fluidly as a big league slugger swings a bat. You didn't speak

NOTES

a black star (par. 4): a black hole. A black hole is created when a massive star consumes all of its energy and collapses; it has such a strong field of gravity that nothing, not even light, can escape from it.

malevolent (par. 4): ill-willed, hostile

icon (par. 4): image or representation, especially of a person considered holy by Christians

badgered (par. 6): harassed

demean (par. 7): humiliate

in Wickham's class unless she spoke to you first. You didn't chew gum, or wear "hood" hair. You didn't drag your feet, curse, pass notes, hold hands with the opposite sex. Most especially, you didn't say anything bad about the Aggies, Governor Connally, LBJ, Sam Houston, or Waco. You did the forbidden and she would get you. It was that simple.

8   She never got me, though. Never gave her reason to. But she could have invented reasons. She did a lot of that. I can't be sure, but I used to think she pitied me because my father was in Viet Nam and my uncle A.J. had recently died there. Whenever she would tell one of her racist jokes, she would always glance at me, preface the joke with, "Now don't you nigra children take offense. This is all in fun, you know. I just want to share with you all something Coach Gilchrest told me th'other day." She would tell her joke, and glance at me again. I'd giggle, feeling a little queasy. "I'm half Irish," she would chuckle, "and you should hear some of those Irish jokes." She never told any, and I never really expected her to. I just did my Tom-thing. I kept my shoes shined, my desk neat, answered her questions as best I could, never brought gum to school, never cursed, never slept in class. I wanted to show her we were not all the same.

9   I tried to show them all, all thirty-odd, that I was different. It worked to some degree, but not very well. When some article was stolen from someone's locker or desk, Marvin, not I, was the first accused. I'd be second. Neither Marvin, nor Ah-so nor I were ever chosen for certain classroom honors— "Pledge leader," "flag holder," "noise monitor," "paper passer outer," but Mrs. Wickham once let me be "eraser duster." I was proud. I didn't even care about the cracks my fellow students made about my finally having turned the right color. I had done something that Marvin, in the deeps of his never-ending sleep, couldn't even dream of doing. Jack Preston, a kid who sat in front of me, asked me one day at recess whether I was embarrassed about Marvin. "Can you believe that guy?" I said. "He's like a pig or something. Makes me sick."

10   "Does it make you ashamed to be colored?"

11   "No," I said, but I meant yes. Yes, if you insist on thinking us all the same. Yes, if his faults are mine, his weaknesses inherent in me.

12   "I'd be," said Jack.

13   I made no reply. I was ashamed. Ashamed for not defending Marvin and ashamed that Marvin even existed. But if it had occurred to me, I would have asked Jack whether he was ashamed of being white because of Oakley. Oakley, "Oak Tree," Kelvin "Oak Tree" Oakley. He was sixteen and proud of it. He made it clear to everyone, including Wickham, that his life's ambition was to stay in school one more year, till he'd be old enough to enlist in the army. "Them slopes got my brother," he would say. "I'mna sign up and git me a

NOTES

"hood" (par. 7): hoodlum, thug

Aggies, Governor Connally, LBJ, Sam Houston, or Waco (par. 7): The *Aggies* is the name of the Texas A & M football team; *Governor John Bowden Connally* (1917–1993) was governor of Texas from 1963–1969; *LBJ,* Lyndon Bains Johnson (1908–1973), a Texan, was President of the United States from 1963–1968; *Sam Houston* (1793–1863) led the struggle to win Texas independence from Mexico and later to make it part of the United States; *Waco* is a city in Texas.

Tom-thing (par. 8): Uncle Tom thing. "Uncle Tom" is a scornful term for an African American who is humiliatingly submissive to white people. Uncle Tom is a character in Harriet Beecher Stowe's *Uncle Tom's Cabin.*

inherent in (par. 11): a part of

slopes (par. 13): a scornful term for Asian people

few slopes. Gonna kill them bastards deader'n shit." Oakley, so far as anyone knew, was and always had been the oldest kid in his family. But no one contradicted him. He would, as anyone would tell you, "snap yer neck jest as soon as look at you." Not a boy in class, excepting Marvin and myself, had been able to avoid Oakley's pink bellies, Texas titty twisters, moon pie punches, or worse. He didn't bother Marvin, I suppose, because Marvin was closer to his size and age, and because Marvin spent five-sixths of the school day asleep. Marvin probably never crossed Oakley's mind. And to say that Oakley hadn't bothered me is not to say he had no intention of ever doing so. In fact, this haphazard sketch of hairy fingers, slash of eyebrow, explosion of acne, elbows, and crooked teeth, swore almost daily that he'd like to kill me.

14   Naturally, I feared him. Though we were about the same height, he outweighed me by no less than forty pounds. He talked, stood, smoked, and swore like a man. No one, except for Mrs. Wickham, the principal, and the coach, ever laid a finger on him. And even Wickham knew that the hot lines she laid on him merely amused him. He would smile out at the classroom, goofy and bashful, as she laid down the two, five or maximum ten strokes on him. Often he would wink, or surreptitiously flash us the thumb as Wickham worked on him. When she was finished, Oakley would walk so cool back to his seat you'd think he was on wheels. He'd slide into his chair, sniff the air, and say, "Somethin's burning. Do y'all smell smoke? I swanee, I smell smoke and fahr back here." If he made these cracks and never threatened me, I might have grown to admire Oakley, even liked him a little. But he hated me, and took every opportunity during the six-hour school day to make me aware of this. "Some Sambo's gittin his ass broke open one of these days," he'd mumble. "I wanna fight somebody. Need to keep in shape till I git to Nam."

15   I never said anything to him for the longest time. I pretended not to hear him, pretended not to notice his sour breath on my neck and ear. "Yep," he'd whisper. "Coonies keep ya in good shape for slope killin." Day in, day out, that's the kind of thing I'd pretend not to hear. But one day when the rain dropped down like lead balls, and the cold air made your skin look plucked, Oakley whispered to me, "My brother tells me it rains like this in Nam. Maybe I oughta go out at recess and break your ass open today. Nice and cool so you don't sweat. Nice and wet to clean up the blood." I said nothing for at least half a minute, then I turned half right and said, "Thought you said your brother was dead." Oakley, silent himself, for a time, poked me in the back with his pencil and hissed, "*Yer* dead." Wickham cut her eyes our way, and it was over.

16   It was hardest avoiding him in gym class. Especially when we played murderball. Oakley always aimed his throws at me. He threw with unblinking intensity, his teeth gritting, his neck veining, his face flushing, his black hair sweeping over one eye. He could throw hard, but the balls were squishy and harmless. In fact, I found his misses more intimidating than his hits. The balls would whizz by, thunder against the folded bleachers. They rattled as though a locomotive were passing through them. I would duck, dodge, leap as if he were throwing grenades. But he always hit me, sooner or later. And after a while I noticed that the other boys would avoid throwing at me, as if I belonged to Oakley.

17   One day, however, I was surprised to see that Oakley was throwing at everyone else but me. He was uncommonly accurate, too; kids were falling

NOTES

surreptitiously (par. 14): secretly

Sambo (par. 14): a scornful term for African Americans. Sambo is a character in Helen Bannerman's *Little Black Sambo.*

Coonies (par. 15): a scornful term for African Americans.

like tin cans. Since no one was throwing at me, I spent most of the game watching Oakley cut this one and that one down. Finally, he and I were the only ones left on the court. Try as he would, he couldn't hit me, nor I him. Coach Gilchrest blew his whistle and told Oakley and me to bring the red rubber balls to the equipment locker. I was relieved I'd escaped Oakley's stinging throws for once. I was feeling triumphant, full of myself. As Oakley and I approached Gilchrest, I thought about saying something friendly to Oakley: Good game, Oak Tree, I would say. Before I could speak, though, Gilchrest said, "All right boys, there's five minutes left in the period. Y'all are so good, looks like, you're gonna have to play like men. No boundaries, no catch outs, and you gotta hit your opponent three times in order to win. Got me?"

18   We nodded.

19   "And you're gonna use these," said Gilchrest, pointing to three volley-balls at his feet. "And you better believe they're pumped full. Oates, you start at that end of the court. Oak Tree, you're at th'other end. Just like usual, I'll set the balls at mid-court, and when I blow my whistle I want y'all to haul your cheeks to the middle and th'ow for all you're worth. Got me?" Gilchrest nodded at our nods, then added, "Remember, no boundaries, right?"

20   I at my end, Oakley at his, Gilchrest blew his whistle. I was faster than Oakley and scooped up a ball before he'd covered three quarters of his side. I aimed, threw, and popped him right on the knee. "One-zip!" I heard Gilchrest shout. The ball bounced off his knee and shot right back into my hands. I hurried my throw and missed. Oakley bent down, clutched the two remaining balls. I remember being amazed that he could palm each ball, run full out, and throw left-handed or right-handed without a shade of awkwardness. I spun, ran, but one of Oakley's throws glanced off the back of my head. "One-one!" hollered Gilchrest. I fell and spun on my ass as the other ball came sailing at me. I caught it. "He's out!" I yelled. Gilchrest's voice boomed, "No catch outs. Three hits. Three hits." I leapt to my feet as Oakley scrambled across the floor for another ball. I chased him down, leapt, and heaved the ball hard as he drew himself erect. The ball hit him dead in the face, and he went down flat. He rolled around, cupping his hands over his nose. Gilchrest sped to his side, helped him to his feet, asked him whether he was OK. Blood flowed from Oakley's nose, dripped in startlingly bright spots on the floor, his shoes, Gilchrest's shirt. The coach removed Oakley's T-shirt and pressed it against the big kid's nose to stanch the bleeding. As they walked past me toward the office I mumbled an apology to Oakley, but couldn't catch his reply. "You watch your filthy mouth, boy," said Gilchrest to Oakley.

21   The locker room was unnaturally quiet as I stepped into its steamy atmosphere. Eyes clicked in my direction, looked away. After I was out of my shorts, had my towel wrapped around me, my shower kit in hand, Jack Preston and Brian Nailor approached me. Preston's hair was combed slick and plastic looking. Nailor's stood up like frozen flames. Nailor smiled at me with his big teeth and pale eyes. He poked my arm with a finger. "You fucked up," he said.

22   "I tried to apologize."

23   "Won't do you no good," said Preston.

24   "I swanee," said Nailor.

25   "It's part of the game," I said. "It was an accident. Wasn't my idea to use volleyballs."

26   "Don't matter," Preston said. "He's jest lookin for an excuse to fight you."

NOTE

I swanee (par. 24): I declare

27   "I never done nothing to him."

28   "Don't matter," said Nailor. "He don't like you."

29   "Brian's right, Clint. He'd jest as soon kill you as look at you."

30   "I never done nothing to him."

31   "Look," said Preston, "I know him pretty good. And jest between you and me, it's cause you're a city boy—"

32   "Whadda you mean? I've never—"

33   "He don't like your clothes—"

34   "And he don't like the fancy way you talk in class."

35   "What fancy—"

36   "I'm tellin him, if you don't mind, Brian."

37   "Tell him then."

38   "He don't like the way you say 'tennis shoes' instead of sneakers. He don't like coloreds. A whole bunch of things, really."

39   "I never done nothing to him. He's got no reason—"

40   *"And,"* said Nailor, grinning, *"and,* he says you're a stuck-up rich kid." Nailor's eyes had crow's-feet, bags beneath them. They were a man's eyes.

41   "My dad's a sergeant," I said.

42   "You chicken to fight him?" said Nailor.

43   "Yeah, Clint, don't be chicken. Jest go on and git it over with. He's whupped pert near ever'body else in the class. It ain't so bad."

44   "Might as well, Oates."

45   "Yeah, yer pretty skinny, but yer jest about his height. Jest git im in a headlock and don't let go."

46   "Goddamn," I said, "he's got no reason to—"

47   Their eyes shot right and I looked over my shoulder. Oakley stood at his locker, turning its tumblers. From where I stood I could see that a piece of cotton was wedged up one of his nostrils, and he already had the makings of a good shiner. His acne burned red like a fresh abrasion. He snapped the locker open and kicked his shoes off without sitting. Then he pulled off his shorts, revealing two paddle stripes on his ass. They were fresh red bars speckled with white, the white speckles being the reverse impression of the paddle's suction holes. He must not have watched his filthy mouth while in Gilchrest's presence. Behind me, I heard Preston and Nailor pad to their lockers.

48   Oakley spoke without turning around. "Somebody's gonna git his skinny black ass kicked, right today, right after school." He said it softly. He slipped his jock off, turned around. I looked away. Out of the corner of my eye I saw him stride off, his hairy nakedness a weapon clearing the younger boys from his path. Just before he rounded the corner of the shower stalls, I threw my toilet kit to the floor and stammered, "I—I never did nothing to you, Oakley." He stopped, turned, stepped closer to me, wrapping his towel around himself. Sweat streamed down my rib cage. It felt like ice water. "You wanna go at it right now, boy?"

49   "I never did nothing to you." I felt tears in my eyes. I couldn't stop them even though I was blinking like mad. "Never."

50   He laughed. "You busted my nose, asshole."

51   "What about before? What'd I ever do to you?"

52   "See you after school, Coonie." Then he turned away, flashing his acne-spotted back like a semaphore. "Why?" I shouted. "Why you wanna fight me?"

NOTES

abrasion (par. 47): scrape

semaphore (par. 52): an apparatus, such as the one used on railways, with lights, flags, or movable arms used to send signals

Oakley stopped and turned, folded his arms, leaned against a toilet stall. "Why you wanna fight *me*, Oakley?" I stepped over the bench. "What'd I do? Why me?" And then unconsciously, as if scratching, as if breathing, I walked toward Marvin, who stood a few feet from Oakley, combing his hair at the mirror. "Why not him?" I said. "How come you're after *me* and not *him?*" The room froze. Froze for a moment that was both evanescent and eternal, somewhere between an eye blink and a week in hell. No one moved, nothing happened; there was no sound at all. And then it was as if all of us at the same moment looked at Marvin. He just stood there, combing away, the only body in motion, I think. He combed his hair and combed it, as if seeing only his image, hearing only his comb scraping his scalp. I knew he'd heard me. There's no way he could not have heard me. But all he did was slide the comb into his pocket and walk out the door.

53   "I got no quarrel with Marvin," I heard Oakley say. I turned toward his voice, but he was already in the shower.

54   I was able to avoid Oakley at the end of the school day. I made my escape by asking Mrs. Wickham if I could go to the restroom.

55   "'Restroom,'" Oakley mumbled. "It's a damn toilet, sissy."

56   "Clinton," said Mrs. Wickham, "Can you *not* wait till the bell rings? It's almost three o'clock."

57   "No ma'am," I said. "I won't make it."

58   "Well, I should make you wait just to teach you to be more mindful about . . . hygiene . . . uh things." She sucked in her cheeks, squinted. "But I'm feeling charitable today. You may go." I immediately left the building, and got on the bus. "Ain't you a little early?" said the bus driver, swinging the door shut. "Just left the office," I said. The driver nodded, apparently not giving me a second thought. I had no idea why I'd told her I'd come from the office, or why she found it a satisfactory answer. Two minutes later the bus filled, rolled and shook its way to Connolly Air Base.

59   When I got home, my mother was sitting in the living room, smoking her Slims, watching her soap opera. She absently asked me how my day had gone and I told her fine. "Hear from Dad?" I said.

60   "No, but I'm sure he's fine." She always said that when we hadn't heard from him in a while. I suppose she thought I was worried about him, or that I felt vulnerable without him. It was neither. I just wanted to discuss something with my mother that we both cared about. If I spoke with her about things that happened at school, or on my weekends, she'd listen with half an ear, say something like, "Is that so?" or "You don't say?" I couldn't stand that sort of thing. But when I mentioned my father, she treated me a bit more like an adult, or at least someone who was worth listening to. I didn't want to feel like a boy that afternoon. As I turned from my mother and walked down the hall I thought about the day my father left for Viet Nam. Sharp in his uniform, sure behind his aviator specs, he slipped a cigar from his pocket and stuck it in mine. "Not till I get back," he said. "We'll have us one when we go fishing. Just you and me, out on the lake all day, smoking and casting and sitting. Don't let Mamma see it. Put in in y'back pocket." He hugged me, shook my hand, and told me I was the man of the house now. He told me he was depending on me to take good care of my mother and sister. "Don't you let me down, now, hear?" And he tapped his thick finger on my chest. "You almost as big as me. Boy, you something else." I believed him when he told

NOTES

evanescent (par. 52): fleeting
Slims (par. 59): Virginia Slims, a brand of cigarettes

me those things. My heart swelled big enough to swallow my father, my mother, Claire. I loved, feared, and respected myself, my manhood. That day I could have put all of Waco, Texas, in my heart. And it wasn't till about three months later that I discovered I really wasn't the man of the house, that my mother and sister, as they always had, were taking care of me.

61   For a brief moment I considered telling my mother about what had happened at school that day, but for one thing, she was deep down in the halls of "General Hospital," and never paid you much mind till it was over. For another thing, I just wasn't the kind of person—I'm still not, really—to discuss my problems with anyone. Like my father I kept things to myself, talked about my problems only in retrospect. Since my father wasn't around, I consciously wanted to be like him, doubly like him, I could say. I wanted to be the man of the house in some respect, even if it had to be in an inward way. I went to my room, changed my clothes, and laid out my homework. I couldn't focus on it. I thought about Marvin, what I'd said about him or done to him—I couldn't tell which. I'd done something to him, said something about him; said something about and done something to myself. *How come you're after* me *and not* him? I kept trying to tell myself I hadn't meant it that way. *That* way. I thought about approaching Marvin, telling him what I really meant was that he was more Oakley's age and weight than I. I would tell him I meant I was no match for Oakley. *See, Marvin, what I meant was that he wants to fight a colored guy, but is afraid to fight you cause you could beat him.* But try as I did, I couldn't for a moment convince myself that Marvin would believe me. I meant it *that* way and no other. Everybody heard. Everybody knew. That afternoon I forced myself to confront the notion that tomorrow I would probably have to fight both Oakley and Marvin. I'd have to be two men.

62   I rose from my desk and walked to the window. The light made my skin look orange, and I started thinking about what Wickham had told us once about light. She said that oranges and apples, leaves and flowers, the whole multi-colored world, was not what it appeared to be. The colors we see, she said, look like they do only because of the light or ray that shines on them. "The color of the thing isn't what you see, but the light that's reflected off it." Then she shut out the lights and shone a white light lamp on a prism. We watched the pale splay of colors on the projector screen; some people ooohed and aaahed. Suddenly, she switched on a black light and the color of everything changed. The prism colors vanished, Wickham's arms were purple, the buttons of her dress were as orange as hot coals, rather than the blue they had been only seconds before. We were all very quiet. "Nothing," she said after a while, "is really what it appears to be." I didn't really understand then. But as I stood at the window, gazing at my orange skin, I wondered what kind of light I could shine on Marvin, Oakley, and me that would reveal us as the same.

63   I sat down and stared at my arms. They were dark brown again. I worked up a bit of saliva under my tongue and spat on my left arm. I spat again, then rubbed the spittle into it, polishing, working till my arm grew warm. As I spat, and rubbed, I wondered why Marvin did this weird, nasty thing to himself, day after day. Was he trying to rub away the black, or deepen it, doll it up? And if he did this weird nasty thing for a hundred years, would he spit-shine himself invisible, rolling away the eggplant skin, revealing the scarlet muscle, blue vein, pink and yellow tendon, white bone? Then disappear? Seen through, all colors, no colors. Spitting and rubbing. Is this the way you do it?

NOTE
talked about my problems only in retrospect (par. 61): talked about my problems only when they were in the past

I leaned forward, sniffed the arm. It smelled vaguely of mayonnaise. After an hour or so, I fell asleep.

64   I saw Oakley the second I stepped off the bus the next morning. He stood outside the gym in his usual black penny loafers, white socks, high water jeans, T-shirt, and black jacket. Nailor stood with him, his big teeth spread across his bottom lip like playing cards. If there was anyone I felt like fighting, that day, it was Nailor. But I wanted to put off fighting for as long as I could. I stepped toward the gymnasium, thinking that I shouldn't run, but if I hurried I could beat Oakley to the door and secure myself near Gilchrest's office. But the moment I stepped into the gym, I felt Oakley's broad palm clap down on my shoulder. "Might as well stay out here, Coonie," he said. "I need me a little target practice." I turned to face him and he slapped me, one-two, with the back, then the palm of his hand, as I'd seen Bogart do to Peter Lorre in "The Maltese Falcon." My heart went wild. I could scarcely breathe. I couldn't swallow.

65   "Call me a nigger," I said. I have no idea what made me say this. All I know is that it kept me from crying. "Call me a nigger, Oakley."

66   "Fuck you, ya black ass slope." He slapped me again, scratching my eye. "I don't do what coonies tell me."

67   "Call me a nigger."

68   "Outside, Coonie."

69   "Call me one. Go ahead."

70   He lifted his hand to slap me again, but before his arm could swing my way, Marvin Pruitt came from behind me and calmly pushed me aside. "Git out my way, boy," he said. And he slugged Oakley on the side of his head. Oakley stumbled back, stiff-legged. His eyes were big. Marvin hit him twice more, once again to the side of the head, once to the nose. Oakley went down and stayed down. Though blood was drawn, whistles blowing, fingers pointing, kids hollering, Marvin just stood there, staring at me with cool eyes. He spat on the ground, licked his lips, and just stared at me, till Coach Gilchrest and Mr. Calderon tackled him and violently carried him away. He never struggled, never took his eyes off me.

71   Nailor and Mrs. Wickham helped Oakley to his feet. His already fattened nose bled and swelled so that I had to look away. He looked around, bemused, wall-eyed, maybe scared. It was apparent he had no idea how bad he was hurt. He didn't even touch his nose. He didn't look like he knew much of anything. He looked at me, looked me dead in the eye in fact, but didn't seem to recognize me.

72   That morning, like all other mornings, we said the Pledge of Allegiance, sang "The Yellow Rose of Texas," "The Eyes of Texas Are upon You," and "Mistress Shady." The room stood strangely empty without Oakley, and without Marvin, but at the same time you could feel their presence more intensely somehow. I felt like I did when I'd walk into my mother's room and could smell my father's cigars, or cologne. He was more palpable, in certain respects, than when there in actual flesh. For some reason, I turned to look at Ah-so, and just this once I let my eyes linger on her face. She had a very gentle-looking face, really. That surprised me. She must have felt my eyes on her because she glanced up at me for a second and smiled, white teeth, downcast eyes. Such a pretty smile. That surprised me too. She held it for a few seconds, then let it fade. She looked down at her desk, and sat still as a photograph.

NOTES
bemused (par. 71): stunned, confused
palpable (par. 72): touchable

Shiloh

Bobbie Ann Mason

1   Leroy Moffitt's wife, Norma Jean, is working on her pectorals. She lifts three-pound dumbbells to warm up, then progresses to a twenty-pound barbell. Standing with her legs apart, she reminds Leroy of Wonder Woman.

2   "I'd give anything if I could just get these muscles to where they're real hard," says Norma Jean. "Feel this arm. It's not as hard as the other one."

3   "That's 'cause you're right-handed," says Leroy, dodging as she swings the barbell in an arc.

4   "Do you think so?"

5   "Sure."

6   Leroy is a truckdriver. He injured his leg in a highway accident four months ago, and his physical therapy, which involves weights and a pulley, prompted Norma Jean to try building herself up. Now she is attending a bodybuilding class. Leroy has been collecting temporary disability since his tractor-trailer jack-knifed in Missouri, badly twisting his left leg in its socket. He has a steel pin in his hip. He will probably not be able to drive his rig again. It sits in the backyard, like a gigantic bird that has flown home to roost. Leroy has been home in Kentucky for three months, and his leg is almost healed, but the accident frightened him and he does not want to drive any more long hauls. He is not sure what to do next. In the meantime, he makes things from craft kits. He started by building a miniature log cabin from notched Popsicle sticks. He varnished it and placed it on the TV set, where it remains. It reminds him of a rustic Nativity scene. Then he tried string art (sailing ships on black velvet), a macrame owl kit, a snap-together B-17 Flying Fortress, and a lamp made out of a model truck, with a light fixture screwed in the top of the cab. At first the kits were diversions, something to kill time, but now he is thinking about building a fullscale log house from a kit. It would be considerably cheaper than building a regular house, and besides, Leroy has grown to appreciate how things are put together. He has begun to realize that in all the years he was on the road he never took time to examine anything. He was always flying past scenery.

7   "They won't let you build a log cabin in any of the new subdivisions," Norma Jean tells him.

8   "They will if I tell them it's for you," he says, teasing her. Ever since they were married, he has promised Norma Jean he would build her a new house one day. They have always rented, and the house they live in is small and nondescript. It does not even feel like a home, Leroy realizes now.

9   Norma Jean works at the Rexall drugstore, and she has acquired an amazing amount of information about cosmetics. When she explains to Leroy the three stages of complexion care, involving creams, toners, and moisturizers, he thinks happily of other petroleum products—axle grease, diesel fuel. This is a connection between him and Norma Jean. Since he has been home, he has felt unusually tender about his wife and guilty over his long absences. But

NOTES

Shiloh (title): a town in Tennessee where over twenty thousand soldiers died during a Civil War battle; the Confederate army was defeated and driven back to Corinth, Mississippi (par. 134).

pectorals (par. 1): chest muscles

jack-knifed (par. 6): twisted sideways

he can't tell what she feels about him. Norma Jean has never complained about his traveling; she has never made hurt remarks, like calling his truck a "widow-maker." He is reasonably certain she has been faithful to him, but he wishes she could celebrate his permanent homecoming more happily. Norma Jean is often startled to find Leroy at home, and he thinks she seems a little disappointed about it. Perhaps it reminds her too much of the early days of their marriage, before he went on the road. They had a child who died as an infant, years ago. They never speak about their memories of Randy, which have almost faded, but now that Leroy is home all the time, they sometimes feel awkward around each other, and Leroy wonders if one of them should mention the child. He has the feeling that they are waking up out of a dream together—that they must create a new marriage, start afresh. They are lucky they are still married. Leroy has read that for most people losing a child destroys the marriage—or else he heard this on *Donahue*. He can't always remember where he learns things anymore.

10   At Christmas, Leroy bought an electric organ for Norma Jean. She used to play the piano when she was in high school. "It don't leave you," she told him once. "It's like riding a bicycle."

11   The new instrument had so many keys and buttons that she was bewildered by it at first. She touched the keys tentatively, pushed some buttons, then pecked out "Chopsticks." It came out in an amplified fox-trot rhythm, with marimba sounds.

12   "It's an orchestra!" she cried.

13   The organ had a pecan-look finish and eighteen preset chords, with optional flute, violin, trumpet, clarinet, and banjo accompaniments. Norma Jean mastered the organ almost immediately. At first she played Christmas songs. Then she bought *The Sixties Songbook* and learned every tune in it, adding variations to each with the rows of brightly colored buttons.

14   "I didn't like these old songs back then," she said. "But I have this crazy feeling I missed something."

15   "You didn't miss a thing," said Leroy.

16   Leroy likes to lie on the couch and smoke a joint and listen to Norma Jean play "Can't Take My Eyes Off You" and "I'll Be Back." He is back again. After fifteen years on the road, he is finally settling down with the woman he loves. She is still pretty. Her skin is flawless. Her frosted curls resemble pencil trimmings.

17   Now that Leroy has come home to stay, he notices how much the town has changed. Subdivisions are spreading across western Kentucky like an oil slick. The sign at the edge of town says "Pop: 11,500"—only seven hundred more than it said twenty years before. Leroy can't figure out who is living in all the new houses. The farmers who used to gather around the courthouse square on Saturday afternoons to play checkers and spit tobacco juice have gone. It has been years since Leroy has thought about the farmers, and they have disappeared without his noticing.

NOTES

startled (par. 9): surprised
bewildered (par. 11): confused
tentatively (par. 11): uncertainly
amplified (par. 11): To "amplify" sounds is to make them louder.
fox-trot (par. 11): a ballroom dance with slow and fast steps
marimba (par. 11): a large xylophone—a musical instrument having wooden bars that are struck to produce sound
a joint (par. 16): a marijuana cigarette

18   Leroy meets a kid named Stevie Hamilton in the parking lot at the new shopping center. While they pretend to be strangers meeting over a stalled car, Stevie tosses an ounce of marijuana under the front seat of Leroy's car. Stevie is wearing orange jogging shoes and a T-shirt that says CHATTAHOOCHEE SUPER-RAT. His father is a prominent doctor who lives in one of the expensive subdivisions in a new white-columned brick house that looks like a funeral parlor. In the phone book under his name there is a separate number, with the listing "Teenagers."

19   "Where do you get this stuff?" asks Leroy. "From your pappy?"

20   "That's for me to know and you to find out," Stevie says. He is slit-eyed and skinny.

21   "What else you got?"

22   "What you interested in?"

23   "Nothing special. Just wondered."

24   Leroy used to take speed on the road. Now he has to go slowly. He needs to be mellow. He leans back against the car and says, "I'm aiming to build me a log house, soon as I get time. My wife, though, I don't think she likes the idea."

25   "Well, let me know when you want me again," Stevie says. He has a cigarette in his cupped palm, as though sheltering it from the wind. He takes a long drag, then stomps it on the asphalt and slouches away.

26   Stevie's father was two years ahead of Leroy in high school. Leroy is thirty-four. He married Norma Jean when they were both eighteen, and their child Randy was born a few months later, but he died at the age of four months and three days. He would be about Stevie's age now. Norma Jean and Leroy were at the drive-in, watching a double feature (*Dr. Strangelove* and *Lover Come Back*), and the baby was sleeping in the back seat. When the first movie ended, the baby was dead. It was the sudden infant death syndrome. Leroy remembers handing Randy to a nurse at the emergency room, as though he were offering her a large doll as a present. A dead baby feels like a sack of flour. "It just happens sometimes," said the doctor, in what Leroy always recalls as a nonchalant tone. Leroy can hardly remember the child anymore, but he still sees vividly a scene from *Dr. Strangelove* in which the President of the United States was talking in a folksy voice on the hot line to the Soviet premier about the bomber accidentally headed toward Russia. He was in the War Room, and the world map was lit up. Leroy remembers Norma Jean standing catatonically beside him in the hospital and himself thinking: Who is this strange girl? He had forgotten who she was. Now scientists are saying that crib death is caused by a virus. Nobody knows anything, Leroy thinks. The answers are always changing.

27   When Leroy gets home from the shopping center, Norma Jean's mother, Mabel Beasley, is there. Until this year, Leroy has not realized how much time she spends with Norma Jean. When she visits, she inspects the closets and then the plants, informing Norma Jean when a plant is droopy or yellow. Mabel calls the plants "flowers," although there are never any blooms. She always notices if Norma Jean's laundry is piling up. Mabel is a short, overweight woman whose tight, brown-dyed curls look more like a wig than the actual wig she sometimes wears. Today she has brought Norma Jean an off-white dust ruffle she made for the bed; Mabel works in a custom-upholstery shop.

NOTES

prominent (par. 18): well-known
nonchalant (par. 26): unconcerned
folksy (par. 26): friendly, personal
catatonically (par. 26): motionless, stunned

28   "This is the tenth one I made this year," Mabel says. "I got started and couldn't stop."

29   "It's real pretty," says Norma Jean.

30   "Now we can hide things under the bed," says Leroy, who gets along with his mother-in-law primarily by joking with her. Mabel has never really forgiven him for disgracing her by getting Norma Jean pregnant. When the baby died, she said that fate was mocking her.

31   "What's that thing?" Mabel says to Leroy in a loud voice, pointing to a tangle of yarn on a piece of canvas.

32   Leroy holds it up for Mabel to see. "It's my needlepoint," he explains. "This is a *Star Trek* pillow cover."

33   "That's what a woman would do," says Mabel. "Great day in the morning!"

34   "All the big football players on TV do it," he says.

35   "Why, Leroy, you're always trying to fool me. I don't believe you for one minute. You don't know what to do with yourself—that's the whole trouble. Sewing!"

36   "I'm aiming to build us a log house," says Leroy. "Soon as my plans come."

37   "Like *heck* you are," says Norma Jean. She takes Leroy's needlepoint and shoves it into a drawer. "You have to find a job first. Nobody can afford to build now anyway."

38   Mabel straightens her girdle and says, "I still think before you get tied down y'all ought to take a little run to Shiloh."

39   "One of these days, Mama," Norma Jean says impatiently.

40   Mabel is talking about Shiloh, Tennessee. For the past few years, she has been urging Leroy and Norma Jean to visit the Civil War battleground there. Mabel went there on her honeymoon—the only real trip she ever took. Her husband died of a perforated ulcer when Norma Jean was ten, but Mabel, who was accepted into the United Daughters of the Confederacy in 1975, is still preoccupied with going back to Shiloh.

41   "I've been to kingdom come and back in that truck out yonder," Leroy says to Mabel, "but we never yet set foot in that battleground. Ain't that something? How did I miss it?"

42   "It's not even that far," Mabel says.

43   After Mabel leaves, Norma Jean reads to Leroy from a list she has made. "Things you could do," she announces. "You could get a job as a guard at Union Carbide, where they'd let you set on a stool. You could get on at the lumberyard. You could do a little carpenter work, if you want to build so bad. You could—"

44   "I can't do something where I'd have to stand up all day."

45   "You ought to try standing up all day behind a cosmetics counter. It's amazing that I have strong feet, coming from two parents that never had strong feet at all." At the moment Norma Jean is holding on to the kitchen counter, raising her knees one at a time as she talks. She is wearing two pound ankle weights.

46   "Don't worry," says Leroy. "I'll do something."

47   "You could truck calves to slaughter for somebody. You wouldn't have to drive any big old truck for that."

48   "I'm going to build you this house," says Leroy. "I want to make you a real home."

NOTES

mocking (par. 30): ridiculing
preoccupied with (par. 40): extremely interested in
kingdom come (par. 41): as far as one can travel

49   "I don't want to live in any log cabin."

50   "It's not a cabin. It's a house."

51   "I don't care. It looks like a cabin."

52   "You and me together could lift those logs. It's just like lifting weights."

53   Norma Jean doesn't answer. Under her breath, she is counting. Now she is marching through the kitchen. She is doing goose steps.

54   Before his accident, when Leroy came home he used to stay in the house with Norma Jean, watching TV in bed and playing cards. She would cook fried chicken, picnic ham, chocolate pie—all his favorites. Now he is home alone much of the time. In the mornings, Norma Jean disappears, leaving a cooling place in the bed. She eats a cereal called Body Buddies, and she leaves the bowl on the table, with the soggy tan balls floating in a milk puddle. He sees things about Norma Jean that he never realized before. When she chops onions, she stares off into a corner, as if she can't bear to look. She puts on her house slippers almost precisely at nine o'clock every evening and nudges her jogging shoes under the couch. She saves bread heels for the birds. Leroy watches the birds at the feeder. He notices the peculiar way goldfinches fly past the window. They close their wings, then fall, then spread their wings to catch and lift themselves. He wonders if they close their eyes when they fall. Norma Jean closes her eyes when they are in bed. She wants the lights turned out. Even then, he is sure she closes her eyes.

55   He goes for long drives around town. He tends to drive a car rather carelessly. Power steering and an automatic shift make a car feel so small and inconsequential that his body is hardly involved in the driving process. His injured leg stretches out comfortably. Once or twice he has almost hit something, but even the prospect of an accident seems minor in a car. He cruises the new subdivisions, feeling like a criminal rehearsing for a robbery. Norma Jean is probably right about a log house being inappropriate here in the new subdivisions. All the houses look grand and complicated. They depress him.

56   One day when Leroy comes home from a drive he finds Norma Jean in tears. She is in the kitchen making a potato and mushroom-soup casserole, with grated-cheese topping. She is crying because her mother caught her smoking.

57   "I didn't hear her coming. I was standing here puffing away pretty as you please," Norma Jean says, wiping her eyes.

58   "I knew it would happen sooner or later," says Leroy, putting his arm around her.

59   "She don't know the meaning of the word 'knock,'" says Norma Jean. "It's a wonder she hadn't caught me years ago."

60   "Think of it this way," Leroy says. "What if she caught me with a joint?"

61   "You better not let her!" Norma Jean shrieks. "I'm warning you, Leroy Moffitt!"

62   "I'm just kidding. Here, play me a tune. That'll help you relax."

63   Norma Jean puts the casserole in the oven and sets the timer. Then she plays a ragtime tune, with horns and banjo, as Leroy lights up a joint and lies on the couch, laughing to himself about Mabel's catching him at it. He thinks of Stevie Hamilton—a doctor's son pushing grass. Everything is funny. The town seems crazy and small. He is reminded of Virgil Mathis, a boastful policeman Leroy used to shoot pool with. Virgil recently led a drug bust in a

NOTES

inconsequential (par. 55): unimportant, insignificant
prospect (par. 55): possibility
pushing grass (par. 63): selling marijuana

back room at a bowling alley, where he seized ten thousand dollars' worth of marijuana. The newspaper had a picture of him holding up the bags of grass and grinning widely. Right now, Leroy can imagine Virgil breaking down the door and arresting him with a lungful of smoke. Virgil would probably have been alerted to the scene because of all the racket Norma Jean is making. Now she sounds like a hard-rock band. Norma Jean is terrific. When she switches to a Latin-rhythm version of "Sunshine Superman," Leroy hums along. Norma Jean's foot goes up and down, up and down.

64   "Well, what do you think?" Leroy says, when Norma Jean pauses to search through her music.

65   "What do I think about what?"

66   His mind has gone blank. Then he says, "I'll sell my rig and build us a house." That wasn't what he wanted to say. He wanted to know what she thought—what she *really* thought—about them.

67   "Don't start in on that again," says Norma Jean. She begins playing "Who'll Be the Next in Line?"

68   Leroy used to tell hitchhikers his whole life story—about his travels, his hometown, the baby. He would end with a question: "Well, what do you think?" It was just a rhetorical question. In time, he had the feeling that he'd been telling the same story over and over to the same hitchhikers. He quit talking to hitchhikers when he realized how his voice sounded—whining and self-pitying, like some teenage-tragedy song. Now Leroy has the sudden impulse to tell Norma Jean about himself, as if he had just met her. They have known each other so long they have forgotten a lot about each other. They could become reacquainted. But when the oven timer goes off and she runs to the kitchen, he forgets why he wants to do this.

69   The next day, Mabel drops by. It is Saturday and Norma Jean is cleaning. Leroy is studying the plans of his log house, which have finally come in the mail. He has them spread out on the table—big sheets of stiff blue paper, with diagrams and numbers printed in white. While Norma Jean runs the vacuum, Mabel drinks coffee. She sets her coffee cup on a blueprint.

70   "I'm just waiting for time to pass," she says to Leroy, drumming her fingers on the table.

71   As soon as Norma Jean switches off the vacuum, Mabel says in a loud voice, "Did you hear about the datsun dog that killed the baby?"

72   Norma Jean says, "The word is 'dachshund.'"

73   "They put the dog on trial. It chewed the baby's legs off. The mother was in the next room all the time." She raises her voice. "They thought it was neglect."

74   Norma Jean is holding her ears. Leroy manages to open the refrigerator and get some Diet Pepsi to offer Mabel. Mabel still has some coffee and she waves away the Pepsi.

75   "Datsuns are like that," Mabel says. "They're jealous dogs. They'll tear a place to pieces if you don't keep an eye on them."

76   "You better watch out what you're saying, Mabel," says Leroy.

77   "Well, facts is facts."

78   Leroy looks out the window at his rig. It is like a huge piece of furniture gathering dust in the backyard. Pretty soon it will be an antique. He hears the vacuum cleaner. Norma Jean seems to be cleaning the living room rug again.

79   Later, she says to Leroy, "She just said that about the baby because she caught me smoking. She's trying to pay me back."

NOTES

rhetorical question (par. 68): a question that is not meant to be answered
impulse (par. 68): desire

80   "What are you talking about?" Leroy says, nervously shuffling blueprints.

81   "You know good and well," Norma Jean says. She is sitting in a kitchen chair with her feet up and her arms wrapped around her knees. She looks small and helpless. She says, "The very idea, her bringing up a subject like that! Saying it was neglect."

82   "She didn't mean that," Leroy says.

83   "She might not have *thought* she meant it. She always says things like that. You don't know how she goes on."

84   "But she didn't really mean it. She was just talking."

85   Leroy opens a king-sized bottle of beer and pours it into two glasses, dividing it carefully. He hands a glass to Norma Jean, and she takes it from him mechanically. For a long time, they sit by the kitchen window watching the birds at the feeder.

86   Something is happening. Norma Jean is going to night school. She has graduated from her six-week body-building course and now she is taking an adult-education course in composition at Paducah Community College. She spends her evenings outlining paragraphs.

87   "First you have a topic sentence," she explains to Leroy. "Then you divide it up. Your secondary topic has to be connected to your primary topic."

88   To Leroy, this sounds intimidating. "I never was any good in English," he says.

89   "It makes a lot of sense."

90   "What are you doing this for, anyhow?"

91   She shrugs. "It's something to do." She stands up and lifts her dumbbells a few times.

92   "Driving a rig, nobody cared about my English."

93   "I'm not criticizing your English."

94   Norma Jean used to say, "If I lose ten minutes' sleep, I just drag all day." Now she stays up late, writing compositions. She got a B on her first paper—a how-to theme on soup-based casseroles. Recently Norma Jean has been cooking unusual foods—tacos, lasagna, Bombay chicken. She doesn't play the organ anymore, though her second paper was called "Why Music Is Important to Me." She sits at the kitchen table, concentrating on her outlines, while Leroy plays with his log house plans, practicing with a set of Lincoln Logs. The thought of getting a truckload of notched, numbered logs scares him, and he wants to be prepared. As he and Norma Jean work together at the kitchen table, Leroy has the hopeful thought that they are sharing something, but he knows he is a fool to think this. Norma Jean is miles away. He knows he is going to lose her. Like Mabel, he is just waiting for time to pass.

95   One day, Mabel is there before Norma Jean gets home from work, and Leroy finds himself confiding in her. Mabel, he realizes, must know Norma Jean better than he does.

96   "I don't know what's got into that girl," Mabel says. "She used to go to bed with the chickens. Now you say she's up all hours. Plus her a-smoking. I like to died."

97   "I want to make her this beautiful home," Leroy says, indicating the Lincoln Logs. "I don't think she even wants it. Maybe she was happier with me gone."

98   "She don't know what to make of you, coming home like this."

99   "Is that it?"

NOTES

intimidating (par. 88): threatening
confiding in (par. 95): talking privately to

100   Mabel takes the roof off his Lincoln Log cabin. "You couldn't get *me* in a log cabin," she says. "I was raised in one. It's no picnic, let me tell you."

101   "They're different now," says Leroy.

102   "I tell you what," Mabel says, smiling oddly at Leroy.

103   "What?"

104   "Take her on down to Shiloh. Y'all need to get out together, stir a little. Her brain's all balled up over them books."

105   Leroy can see traces of Norma Jean's features in her mother's face. Mabel's worn face has the texture of crinkled cotton, but suddenly she looks pretty. It occurs to Leroy that Mabel has been hinting all along that she wants them to take her with them to Shiloh.

106   "Let's all go to Shiloh," he says. "You and me and her. Come Sunday."

107   Mabel throws up her hands in protest. "Oh, no, not me. Young folks want to be by themselves."

108   When Norma Jean comes in with groceries, Leroy says excitedly, "Your mama here's been dying to go to Shiloh for thirty-five years. It's about time we went, don't you think?"

109   "I'm not going to butt in on anybody's second honeymoon," Mabel says.

110   "Who's going on a honeymoon, for Christ's sake?" Norma Jean says loudly.

111   "I never raised no daughter of mine to talk that-a-way," Mabel says.

112   "You ain't seen nothing yet," says Norma Jean. She starts putting away boxes and cans, slamming cabinet doors.

113   "There's a log cabin at Shiloh," Mabel says. "It was there during the battle. There's bullet holes in it."

114   "When are you going to *shut up* about Shiloh, Mama?" asks Norma Jean.

115   "I always thought Shiloh was the prettiest place, so full of history," Mabel goes on. "I just hoped y'all could see it once before I die, so you could tell me about it." Later, she whispers to Leroy, "You do what I said. A little change is what she needs."

116   "Your name means 'the king,'" Norma Jean says to Leroy that evening. He is trying to get her to go to Shiloh, and she is reading a book about another century.

117   "Well, I reckon I ought to be right proud."

118   "I guess so."

119   "Am I still king around here?"

120   Norma Jean flexes her biceps and feels them for hardness. "I'm not fooling around with anybody, if that's what you mean," she says.

121   "Would you tell me if you were?"

122   "I don't know."

123   "What does *your* name mean?"

124   "It was Marilyn Monroe's real name."

125   "No kidding!"

126   "Norma comes from the Normans. They were invaders," she says. She closes her book and looks hard at Leroy. "I'll go to Shiloh with you if you'll stop staring at me."

127   On Sunday, Norma Jean packs a picnic and they go to Shiloh. To Leroy's relief, Mabel says she does not want to come with them. Norma Jean drives, and Leroy, sitting beside her, feels like some boring hitchhiker she has picked up. He tries some conversation, but she answers him in monosyllables.

NOTES

biceps (par. 120): upper arm muscles

Normans (par. 126): Scandinavian invaders of Normandy (in France); the French Normans later invaded England (in 1066).

monosyllables (par. 127): one-syllable sounds or words

At Shiloh, she drives aimlessly through the park, past bluffs and trails and steep ravines. Shiloh is an immense place, and Leroy cannot see it as a battleground. It is not what he expected. He thought it would look like a golf course. Monuments are everywhere, showing through the thick clusters of trees. Norma Jean passes the log cabin Mabel mentioned. It is surrounded by tourists looking for bullet holes.

128   "That's not the kind of log house I've got in mind," says Leroy apologetically.

129   "I know *that*."

130   "This is a pretty place. Your mama was right."

131   "It's O.K.," says Norma Jean. "Well, we've seen it. I hope she's satisfied."

132   They burst out laughing together.

133   At the park museum, a movie on Shiloh is shown every half hour, but they decide that they don't want to see it. They buy a souvenir Confederate flag for Mabel, and then they find a picnic spot near the cemetery. Norma Jean has brought a picnic cooler, with pimiento sandwiches, soft drinks, and Yodels. Leroy eats a sandwich and then smokes a joint, hiding it behind the picnic cooler. Norma Jean has quit smoking altogether. She is picking cake crumbs from the cellophane wrapper, like a fussy bird.

134   Leroy says, "So the boys in gray ended up in Corinth. The Union soldiers zapped 'em finally, April 7, 1862."

135   They both know he doesn't know any history. He is just talking about some of the historical plaques they have read. He feels awkward, like a boy on a date with an older girl. They are still just making conversation.

136   "Corinth is where Mama eloped to," says Norma Jean.

137   They sit in silence and stare at the cemetery for the Union dead and, beyond, at a tall cluster of trees. Campers are parked nearby, bumper to bumper, and small children in bright clothing are cavorting and squealing. Norma Jean wads up the cake wrapper and squeezes it tightly in her hand. Without looking at Leroy, she says, "I want to leave you."

138   Leroy takes a bottle of Coke out of the cooler and flips off the cap. He holds the bottle poised near his mouth but cannot remember to take a drink. Finally he says, "No, you don't."

139   "Yes, I do."

140   "I won't let you."

141   "You can't stop me."

142   "Don't do me that way."

143   Leroy knows Norma Jean will have her own way. "Didn't I promise to be home from now on?" he says.

144   "In some ways, a woman prefers a man who wanders," says Norma Jean. "That sounds crazy, I know."

145   "You're not crazy."

146   Leroy remembers to drink from his Coke. Then he says, "Yes, you *are* crazy. You and me could start all over again. Right back at the beginning."

147   "We *have* started all over again," says Norma Jean. "And this is how it turned out."

148   "What did I do wrong?"

149   "Nothing."

150   "Is this one of those women's lib things?" Leroy asks.

NOTES

aimlessly (par. 127): without purpose or direction
immense (par. 127): huge
the boys in gray (par. 134): Confederate soldiers
cavorting (par. 137): leaping, hopping, etc.

151   "Don't be funny."

152   The cemetery, a green slope dotted with white markers, looks like a subdivision site. Leroy is trying to comprehend that his marriage is breaking up, but for some reason he is wondering about white slabs in a graveyard.

153   "Everything was fine till Mama caught me smoking," says Norma Jean, standing up. "That set something off."

154   "What are you talking about?"

155   "She won't leave me alone—*you* won't leave me alone." Norma Jean seems to be crying, but she is looking away from him. "I feel eighteen again. I can't face that all over again." She starts walking away. "No, it *wasn't* fine. I don't know what I'm saying. Forget it."

156   Leroy takes a lungful of smoke and closes his eyes as Norma Jean's words sink in. He tries to focus on the fact that thirty-five hundred soldiers died on the grounds around him. He can only think of that war as a board game with plastic soldiers. Leroy almost smiles, as he compares the Confederates' daring attack on the Union camps and Virgil Mathis's raid on the bowling alley. General Grant, drunk and furious, shoved the Southerners back to Corinth, where Mabel and Jet Beasley were married years later, when Mabel was still thin and good-looking. The next day Mabel and Jet visited the battleground and then Norma Jean was born, and then she married Leroy and they had a baby, which they lost, and now Leroy and Norma Jean are here at the same battleground. Leroy knows he is leaving out a lot. He is leaving out the insides of history. History was always just names and dates to him. It occurs to him that building a house out of logs is similarly empty—too simple. And the real inner workings of a marriage, like most of history, have escaped him. Now he sees that building a log house is the dumbest idea he could have had. It was clumsy of him to think Norma Jean would want a log house. It was a crazy idea. He'll have to think of something else, quickly. He will wad the blueprints into tight balls and fling them into the lake. Then he'll get moving again. He opens his eyes. Norma Jean has moved away and is walking through the cemetery, following a serpentine brick path.

157   Leroy gets up to follow his wife, but his good leg is asleep and his bad leg still hurts him. Norma Jean is far away, walking rapidly toward the bluff by the river, and he tries to hobble toward her. Some children run past him, screaming noisily. Norma Jean has reached the bluff, and she is looking out over the Tennessee River. Now she turns toward Leroy and waves her arms. Is she beckoning to him? She seems to be doing an exercise for her chest muscles. The sky is unusually pale—the color of the dust ruffle Mabel made for their bed.

NOTES
General Grant (par. 156): commander of the Union army
serpentine (par. 156): twisting, like a snake

The Fat Girl

Andre Dubus

1   Her name was Louise. Once when she was sixteen a boy kissed her at a barbecue; he was drunk and he jammed his tongue into her mouth and ran his hands up and down her hips. Her father kissed her often. He was thin and

kind and she could see in his eyes when he looked at her the lights of love and pity.

2   It started when Louise was nine. You must start watching what you eat, her mother would say. I can see you have my metabolism. Louise also had her mother's pale blonde hair. Her mother was slim and pretty, carried herself erectly, and ate very little. The two of them would eat bare lunches, while her older brother ate sandwiches and potato chips, and then her mother would sit smoking while Louise eyed the bread box, the pantry, the refrigerator. Wasn't that good, her mother would say. In five years you'll be in high school and if you're fat the boys won't like you; they won't ask you out. Boys were as far away as five years, and she would go to her room and wait for nearly an hour until she knew her mother was no longer thinking of her, then she would creep into the kitchen and, listening to her mother talking on the phone, or her footsteps upstairs, she would open the bread box, the pantry, the jar of peanut butter. She would put the sandwich under her shirt and go outside or to the bathroom to eat it.

3   Her father was a lawyer and made a lot of money and came home looking pale and happy. Martinis put color back in his face, and at dinner he talked to his wife and two children. Oh give her a potato, he would say to Louise's mother. She's a growing girl. Her mother's voice then became tense: If she has a potato she shouldn't have dessert. She should have both, her father would say, and he would reach over and touch Louise's cheek or hand or arm.

4   In high school she had two girl friends and at night and on week-ends they rode in a car or went to movies. In movies she was fascinated by fat actresses. She wondered why they were fat. She knew why she was fat: she was fat because she was Louise. Because God had made her that way. Because she wasn't like her friends Joan and Marjorie, who drank milk shakes after school and were all bones and tight skin. But what about those actresses, with their talents, with their broad and profound faces? Did they eat as heedlessly as Bishop Humphries and his wife who sometimes came to dinner and, as Louise's mother said, gorged between amenities? Or did they try to lose weight, did they go about hungry and angry and thinking of food? She thought of them eating lean meats and salads with friends, and then going home and building strange large sandwiches with French bread. But mostly she believed they did not go through these failures; they were fat because they chose to be. And she was certain of something else too: she could see it in their faces: they did not eat secretly. Which she did: her creeping to the kitchen when she was nine became, in high school, a ritual of deceit and pleasure. She was furtive eater of sweets. Even her two friends did not know her secret.

5   Joan was thin, gangling, and flat-chested; she was attractive enough and all she needed was someone to take a second look at her face, but the school was large and there were pretty girls in every classroom and walking all the corridors, so no one ever needed to take a second look at Joan. Marjorie was thin too, an intense, heavy-smoking girl with brittle laughter. She was very intelligent, and with boys she was shy because she knew she made them uncomfortable, and because she was smarter than they were and so could not

NOTES

metabolism (par. 2): the chemical process through which the body breaks down and uses food

heedlessly (par. 4): unconcerned

gorged (par. 4): stuffed themselves

amenities (par. 4): polite conversations

furtive (par. 4): secret

gangling (par. 5): tall and awkward

understand or could not believe the levels they lived on. She was to have a nervous breakdown before earning her PhD. in philosophy at the University of California, where she met and married a physicist and discovered within herself an untrammelled passion: she made love with her husband on the couch, the carpet, in the bathtub, and on the washing machine. By that time much had happened to her and she never thought of Louise. Joan would finally stop growing and begin moving with grace and confidence. In college she would have two lovers and then several more during the six years she spent in Boston before marrying a middle-aged editor who had two sons in their early teens, who drank too much, who was tenderly, boyishly grateful for her love, and whose wife had been killed while rock-climbing in New Hampshire with her lover. She would not think of Louise either, except in an earlier time, when lovers were still new to her and she was ecstatically surprised each time one of them loved her and, sometimes at night, lying in a man's arms, she would tell how in high school no one dated her, she had been thin and plain (she would still believe that: that she had been plain; it had never been true) and so had been forced into the week-end and night-time company of a neurotic smart girl and a shy fat girl. She would say this with self-pity exaggerated by Scotch and her need to be more deeply loved by the man who held her.

6   She never eats, Joan and Marjorie said of Louise. They ate lunch with her at school, watched her refusing potatoes, ravioli, fried fish. Sometimes she got through the cafeteria line with only a salad. That is how they would remember her: a girl whose hapless body was destined to be fat. No one saw the sandwiches she made and took to her room when she came home from school. No one saw the store of Milky Ways, Butterfingers, Almond Joys, and Hersheys far back on her closet shelf, behind the stuffed animals of her childhood. She was not a hypocrite. When she was out of the house she truly believed she was dieting; she forgot about the candy, as a man speaking into his office dictaphone may forget the lewd photographs hidden in an old shoe in his closet. At other times, away from home, she thought of the waiting candy with near lust. One night driving home from a movie, Marjorie said: "You're lucky you don't smoke; it's in*cred*ible what I go through to hide it from my parents." Louise turned to her a smile which was elusive and mysterious; she yearned to be home in bed, eating chocolate in the dark. She did not need to smoke; she already had a vice that was insular and destructive.

7   She brought it with her to college. She thought she would leave it behind. A move from one place to another, a new room without the haunted closet shelf, would do for her what she could not do for herself. She packed her large dresses and went. For two weeks she was busy with registration, with shyness, with classes; then she began to feel at home. Her room was no longer like a motel. Its walls had stopped watching her, she felt they were her friends, and she gave them her secret. Away from her mother, she did not have to be as elaborate; she kept the candy in her drawer now.

NOTES

untrammelled (par. 5): unrestricted
ecstatically (par. 5): overwhelmingly, joyfully
hapless (par. 6): unfortunate
hypocrite (par. 6): a person who says one thing and does the opposite
lewd (par. 6): obscene
elusive (par. 6): deceptive
insular (par. 6): concealed
elaborate (par. 7): careful

8   The school was in Massachusetts, a girls' school. When she chose it, when she and her father and mother talked about it in the evenings, everyone so carefully avoided the word boys that sometimes the conversations seemed to be about nothing but boys. There are no boys there, the neuter words said; you will not have to contend with that. In her father's eyes were pity and encouragement; in her mother's was disappointment, and her voice was crisp. They spoke of courses, of small classes where Louise would get more attention. She imagined herself in those small classes; she saw herself as a teacher would see her, as the other girls would; she would get no attention.

9   The girls at the school were from wealthy families, but most of them wore the uniform of another class: blue jeans and work shirts, and many wore overalls. Louise bought some overalls, washed them until the dark blue faded, and wore them to classes. In the cafeteria she ate as she had in high school, not to lose weight nor even to sustain her lie, but because eating lightly in public had become as habitual as good manners. Everyone had to take gym, and in the locker room with the other girls, and wearing shorts on the volleyball and badminton courts, she hated her body. She liked her body most when she was unaware of it: in bed at night, as sleep gently took her out of her day, out of herself. And she liked parts of her body. She liked her brown eyes and sometimes looked at them in the mirror: they were not shallow eyes, she thought; they were indeed windows of a tender soul, a good heart. She liked her lips and nose, and her chin, finely shaped between her wide and sagging cheeks. Most of all she liked her long pale blonde hair, she liked washing and drying it and lying naked on her bed, smelling of shampoo, and feeling the soft hair at her neck and shoulders and back.

10   Her friend at college was Carrie, who was thin and wore thick glasses and often at night she cried in Louise's room. She did not know why she was crying. She was crying, she said, because she was unhappy. She could say no more. Louise said she was unhappy too, and Carrie moved in with her. One night Carrie talked for hours, sadly and bitterly, about her parents and what they did to each other. When she finished she hugged Louise and they went to bed. Then in the dark Carrie spoke across the room: "Louise? I just wanted to tell you. One night last week I woke up and smelled chocolate. You were eating chocolate, in your bed. I wish you'd eat it in front of me, Louise, whenever you feel like it."

11   Stiffened in her bed, Louise could think of nothing to say. In the silence she was afraid Carrie would think she was asleep and would tell her again in the morning or tomorrow night. Finally she said Okay. Then after a moment she told Carrie if she ever wanted any she could feel free to help herself; the candy was in the top drawer. Then she said Thank you.

12   They were roommates for four years and in the summers they exchanged letters. Each fall they greeted with embraces, laughter, tears, and moved into their old room, which had been stripped and cleansed of them for the summer. Neither girl enjoyed summer. Carrie did not like being at home because her parents did not love each other. Louise lived in a small city in Louisiana. She did not like summer because she had lost touch with Joan and Marjorie; they saw each other, but it was not the same. She liked being with her father but with no one else. The flicker of disappointment in her mother's eyes at the airport was a vanguard of the army of relatives and acquaintances who awaited her: they would see her on the streets, in stores, at the country club,

NOTES

neuter (par. 8): literally, having neither male nor female characteristics
sustain (par. 9): maintain
vanguard (par. 12): literally, the troops at the head of an army

in her home, and in theirs; in the first moments of greeting, their eyes would tell her she was still fat Louise, who had been fat as long as they could remember, who had gone to college and returned as fat as ever. Then their eyes dismissed her, and she longed for school and Carrie, and she wrote letters to her friend. But that saddened her too. It wasn't simply that Carrie was her only friend, and when they finished college they might never see each other again. It was that her existence in the world was so divided; it had begun when she was a child creeping to the kitchen; now that division was much sharper, and her friendship with Carrie seemed disproportionate and perilous. The world she was destined to live in had nothing to do with the intimate nights in their room at school.

13   In the summer before their senior year, Carrie fell in love. She wrote to Louise about him, but she did not write much, and this hurt Louise more than if Carrie had shown the joy her writing tried to conceal. That fall they returned to their room; they were still close and warm, Carrie still needed Louise's ears and heart at night as she spoke of her parents and her recurring malaise whose source the two friends never discovered. But on most weekends Carrie left, and caught a bus to Boston where her boy friend studied music. During the week she often spoke hesitantly of sex; she was not sure if she liked it. But Louise, eating candy and listening, did not know whether Carrie was telling the truth or whether, as in her letters of the past summer, Carrie was keeping from her those delights she may never experience.

14   Then one Sunday night when Carrie had just returned from Boston and was unpacking her overnight bag, she looked at Louise and said: "I was thinking about you. On the bus coming home tonight." Looking at Carrie's concerned, determined face, Louise prepared herself for humiliation. "I was thinking about when we graduate. What you're going to do. What's to become of you. I want you to be loved the way I love you. Louise, if I help you, *really* help you, will you go on a diet?"

15   Louise entered a period of her life she would remember always, the way some people remember having endured poverty. Her diet did not begin the next day. Carrie told her to eat on Monday as though it were the last day of her life. So for the first time since grammar school Louise went into a school cafeteria and ate everything she wanted. At breakfast and lunch and dinner she glanced around the table to see if the other girls noticed the food on her tray. They did not. She felt there was a lesson in this, but it lay beyond her grasp. That night in their room she ate the four remaining candy bars. During the day Carrie rented a small refrigerator, bought an electric skillet, an electric broiler, and bathroom scales.

16   On Tuesday morning Louise stood on the scales, and Carrie wrote in her notebook: *October 14: 184 lbs.* Then she made Louise a cup of black coffee and scrambled one egg and sat with her while she ate. When Carrie went to the dining room for breakfast, Louise walked about the campus for thirty minutes. That was part of the plan. The campus was pretty, on its lawns grew at least one of every tree native to New England, and in the warm morning sun Louise felt a new hope. At noon they met in their room, and Carrie broiled her a piece of hamburger and served it with lettuce. Then while Carrie ate in the dining room Louise walked again. She was weak with hunger and she felt queasy. During her afternoon classes she was nervous and tense and she

NOTES
perilous (par. 12): risky
destined (par. 12): certain
intimate (par. 12): very personal
malaise (par. 13): depression
queasy (par. 16): nauseated

chewed her pencil and tapped her heels on the floor and tightened her calves. When she returned to her room late that afternoon, she was so glad to see Carrie that she embraced her; she had felt she could not bear another minute of hunger, but now with Carrie she knew she could make it at least through tonight. Then she would sleep and face tomorrow when it came. Carrie broiled her a steak and served it with lettuce. Louise studied while Carrie ate dinner, then they went for a walk.

17   That was her ritual and her diet for the rest of the year, Carrie alternating fish and chicken breasts with the steaks for dinner, and every day was nearly as bad as the first. In the evenings she was irritable. In all her life she had never been afflicted by ill temper and she looked upon it now as a demon which, along with hunger, was taking possession of her soul. Often she spoke sharply to Carrie. One night during their after-dinner walk Carrie talked sadly of night, of how darkness made her more aware of herself, and at night she did not know why she was in college, why she studied, why she was walking the earth with other people. They were standing on a wooden foot bridge looking down at a dark pond. Carrie kept talking; perhaps soon she would cry. Suddenly Louise said: "I'm sick of lettuce. I never want to see a piece of lettuce for the rest of my life. I hate it. We shouldn't even buy it, it's immoral."

18   Carrie was quiet. Louise glanced at her, and the pain and irritation in Carrie's face soothed her. Then she was ashamed. Before she could say she was sorry, Carrie turned to her and said gently: "I know. I know how terrible it is."

19   Carrie did all the shopping, telling Louise she knew how hard it was to go into a supermarket when you were hungry. And Louise was always hungry. She drank diet soft drinks and started smoking Carrie's cigarettes, learned to enjoy inhaling, thought of cancer and emphysema but they were as far away as those boys her mother had talked about when she was nine. By Thanksgiving she was smoking over a pack a day and her weight in Carrie's notebook was one hundred and sixty-two pounds. Carrie was afraid if Louise went home at Thanksgiving she would lapse from the diet, so Louise spent the vacation with Carrie, in Philadelphia. Carrie wrote her family about the diet, and told Louise that she had. On the phone to Philadelphia, Louise said: "I feel like a bedwetter. When I was a little girl I had a friend who used to come spend the night and Mother would put a rubber sheet on the bed and we all pretended there wasn't a rubber sheet and that she hadn't wet the bed. Even me, and I slept with her." At Thanksgiving dinner she lowered her eyes as Carrie's father put two slices of white meat on her plate and passed it to her over the bowls of steaming food.

20   When she went home at Christmas she weighed a hundred and fifty-five pounds; at the airport her mother marvelled. Her father laughed and hugged her and said: "But now there's less of you to love." He was troubled by her smoking but only mentioned it once; he told her she was beautiful and, as always, his eyes bathed her with love. During the long vacation her mother cooked for her as Carrie had, and Louise returned to school weighing a hundred and forty-six pounds.

21   Flying north on the plane she warmly recalled the surprised and congratulatory eyes of her relatives and acquaintances. She had not seen Joan or Marjorie. She thought of returning home in May, weighing the hundred and fifteen pounds which Carrie had in October set as their goal. Looking toward the stoic days ahead, she felt strong. She thought of those hungry days of fall and

NOTES

afflicted (par. 17): troubled

stoic (par. 21): literally, showing no reaction to pleasure or pain

early winter (and now: she was hungry now: with almost a frown, almost a brusque shake of the head, she refused peanuts from the stewardess): those first weeks of the diet when she was the pawn of an irascibility which still, conditioned to her ritual as she was, could at any moment take command of her. She thought of the nights of trying to sleep while her stomach growled. She thought of her addiction to cigarettes. She thought of the people at school: not one teacher, not one girl, had spoken to her about her loss of weight, not even about her absence from meals. And without warning her spirit collapsed. She did not feel strong, she did not feel she was committed to and within reach of achieving a valuable goal. She felt that somehow she had lost more than pounds of fat; that some time during her dieting she had lost herself too. She tried to remember what it had felt like to be Louise before she had started living on meat and fish, as an unhappy adult may look sadly in the memory of childhood for lost virtues and hopes. She looked down at the earth far below, and it seemed to her that her soul, like her body aboard the plane, was in some rootless flight. She neither knew its destination nor where it had departed from; it was on some passage she could not even define.

22 During the next few weeks she lost weight more slowly and once for eight days Carrie's daily recording stayed at a hundred and thirty-six. Louise woke in the morning thinking of one hundred and thirty-six and then she stood on the scales and they echoed her. She became obsessed with that number, and there wasn't a day when she didn't say it aloud, and through the days and nights the number stayed in her mind, and if a teacher had spoken those digits in a classroom she would have opened her mouth to speak. What if that's me, she said to Carrie. I mean what if a hundred and thirty-six is my real weight and I just can't lose anymore. Walking hand-in-hand with her despair was a longing for this to be true, and that longing angered her and wearied her, and every day she was gloomy. On the ninth day she weighed a hundred and thirty-five and a half pounds. She was not relieved; she thought bitterly of the months ahead, the shedding of the last twenty and a half pounds.

23 On Easter Sunday, which she spent at Carrie's, she weighed one hundred and twenty pounds, and she ate one slice of glazed pineapple with her ham and lettuce. She did not enjoy it: she felt she was being friendly with a recalcitrant enemy who had once tried to destroy her. Carrie's parents were laudative. She liked them and she wished they would touch sometimes, and look at each other when they spoke. She guessed they would divorce when Carrie left home, and she vowed that her own marriage would be one of affection and tenderness. She could think about that now: marriage. At school she had read in a Boston paper that this summer the cicadas would come out of their seventeen year hibernation on Cape Cod, for a month they would mate and then die, leaving their young to burrow into the ground where they would stay for seventeen years. That's me, she had said to Carrie. Only my hibernation lasted twenty-one years.

24 Often her mother asked in letters and on the phone about the diet, but Louise answered vaguely. When she flew home in late May she weighed a hundred and thirteen pounds, and at the airport her mother cried and hugged her and said again and again: You're so *beau*tiful. Her father blushed and

NOTES

brusque (par. 21): abrupt, rude
pawn (par. 21): literally, one who is controlled by another
irascibility (par. 21): anger, irritability
recalcitrant (par. 23): difficult to control or overcome
laudative (par. 23): extremely complimentary
cicadas (par. 23): an insect

bought her a martini. For days her relatives and acquaintances congratulated her, and the applause in their eyes lasted the entire summer, and she loved their eyes, and swam in the country club pool, the first time she had done this since she was a child.

25   She lived at home and ate the way her mother did and every morning she weighed herself on the scales in her bathroom. Her mother liked to take her shopping and buy her dresses and they put her old ones in the Goodwill box at the shopping center; Louise thought of them existing on the body of a poor woman whose cheap meals kept her fat. Louise's mother had a photographer come to the house, and Louise posed on the couch and standing beneath a live oak and sitting in a wicker lawn chair next to an azalea bush. The new clothes and the photographer made her feel she was going to another country or becoming a citizen of a new one. In the fall she took a job of no consequence, to give herself something to do.

26   Also in the fall a young lawyer joined her father's firm, he came one night to dinner, and they started seeing each other. He was the first man outside her family to kiss her since the barbecue when she was sixteen. Louise celebrated Thanksgiving not with rice dressing and candied sweet potatoes and mince meat and pumpkin pies, but by giving Richard her virginity which she realized, at the very last moment of its existence, she had embarked on giving him over thirteen months ago, on that Tuesday in October when Carrie had made her a cup of black coffee and scrambled one egg. She wrote this to Carrie, who replied happily by return mail. She also, through glance and smile and innuendo, tried to tell her mother too. But finally she controlled that impulse, because Richard felt guilty about making love with the daughter of his partner and friend. In the spring they married. The wedding was a large one, in the Episcopal church, and Carrie flew from Boston to be maid of honor. Her parents had recently separated and she was living with the musician and was still victim of her unpredictable malaise. It overcame her on the night before the wedding, so Louise was up with her until past three and woke next morning from a sleep so heavy that she did not want to leave it.

27   Richard was a lean, tall, energetic man with the metabolism of a pencil sharpener. Louise fed him everything he wanted. He liked Italian food and she got recipes from her mother and watched him eating spaghetti with the sauce she had only tasted, and ravioli and lasagna, while she ate antipasto with her chianti. He made a lot of money and borrowed more and they bought a house whose lawn sloped down to the shore of a lake; they had a wharf and a boathouse, and Richard bought a boat and they took friends waterskiing. Richard bought her a car and they spent his vacations in Mexico, Canada, the Bahamas, and in the fifth year of their marriage they went to Europe and, according to their plan, she conceived a child in Paris. On the plane back, as she looked out the window and beyond the sparkling sea and saw her country, she felt that it was waiting for her, as her home by the lake was, and her parents, and her good friends who rode in the boat and waterskied; she thought of the accumulated warmth and pelf of her marriage, and how by slimming her body she had bought into the pleasures of the nation. She felt cunning, and she smiled to herself, and took Richard's hand.

28   But these moments of triumph were sparse. On most days she went about her routine of leisure with a sense of certainty about herself that came merely

NOTES
had embarked on (par. 26): had begun
innuendo (par. 26): suggestion
pelf (par. 27): wealth
sparse (par. 28): few

from not thinking. But there were times, with her friends, or with Richard, or alone in the house, when she was suddenly assaulted by the feeling that she had taken the wrong train and arrived at a place where no one knew her, and where she ought not to be. Often, in bed with Richard, she talked of being fat: "I was the one who started the friendship with Carrie, I chose her, I started the conversations. When I understood that she was my friend I understood something else: I had chosen her for the same reason I'd chosen Joan and Marjorie. They were all thin. I was always thinking about what people saw when they looked at me and I didn't want them to see two fat girls. When I was alone I didn't mind being fat but then I'd have to leave the house again and then I didn't want to look like me. But at home I didn't mind except when I was getting dressed to go out of the house and when Mother looked at me. But I stopped looking at her when she looked at me. And in college I felt good with Carrie; there weren't any boys and I didn't have any other friends and so when I wasn't with Carrie I thought about her and I tried to ignore the other people around me, I tried to make them not exist. A lot of the time I could do that. It was strange, and I felt like a spy."

29   If Richard was bored by her repetition he pretended not to be. But she knew the story meant very little to him. She could have been telling him of a childhood illness, or wearing braces, or a broken heart at sixteen. He could not see her as she was when she was fat. She felt as though she were trying to tell a foreign lover about her life in the United States, and if only she could command the language he would know and love all of her and she would feel complete. Some of the acquaintances of her childhood were her friends now, and even they did not seem to remember her when she was fat.

30   Now her body was growing again, and when she put on a maternity dress for the first time she shivered with fear. Richard did not smoke and he asked her, in a voice just short of demand, to stop during her pregnancy. She did. She ate carrots and celery instead of smoking, and at cocktail parties she tried to eat nothing, but after her first drink she ate nuts and cheese and crackers and dips. Always at these parties Richard had talked with his friends and she had rarely spoken to him until they drove home. But now when he noticed her at the hors d'oeuvres table he crossed the room and, smiling, led her back to his group. His smile and his hand on her arm told her he was doing his clumsy, husbandly best to help her through a time of female mystery.

31   She was gaining weight but she told herself it was only the baby, and would leave with its birth. But at other times she knew quite clearly that she was losing the discipline she had fought so hard to gain during her last year with Carrie. She was hungry now as she had been in college, and she ate between meals and after dinner and tried to eat only carrots and celery, but she grew to hate them, and her desire for sweets was as vicious as it had been long ago. At home she ate bread and jam and when she shopped for groceries she bought a candy bar and ate it driving home and put the wrapper in her purse and then in the garbage can under the sink. Her cheeks had filled out, there was loose flesh under her chin, her arms and legs were plump, and her mother was concerned. So was Richard. One night when she brought pie and milk to the living room where they were watching television, he said: "You already had a piece. At dinner."

32   She did not look at him.

33   "You're gaining weight. It's not all water, either. It's fat. It'll be summertime. You'll want to get into your bathing suit."

34   The pie was cherry. She looked at it as her fork cut through it; she speared the piece and rubbed it in the red juice on the plate before lifting it to her mouth.

35   "You never used to eat pie," he said. "I just think you ought to watch it a bit. It's going to be tough on you this summer."

36   In her seventh month, with a delight reminiscent of climbing the stairs to Richard's apartment before they were married, she returned to her world of secret gratification. She began hiding candy in her underwear drawer. She ate it during the day and at night while Richard slept, and at breakfast she was distracted, waiting for him to leave.

37   She gave birth to a son, brought him home, and nursed both him and her appetites. During this time of celibacy she enjoyed her body through her son's mouth; while he suckled she stroked his small head and back. She was hiding candy but she did not conceal her other indulgences: she was smoking again but still she ate between meals, and at dinner she ate what Richard did, and coldly he watched her, he grew petulant, and when the date marking the end of their celibacy came they let it pass. Often in the afternoons her mother visited and scolded her and Louise sat looking at the baby and said nothing until finally, to end it, she promised to diet. When her mother and father came for dinners, her father kissed her and held the baby and her mother said nothing about Louise's body, and her voice was tense. Returning from work in the evenings Richard looked at a soiled plate and glass on the table beside her chair as if detecting traces of infidelity, and at every dinner they fought.

38   "Look at you," he said. "Lasagna, for God's sake. When are you going to start? It's not simply that you haven't lost any weight. You're gaining. I can see it. I can feel it when you get in bed. Pretty soon you'll weigh more than I do and I'll be sleeping on a trampoline."

39   "You never touch me anymore."

40   "I don't want to touch you. Why should I? Have you *looked* at yourself?"

41   "You're cruel," she said. "I never knew how cruel you were."

42   She ate, watching him. He did not look at her. Glaring at his plate, he worked with fork and knife like a hurried man at a lunch counter.

43   "I bet you didn't either," she said.

44   That night when he was asleep she took a Milky Way to the bathroom. For a while she stood eating in the dark, then she turned on the light. Chewing, she looked at herself in the mirror; she looked at her eyes and hair. Then she stood on the scales and looking at the numbers between her feet, one hundred and sixty-two, she remembered when she had weighed a hundred and thirty-six pounds for eight days. Her memory of those eight days was fond and amusing, as though she were recalling an Easter egg hunt when she was six. She stepped off the scales and pushed them under the lavatory and did not stand on them again.

45   It was summer and she bought loose dresses and when Richard took friends out on the boat she did not wear a bathing suit or shorts; her friends gave her mischievous glances, and Richard did not look at her. She stopped riding on the boat. She told them she wanted to stay with the baby, and she sat inside holding him until she heard the boat leave the wharf. Then she took him to the front lawn and walked with him in the shade of the trees and talked to him about the blue jays and mockingbirds and cardinals she saw on their branches. Sometimes she stopped and watched the boat out on the lake and the friend skiing behind it.

NOTES

reminiscent of (par. 36): remindful of and similar to
gratification (par. 36): pleasure
distracted (par. 36): occupied with other thoughts
celibacy (par. 37): refraining from sexual intercourse
petulant (par. 37): irritable
infidelity (par. 37): adultery

46   Every day Richard quarrelled, and because his rage went no further than her weight and shape, she felt excluded from it, and she remained calm within layers of flesh and spirit, and watched his frustration, his impotence. He truly believed they were arguing about her weight. She knew better: she knew that beneath the argument lay the question of who Richard was. She thought of him smiling at the wheel of his boat, and long ago courting his slender girl, the daughter of his partner and friend. She thought of Carrie telling her of smelling chocolate in the dark and, after that, watching her eat it night after night. She smiled at Richard, teasing his anger.

47   He is angry now. He stands in the center of the living room, raging at her, and he wakes the baby. Beneath Richard's voice she hears the soft crying, feels it in her heart, and quietly she rises from her chair and goes upstairs to the child's room and takes him from the crib. She brings him to the living room and sits holding him in her lap, pressing him gently against the folds of fat at her waist. Now Richard is pleading with her. Louise thinks tenderly of Carrie broiling meat and fish in their room, and walking with her in the evenings. She wonders if Carrie still has the malaise. Perhaps she will come for a visit. In Louise's arms now the boy sleeps.

48   "I'll help you, Richard says. "I'll eat the same things you eat."

49   But his face does not approach the compassion and determination and love she had seen in Carrie's during what she now recognizes as the worst year of her life. She can remember nothing about that year except hunger, and the meals in her room. She is hungry now. When she puts the boy to bed she will get a candy bar from her room. She will eat it here, in front of Richard. This room will be hers soon. She considers the possibilities: all these rooms and the lawn where she can do whatever she wishes. She knows he will leave soon. It has been in his eyes all summer. She stands, using one hand to pull herself out of the chair. She carries the boy to his crib, feels him against her large breasts, feels that his sleeping body touches her soul. With a surge of vindication and relief she holds him. Then she kisses his forehead and places him in the crib. She goes to the bedroom and in the dark takes a bar of candy from her drawer. Slowly she descends the stairs. She knows Richard is waiting but she feels his departure so happily that, when she enters the living room, unwrapping the candy, she is surprised to see him standing there.

NOTES
impotence (par. 46): powerlessness
vindication (par. 49): a feeling of being right or blameless

A Sudden Trip Home in the Spring

Alice Walker

(For The Wellesley Class)

I

1   Sarah walked slowly off the tennis court, fingering the back of her head, feeling the sturdy dark hair that grew there. She was popular. As she walked along the path toward Talfinger Hall, her friends fell into place around her.

They formed a warm, jostling group of six. Sarah, because she was taller than the rest, saw the messenger first.

2   "Miss Davis," he said, standing still until the group came abreast of him, "I've got a telegram for ye." Brian was Irish and always quite respectful. He stood with his cap in his hand until Sarah took the telegram. Then he gave a nod that included all the young ladies before he turned away. He was young and good-looking, though annoyingly servile, and Sarah's friends twittered.

3   "Well, open it!" someone cried, for Sarah stood staring at the yellow envelope, turning it over and over in her hand.

4   "Look at her," said one of the girls, "isn't she beautiful! Such eyes, and hair, and *skin!*"

5   Sarah's tall, caplike hair framed a face of soft brown angles, high cheekbones, and large, dark eyes. Her eyes enchanted her friends because they always seemed to know more, and to find more of life amusing, or sad, than Sarah cared to tell.

6   Her friends often teased Sarah about her beauty; they loved dragging her out of her room so that their boy friends, naïve and worldly young men from Princeton and Yale, could see her. They never guessed she found this distasteful. She was gentle with her friends, and her outrage at their tactlessness did not show. She was most often inclined to pity them, though embarrassment sometimes drove her to fraudulent expressions. Now she smiled and raised eyes and arms to heaven. She acknowledged their unearned curiosity as a mother endures the prying impatience of a child. Her friends beamed love and envy upon her as she tore open the telegram.

7   "He's dead," she said.

8   Her friends reached out for the telegram, their eyes on Sarah.

9   "It's her father," one of them said softly. "He died yesterday. Oh, Sarah," the girl whimpered, "I'm so sorry!"

10   "Me too." "So am I." "Is there anything we can do?"

11   But Sarah had walked away, head high and neck stiff.

12   "So graceful!" one of her friends said.

13   "Like a proud gazelle," said another. Then they all trooped to their dormitories to change for supper.

14   Talfinger Hall was a pleasant dorm. The common room just off the entrance had been made into a small modern-art gallery with some very good original paintings, lithographs, and collages. Pieces were constantly being stolen. Some of the girls could not resist an honest-to-God Chagall, signed (in the plate) by his own hand, though they could have afforded to purchase one from the gallery in town. Sarah Davis' room was next door to the gallery, but her walls were covered with inexpensive Gauguin reproductions, a Rubens

NOTES

jostling (par. 1): gently pushing

servile (par. 2): like an obedient servant

twittered (par. 2): giggled

naïve (par. 6): inexperienced

tactlessness (par. 6): lack of sensitivity

fraudulent (par. 6): false

gazelle (par. 13): a type of antelope noted for its gracefulness

lithographs (par. 14): a print made by lithography: The artist etches an image on a metal surface; the image retains ink while the unetched surface does not.

collages (par. 14): an artistic work in which materials such as wood, cloth, and paper are glued onto a surface

Chagall (par. 14): Mark Chagall (1887–1985), Russian painter who lived in France

Gauguin (par. 14): Henri Gauguin (1848–1903), French painter

Rubens (par. 14): Peter Paul Rubens (1577–1640), Flemish painter

("The Head of a Negro"), a Modigliani, and a Picasso. There was a full wall of her own drawings, all of black women. She found black men impossible to draw or to paint; she could not bear to trace defeat onto blank pages. Her women figures were matronly, massive of arm, with a weary victory showing in their eyes. Surrounded by Sarah's drawings was a red SNCC poster of an old man holding a small girl whose face nestled in his shoulder. Sarah often felt she was the little girl whose face no one could see.

15   To leave Talfinger even for a few days filled Sarah with fear. Talfinger was her home now; it suited her better than any home she'd ever known. Perhaps she loved it because in winter there was a fragrant fireplace and snow outside her window. When hadn't she dreamed of fireplaces that really warmed, snow that almost pleasantly froze? Georgia seemed far away as she packed; she did not want to leave New York, where, her grandfather had liked to say, "the devil hangs out and catches young gals by the front of their dresses." He had always believed the South the best place to live on earth (never mind that certain people invariably marred the landscape), and swore he expected to die no more than a few miles from where he had been born. There was tenacity even in the gray frame house he lived in, and in scrawny animals on his farm who regularly reproduced. He was the first person Sarah wanted to see when she got home.

16   There was a knock on the door of the adjoining bathroom, and Sarah's suite mate entered, a loud Bach Concerto just finishing behind her. At first she stuck just her head into the room, but seeing Sarah fully dressed she trudged in and plopped down on the bed. She was a heavy blond girl with large, milk-white legs. Her eyes were small and her neck usually gray with grime.

17   "My, don't you look gorgeous," she said.

18   "Ah, Pam," said Sarah, waving her hand in disgust. In Georgia she knew that even to Pam she would be just another ordinarily attractive *colored* girl. In Georgia there were a million girls better looking. Pam wouldn't know that, of course, she'd never been to Georgia; she'd never even seen a black person to speak to—that is, before she met Sarah. One of her first poetic observations about Sarah was that she was "a poppy in a field of winter roses." She had found it weird that Sarah did not own more than one coat.

19   "Say, listen, Sarah," said Pam, "I heard about your father. I'm sorry. I really am."

20   "Thanks," said Sarah.

21   "Is there anything we can do? I thought, well, maybe you'd want my father to get somebody to fly you down. He'd go himself but he's taking mother to Madeira this week. You wouldn't have to worry about trains and things."

NOTES
Modigliani (par. 14): Amedeo Modigliani (1884–1920), Italian painter who lived in France
Picasso (par. 14): Pablo Picasso (1881–1973), Spanish painter who lived in France
matronly (par. 14): dignified, motherly
SNCC (par. 14): Student Nonviolent Coordinating Committee
invariably (par. 15): always
marred (par. 15): spoiled
tenacity (par. 15): strength, determination
scrawny (par. 15): skinny
Bach (par. 16): Johann Sebastian Bach (1685–1750), German composer and organist
Concerto (par. 16): a piece written for an orchestra and at least one solo instrument
poppy (par. 18): a bright flower
Madeira (par. 21): an island in the Atlantic Ocean

22   Pamela's father was one of the richest men in the world, though no one ever mentioned it. Pam only alluded to it at times of crisis, when a friend might benefit from the use of a private plane, train, or ship; or, if someone wanted to study the characteristics of a totally secluded village, island, or mountain, she might offer one of theirs. Sarah could not comprehend such wealth, and was always annoyed because Pam didn't look more like a billionaire's daughter. A billionaire's daughter, Sarah thought, should really be less horsy and brush her teeth more often.

23   "Gonna tell me what you're brooding about?" asked Pam.

24   Sarah stood in front of the radiator, her fingers resting on the window seat. Down below, girls were coming up the hill from supper.

25   "I'm thinking," she said, "of the child's duty to his parents after they are dead."

26   "Is that all?"

27   "Do you know," asked Sarah, "about Richard Wright and his father?"

28   Pamela frowned. Sarah looked down at her.

29   "Oh, I forgot," she said with a sigh, "they don't teach Wright here. The poshest school in the U.S. and the girls come out ignorant." She looked at her watch, saw she had twenty minutes before her train. "Really," she said almost inaudibly, "why Tears Eliot, Ezratic Pound, and even Sara Teacake, and no Wright?" She and Pamela thought e. e. cummings very clever with his perceptive spelling of great literary names.

30   "Is he a poet, then?" asked Pam. She adored poetry, all poetry. Half of America's poetry she had, of course, not read, for the simple reason that she had never heard of it.

31   "No," said Sarah, "he wasn't a poet." She felt weary. "He was a man who wrote, a man who had trouble with his father." She began to walk about the room, and came to stand below the picture of the old man and the little girl.

32   "When he was a child," she continued, "his father ran off with another woman, and one day when Richard and his mother went to ask him for money to buy food, he laughingly rejected them. Richard, being very young, thought his father Godlike—big, omnipotent, unpredictable, undependable, and cruel; entirely in control of his universe; just like God. But, many years later, after Wright had become a famous writer, he went down to Mississippi to visit his father. He found, instead of God, just an old, watery-eyed field hand, bent from plowing, his teeth gone, smelling of manure. Richard realized that the most daring thing his 'God' had done was run off with that other woman."

33   "So?" asked Pam. "What 'duty' did he feel he owed the old man?"

34   "So," said Sarah, "that's what Wright wondered as he peered into that old, shifty-eyed Mississippi Negro face. What was the duty of the son of a destroyed man? The son of a man whose vision had stopped at the edge of fields that weren't even his. Who was Wright without his father? Was he Wright the great writer? Wright the Communist? Wright the French farmer? Wright whose wife could never accompany him to Mississippi? Was he, in fact, still his fa-

NOTES

secluded (par. 22): isolated
brooding about (par. 23): thinking seriously about
Richard Wright (par. 27): American writer (1908–1960)
poshest (par. 29): most expensive
inaudibly (par. 29): incapable of being heard
Tears Eliot, Ezratic Pound . . . Sara Teacake (par. 29): T. S. Eliot (1888–1965), American-born British poet; Ezra Pound (1885–1972), American poet and critic; Sara Teasdale (1884–1933), American poet
e.e. cummings (par. 29): American poet (1894–1962)
omnipotent (par. 32): all-powerful

ther's son? Or was he freed by his father's desertion to be nobody's son, to be his own father? Could he disavow his father and live? And if so, live as what? As whom? And for what purpose?"

35   "Well," said Pam, swinging her hair over her shoulders and squinting her small eyes, "if his father rejected him I don't see why Wright even bothered to go see him again. From what you've said, Wright earned the freedom to be whoever he wanted to be. To a strong man a father is not essential."

36   "Maybe not," said Sarah, "but Wright's father was one faulty door in a house of many ancient rooms. Was that one faulty door to shut him off forever from the rest of the house? That was the question. And though he answered this question eloquently in his work, where it really counted, one can only wonder if he was able to answer it satisfactorily—or at all—in his life."

37   "You're thinking of his father more as a symbol of something, aren't you?" asked Pam.

38   "I suppose," said Sarah, taking a last look around her room. "I see him as a door that refused to open, a hand that was always closed. A fist."

39   Pamela walked with her to one of the college limousines, and in a few minutes she was at the station. The train to the city was just arriving.

40   "Have a nice trip," said the middle-aged driver courteously as she took her suitcase from him. But, for about the thousandth time since she'd seen him, he winked at her.

41   Once away from her friends, she did not miss them. The school was all they had in common. How could they ever know her if they were not allowed to know Wright? she wondered. She was interesting, "beautiful," only because they had no idea what made her, charming only because they had no idea from where she came. And where they came from, though she glimpsed it—in themselves and in F. Scott Fitzgerald—she was never to enter. She hadn't the inclination or the proper ticket.

II

42   Her father's body was in Sarah's old room. The bed had been taken down to make room for the flowers and chairs and casket. Sarah looked for a long time into the face, as if to find some answer to her questions written there. It was the same face, a dark, Shakespearean head framed by gray, woolly hair and split almost in half by a short, gray mustache. It was a completely silent face, a shut face. But her father's face also looked fat, stuffed, and ready to burst. He wore a navy-blue suit, white shirt, and black tie. Sarah bent and loosened the tie. Tears started behind her shoulder blades but did not reach her eyes.

43   "There's a rat here under the casket," she called to her brother, who apparently did not hear her, for he did not come in. She was alone with her father, as she had rarely been when he was alive. When he was alive she had avoided him.

44   "Where's that girl at?" her father would ask. "Done closed herself up in her room again," he would answer himself.

45   For Sarah's mother had died in her sleep one night. Just gone to bed tired and never got up. And Sarah had blamed her father.

46   Stare the rat down, thought Sarah; surely that will help. *Perhaps it doesn't matter whether I misunderstood or never understood.*

NOTES
disavow (par. 34): disown
F. Scott Fitzgerald (par. 41): American novelist (1896–1940)
inclination (par. 41): desire

47   "We moved so much, looking for crops, a place to *live*," her father had moaned, accompanied by Sarah's stony silence. "The moving killed her. And now we have a real house, with *four* rooms, and a mailbox on the *porch*, and it's too late. She gone. *She* ain't here to see it." On very bad days her father would not eat at all. At night he did not sleep.

48   *Whatever had made her think she knew what love was or was not?*

49   Here she was, Sarah Davis, immersed in Camusian philosophy, versed in many languages, a poppy, of all things, among winter roses. But before she became a poppy she was a native Georgian sunflower, but still had not spoken the language they both knew. Not to him.

50   *Stare the rat down*, she thought, and did. The rascal dropped his bold eyes and slunk away. Sarah felt she had, at least, accomplished something.

51   Why did she have to see the picture of her mother, the one on the mantel among all the religious doodads, come to life? Her mother had stood stout against the years, clean gray braids shining across the top of her head, her eyes snapping, protective. Talking to her father.

52   "He called you out your name, we'll leave this place today. Not tomorrow. That be too late. Today!" Her mother was magnificent in her quick decisions.

53   "But what about your garden, the children, the change of schools?" Her father would be holding, most likely, the wide brim of his hat in nervously twisting fingers.

54   "He called you out your name, we go!"

55   And go they would. Who knew exactly where, before they moved? Another soundless place, walls falling down, roofing gone; another face to please without leaving too much of her father's pride at his feet. But to Sarah then, no matter with what alacrity her father moved, foot-dragging alone was visible.

56   *The moving killed her*, her father had said, but the moving was also love.

57   Did it matter now that often he had threatened their lives with the rage of his despair? That once he had spanked the crying baby violently, who later died of something else altogether . . . and that the next day they moved?

58   "No," said Sarah aloud, "I don't think it does."

59   "Huh?" It was her brother, tall, wiry, black, deceptively calm. As a child he'd had an irrepressible temper. As a grown man he was tensely smooth, like a river that any day will overflow its bed.

60   He had chosen a dull gray casket. Sarah wished for red. Was it Dylan Thomas who had said something grand about the dead offering "deep, dark defiance"? It didn't matter; there were more ways to offer defiance than with a red casket.

61   "I was just thinking," said Sarah, "that with us Mama and Daddy were saying NO with capital letters."

62   "I don't follow you," said her brother. He had always been the activist in the family. He simply directed his calm rage against any obstacle that might exist, and awaited the consequences with the same serenity he awaited his

NOTES

immersed (par. 49): deeply involved
Camusian philosophy (par. 49): philosophy of French novelist Albert Camus (1913–1960)
"He called you out your name" (par. 52): That is, he called you an insulting name.
alacrity (par. 55): promptness
irrepressible (par. 59): impossible to control
Dylan Thomas (par. 60): Welsh poet (1914–1953)
serenity (par. 62): calmness

sister's answer. Not for him the philosophical confusions and poetic observations that hung his sister up.

63   "That's because you're a radical preacher," said Sarah, smiling up at him. "You deliver your messages in person with your own body." It excited her that her brother had at last imbued their childhood Sunday sermons with the reality of fighting for change. And saddened her that no matter how she looked at it this seemed more important than Medieval Art, Course 201.

III

64   "Yes, Grandma," Sarah replied. "Cresselton is for girls only, and *No,* Grandma, I am not pregnant."

65   Her grandmother stood clutching the broad, wooden handle of her black bag, which she held, with elbows bent, in front of her stomach. Her eyes glinted through round, wire-framed glasses. She spat into the grass outside the privy. She had insisted that Sarah accompany her to the toilet while the body was being taken into the church. She had leaned heavily on Sarah's arm, her own arm thin and the flesh like crepe.

66   "I guess they teach you how to really handle the world," she said. "And who knows, the Lord is everywhere. I would like a whole lot to see a great-grand. You don't specially have to be married, you know. That's why I felt free to ask." She reached into her bag and took out a Three Sixes bottle, which she proceeded to drink from, taking deep, swift swallows with her head thrown back.

67   "There are very few black boys near Cresselton," Sarah explained, watching the corn liquor leave the bottle in spurts and bubbles. "Besides, I'm really caught up now in my painting and sculpturing . . . " Should she mention how much she admired Giacometti's work? No, she decided. Even if her grandmother had heard of him, and Sarah was positive she had not, she would surely think his statues much too thin. This made Sarah smile and remember how difficult it had been to convince her grandmother that even if Cresselton had not given her a scholarship she would have managed to go there anyway. Why? Because she wanted somebody to teach her to paint and to sculpture, and Cresselton had the best teachers. Her grandmother's notion of a successful granddaughter was a married one, pregnant the first year.

68   "Well," said her grandmother, placing the bottle with dignity back into her purse and gazing pleadingly into Sarah's face, "I sure would 'preshate a great-grand." Seeing her granddaughter's smile, she heaved a great sigh, and walking rather haughtily over the stones and grass, made her way to the church steps.

69   As they walked down the aisle, Sarah's eyes rested on the back of her grandfather's head. He was sitting on the front middle bench in front of the casket, his hair extravagantly long and white and softly kinked. When she sat down beside him, her grandmother sitting next to him on the other side, he turned toward her and gently took her hand in his. Sarah briefly leaned her cheek against his shoulder and felt like a child again.

NOTES
imbued (par. 63): filled
crepe (par. 65): a thin, crinkled fabric
Three Sixes (par. 66): a cold medicine
Giacometti (par. 67): Alberto Giacometti (1901–1966), Swiss sculptor and painter
'preshate (par. 68): appreciate
haughtily (par. 68): with an attitude of superiority

IV

70 They had come twenty miles from town, on a dirt road, and the hot spring sun had drawn a steady rich scent from the honeysuckle vines along the way. The church was a bare, weatherbeaten ghost of a building with hollow windows and a sagging door. Arsonists had once burned it to the ground, lighting the dry wood of the walls with the flames from the crosses they carried. The tall, spreading red-oak tree under which Sarah had played as a child still dominated the churchyard, stretching its branches widely from the roof of the church to the other side of the road.

71 After a short and eminently dignified service, during which Sarah and her grandfather alone did not cry, her father's casket was slid into the waiting hearse and taken the short distance to the cemetery, an overgrown wilderness whose stark white stones appeared to be the small ruins of an ancient civilization. There Sarah watched her grandfather from the corner of her eye. He did not seem to bend under the grief of burying a son. His back was straight, his eyes dry and clear. He was simply and solemnly heroic, a man who kept with pride his family's trust and his own grief. *It is strange,* Sarah thought, *that I never thought to paint him like this, simply as he stands; without anonymous, meaningless people hovering beyond his profile; his face turned proud and brownly against the light.* The defeat that had frightened her in the faces of black men was the defeat of black forever defined by white. But that defeat was nowhere on her grandfather's face. He stood like a rock, outwardly calm, the grand patriarch of the Davis family. The family alone defined him, and he was not about to let them down.

72 "One day I will paint you, Grandpa," she said as they turned to go. "Just as you stand here now, with just," she moved closer and touched his face with her hand, "just the right stubborn tenseness of your cheek. Just that look of Yes and No in your eyes."

73 "You wouldn't want to paint an old man like me," he said, looking deep into her eyes from wherever his mind had been. "If you want to make me, make me up in stone."

74 The completed grave was plump and red. The wreaths of flowers were arranged all on one side, so that from the road there appeared to be only a large mass of flowers. But already the wind was tugging at the rose petals and the rain was making dabs of faded color all over the greenfoam frames. In a week, the displaced honeysuckle vines, the wild roses, the grapevines, the grass, would be back. Nothing would seem to have changed.

V

75 "What do you mean, come *home?*" Her brother seemed genuinely amused. "We're all proud of you. How many black girls are at that school? Just *you?* Well, just one more besides you, and she's from the North. That's really something!"

76 "I'm glad you're pleased," said Sarah.

77 "Pleased! Why, it's what Mama would have wanted, a good education for little Sarah; and what Dad would have wanted too, if he could have wanted anything after Mama died. You were always smart. When you were two and I was five you showed me how to eat ice cream without getting it all over me. First, you said, nip off the bottom of the cone with your teeth, and suck

NOTES
eminently (par. 71): highly
patriarch (par. 71): male leader

the ice cream down. I never knew *how* you were supposed to eat the stuff once it began to melt."

78 "I don't know," she said; "sometimes you can want something a whole lot, only to find out later that it wasn't what you *needed* at all."

79 Sarah shook her head, a frown coming between her eyes. "I sometimes spend *weeks,*" she said, "trying to sketch or paint a face that is unlike every other face around me, except, vaguely, for one. Can I help but wonder if I'm in the right place?"

80 Her brother smiled. "You mean to tell me you spend *weeks* trying to draw one face, and you still wonder whether you're in the right place? You must be kidding!" He chucked her under the chin and laughed out loud. "You learn how to draw the face," he said, "then you learn how to paint me and how to make Grandpa up in stone. Then you can come home or go live in Paris, France. It'll be the same thing."

81 It was the unpreacher-like gaiety of his affection that made her cry. She leaned peacefully into her brother's arms. She wondered if Richard Wright had had a brother.

82 "You are my door to all the rooms." she said. "Don't ever close."

83 And he said, "I won't," as if he understood what she meant.

VI

84 "When will we see you again, young woman?" he asked later as he drove her to the bus stop.

85 "I'll sneak up one day and surprise you," she said.

86 At the bus stop, in front of a tiny service station, Sarah hugged her brother with all her strength. The white station attendant stopped his work to leer at them, his eyes bold and careless.

87 "Did you ever think," said Sarah, "that we are a very old people in a very young place?"

88 She watched her brother from a window on the bus; her eyes did not leave his face until the little station was out of sight and the big Greyhound lurched on its way toward Atlanta. She would fly from there to New York.

VII

89 She took the train to the campus.

90 "My," said one of her friends, "you look wonderful! Home sure must agree with you!"

91 "Sarah was home?" someone who didn't know asked. "Oh, *great,* how was it?"

92 *Well, how was it?* went an echo in Sarah's head. The noise of the echo almost made her dizzy.

93 "How was it?" she asked aloud, searching for, and regaining, her balance.

94 "How was it?" She watched her reflection in a pair of smiling hazel eyes.

95 "It was fine," she said slowly, returning the smile, thinking of her grandfather. "Just fine."

96 The girl's smile deepened. Sarah watched her swinging along toward the back tennis courts, hair blowing in the wind.

97 *Stare the rat down,* thought Sarah; *and whether it disappears or not, I am a woman in the world. I have buried my father, and shall soon know how to make my grandpa up in stone.*

NOTES
chucked (par. 80): patted
leer (par. 86): stare

A Rose for Emily

William Faulkner

I

1   When Miss Emily Grierson died, our whole town went to her funeral: the men through a sort of respectful affection for a fallen monument, the women mostly out of curiosity to see the inside of her house, which no one save an old man-servant—a combined gardener and cook—had seen in at least ten years.

2   It was a big, squarish frame house that had once been white, decorated with cupolas and spires and scrolled balconies in the heavily lightsome style of the seventies, set on what had once been our most select street. But garages and cotton gins had encroached and obliterated even the august names of that neighborhood; only Miss Emily's house was left, lifting its stubborn and coquettish decay above the cotton wagons and the gasoline pumps—an eyesore among eyesores. And now Miss Emily had gone to join the representatives of those august names where they lay in the cedar-bemused cemetery among the ranked and anonymous graves of Union and Confederate soldiers who fell at the battle of Jefferson.

3   Alive, Miss Emily had been a tradition, a duty, and a care; a sort of hereditary obligation upon the town, dating from that day in 1894 when Colonel Sartoris, the mayor—he who fathered the edict that no Negro woman should appear on the street without an apron—remitted her taxes, the dispensation dating from the death of her father on into perpetuity. Not that Miss Emily would have accepted charity. Colonel Sartoris invented an involved tale to the effect that Miss Emily's father had loaned money to the town, which the town, as a matter of business, preferred this way of repaying. Only a man of Colonel Sartoris' generation and thought could have invented it, and only a woman could have believed it.

4   When the next generation, with its more modern ideas, became mayors and aldermen, this arrangement created some little dissatisfaction. On the first of the year they mailed her a tax notice. February came, and there was no reply. They wrote her a formal letter, asking her to call at the sheriff's office at her convenience. A week later the mayor wrote her himself, offering to call or to send his car for her, and received in reply a note on paper of an archaic shape, in a thin, flowing calligraphy in faded ink, to the effect that

NOTES

cupolas (par. 2): a rounded structure forming part of the roof of a house
spires (par. 2): small steeples
scrolled balconies (par. 2): balconies with fancy designs or "scrollwork"
lightsome (par. 2): graceful
encroached (par. 2): moved in
obliterated (par. 2): destroyed
august (par. 2): grand
coquettish (par. 2): literally, a flirtatious woman
cedar-bemused (par. 2): overgrown with cedars
hereditary (par. 3): inherited
remitted (par. 3): cancelled
dispensation (par. 3): exemption
perpetuity (par. 3): eternity
archaic (par. 4): old fashioned
calligraphy (par. 4): fancy writing

she no longer went out at all. The tax notice was also enclosed, without comment.

5   They called a special meeting of the Board of Aldermen. A deputation waited upon her, knocked at the door through which no visitor had passed since she ceased giving china-painting lessons eight or ten years earlier. They were admitted by the old Negro into a dim hall from which a stairway mounted into still more shadow. It smelled of dust and disuse—a close, dank smell. The Negro led them into the parlor. It was furnished in heavy, leather-covered furniture. When the Negro opened the blinds of one window, they could see that the leather was cracked; and when they sat down, a faint dust rose sluggishly about their thighs, spinning with slow motes in the single sun-ray. On a tarnished gilt easel before the fireplace stood a crayon portrait of Miss Emily's father.

6   They rose when she entered—a small, fat woman in black, with a thin gold chain descending to her waist and vanishing into her belt, leaning on an ebony cane with a tarnished gold head. Her skeleton was small and spare; perhaps that was why what would have been merely plumpness in another was obesity in her. She looked bloated, like a body long submerged in motionless water, and of that pallid hue. Her eyes, lost in the fatty ridges of her face, looked like two small pieces of coal pressed into a lump of dough as they moved from one face to another while the visitors stated their errand.

7   She did not ask them to sit. She just stood in the door and listened quietly until the spokesman came to a stumbling halt. Then they could hear the invisible watch ticking at the end of the gold chain.

8   Her voice was dry and cold. "I have no taxes in Jefferson. Colonel Sartoris explained it to me. Perhaps one of you can gain access to the city records and satisfy yourselves."

9   "But we have. We are the city authorities, Miss Emily. Didn't you get a notice from the sheriff, signed by him?"

10   "I received a paper, yes," Miss Emily said. "Perhaps he considers himself the sheriff . . . I have no taxes in Jefferson."

11   "But there is nothing on the books to show that, you see. We must go by the—"

12   "See Colonel Sartoris. I have no taxes in Jefferson."

13   "But, Miss Emily—"

14   "See Colonel Sartoris." (Colonel Sartoris had been dead almost ten years.) "I have no taxes in Jefferson. Tobe!" The Negro appeared. "Show these gentlemen out."

II

15   So she vanquished them, horse and foot, just as she had vanquished their fathers thirty years before about the smell. That was two years after her father's death and a short time after her sweetheart—the one we believed would marry her—had deserted her. After her father's death she went out very little; after her sweetheart went away, people hardly saw her at all. A few of the

NOTES

deputation (par. 5): a group of citizens that represents others
dank (par. 5): damp
motes (par. 5): specks
gilt (par. 5): a gold coating
ebony (par. 6): a black wood
pallid hue (par. 6): pale color
vanquished (par. 15): defeated

ladies had the temerity to call, but were not received, and the only sign of life about the place was the Negro man—a young man then—going in and out with a market basket.

16   "Just as if a man—any man—could keep a kitchen properly," the ladies said; so they were not surprised when the smell developed. It was another link between the gross, teeming world and the high and mighty Griersons.

17   A neighbor, a woman, complained to the mayor, Judge Stevens, eighty years old.

18   "But what will you have me to do about it, madam?" he said.

19   "Why, send her word to stop it," the woman said. "Isn't there a law?"

20   "I'm sure that won't be necessary," Judge Stevens said. "It's probably just a snake or a rat that nigger of hers killed in the yard. I'll speak to him about it."

21   The next day he received two more complaints, one from a man who came in diffident deprecation. "We really must do something about it, Judge. I'd be the last one in the world to bother Miss Emily, but we've got to do something." That night the Board of Aldermen met—three graybeards and one younger man, a member of the rising generation.

22   "It's simple enough," he said. "Send her word to have her place cleaned up. Give her a certain time to do it in, and if she don't . . . "

23   "Dammit, sir," Judge Stevens said, "will you accuse a lady to her face of smelling bad?"

24   So the next night, after midnight, four men crossed Miss Emily's lawn and slunk about the house like burglars, sniffing along the base of the brickwork and at the cellar openings while one of them performed a regular sowing motion with his hand out of a sack slung from his shoulder. They broke open the cellar door and sprinkled lime there, and in all the outbuildings. As they recrossed the lawn, a window that had been dark was lighted and Miss Emily sat in it, the light behind her, and her upright torso motionless as that of an idol. They crept quietly across the lawn and into the shadow of the locusts that lined the street. After a week or two the smell went away.

25   That was when people had begun to feel really sorry for her. People in our town, remembering how old lady Wyatt, her great-aunt, had gone completely crazy at last, believed that the Griersons held themselves a little too high for what they really were. None of the young men were quite good enough for Miss Emily and such. We had long thought of them as a tableau, Miss Emily a slender figure in white in the background, her father a spraddled silhouette in the foreground, his back to her and clutching a horsewhip, the two of them framed by the back-flung front door. So when she got to be thirty and was still single, we were not pleased exactly, but vindicated; even with insanity in the family she wouldn't have turned down all of her chances if they had really materialized.

NOTES

temerity (par. 15): nerve
teeming (par. 16): crowded
diffident (par. 21): hesitant
deprecation (par. 21): mild disapproval
sowing (par. 24): scattering
torso (par. 24): upper body
tableau (par. 25): like a posed picture
spraddled (par. 25): spread out
silhouette (par. 25): literally, the outline of some figure
vindicated (par. 25): proven correct
materialized (par. 25): occurred

26   When her father died, it got about that the house was all that was left to her, and in a way, people were glad. At last they could pity Miss Emily. Being left alone, and a pauper, she had become humanized. Now she too would know the old thrill and the old despair of a penny more or less.

27   The day after his death all the ladies prepared to call at the house and offer condolence and aid, as is our custom. Miss Emily met them at the door, dressed as usual and with no trace of grief on her face. She told them that her father was not dead. She did that for three days, with the ministers calling on her, and the doctors, trying to persuade her to let them dispose of the body. Just as they were about to resort to law and force, she broke down, and they buried her father quickly.

28   We did not say she was crazy then. We believed she had to do that. We remembered all the young men her father had driven away, and we knew that with nothing left, she would have to cling to that which had robbed her, as people will.

III

29   She was sick for a long time. When we saw her again, her hair was cut short, making her look like a girl, with a vague resemblance to those angels in colored church windows—sort of tragic and serene.

30   The town had just let the contracts for paving the sidewalks, and in the summer after her father's death they began the work. The construction company came with niggers and mules and machinery, and a foreman named Homer Barron, a Yankee—a big, dark, ready man, with a big voice and eyes lighter than his face. The little boys would follow in groups to hear him cuss the niggers, and the niggers singing in time to the rise and fall of picks. Pretty soon he knew everybody in town. Whenever you heard a lot of laughing anywhere about the square, Homer Barron would be in the center of the group. Presently, we began to see him and Miss Emily on Sunday afternoons driving in the yellow-wheeled buggy and the matched team of bays from the livery stable.

31   At first we were glad that Miss Emily would have an interest, because the ladies all said, "Of course a Grierson would not think seriously of a Northerner, a day laborer." But there were still others, older people, who said that even grief could not cause a real lady to forget *noblesse oblige*—without calling it *noblesse oblige*. They just said, "Poor Emily. Her kinsfolk should come to her." She had some kin in Alabama; but years ago her father had fallen out with them over the estate of old lady Wyatt, the crazy woman, and there was no communication between the two families. They had not even been represented at the funeral.

32   And as soon as the old people said, "Poor Emily," the whispering began. "Do you suppose it's really so?" they said to one another. "Of course it is. What else could . . . " This behind their hands; rustling of craned silk and satin behind jalousies closed upon the sun of Sunday afternoon as the thin, swift clop-clop-clop of the matched team passed: "Poor Emily."

NOTES

pauper (par. 26): a very poor person
condolence (par. 27): sympathy
serene (par. 29): peaceful
let (par. 30): issued
noblesse oblige (par. 31): literally, "nobility obligates": The term refers to the obligation of a person of high standing to be honorable and generous.
jalousies (par. 32): blinds

33   She carried her head high enough—even when we believed that she was fallen. It was as if she demanded more than ever the recognition of her dignity as the last Grierson; as if it had wanted that touch of earthiness to reaffirm her imperviousness. Like when she bought the rat poison, the arsenic. That was over a year after they had begun to say "Poor Emily," and while the two female cousins were visiting her.

34   "I want some poison," she said to the druggist. She was over thirty then, still a slight woman, though thinner than usual, with cold, haughty black eyes in a face the flesh of which was strained across the temples and about the eyesockets as you imagine a lighthouse-keeper's face ought to look. "I want some poison," she said.

35   "Yes, Miss Emily. What kind? For rats and such? I'd recom—"

36   "I want the best you have. I don't care what kind."

37   The druggist named several. "They'll kill anything up to an elephant. But what you want is—"

38   "Arsenic," Miss Emily said. "Is that a good one?"

39   "Is . . . arsenic? Yes, ma'am. But what you want—"

40   "I want arsenic."

41   The druggist looked down at her. She looked back at him, erect, her face like a strained flag. "Why, of course," the druggist said. "If that's what you want. But the law requires you to tell what you are going to use it for."

42   Miss Emily just stared at him, her headed tilted back in order to look him eye for eye, until he looked away and went and got the arsenic and wrapped it up. The Negro delivery boy brought her the package; the druggist didn't come back. When she opened the package at home there was written on the box, under the skull and bones: "For rats."

IV

43   So the next day we all said, "She will kill herself"; and we said it would be the best thing. When she had first begun to be seen with Homer Barron, we had said, "She will marry him." Then we said, "She will persuade him yet," because Homer himself had remarked—he liked men, and it was known that he drank with the younger men in the Elks' Club—that he was not a marrying man. Later we said, "Poor Emily" behind the jalousies as they passed on Sunday afternoon in the glittering buggy, Miss Emily with her head high and Homer Barron with his hat cocked and a cigar in his teeth, reins and whip in a yellow glove.

44   Then some of the ladies began to say that it was a disgrace to the town and a bad example to the young people. The men did not want to interfere, but at last the ladies forced the Baptist minister—Miss Emily's people were Episcopal—to call upon her. He would never divulge what happened during that interview, but he refused to go back again. The next Sunday they again drove about the streets, and the following day the minister's wife wrote to Miss Emily's relations in Alabama.

45   So she had blood-kin under her roof again and we sat back to watch developments. At first nothing happened. Then we were sure that they were to be married. We learned that Miss Emily had been to the jeweler's and ordered a man's toilet set in silver, with the letters H. B. on each piece. Two days later

NOTES

reaffirm (par. 33): prove again
imperviousness (par. 33): ability to be affected by nothing
divulge (par. 44): reveal
a man's toilet set (par. 45): personal items such as a hair brush, a razor, etc.

we learned that she had bought a complete outfit of men's clothing, including a nightshirt, and we said, "They are married." We were really glad. We were glad because the two female cousins were even more Grierson than Miss Emily had ever been.

46   So we were not surprised when Homer Barron—the streets had been finished some time since—was gone. We were a little disappointed that there was not a public blowing-off, but we believed that he had gone on to prepare for Miss Emily's coming, or to give her a chance to get rid of the cousins. (By that time it was a cabal, and we were all Miss Emily's allies to help circumvent the cousins.) Sure enough, after another week they departed. And, as we had expected all along, within three days Homer Barron was back in town. A neighbor saw the Negro man admit him at the kitchen door at dusk one evening.

47   And that was the last we saw of Homer Barron. And of Miss Emily for some time. The Negro man went in and out with the market basket, but the front door remained closed. Now and then we would see her at the window for a moment, as the men did that night when they sprinkled the lime, but for almost six months she did not appear on the streets. Then we knew that this was to be expected too; as if that quality of her father which had thwarted her woman's life so many times had been too virulent and too furious to die.

48   When we next saw Miss Emily, she had grown fat and her hair was turning gray. During the next few years it grew grayer and grayer until it attained an even pepper-and-salt iron-gray, when it ceased turning. Up to the day of her death at seventy-four it was still that vigorous iron-gray, like the hair of an active man.

49   From that time on her front door remained closed, save for a period of six or seven years, when she was about forty, during which she gave lessons in china-painting. She fitted up a studio in one of the downstairs rooms, where the daughters and granddaughters of Colonel Sartoris' contemporaries were sent to her with the same regularity and in the same spirit that they were sent to church on Sundays with a twenty-five-cent piece for the collection plate. Meanwhile her taxes had been remitted.

50   Then the newer generation became the backbone and the spirit of the town, and the painting pupils grew up and fell away and did not send their children to her with boxes of color and tedious brushes and pictures cut from the ladies' magazines. The front door closed upon the last one and remained closed for good. When the town got free postal delivery, Miss Emily alone refused to let them fasten the metal numbers above her door and attach a mailbox to it. She would not listen to them.

51   Daily, monthly, yearly we watched the Negro grow grayer and more stooped, going in and out with the market basket. Each December we sent her a tax notice, which would be returned by the post office a week later, unclaimed. Now and then we would see her in one of the downstairs windows—she had evidently shut up the top floor of the house—like the carven torso of an idol in a niche, looking or not looking at us, we could never tell which. Thus she passed from generation to generation—dear, inescapable, impervious, tranquil, and perverse.

NOTES

cabal (par. 46): a group of people united to bring about a certain result
circumvent (par. 46): outsmart
thwarted (par. 47): frustrated
virulent (par. 47): poisonous
tedious (par. 50): tiresome
niche (par. 51): literally, a recess in a wall in which a statue is usually placed
tranquil (par. 51): calm
perverse (par. 51): extremely strange

52   And so she died. Fell ill in the house filled with dust and shadows, with only a doddering Negro man to wait on her. We did not even know she was sick; we had long since given up trying to get any information from the Negro. He talked to no one, probably not even to her, for his voice had grown harsh and rusty, as if from disuse.

53   She died in one of the downstairs rooms, in a heavy walnut bed with a curtain, her gray head propped on a pillow yellow and moldy with age and lack of sunlight.

V

54   The Negro met the first of the ladies at the front door and let them in, with their hushed, sibilant voices and their quick, curious glances, and then he disappeared. He walked right through the house and out the back and was not seen again.

55   The two female cousins came at once. They held the funeral on the second day, with the town coming to look at Miss Emily beneath a mass of bought flowers, with the crayon face of her father musing profoundly above the bier and the ladies sibilant and macabre; and the very old men—some in their brushed Confederate uniforms—on the porch and the lawn, talking of Miss Emily as if she had been a contemporary of theirs, believing that they had danced with her and courted her perhaps, confusing time with its mathematical progression, as the old do, to whom all the past is not a diminished road but, instead, a huge meadow which no winter ever quite touches, divided from them now by the narrow bottleneck of the most recent decade of years.

56   Already we knew that there was one room in that region above stairs which no one had seen in forty years, and which would have to be forced. They waited until Miss Emily was decently in the ground before they opened it.

57   The violence of breaking down the door seemed to fill this room with pervading dust. A thin, acrid pall as of the tomb seemed to lie everywhere upon this room decked and furnished as for a bridal: upon the valance curtains of faded rose color, upon the rose-shaded lights, upon the dressing table, upon the delicate array of crystal and the man's toilet things backed with tarnished silver, silver so tarnished that the monogram was obscured. Among them lay a collar and tie, as if they had just been removed, which lifted, left upon the surface a pale crescent in the dust. Upon a chair hung the suit, carefully folded; beneath it the two mute shoes and the discarded socks.

58   The man himself lay in the bed.

59   For a long while we just stood there, looking down at the profound and fleshless grin. The body had apparently once lain in the attitude of an embrace, but now the long sleep that outlasts love, that conquers even the grimace of love, had cuckolded him. What was left of him, rotted beneath what was left of the nightshirt, had become inextricable from the bed in which

NOTES
sibilant (par. 54): hissing
bier (par. 55): a stand upon which a coffin is placed
macabre (par. 55): fascinated with death
a contemporary (par. 55): a person of approximately the same age
acrid (par. 57): harsh, irritating
pall (par. 57): atmosphere of gloom
profound (par. 59): difficult to understand
grimace (par. 59): a facial expression
cuckolded (par. 59): literally, a man whose wife is unfaithful to him
inextricable (par. 59): inseparable

he lay; and upon him and upon the pillow beside him lay that even coating of the patient and bidding dust.

60   Then we noticed that in the second pillow was the indentation of a head. One of us lifted something from it, and leaning forward, that faint and invisible dust dry and acrid in the nostrils, we saw a long strand of iron-gray hair.

Revelation

Flannery O'Connor

1   The doctor's waiting room, which was very small, was almost full when the Turpins entered and Mrs. Turpin, who was very large, made it look even smaller by her presence. She stood looming at the head of the magazine table set in the center of it, a living demonstration that the room was inadequate and ridiculous. Her little bright black eyes took in all the patients as she sized up the seating situation. There was one vacant chair and a place on the sofa occupied by a blond child in a dirty blue romper who should have been told to move over and make room for the lady. He was five or six, but Mrs. Turpin saw at once that no one was going to tell him to move over. He was slumped down in the seat, his arms idle at his sides and his eyes idle in his head; his nose ran unchecked.

2   Mrs. Turpin put a firm hand on Claud's shoulder and said in a voice that included anyone who wanted to listen, "Claud, you sit in that chair there," and gave him a push down into the vacant one. Claud was florid and bald and sturdy, somewhat shorter than Mrs. Turpin, but he sat down as if he were accustomed to doing what she told him to.

3   Mrs. Turpin remained standing. The only man in the room besides Claud was a lean stringy old fellow with a rusty hand spread out on each knee, whose eyes were closed as if he were asleep or dead or pretending to be so as not to get up and offer her his seat. Her gaze settled agreeably on a well-dressed gray-haired lady whose eyes met hers and whose expression said: if that child belonged to me, he would have some manners and move over—there's plenty of room there for you and him too.

4   Claud looked up with a sigh and made as if to rise.

5   "Sit down," Mrs. Turpin said. "You know you're not supposed to stand on that leg. He has an ulcer on his leg," she explained.

6   Claud lifted his foot onto the magazine table and rolled his trouser leg up to reveal a purple swelling on a plump marble-white calf.

7   "My!" the pleasant lady said. "How did you do that?"

8   "A cow kicked him," Mrs. Turpin said.

9   "Goodness!" said the lady.

10   Claud rolled his trouser leg down.

11   "Maybe the little boy would move over," the lady suggested, but the child did not stir.

NOTES
Revelation (title): something that is revealed by God to man
looming (par. 1): impressively
romper (par. 1): one piece outfit for children
idle (par. 1): inactive
unchecked (par. 1): freely
florid (par. 2): ruddy, a red complexion
ulcer (par. 5): infected, festering wound

12   "Somebody will be leaving in a minute," Mrs. Turpin said. She could not understand why a doctor—with as much money as they made charging five dollars a day to just stick their head in the hospital door and look at you— couldn't afford a decent-sized waiting room. This one was hardly bigger than a garage. The table was cluttered with limp-looking magazines and at one end of it there was a big green glass ash tray full of cigarette butts and cotton wads with little blood spots on them. If she had had anything to do with the running of the place, that would have been emptied every so often. There were no chairs against the wall at the head of the room. It had a rectangular-shaped panel in it that permitted a view of the office where the nurse came and went and the secretary listened to the radio. A plastic fern in a gold pot sat in the opening and trailed its fronds down almost to the floor. The radio was softly playing gospel music.

13   Just then the inner door opened and a nurse with the highest stack of yellow hair Mrs. Turpin had ever seen put her face in the crack and called for the next patient. The woman sitting beside Claud grasped the two arms of her chair and hoisted herself up; she pulled her dress free from her legs and lumbered through the door where the nurse had disappeared.

14   Mrs. Turpin eased into the vacant chair, which held her tight as a corset. "I wish I could reduce," she said, and rolled her eyes and gave a comic sigh.

15   "Oh, *you* aren't fat," the stylish lady said.

16   "Ooooo I am too," Mrs. Turpin said. "Claud he eats all he wants to and never weighs over one hundred and seventy-five pounds, but me I just look at something good to eat and I gain some weight," and her stomach and shoulders shook with laughter. "You can eat all you want to, can't you, Claud?" she asked, turning to him.

17   Claud only grinned.

18   "Well, as long as you have such a good disposition," the stylish lady said, "I don't think it makes a bit of difference what size you are. You just can't beat a good disposition."

19   Next to her was a fat girl of eighteen or nineteen, scowling into a thick blue book which Mrs. Turpin saw was entitled *Human Development.* The girl raised her head and directed her scowl at Mrs. Turpin as if she did not like her looks. She appeared annoyed that anyone should speak while she tried to read. The poor girl's face was blue with acne and Mrs. Turpin thought how pitiful it was to have a face like that at that age. She gave the girl a friendly smile but the girl only scowled the harder. Mrs. Turpin herself was fat but she had always had good skin, and though she was forty-seven years old, there was not a wrinkle in her face except around her eyes from laughing too much.

20   Next to the ugly girl was the child, still in exactly the same position, and next to him was a thin leathery old woman in a cotton print dress. She and Claud had three sacks of chicken feed in their pump house that was in the same print. She had seen from the first that the child belonged with the old woman. She could tell by the way they sat—kind of vacant and white-trashy, as if they would sit there until Doomsday if nobody called and told them to get up. And at right angles but next to the well-dressed pleasant lady was a lank-faced

NOTES
fronds (par. 12): leaves (of ferns)
hoisted (par. 13): raised
corset (par. 14): girdle
disposition (par. 18): temperament, personality
scowling (par. 19): frowning
white-trashy (par. 20): like worthless white people
Doomsday (par. 20): Judgment day, the end of the world
lank-faced (par. 20): thin

woman who was certainly the child's mother. She had on a yellow sweat shirt and wine-colored slacks, both gritty-looking, and the rims of her lips were stained with snuff. Her dirty yellow hair was tied behind with a little piece of red paper ribbon. Worse than niggers any day, Mrs. Turpin thought.

21   The gospel hymn playing was, "When I looked up and He looked down," and Mrs. Turpin, who knew it, supplied the last line mentally, "And wona these days I know's I'll we-eara crown."

22   Without appearing to, Mrs. Turpin always noticed people's feet. The well-dressed lady had on red and gray suede shoes to match her dress. Mrs. Turpin had on her good black patent leather pumps. The ugly girl had on Girl Scout shoes and heavy socks. The old woman had on tennis shoes and the white-trashy mother had on what appeared to be bedroom slippers, black straw with gold braid threaded through them—exactly what you would have expected her to have on.

23   Sometimes at night when she couldn't go to sleep, Mrs. Turpin would occupy herself with the question of who she would have chosen to be if she couldn't have been herself. If Jesus had said to her before he made her, "There's only two places available for you. You can either be a nigger or white-trash," what would she have said? "Please, Jesus, please," she would have said, "just let me wait until there's another place available," and he would have said, "No, you have to go right now and I have only those two places so make up your mind." She would have wiggled and squirmed and begged and pleaded but it would have been no use and finally she would have said, "All right, make me a nigger then—but that don't mean a trashy one." And he would have made her a neat clean respectable Negro woman, herself but black.

24   Next to the child's mother was a red-headed youngish woman, reading one of the magazines and working a piece of chewing gum, hell for leather, as Claud would say. Mrs. Turpin could not see the woman's feet. She was not white-trash, just common. Sometimes Mrs. Turpin occupied herself at night naming the classes of people. On the bottom of the heap were most colored people, not the kind she would have been if she had been one, but most of them; then next to them—not above, just away from—were the white-trash; then above them were the homeowners, and above them the home-and-land owners, to which she and Claud belonged. Above she and Claud were people with a lot of money and much bigger houses and much more land. But here the complexity of it would begin to bear in on her, for some of the people with a lot of money were common and ought to be below she and Claud and some of the people who had good blood had lost their money and had to rent and then there were colored people who owned their homes and land as well. There was a colored dentist in town who had two red Lincolns and a swimming pool and a farm with registered white-face cattle on it. Usually by the time she had fallen asleep all the classes of people were moiling and roiling around in her head, and she would dream they were all crammed in together in a box car being ridden off to be put in a gas oven.

25   "That's a beautiful clock," she said and nodded to her right. It was a big wall clock, the face encased in a brass sunburst.

26   "Yes, it's very pretty," the stylish lady said agreeably. "And right on the dot too," she added, glancing at her watch.

NOTES

snuff (par. 20): ground tobacco that is inhaled or placed inside the lip or cheek
pumps (par. 22): a low-heel shoe without straps or laces
hell for leather (par. 24): as fast as possible
moiling and roiling (par. 24): swirling and mixing
encased (par. 25): enclosed

27   The ugly girl beside her cast an eye upward at the clock, smirked, then looked directly at Mrs. Turpin and smirked again. Then she returned her eyes to her book. She was obviously the lady's daughter because, although they didn't look anything alike as to disposition, they both had the same shape of face and the same blue eyes. On the lady they sparkled pleasantly but in the girl's seared face they appeared alternately to smolder and to blaze.

28   What if Jesus had said, "All right, you can be white-trash or a nigger or ugly!"

29   Mrs. Turpin felt an awful pity for the girl, though she thought it was one thing to be ugly and another to act ugly.

30   The woman with the snuff-stained lips turned around in her chair and looked up at the clock. Then she turned back and appeared to look a little to the side of Mrs. Turpin. There was a cast in one of her eyes. "You want to know wher you can get you one of themther clocks?" she asked in a loud voice.

31   "No, I already have a nice clock," Mrs. Turpin said. Once somebody like her got a leg in the conversation, she would be all over it.

32   "You can get you one with green stamps," the woman said. "That's most likely wher he got hisn. Save you up enough, you can get you most anythang. I got me some joo-ry."

33   Ought to have got you a wash rag and some soap, Mrs. Turpin thought.

34   "I get contour sheets with mine," the pleasant lady said.

35   The daughter slammed her book shut. She looked straight in front of her, directly through Mrs. Turpin and on through the yellow curtain and the plate glass window which made the wall behind her. The girl's eyes seemed lit all of a sudden with a peculiar light, an unnatural light like night road signs give. Mrs. Turpin turned her head to see if there was anything going on outside that she should see, but she could not see anything. Figures passing cast only a pale shadow through the curtain. There was no reason the girl should single her out for her ugly looks.

36   "Miss Finley," the nurse said, cracking the door. The gum-chewing woman got up and passed in front of her and Claud and went into the office. She had on red high-heeled shoes.

37   Directly across the table, the ugly girl's eyes were fixed on Mrs. Turpin as if she had some very special reason for disliking her.

38   "This is wonderful weather, isn't it?" the girl's mother said.

39   "It's good weather for cotton if you can get the niggers to pick it," Mrs. Turpin said, "but niggers don't want to pick cotton any more. You can't get the white folks to pick it and now you can't get the niggers—because they got to be right up there with the white folks."

40   "They gonna *try* anyways," the white-trash woman said, leaning forward.

41   "Do you have one of the cotton-picking machines?" the pleasant lady asked.

42   "No," Mrs. Turpin said, "they leave half the cotton in the field. We don't have much cotton anyway. If you want to make it farming now, you have to have a little of everything. We got a couple of acres of cotton and a few hogs

NOTES

smirked (par. 27): smiled insincerely

seared (par. 27): scorched

smolder (par. 27): literally, to burn slowly and without flame

green stamps (par. 32): stamps given by stores as a bonus: The shopper collects the stamps and exchanges them for merchandise at the green stamp store.

joo'ry (par. 32): jewelry

contour sheets (par. 34): sheets that fit the shape of a bed

and chickens and just enough white-face that Claud can look after them himself."

43   "One thang I don't want," the white-trash woman said, wiping her mouth with the back of her hand. "Hogs. Nasty stinking things, a-gruntin and a-rootin all over the place."

44   Mrs. Turpin gave her the merest edge of her attention. "Our hogs are not dirty and they don't stink," she said. "They're cleaner than some children I've seen. Their feet never touch the ground. We have a pig-parlor—that's where you raise them on concrete," she explained to the pleasant lady, "and Claud scoots them down with the hose every afternoon and washes off the floor." Cleaner by far than that child right there, she thought. Poor nasty little thing. He had not moved except to put the thumb of his dirty hand into his mouth.

45   The woman turned her face away from Mrs. Turpin. "I know I wouldn't scoot down no hog with no hose," she said to the wall.

46   You wouldn't have no hog to scoot down, Mrs. Turpin said to herself.

47   "A-gruntin and a-rootin and a-groanin," the woman muttered.

48   "We got a little of everything," Mrs. Turpin said to the pleasant lady. "It's no use in having more than you can handle yourself with help like it is. We found enough niggers to pick our cotton this year but Claud he has to go after them and take them home again in the evening. They can't walk that half a mile. No they can't. I tell you," she said and laughed merrily, "I sure am tired of buttering up niggers, but you got to love em if you want em to work for you. When they come in the morning, I run out and I say, 'Hi yawl this morning?' and when Claud drives them off to the field I just wave to beat the band and they just wave back." And she waved her hand rapidly to illustrate.

49   "Like you read out of the same book," the lady said showing she understood perfectly.

50   "Child, yes," Mrs. Turpin said. "And when they come in from the field, I run out with a bucket of icewater. That's the way it's going to be from now on," she said. "You may as well face it."

51   "One thang I know," the white-trash woman said. "Two things I ain't going to do: love no niggers or scoot down no hog with no hose." And she let out a bark of contempt.

52   The look that Mrs. Turpin and the pleasant lady exchanged indicated they both understood that you had to *have* certain things before you could *know* certain things. But every time Mrs. Turpin exchanged a look with the lady, she was aware that the ugly girl's peculiar eyes were still on her, and she had trouble bringing her attention back to the conversation.

53   "When you got something," she said, "you got to look after it." And when you ain't got a thing but breath and britches, she added to herself, you can afford to come to town every morning and just sit on the Court House coping and spit.

54   A grotesque revolving shadow passed across the curtain behind her and was thrown palely on the opposite wall. Then a bicycle clattered down against the outside of the building. The door opened and a colored boy glided in with a tray from the drugstore. It had two large red and white paper cups on it with

NOTES

merest (par. 44): slightest
buttering up (par. 48): flattering
to beat the band (par. 48): as fast and as much as possible
contempt (par. 51): disgust
peculiar (par. 52): strange
coping (par. 53): the top of a short wall
grotesque (par. 54): bizarre, twisted

tops on them. He was a tall, very black boy in discolored white pants and a green nylon shirt. He was chewing gum slowly, as if to music. He set the tray down in the office opening next to the fern and stuck his head through to look for the secretary. She was not in there. He rested his arms on the ledge and waited, his narrow bottom stuck out, swaying to the left and right. He raised a hand over his head and scratched the base of his skull.

55   "You see that button there, boy?" Mrs. Turpin said. "You can punch that and she'll come. She's probably in the back somewhere."

56   "Is that right?" the boy said agreeably, as if he had never seen the button before. He leaned to the right and put his finger on it. "She sometime out," he said and twisted around to face his audience, his elbows behind him on the counter. The nurse appeared and he twisted back again. She handed him a dollar and he rooted in his pocket and made the change and counted it out to her. She gave him fifteen cents for a tip and he went out with the empty tray. The heavy door swung to slowly and closed at length with the sound of suction. For a moment no one spoke.

57   "They ought to send all them niggers back to Africa," the white-trash woman said. "That's where they come from in the first place."

58   "Oh, I couldn't do without my good colored friends," the pleasant lady said.

59   "There's a heap of things worse than a nigger," Mrs. Turpin agreed. "It's all kinds of them just like it's all kinds of us."

60   "Yes, and it takes all kinds to make the world go round," the lady said in her musical voice.

61   As she said it, the raw-complexioned girl snapped her teeth together. Her lower lip turned downwards and inside out, revealing the pale pink inside of her mouth. After a second it rolled back up. It was the ugliest face Mrs. Turpin had ever seen anyone make and for a moment she was certain that the girl had made it at her. She was looking at her as if she had known and disliked her all her life—all of Mrs. Turpin's life, it seemed too, not just all the girl's life. Why, girl, I don't even know you, Mrs. Turpin said silently.

62   She forced her attention back to the discussion. "It wouldn't be practical to send them back to Africa," she said. "They wouldn't want to go. They got it too good here."

63   "Wouldn't be what they wanted—if I had anythang to do with it," the woman said.

64   "It wouldn't be a way in the world you could get all the niggers back over there," Mrs. Turpin said. "They'd be hiding out and lying down and turning sick on you and wailing and hollering and raring and pitching. It wouldn't be a way in the world to get them over there."

65   "They got over here," the trashy woman said. "Get back like they got over."

66   "It wasn't so many of them then," Mrs. Turpin explained.

67   The woman looked at Mrs. Turpin as if here was an idiot indeed but Mrs. Turpin was not bothered by the look, considering where it came from.

68   "Nooo," she said, "they're going to stay here where they can go to New York and marry white folks and improve their color. That's what they all want to do, every one of them, improve their color."

69   "You know what comes of that, don't you?" Claud asked.

NOTES

raw-complexioned (par. 61): red-faced

wailing (par. 64): crying

raring and pitching (par. 64): jumping up and down

70   "No, Claud, what?" Mrs. Turpin said.

71   Claud's eyes twinkled. "White-faced niggers," he said with never a smile.

72   Everybody in the office laughed except the white-trash and the ugly girl. The girl gripped the book in her lap with white fingers. The trashy woman looked around her from face to face as if she thought they were all idiots. The old woman in the feed sack dress continued to gaze expressionless across the floor at the high-top shoes of the man opposite her, the one who had been pretending to be asleep when the Turpins came in. He was laughing heartily, his hands still spread out on his knees. The child had fallen to the side and was lying now almost face down in the old woman's lap.

73   While they recovered from their laughter, the nasal chorus on the radio kept the room from silence.

"You go to blank blank
And I'll go to mine
But we'll all blank along
To-geth-ther,
And all along the blank
We'll hep eachother out
Smile-ling in any kind of
Weath-ther!"

74   Mrs. Turpin didn't catch every word but she caught enough to agree with the spirit of the song and it turned her thoughts sober. To help anybody out that needed it was her philosophy of life. She never spared herself when she found somebody in need, whether they were white or black, trash or decent. And of all she had to be thankful for, she was most thankful that this was so. If Jesus had said, "You can be high society and have all the money you want and be thin and svelte-like, but you can't be a good woman with it," she would have had to say, "Well don't make me that then. Make me a good woman and it don't matter what else, how fat or how ugly or how poor!" Her heart rose. He had not made her a nigger or white-trash or ugly! He had made her herself and given her a little of everything. Jesus, thank you! she said. Thank you thank you thank you! Whenever she counted her blessings she felt as buoyant as if she weighed one hundred and twenty-five pounds instead of one hundred and eighty.

75   "What's wrong with your little boy?" the pleasant lady asked the white-trashy woman.

76   "He has a ulcer," the woman said proudly. "He ain't give me a minute's peace since he was born. Him and her are just alike," she said, nodding at the old woman, who was running her leathery fingers through the child's pale hair. "Look like I can't get nothing down them two but Co'Cola and candy."

77   That's all you try to get down em, Mrs. Turpin said to herself. Too lazy to light the fire. There was nothing you could tell her about people like them that she didn't know already. And it was not just that they didn't have anything. Because if you gave them everything, in two weeks it would all be broken or filthy or they would have chopped it up for lightwood. She knew all this from her own experience. Help them you must, but help them you couldn't.

78   All at once the ugly girl turned her lips inside out again. Her eyes fixed like two drills on Mrs. Turpin. This time there was no mistaking that there was something urgent behind them.

NOTES

svelte-like (par. 74): well shaped
buoyant (par. 74): cheerful, light
Co'Cola (par. 76): Coca Cola
lightwood (par. 77): kindling; small pieces of wood used to start fires

79   Girl, Mrs. Turpin exclaimed silently, I haven't done a thing to you! The girl might be confusing her with somebody else. There was no need to sit by and let herself be intimidated. "You must be in college," she said boldly, looking directly at the girl. "I see you reading a book there."

80   The girl continued to stare and pointedly did not answer.

81   Her mother blushed at this rudeness. "The lady asked you a question, Mary Grace," she said under her breath.

82   "I have ears," Mary Grace said.

83   The poor mother blushed again. "Mary Grace goes to Wellesley College," she explained. She twisted one of the buttons on her dress. "In Massachusetts," she added with a grimace. "And in the summer she just keeps right on studying. Just reads all the time, a real book worm. She's done real well at Wellesley; she's taking English and Math and History and Psychology and Social Studies," she rattled on, "and I think it's too much. I think she ought to get out and have fun."

84   The girl looked as if she would like to hurl them all through the plate glass window.

85   "Way up north," Mrs. Turpin murmured and thought, well, it hasn't done much for her manners.

86   "I'd almost rather to have him sick," the white-trash woman said, wrenching the attention back to herself. "He's so mean when he ain't. Look like some children just take natural to meanness. It's some gets bad when they get sick but he was the opposite. Took sick and turned good. He don't give me no trouble now. It's me waitin to see the doctor," she said.

87   If I was going to send anybody back to Africa, Mrs. Turpin thought, it would be your kind, woman. "Yes, indeed," she said aloud, but looking up at the ceiling, "It's a heap of things worse than a nigger." And dirtier than a hog, she added to herself.

88   "I think people with bad dispositions are more to be pitied than anyone on earth," the pleasant lady said in a voice that was decidedly thin.

89   "I thank the Lord he has blessed me with a good one," Mrs. Turpin said. "The day has never dawned that I couldn't find something to laugh at."

90   "Not since she married me anyways," Claud said with a comical straight face.

91   Everybody laughed except the girl and the white-trash.

92   Mrs. Turpin's stomach shook. "He's such a caution," she said, "that I can't help but laugh at him."

93   The girl made a loud ugly noise through her teeth.

94   Her mother's mouth grew thin and tight. "I think the worst thing in the world," she said, "is an ungrateful person. To have everything and not appreciate it. I know a girl," she said, "who has parents who would give her anything, a little brother who loves her dearly, who is getting a good education, who wears the best clothes, but who can never say a kind word to anyone, who never smiles, who just criticizes and complains all day long."

95   "Is she too old to paddle?" Claud asked.

96   The girl's face was almost purple.

97   "Yes," the lady said, "I'm afraid there's nothing to do but leave her to her folly. Some day she'll wake up and it'll be too late."

NOTES
intimidated (par. 79): threatened, bullied
grimace (par. 83): a facial expression showing disapproval or disbelief
a caution (par. 92): one that does something unexpectedly
folly (par. 97): foolishness

98   "It never hurt anyone to smile," Mrs. Turpin said. "It just makes you feel better all over."

99   "Of course," the lady said sadly, "but there are just some people you can't tell anything to. They can't take criticism."

100   "If it's one thing I am," Mrs. Turpin said with feeling, "it's grateful. When I think who all I could have been besides myself and what all I got, a little of everything, and a good disposition besides, I just feel like shouting, 'Thank you, Jesus, for making everything the way it is!' It could have been different!" For one thing, somebody else could have got Claud. At the thought of this, she was flooded with gratitude and a terrible pang of joy ran through her. "Oh thank you, Jesus, Jesus, thank you!" she cried aloud.

101   The book struck her directly over her left eye. It struck almost at the same instant that she realized the girl was about to hurl it. Before she could utter a sound, the raw face came crashing across the table toward her, howling. The girl's fingers sank like clamps into the soft flesh of her neck. She heard the mother cry out and Claud shout, "Whoa!" There was an instant when she was certain that she was about to be in an earthquake.

102   All at once her vision narrowed and she saw everything as if it were happening in a small room far away, or as if she were looking at it through the wrong end of a telescope. Claud's face crumpled and fell out of sight. The nurse ran in, then out, then in again. Then the gangling figure of the doctor rushed out of the inner door. Magazines flew this way and that as the table turned over. The girl fell with a thud and Mrs. Turpin's vision suddenly reversed itself and she saw everything large instead of small. The eyes of the white-trashy woman were staring hugely at the floor. There the girl, held down on one side by the nurse and on the other by her mother, was wrenching and turning in their grasp. The doctor was kneeling astride her, trying to hold her arm down. He managed after a second to sink a long needle into it.

103   Mrs. Turpin felt entirely hollow except for her heart which swung from side to side as if it were agitated in a great empty drum of flesh.

104   "Somebody that's not busy call for the ambulance," the doctor said in the off-hand voice young doctors adopt for terrible occasions.

105   Mrs. Turpin could not have moved a finger. The old man who had been sitting next to her skipped nimbly into the office and made the call, for the secretary still seemed to be gone.

106   "Claud!" Mrs. Turpin called.

107   He was not in his chair. She knew she must jump up and find him but she felt like someone trying to catch a train in a dream, when everything moves in slow motion and the faster you try to run the slower you go.

108   "Here I am," a suffocated voice, very unlike Claud's said.

109   He was doubled up in the corner on the floor, pale as paper, holding his leg. She wanted to get up and go to him but she could not move. Instead, her gaze was drawn slowly downward to the churning face on the floor, which she could see over the doctor's shoulder.

110   The girl's eyes stopped rolling and focused on her. They seemed a much lighter blue than before, as if a door that had been tightly closed behind them was now open to admit light and air.

111   Mrs. Turpin's head cleared and her power of motion returned. She leaned forward until she was looking directly into the fierce brilliant eyes. There was

NOTES

gangling (par. 102): thin and awkward
astride (par. 102): with one leg on each side
agitated (par. 103): shaking

no doubt in her mind that the girl did know her, knew her in some intense and personal way, beyond time and place and condition. "What you got to say to me?" she asked hoarsely and held her breath, waiting, as for a revelation.

112   The girl raised her head. Her gaze locked with Mrs. Turpin's. "Go back to hell where you came from you old wart hog," she whispered. Her voice was low but clear. Her eyes burned for a moment as if she saw with pleasure that her message had struck its target.

113   Mrs. Turpin sank back in her chair.

114   After a moment the girl's eyes closed and she turned her head wearily to the side.

115   The doctor rose and handed the nurse the empty syringe. He leaned over and put both hands for a moment on the mother's shoulders, which were shaking. She was sitting on the floor, her lips pressed together, holding Mary Grace's hand in her lap. The girl's fingers were gripped like a baby's around her thumb. "Go on to the hospital," he said. "I'll call and make the arrangements."

116   "Now let's see that neck," he said in a jovial voice to Mrs. Turpin. He began to inspect her neck with his first two fingers. Two little moon-shaped lines like pink fish bones were indented over her windpipe. There was the beginning of an angry red swelling above her eye. His fingers passed over this also.

117   "Lea' me be," she said thickly and shook him off. "See about Claud. She kicked him."

118   "I'll see about him in a minute," he said and felt her pulse. He was a thin gray-haired man, given to pleasantries. "Go home and have yourself a vacation the rest of the day," he said and patted her on the shoulder.

119   Quit your pattin me, Mrs. Turpin growled to herself.

120   "And put an ice pack over that eye," he said. Then he went and squatted down beside Claud and looked at his leg. After a moment he pulled him up and Claud limped after him into the office.

121   Until the ambulance came, the only sounds in the room were the tremulous moans of the girl's mother, who continued to sit on the floor. The white-trash woman did not take her eyes off the girl. Mrs. Turpin looked straight ahead at nothing. Presently the ambulance drew up, a long dark shadow, behind the curtain. The attendants came in and set the stretcher down beside the girl and lifted her expertly onto it and carried her out. The nurse helped the mother gather up her things. The shadow of the ambulance moved silently away and the nurse came back in the office.

122   "That ther girl is going to be a lunatic, ain't she" the white-trash woman asked the nurse, but the nurse kept on to the back and never answered her.

123   "Yes, she's going to be a lunatic," the white-trash woman said to the rest of them.

124   "Po'critter," the old woman murmured. The child's face was still in her lap. His eyes looked idly out over her knees. He had not moved during the disturbance except to draw one leg up under him.

125   "I thank Gawd," the white-trash woman said fervently, "I ain't a lunatic."

126   Claud came limping out and the Turpins went home.

127   As their pick-up truck turned into their own dirt road and made the crest of the hill, Mrs. Turpin gripped the window ledge and looked out suspiciously.

NOTES

jovial (par. 116): jolly
tremulous (par. 121): trembling
a lunatic (par. 122): an insane person
Po'critter (par. 124): poor creature
fervently (par. 125): passionately

The land sloped gracefully down through a field dotted with lavender weeds and at the start of the rise their small yellow frame house with its little flower beds spread out around it like a fancy apron sat primly in its accustomed place between two giant hickory trees. She would not have been startled to see a burnt wound between two blackened chimneys.

128   Neither of them felt like eating so they put on their house clothes and lowered the shade in the bedroom and lay down, Claud with his leg on a pillow and herself with a damp washcloth over her eye. The instant she was flat on her back, the image of a razor-backed hog with warts on its face and horns coming out behind its ears snorted into her head. She moaned, a low quiet moan.

129   "I am not," she said tearfully, "a wart hog. From hell." But the denial had no force. The girl's eyes and her words, even the tone of her voice, low but clear, directed only to her, brooked no repudiation. She had been singled out for the message, though there was trash in the room to whom it might justly have been applied. The full force of this fact struck her only now. There was a woman there who was neglecting her own child but she had been overlooked. The message had been given to Ruby Turpin, a respectable, hard-working, church-going woman. The tears dried. Her eyes began to burn instead with wrath.

130   She rose on her elbow and the washcloth fell into her hand. Claud was lying on his back, snoring. She wanted to tell him what the girl had said. At the same time, she did not wish to put the image of herself as a wart hog from hell into his mind.

131   "Hey, Claud," she muttered and pushed his shoulder.

132   Claud opened one pale baby blue eye.

133   She looked into it warily. He did not think about anything. He just went his way.

134   "Wha, whasit?" he said and closed the eye again.

135   "Nothing," she said. "Does your leg pain you?"

136   "Hurts like hell," Claud said.

137   "It'll quit terreckly," she said and lay back down. In a moment Claud was snoring again. For the rest of the afternoon they lay there. Claud slept. She scowled at the ceiling. Occasionally she raised her fist and made a small stabbing motion over her chest as if she was defending her innocence to invisible guests who were like the comforters of Job, reasonable-seeming but wrong.

138   About five-thirty Claud stirred. "Got to go after those niggers," he sighed, not moving.

139   She was looking straight up as if there were unintelligible handwriting on the ceiling. The protuberance over her eye had turned a greenish-blue. "Listen here," she said.

NOTES

the rise (par. 127): the hill

primly (par. 127): neatly

brooked (par. 129): allowed

repudiation (par. 129): denial

wrath (par. 129): anger

warily (par. 133): cautiously

terreckly (par. 137): directly, soon

Job (par. 137): hero of the book of Job in the Old Testament: Job endures many hardships but keeps his faith in God.

handwriting on the ceiling (par. 139): In the Bible, Belshazzar's doom is foretold by mysterious handwriting that appears on the wall of his palace (Daniel 5).

protuberance (par. 139): lump

140   "What?"

141   "Kiss me."

142   Claud leaned over and kissed her loudly on the mouth. He pinched her side and their hands interlocked. Her expression of ferocious concentration did not change. Claud got up, groaning and growling, and limped off. She continued to study the ceiling.

143   She did not get up until she heard the pick-up truck coming back with the Negroes. Then she rose and thrust her feet in her brown oxfords, which she did not bother to lace, and stumped out onto the back porch and got her red plastic bucket. She emptied a tray of ice cubes into it and filled it half full of water and went out into the back yard. Every afternoon after Claud brought the hands in, one of the boys helped him put out hay and the rest waited in the back of the truck until he was ready to take them home. The truck was parked in the shade under one of the hickory trees.

144   "Hi yawl this morning?" Mrs. Turpin asked grimly, appearing with the bucket and the dipper. There were three woman and a boy in the truck.

145   "Us doin nicely," the oldest woman said. "Hi you doin?" and her gaze struck immediately on the dark lump on Mrs. Turpin's forehead. "You done fell down, ain't you?" she asked in a solicitous voice. The old woman was dark and almost toothless. She had on an old felt hat of Claud's set back on her head. The other two women were younger and lighter and they both had new bright green sunhats. One of them had hers on her head; the other had taken hers off and the boy was grinning beneath it.

146   Mrs. Turpin set the bucket down on the floor of the truck. "Yawl hep yourselves," she said. She looked around to make sure Claud had gone. "No, I didn't fall down," she said, folding her arms. "It was something worse than that."

147   "Ain't nothing bad happen to you!" the old woman said. She said it as if they all knew that Mrs. Turpin was protected in some special way by Divine Providence. "You just had you a little fall."

148   "We were in town at the doctor's office for where the cow kicked Mr. Turpin," Mrs. Turpin said in a flat tone that indicated they could leave off their foolishness. "And there was this girl there. A big fat girl with her face all broke out. I could look at that girl and tell she was peculiar but I couldn't tell how. And me and her mama was just talking and going along and all of a sudden WHAM! She throws this big book she was reading at me and . . ."

149   "Naw!" the old woman cried out.

150   "And then she jumps over the table and commences to choke me."

151   "Naw!" they all exclaimed, "naw!"

152   "Hi come she do that?" the old woman asked. "What ail her?"

153   Mrs. Turpin only glared in front of her.

154   "Somethin ail her," the old woman said.

155   "They carried her off in an ambulance," Mrs. Turpin continued, "but before she went she was rolling on the floor and they were trying to hold her down to give her a shot and she said something to me." She paused. "You know what she said to me?"

156   "What she say?" they asked.

NOTES
ferocious (par. 142): intense
grimly (par. 144): coldly
solicitous (par. 145): concerned
Divine Providence (par. 147): God
ail (par. 152): troubles

157   "She said," Mrs. Turpin began, and stopped, her face very dark and heavy. The sun was getting whiter and whiter, blanching the sky overhead so that the leaves of the hickory tree were black in the face of it. She could not bring forth the words. "Something real ugly," she muttered.

158   "She sho shouldn't said nothin ugly to you," the old woman said. "You so sweet. You the sweetest lady I know."

159   "She pretty too," the one with the hat on said.

160   "And stout," the other one said. "I never knowed no sweeter white lady."

161   "That's the truth befo' Jesus," the old woman said. "Amen! You des as sweet and pretty as you can be."

162   Mrs. Turpin knew exactly how much Negro flattery was worth and it added to her rage. "She said," she began again and finished this time with a fierce rush of breath, "that I was an old wart hog from hell."

163   There was an astounded silence.

164   "Where she at?" the youngest woman cried in a piercing voice.

165   "Lemme see her. I'll kill her!"

166   "I'll kill her with you!" the other one cried.

167   "She b'long in the sylum," the old woman said emphatically. "You the sweetest white lady I know."

168   "She pretty too," the other two said. "Stout as she can be and sweet. Jesus satisfied with her!"

169   "Deed he is," the old woman declared.

170   Idiots! Mrs. Turpin growled to herself. You could never say anything intelligent to a nigger. You could talk at them but not with them. "Yawl ain't drunk your water," she said shortly. "Leave the bucket in the truck when you're finished with it. I got more to do than just stand around and pass the time of day," and she moved off and into the house.

171   She stood for a moment in the middle of the kitchen. The dark protuberance over her eye looked like a miniature tornado cloud which might any moment sweep across the horizon of her brow. Her lower lip protruded dangerously. She squared her massive shoulders. Then she marched into the front of the house and out the side door and started down the road to the pig parlor. She had the look of a woman going single-handed, weaponless, into battle.

172   The sun was deep yellow now like a harvest moon and was riding westward very fast over the far tree line as if it meant to reach the hogs before she did. The road was rutted and she kicked several good-sized stones out of her path as she strode along. The pig parlor was on a little knoll at the end of a lane that ran off from the side of the barn. It was a square of concrete as large as a small room, with a board fence about four feet high around it. The concrete floor sloped slightly so that the hog wash could drain off into a trench where it was carried to the field for fertilizer. Claud was standing on the outside, on the edge of the concrete, hanging onto the top board, hosing down the floor inside. The hose was connected to the faucet of a water trough nearby.

173   Mrs. Turpin climbed up beside him and glowered down at the hogs inside. There were seven long-snouted bristly shoats in it—tan with liver-colored

NOTES

astounded (par. 163): shocked

sylum (par. 167): asylum, an institution for the care of the insane

emphatically (par. 167): forcefully

protruded (par. 171): stuck out

rutted (par. 172): contained ruts (tracks worn by wheels)

knoll (par. 172): a little hill

glowered (par. 173): stared angrily

shoats (par. 173): young hogs

spots—and an old sow a few weeks off from farrowing. She was lying on her side grunting. The shoats were running about shaking themselves like idiot children, their little slit pig eyes searching the floor for anything left. She had read that pigs were the most intelligent animal. She doubted it. They were supposed to be smarter than dogs. There had even been a pig astronaut. He had performed his assignment perfectly but died of a heart attack afterwards because they left him in his electric suit, sitting upright throughout his examination when naturally a hog should be on all fours.

174   A-gruntin and a-rooting and a-groanin.

175   "Gimme that hose," she said, yanking it away from Claud. "Go on and carry them niggers home and then get off that leg."

176   "You look like you might have swallowed a mad dog," Claud observed, but he got down and limped off. He paid no attention to her humors.

177   Until he was out of earshot, Mrs. Turpin stood on the side of the pen, holding the hose and pointing the stream of water at the hind quarters of any shoat that looked as if it might try to lie down. When he had had time to get over the hill, she turned her head slightly and her wrathful eyes scanned the path. He was nowhere in sight. She turned back again and seemed to gather herself up. Her shoulders rose and she drew in her breath.

178   "What do you send a message like that for?" she said in a low fierce voice, barely above a whisper but with the force of a shout in its concentrated fury. "How am I a hog and me both? How am I saved and from hell too?" Her free fist was knotted and with the other she gripped the hose, blindly pointing the stream of water in and out of the eye of the old sow whose outraged squeal she did not hear.

179   The pig parlor commanded a view of the back pasture where their twenty beef cows were gathered around the hay-bales Claud and the boy had put out. The freshly cut pasture sloped down to the highway. Across it was their cotton field and beyond that a dark green dusty wood which they owned as well. The sun was behind the wood, very red, looking over the paling of the trees like a farmer inspecting his own hogs.

180   "Why me?" she rumbled. "It's no trash around here, black or white, that I haven't given to. And break my back to the bone every day working. And do for the church."

181   She appeared to be the right size woman to command the arena before her. "How am I a hog?" she demanded. "Exactly how am I like them?" and she jabbed the stream of water at the shoats. "There was plenty of trash there. It didn't have to be me,"

182   "If you like trash better, go get yourself some trash then," she railed. "You could have made me trash. Or a nigger. If trash is what you wanted why didn't you make me trash?" She shook her fist with the hose in it and a watery snake appeared momentarily in the air. "I could quit working and take it easy and be filthy," she growled. "Lounge about the sidewalks all day drinking root beer. Dip snuff and spit in every puddle and have it all over my face. I could be nasty.

183   "Or you could have made me a nigger. It's too late for me to be a nigger," she said with deep sarcasm, "but I could act like one. Lay down in the middle of the road and stop traffic. Roll on the ground."

NOTES
farrowing (par. 173): giving birth
mad (par. 176): rabid
humors (par. 176): moods
railed (par. 182): said angrily

184   In the deepening light everything was taking on a mysterious hue. The pasture was growing a peculiar glassy green and the streak of highway had turned lavender. She braced herself for a final assault and this time her voice rolled out over the pasture. "Go on," she yelled, "call me a hog! Call me a hog again. From hell. Call me a wart hog from hell. Put that bottom rail on top. There'll still be a top and bottom!"

185   A garbled echo returned to her.

186   A final surge of fury shook her and she roared, "Who do you think you are?"

187   The color of everything, field and crimson sky, burned for a moment with a transparent intensity. The question carried over the pasture and across the highway and the cotton field and returned to her clearly like an answer from beyond the wood.

188   She opened her mouth but no sound came out of it.

189   A tiny truck, Claud's, appeared on the highway, heading rapidly out of sight. Its gears scraped thinly. It looked like a child's toy. At any moment a bigger truck might smash into it and scatter Claud's and the niggers' brains all over the road.

190   Mrs. Turpin stood there, her gaze fixed on the highway, all her muscles rigid, until in five or six minutes the truck reappeared, returning. She waited until it had had time to turn into their own road. Then like a monumental statue coming to life, she bent her head slowly and gazed, as if through the very heart of mystery, down into the pig parlor at the hogs. They had settled all in one corner around the old sow who was grunting softly. A red glow suffused them. They appeared to pant with a secret life.

191   Until the sun slipped finally behind the tree line, Mrs. Turpin remained there with her gaze bent to them as if she were absorbing some abysmal life-giving knowledge. At last she lifted her head. There was only a purple streak in the sky, cutting through a field of crimson and leading, like an extension of the highway, into the descending dusk. She raised her hands from the side of the pen in a gesture hieratic and profound. A visionary light settled in her eyes. She saw the streak as a vast swinging bridge extending upward from the earth through a field of living fire. Upon it a vast horde of souls were rumbling toward heaven. There were whole companies of white-trash, clean for the first time in their lives, and bands of black niggers in white robes, and battalions of freaks and lunatics shouting and clapping and leaping like frogs. And bringing up the end of the procession was a tribe of people whom she recognized at once as those who, like herself and Claud, had always had a little of everything and the God-given wit to use it right. She leaned forward to observe them closer. They were marching behind the others with great dignity, accountable as they had always been for good order and common sense

NOTES

hue (par. 184): color
garbled (par. 185): confused, jumbled
transparent (par. 187): obvious
mystery (par. 190): A religious truth that can only be known if revealed by God to humans.
suffused (par. 190): spread over
abysmal (par. 191): deep
hieratic (par. 191): priestly
visionary light (par. 191): the light associated with having a vision (a supernatural appearance that reveals a truth)
horde (par. 191): crowd
battalions (par. 191): armies, large groups

and respectable behavior. They alone were on key. Yet she could see by their shocked and altered faces that even their virtues were being burned away. She lowered her hands and gripped the rail of the hog pen, her eyes small but fixed unblinkingly on what lay ahead. In a moment the vision faded but she remained where she was, immobile.

192   At length she got down and turned off the faucet and made her slow way on the darkening path to the house. In the woods around her the invisible cricket choruses had struck up, but what she heard were the voices of the souls climbing upward into the starry field and shouting hallelujah.

NOTES
altered (par. 191): changed
virtues (par. 191): merits, praiseworthy qualities
hallelujah (par. 192): Hebrew for "praise the Lord"

The Chrysanthemums

John Steinbeck

1   The high grey-flannel fog of winter closed off the Salinas Valley from the sky and from all the rest of the world. On every side it sat like a lid on the mountains and made of the great valley a closed pot. On the broad, level land floor the gang plows bit deep and left the black earth shining like metal where the shares had cut. On the foothill ranches across the Salinas River, the yellow stubble fields seemed to be bathed in pale cold sunshine, but there was no sunshine in the valley now in December. The thick willow scrub along the river flamed with sharp and positive yellow leaves.

2   It was a time of quiet and of waiting. The air was cold and tender. A light wind blew up from the southwest so that the farmers were mildly hopeful of a good rain before long; but fog and rain do not go together.

3   Across the river, on Henry Allen's foothill ranch there was little work to be done, for the hay was cut and stored and the orchards were plowed up to receive the rain deeply when it should come. The cattle on the higher slopes were becoming shaggy and rough-coated.

4   Elisa Allen, working in her flower garden, looked down across the yard and saw Henry, her husband, talking to two men in business suits. The three of them stood by the tractor shed, each man with one foot on the side of the little Fordson. They smoked cigarettes and studied the machine as they talked.

5   Elisa watched them for a moment and then went back to her work. She was thirty-five. Her face was lean and strong and her eyes were as clear as water. Her figure looked blocked and heavy in her gardening costume, a man's black hat pulled low down over her eyes, clodhopper shoes, a figured print dress almost completely covered by a big corduroy apron with four big pockets to hold the snips, the trowel and scratcher, the seeds and the knife she

NOTES
gang plows (par. 1): plows that turn more than one furrow (row) at a time
scrub (par. 1): underdeveloped shrubs and trees
clodhopper shoes (par. 5): large work shoes
snips, trowel, scratcher (par. 5): gardening tools

worked with. She wore heavy leather gloves to protect her hands while she worked.

6   She was cutting down the old year's chrysanthemum stalks with a pair of short and powerful scissors. She looked down toward the men by the tractor shed now and then. He face was eager and mature and handsome; even her work with the scissors was over-eager, over-powerful. The chrysanthemum stems seemed too small and easy for her energy.

7   She brushed a cloud of hair out of her eyes with the back of her glove, and left a smudge of earth on the cheek in doing it. Behind her stood the neat white farm house with red geraniums close-banked around it as high as the windows. It was a hard-swept looking little house, with hard-polished windows, and a clean mud-mat on the front steps.

8   Elisa cast another glance toward the tractor shed. The strangers were getting into their Ford coupe. She took off a glove and put her strong fingers down into the forest of new green chrysanthemum sprouts that were growing around the old roots. She spread the leaves and looked down among the close-growing stems. No aphids were there, no sowbugs or snails or cutworms. Her terrier fingers destroyed such pests before they could get started.

9   Elisa started at the sound of her husband's voice. He had come near quietly, and he leaned over the wire fence that protected her flower garden from cattle and dogs and chickens.

10   "At it again," he said. "You've got a strong new crop coming."

11   Elisa straightened her back and pulled on the gardening glove again. "Yes. They'll be strong this coming year." In her tone and on her face there was a little smugness.

12   "You've got a gift with things," Henry observed. "Some of those yellow chrysanthemums you had this year were ten inches across. I wish you'd work out in the orchard and raise some apples that big."

13   Her eyes sharpened. "Maybe I could do it, too. I've a gift with things, all right. My mother had it. She could stick anything in the ground and make it grow. She said it was having planters' hands that knew how to do it."

14   "Well, it sure works with flowers," he said.

15   "Henry, who were those men you were talking to?"

16   "Why, sure, that's what I came to tell you. They were from the Western Meat Company. I sold those thirty head of three-year-old steers. Got nearly my own price, too."

17   "Good," she said. "Good for you."

18   "And I thought," he continued, "I thought how it's Saturday afternoon, and we might go to Salinas for dinner at a restaurant, and then to a picture show—to celebrate, you see."

19   "Good," she repeated. "Oh, yes. That will be good."

20   Henry put on his joking tone. "There's fights tonight. How'd you like to go to the fights?"

21   "Oh, no," she said breathlessly. "No, I wouldn't like fights."

22   "Just fooling, Elisa. We'll go to a movie. Let's see. It's two now. I'm going to take Scotty and bring down those steers from the hill. It'll take us maybe two hours. We'll go in town about five and have dinner at the Cominos Hotel. Like that?"

NOTES

coupe (par. 8): a two-door automobile
aphids, sowbugs, snails, cutworms (par. 8): garden pests
terrier fingers (par. 8): fingers that work like a terrier's claws; a terrier is known for its digging ability.
smugness (par. 11): self-satisfaction

23   "Of course, I'll like it. It's good to eat away from home."

24   "All right, then. I'll go get up a couple of horses."

25   She said, "I'll have plenty of time to transplant some of these sets, I guess."

26   She heard her husband calling Scotty down by the barn. And a little later she saw the two men ride up the pale yellow hillside in search of the steers.

27   There was a little square sandy bed kept for rooting the chrysanthemums. With her trowel she turned the soil over and over, and smoothed it and patted it firm. Then she dug ten parallel trenches to receive the sets. Back at the chrysanthemum bed she pulled out the little crisp shoots, trimmed off the leaves of each one with her scissors and laid it on a small orderly pile.

28   A squeak of wheels and plod of hoofs came from the road. Elisa looked up. The country road ran along the dense bank of willows and cottonwoods that bordered the river, and up this road came a curious vehicle, curiously drawn. It was an old spring-wagon, with a round canvas top on it like the cover of a prairie schooner. It was drawn by an old bay horse and a little grey-and-white burro. A big stubble-bearded man sat between the cover flaps and drove the crawling team. Underneath the wagon, between the hind wheels, a lean and rangy mongrel dog walked sedately. Words were painted on the canvas in clumsy, crooked letters. "Pots, pans, knives, sisors, lawn mores. Fixed." Two rows of articles and the triumphantly definitive "Fixed" below. The black paint had run down in little sharp points beneath each letter.

29   Elisa, squatting on the ground, watched to see the crazy, loose-jointed wagon pass by. But it didn't pass. It turned into the farm road in front of her house, crooked old wheels skirling and squeaking. The rangy dog darted from between the wheels and ran ahead. Instantly the two ranch shepherds flew out at him. Then all three stopped, and with stiff and quivering tails, with taut straight legs, with ambassadorial dignity, they slowly circled, sniffing daintily. The caravan pulled up to Elisa's wire fence and stopped. Now the newcomer dog, feeling outnumbered, lowered his tail and retired under the wagon with raised hackles and bared teeth.

30   The man on the wagon seat called out. "That's a bad dog in a fight when he gets started."

31   Elisa laughed. "I see he is. How soon does he generally get started?"

32   The man caught up her laughter and echoed it heartily. "Sometimes not for weeks and weeks," he said. He climbed stiffly down, over the wheel. The horse and the donkey drooped like unwatered flowers.

33   Elisa saw that he was a very big man. Although his hair and beard were greying, he did not look old. His worn black suit was wrinkled and spotted with grease. The laughter had disappeared from his face and eyes the moment his laughing voice ceased. His eyes were dark and they were full of the brooding that gets in the eyes of teamsters and of sailors. The calloused hands he

NOTES

spring-wagon (par. 28): a farm wagon equipped with springs
prairie schooner (par. 28): a covered wagon
rangy (par. 28): long-limbed
mongrel dog (par. 28): a mutt
sedately (par. 28): calmly
skirling (par. 29): squealing
quivering (par. 29): trembling
taut (par. 29): tight
caravan (par. 29): a travelling group
hackles (par. 29): hair on the neck and back of a dog
brooding (par. 33): serious
teamsters (par. 33): people who drive teams or trucks as an occupation

rested on the wire fence were cracked, and every crack was a black line. He took off his battered hat.

34   "I'm off my general road, ma'am," he said. "Does this dirt road cut over across the river to the Los Angeles highway?"

35   Elisa stood up and shoved the thick scissors in her apron pocket. "Well, yes, it does, but it winds around and then fords the river. I don't think your team could pull through the sand."

36   He replied with some asperity, "It might surprise you what them beasts can pull through."

37   "When they get started?" she asked.

38   He smiled for a second. "Yes. When they get started."

39   "Well," said Elisa, "I think you'll save time if you go back to the Salinas road and pick up the highway there."

40   He drew a big finger down the chicken wire and made it sing. "I ain't in any hurry, ma'am. I go from Seattle to San Diego and back every year. Takes all my time. About six months each way. I aim to follow nice weather."

41   Elisa took off her gloves and stuffed them in the apron pocket with the scissors. She touched the under edge of her man's hat, searching for fugitive hairs. "That sounds like a nice kind of a way to live," she said.

42   He leaned confidentially over the fence. "Maybe you noticed the writing on my wagon. I mend pots and sharpen knives and scissors. You got any of them things to do?"

43   "Oh, no," she said quickly. "Nothing like that." Her eyes hardened with resistance.

44   "Scissors is the worst thing," he explained. "Most people just ruin scissors trying to sharpen 'em, but I know how. I got a special tool. It's a little bobbit kind of thing, and patented. But it sure does the trick."

45   "No. My scissors are all sharp."

46   "All right, then. Take a pot," he continued earnestly, "a bent pot, or a pot with a hole. I can make it like new so you don't have to buy no new ones. That's a saving for you."

47   "No," she said shortly. "I tell you I have nothing like that for you to do."

48   His face fell to an exaggerated sadness. His voice took on a whining undertone. "I ain't had a thing to do today. Maybe I won't have no supper tonight. You see I'm off my regular road. I know folks on the highway clear from Seattle to San Diego. They save their things for me to sharpen up because they know I do it so good and save them money."

49   "I'm sorry," Elisa said irritably. "I haven't anything for you to do."

50   His eyes left her face and fell to searching the ground. They roamed about until they came to the chrysanthemum bed where she had been working. "What's them plants, ma'am?"

51   The irritation and resistance melted from Elisa's face. "Oh, those are chrysanthemums, giant whites and yellows. I raise them every year, bigger than anybody around here."

52   "Kind of a long-stemmed flower? Looks like a quick puff of colored smoke?" he asked.

53   "That's it. What a nice way to describe them."

54   "They smell kind of nasty till you get used to them," he said.

55   "It's a good bitter smell," she retorted, "not nasty at all."

56   He changed his tone quickly. "I like the smell myself."

NOTES

fords (par. 35): crosses
asperity (par. 36): harshness

57   "I had ten-inch blooms this year," she said.

58   The man leaned farther over the fence. "Look. I know a lady down the road a piece, has got the nicest garden you ever seen. Got nearly every kind of flower but no chrysanthemums. Last time I was mending a copper-bottom washtub for her (that's a hard job but I do it good), she said to me, 'If you ever run acrost some nice chrysanthemums I wish you'd try to get me a few seeds.' That's what she told me."

59   Elisa's eyes grew alert and eager. "She couldn't have known much about chrysanthemums. You can raise them from seed, but it's much easier to root the little sprouts you see there."

60   "Oh," he said. "I s'pose I can't take none to her, then."

61   "Why yes you can," Elisa cried. "I can put some in damp sand, and you can carry them right along with you. They'll take root in the pot if you keep them damp. And then she can transplant them."

62   "She'd sure like to have some, ma'am. You say they're nice ones?"

63   "Beautiful," she said. "Oh, beautiful." Her eyes shone. She tore off the battered hat and shook out her dark pretty hair. "I'll put them in a flower pot, and you can take them right with you. Come into the yard."

64   While the man came through the picket gate Elisa ran excitedly along the geranium-bordered path to the back of the house. And she returned carrying a big red flower pot. The gloves were forgotten now. She kneeled on the ground by the starting bed and dug up the sandy soil with her fingers and scooped it into the bright new flower pot. Then she picked up the little pile of shoots she had prepared. With her strong fingers she pressed them into the sand and tamped around them with her knuckles. The man stood over her. "I'll tell you what to do," she said. "You remember so you can tell the lady."

65   "Yes, I'll try to remember."

66   "Well, look. These will take root in about a month. Then she must set them out, about a foot apart in good rich earth like this, see?" She lifted a handful of dark soil for him to look at. "They'll grow fast and tall. Now remember this. In July tell her to cut them down, about eight inches from the ground."

67   "Before they bloom?" he asked.

68   "Yes, before they bloom." Her face was tight with eagerness. "They'll grow right up again. About the last of September the buds will start."

69   She stopped and seemed perplexed. "It's the budding that takes the most care," she said hesitantly. "I don't know how to tell you." She looked deep into his eyes, searchingly. Her mouth opened a little, and she seemed to be listening. "I'll try to tell you," she said. "Did you ever hear of planting hands?"

70   "Can't say I have, ma'am."

71   "Well, I can only tell you what it feels like. It's when you're picking off the buds you don't want. Everything goes right down into your fingertips. You watch your fingers work. They do it themselves. You can feel how it is. They pick and pick the buds. They never make a mistake. They're with the plant. Do you see? Your fingers and the plant. You can feel that, right up your arm. They know. They never make a mistake. You can feel it. When you're like that you can't do anything wrong. Do you see that? Can you understand that?"

72   She was kneeling on the ground looking up at him. Her breast swelled passionately.

73   The man's eyes narrowed. He looked away self-consciously. "Maybe I know," he said. "Sometimes in the night in the wagon there—"

74   Elisa's voice grew husky. She broke in on him. "I've never lived as you do, but I know what you mean. When the night is dark—why, the stars are sharp-pointed, and there's a quiet. Why, you rise up and up! Every pointed star gets driven into your body. It's like that. Hot and sharp and—lovely."

75   Kneeling there, her hand went out toward his legs in the greasy black trousers. Her hesitant fingers almost touched the cloth. Then her hand dropped to the ground. She crouched low like a fawning dog.

76   He said, "It's nice, just like you say. Only when you don't have no dinner, it ain't."

77   She stood up then, very straight, and her face was ashamed. She held the flower pot out to him and placed it gently in his arms. "Here. Put it in your wagon, on the seat, where you can watch it. Maybe I can find something for you to do."

78   At the back of the house she dug in the can pile and found two old and battered aluminum saucepans. She carried them back and gave them to him. "Here, maybe you can fix these."

79   His manner changed. He became professional. "Good as new I can fix them." At the back of his wagon he set a little anvil, and out of an oily tool box dug a small machine hammer. Elisa came through the gate to watch him while he pounded out the dents in the kettles. His mouth grew sure and knowing. At a difficult part of the work he sucked his under-lip.

80   "You sleep right in the wagon?" Elisa asked.

81   "Right in the wagon, ma'am. Rain or shine I'm dry as a cow in there."

82   "It must be nice," she said. "It must be very nice. I wish women could do such things."

83   "It ain't the right kind of a life for a woman."

84   Her upper lip raised a little, showing her teeth. "How do you know? How can you tell?" she said.

85   "I don't know ma'am," he protested. "Of course I don't know. Now here's your kettles, done. You don't have to buy no new ones."

86   "How much?"

87   "Oh, fifty cents'll do. I keep my prices down and my work good. That's why I have all them satisfied customers up and down the highway."

88   Elisa brought him a fifty-cent piece from the house and dropped it in his hand. "You might be surprised to have a rival some time. I can sharpen scissors, too. And I can beat the dents out of little pots. I could show you what a woman might do."

89   He put his hammer back in the oily box and shoved the little anvil out of sight. "It would be a lonely life for a woman, ma'am, and a scarey life, too, with animals creeping under the wagon all night." He climbed over the single-tree, steadying himself with a hand on the burro's white rump. He settled himself in the seat, picked up the lines. "Thank you kindly, ma'am," he said. "I'll do like you told me; I'll go back and catch the Salinas road."

90   "Mind," she called, "if you're long in getting there, keep the sand damp."

91   "Sand, ma'am? . . . Sand? Oh, sure. You mean round the chrysanthemums. Sure I will." He clucked his tongue. The beasts leaned luxuriously into their collars. The mongrel dog took his place between the back wheels. The wagon turned and crawled out the entrance road and back the way it had come, along the river.

92   Elisa stood in front of her wire fence watching the slow progress of the caravan. Her shoulders were straight, her head thrown back, her eyes half-closed, so that the scene came vaguely into them. Her lips moved silently forming the words "Good-bye—good-bye." Then she whispered, "That's a bright direction. There's a glowing there." The sound of her whisper startled her. She shook herself free and looked about to see whether anyone had been

NOTE
fawning (par. 75): timid

listening. Only the dogs had heard. They lifted their heads toward her from their sleeping in the dust, and then stretched out their chins and settled asleep again. Elisa turned and ran hurriedly into the house.

93   In the kitchen she reached behind the stove and felt the water tank. It was full of hot water from the noonday cooking. In the bathroom she tore off her soiled clothes and flung them into the corner. And then she scrubbed herself with a little block of pumice, legs and thighs, loins and chest and arms, until her skin was scratched and red. When she had dried herself she stood in front of a mirror in her bedroom and looked at her body. She tightened her stomach and threw out her chest. She turned and looked over her shoulder at her back.

94   After a while she began to dress, slowly. She put on her newest under-clothing and her nicest stockings and the dress which was the symbol of her prettiness. She worked carefully on her hair, pencilled her eyebrows and rouged her lips.

95   Before she was finished she heard the little thunder of hoofs and the shouts of Henry and his helper as they drove the red steers into the corral. She heard the gate bang shut and set herself for Henry's arrival.

96   His steps sounded on the porch. He entered the house calling "Elisa, where are you?"

97   "In my room, dressing. I'm not ready. There's hot water for your bath. Hurry up. It's getting late."

98   When she heard him splashing in the tub, Elisa laid his dark suit on the bed, and shirt and socks and tie beside it. She stood his polished shoes on the floor beside the bed. Then she went to the porch and sat primly and stiffly down. She looked toward the river road where the willow-line was still yellow with frosted leaves so that under the high grey fog they seemed a thin band of sunshine. This was the only color in the grey afternoon. She sat unmoving for a long time. Her eyes blinked rarely.

99   Henry came banging out of the door, shoving his tie inside his vest as he came. Elisa stiffened and her face grew tight. Henry stopped short and looked at her. "Why—why, Elisa. You look so nice!"

100   "Nice? You think I look nice? What do you mean by 'nice'?"

101   Henry blundered on. "I don't know. I mean you look different, strong and happy."

102   "I am strong? Yes, strong. What do you mean 'strong'?"

103   He looked bewildered. "You're playing some kind of a game," he said helplessly. "It's a kind of a play. You look strong enough to break a calf over your knee, happy enough to eat it like watermelon."

104   For a second she lost her rigidity. "Henry! Don't talk like that. You didn't know what you said." She grew complete again. "I'm strong," she boasted. "I never knew before how strong."

105   Henry looked down toward the tractor shed, and when he brought his eyes back to her, they were his own again. "I'll get out the car. You can put on your coat while I'm starting."

106   Elisa went into the house. She heard him drive to the gate and idle down his motor, and then she took a long time to put on her hat. She pulled it here and pressed it there. When Henry turned the motor off she slipped into her coat and went out.

NOTES
pumice (par. 93): a rough, light-weight stone
rouged (par. 94): reddened
bewildered (par. 103): confused

107   The little roadster bounced along on the dirt road by the river, raising the birds and driving the rabbits into the brush. Two cranes flapped heavily over the willow-line and dropped into the riverbed.

108   Far ahead on the road Elisa saw a dark speck. She knew.

109   She tried not to look as they passed it, but her eyes would not obey. She whispered to herself sadly. "He might have thrown them off the road. That wouldn't have been much trouble, not very much. But he kept the pot," she explained. "He had to keep the pot. That's why he couldn't get them off the road."

110   The roadster turned a bend and she saw the caravan ahead. She swung full around toward her husband so she could not see the little covered wagon and the mismatched team as the car passed them.

111   In a moment it was over. The thing was done. She did not look back. She said loudly, to be heard above the motor, "It will be good, tonight, a good dinner."

112   "Now you're changed again," Henry complained. He took one hand from the wheel and patted her knee. "I ought to take you in to dinner oftener. It would be good for both of us. We get so heavy out on the ranch."

113   "Henry," she asked, "could we have wine at dinner?"

114   "Sure we could. Say! That will be fine."

115   She was silent for a little while; then she said, "Henry, at those prize fights, do the men hurt each other very much?"

116   "Sometimes a little, not often. Why?"

117   "Well, I've read how they break noses, and blood runs down their chests. I've read how the fighting gloves get heavy and soggy with blood."

118   He looked around at her. "What's the matter, Elisa? I didn't know you read things like that." He brought the car to a stop then turned to the right over the Salinas River bridge.

119   "Do any women ever go to the fights?" she asked.

120   "Oh, sure, some. What's the matter, Elisa? Do you want to go? I don't think you'd like it, but I'll take you if you really want to go."

121   She relaxed limply in the seat. "Oh, no. No. I don't want to go. I'm sure I don't." Her face was turned away from him. "It will be enough if we can have wine. It will be plenty." She turned up her coat collar so he could not see that she was crying weakly—like an old woman.

Smeltertown

Carlos Nicolás Flores

I

1   "Your mother says we won't be able to have the *carne asada*."

2   "Why not?"

3   "Your mother had a fight with your sister. Your brothers have gone out with their friends. Your father may not be back until late."

4   Américo laid the razor on the washbasin's rim, then lowered the toilet seat and sat down.

5   "I told you there would be no point in having a *carne asada* with my people," he said.

NOTE
carne asada (par. 1): barbecue

6   Jovita's gaze fell. The *carne asada* had been her idea, a family cookout like those they had enjoyed so often at home with her family.

7   "*Ni modo*," she said, resting her sad face against the doorjamb.

8   Américo pulled his socks from out of his cowboy boots, crossed his legs, and dusted off the bottom of his foot. He was not accustomed to boots, but he wore them to please Jovita, who had grown up close to the ranch life of South Texas. She enjoyed seeing him dress like the men from Escandon. He did not particularly like the boots although the riding heels did give him a bit of height, and illusion of stature, and another illusion—that he belonged with Jovita, with her relatives, and with the other Mexicans in Escandon who had looked upon him as an outsider. He slipped on his socks, put on his boots, and looked up at Jovita.

9   "What do you want to do?" he asked.

10   "We could go eat in Júarez."

11   "Too much traffic on the bridge. Remember, it's Sunday. Besides, I don't want to touch another drink."

12   "What about a movie?"

13   "*Chula*," he said, wanting to reach for her and hold her tenderly so he wouldn't hurt her, "I didn't drive six hundred miles to El Paso just to see a movie. Maybe we could go for a ride."

14   "But where?"

15   "Anywhere," he said.

16   They were silent for a moment. Américo thought about the lake. He decided against it when he remembered its muddy waters and gangs of shirtless Mexican men, beer cans in hand. Then he thought about a ride out to his father's acreage down the valley. No, he didn't want to go there either, having been there with his father several times, politely listening to his impractical dream about how one day the whole family might move there, build their homes, and live happily ever after. Instead, the image of a cross atop a peak popped into Américo's mind.

17   "How about Smeltertown?" he said.

18   "Smeltertown? What's that? An oil refinery?"

19   Américo laughed.

20   "No, *mijita*," he said. "It's where my mother was born. A little Mexican village upriver."

21   "Is it the place you pointed out when we were coming back from New Mexico on our honeymoon?"

22   "Did I?"

23   "Don't you remember, Américo? It was the first time you brought me to El Paso to meet your parents. We drove up to New Mexico and got stuck in the snow."

24   "I didn't get stuck. The car just skidded all over the place, that's all."

25   "Well, whatever. When we drove back, you said, 'Look that's where my mother was born,' and then we went to eat at that restaurant nearby."

26   "La Hacienda."

27   "Yes."

28   "Would you like to eat there again?"

29   "Great."

NOTES

Ni modo (par. 7): You can talk.
illusion (par. 8): appearance
stature (par. 8): height
Chula (par. 13): pretty one
mijita (par. 20): my little one

30   Américo loved to see Jovita happy, the way her smile revealed a sparkling set of white teeth, the girlish delight in her dark eyes. Though she was twenty-two years old, she looked eighteen and was, to his continuing astonishment, one of the most beautiful women he had ever seen. He felt better now that the *carne asada* was no longer an issue.

31   Américo got up and kissed her cheek.

32   "I'll be ready in a minute," he said, stepping to the washbasin.

33   "Maybe we should stay and talk to your mother before we go."

34   Américo had forgotten.

35   "Yes," he said. It was unconvincing.

36   "It's our last day here," she said. "I don't want to offend her by taking off like the rest of your family."

37   "You're right, *chula*," he said.

38   "I'll be in the kitchen."

39   Américo turned to the mirror and saw a Mexican face the color and shape of a chunk of adobe, his black hair unmanageably aflame. With his fingers he spread the aerosol spurt of white cream against the *tierra-cafe* of his skin. As he shaved, he decided that their three-day visit to El Paso had not been as unpleasant as others in the past. Still he knew that if Jovita had not insisted upon these yearly visits from the beginning of their marriage, he would never have set foot in El Paso again. He cleared the lather, rinsed the razor and his hands, and put the shaving things away. After combing his hair, he slipped on his gold-rimmed, green-tinted glasses. Dressed in dark blue pants and a white *guayabera* embroidered with blue and black pyramids, Américo prepared himself to face his mother in the kitchen.

40   "Look how handsome my son looks!"

41   "Good morning," he said.

42   "Good morning?" responded Señora Izquierdo. "You mean good afternoon."

43   "What time is it?"

44   "There's a clock on the wall."

45   It was already past 1:00 PM.

46   "Señora," said Américo, inhaling self-consciously, "I'm on vacation. It's Sunday." Américo never said "Mom."

47   "At home," Jovita said, her eyes gliding on a smile from Américo to his mother, "he never gets up earlier than twelve on weekends."

48   "You don't go to church on Sunday?" asked Señora Izquierdo. Her eyes widened with feigned shock at what she had always known to be Américo's indifference towards church. She attended when she could, by herself.

49   Américo rolled his eyes.

50   "Too much of this," said Señora Izquierdo, cocking her hand so that her thumb almost touched her lips and her pinky stuck out like an upended bottle.

51   "Nonsense," said Américo. He smiled. "It's just that Jovita never lets me out of bed in the morning."

52   "You lie, Américo," said Jovita, embarrassed.

53   "It's true, Señora," he said. "What else can a man who wakes up with a beautiful woman do except stay in bed?"

NOTES

adobe (par. 39): clay
tierra-cafe (par. 39): dark brown
guayabera (par. 39): shirt
feigned (par. 48): pretended

54   "Américo, *te sales*," said Jovita, ready to spring at him and put her hand over his mouth.

55   "Jovita, why are you so mean with my son?" said Señora Izquierdo, chuckling. "Why don't you let him out of bed in the morning?"

56   Señora, it's your son," said Jovita. "The Izquierdo men are terrible."

57   Señora Izquierdo blinked. "You can say that again." She addressed Jovita. "Jesus Christ, my husband was worse than a bull. Puerto Rican men are like that."

58   "Is there any coffee?" asked Américo.

59   Señora Izquierdo's face changed "*Sí, mijito*," she said, bundling toward the stove. "Do you want any breakfast?"

60   "No thanks," said Américo.

61   He took a chair at the table next to Jovita, who yanked lightly at his hair. Smiling, he pushed her gently away. As his mother poured the coffee into the cup, it steamed. Señora Izquierdo returned the coffeepot to the stove, walked to her place by the kitchen sink, and began peeling potatoes. She had been a maid before she married. Her short, pudgy body was at home in cheap cotton dresses and flat sandals. Her fingers were stubby from housework.

62   "*Bueno*," she said, talking seriously now, though with a mischievous sideways grin, her eyes upon the blade sliding beneath the potato's skin, "since both of you have such a difficult time getting out of bed, when, I would like to know, are you going to give me"—she looked up—"a grandson?"

63   "First, we need to buy a house," said Américo. "We want to travel too, maybe Europe."

64   "Naw," said Señora Izquierdo irritably, "that'll take too long. I may die before I see my first grandson."

65   "You're not that old, Señora," said Américo.

66   "You never know."

67   "Tonight," said Jovita.

68   Américo looked at Jovita with a what-are-you-talking-about frown.

69   "That's better," said Señora Izquierdo. "Did you hear that, Américo?"

70   "Well," Américo said, an earnest tone in his voice now, "we have been thinking about a child. We just don't know when or how soon."

71   "It'll be a surprise," said Jovita.

72   "Can you imagine that?" Señora Izquierdo paused, her eyes filled with sights of the future. "A little Américo walking around. A house without children has no *chiste*."

73   Américo took out a cigarette. When he looked around for a place to dump the match, his mother found an ashtray hidden in one of the kitchen cabinets. White-edged streams of smoke filled the bright kitchen. Américo knew what she thought about his smoking, but he couldn't put off the cigarette much longer. Besides, his father wasn't home.

74   "You and Jovita are going to eat here, no?" asked Señora Izquierdo, her eyes on Américo.

75   "We are going out to dinner," said Américo.

76   "Oooooooo!" Señora Izquierdo stopped peeling potatoes.

77   "I want to take Jovita to see Smeltertown."

78   Señora Izquierdo's face registered dismay.

NOTES

te sales (par. 54): You should be ashamed of yourself.
Bueno (par. 62): good
chiste (par. 72): life
registered dismay (par. 78): showed concern

79   "Smeltertown? What are you going to do in Smeltertown? There is nothing there."

80   "Américo wants to show me where you were born," Jovita said.

81   Señora Izquierdo's eyes flared at Américo.

82   "Américo," she demanded, one arm akimbo, "when was I born in Smeltertown?"

83   "I meant to say that you were raised there," Américo apologized.

84   "Your father put that idea in your head," she said. "He thinks I was born in Mexico. No, señor—I know where I was born. It was not in Mexico. It was not Smeltertown. I was born in Williams, Arizona."

85   No one in the family knew anything about Williams, Arizona, not even his mother, as far as Américo could tell, but Señora Izquierdo had always made it a point to say that she had been born there. Not El Paso, not Cd. Juárez across the river where most of her surviving family lived in a three-room adobe hovel. Not Smeltertown where she had been raised from early childhood by *la abuela* and Tía Rosaura.

86   "*Ay qué* Américo," sighed Señora Izquierdo, "you don't even know where your mother was born." Her eyes flashed upon him again. "Do you know who your mother is?"

87   "No, I don't," he said. He loved the banter. It brought him close to his mother.

88   "Américo!" Her black hair shook in every direction, then settled around her bright eyes. "I'm your mother."

89   Jovita laughed. "Are you sure, Señora Izquierdo?" she said.

90   "What?" Señora Izquierdo's eyes flashed at Jovita. A smile glimmered. "I know my children like the palm of my hand. I should. I cleaned them enough times with it."

91   Américo grinned and shook his head.

92   "I can prove I'm from Williams, Arizona," insisted Señora Izquierdo. "It's your father I worry about. He's such a liar I wonder sometimes if he's really where he says he's from."

93   But Américo knew better. Señor Izquierdo was not born in El Paso either. He was from Puerto Rico, a potato-shaped island in the Caribbean sea. Américo had visited it once in a disappointing attempt to find out more about the old man. Señor Izquierdo hated El Paso, an empty desert surrounded by arid mountains, so unlike the lush green of Puerto Rico, *la perla del Caribe*. He sometimes talked of abandoning his family and returning to his *Borinquen querido*. In that threat and others, he reminded them that he was no Mexican.

94   They heard a car in the carport. Its engine died abruptly, and someone got out. Señora Izquierdo peeped outside the kitchen door.

95   "It's Papi," she said, running back to her place. Her knife whipped around the fresh potato she took from the kitchen counter, and her face became self-absorbed.

NOTES

one arm akimbo (par. 82): with her hand on her hip
Cd. (par. 85): an abbreviation for *Ciudad,* city
hovel (par. 85): run-down house
la abuela (par. 85): the grandmother
Ay qué (par. 86): oh what
banter (par. 87): teasing
arid (par. 93): dry and barren
la perla del Caribe (par. 93): the pearl of the Caribbean
Borinquen querido (par. 93): beloved Puerto Rico

96   Américo put out his cigarette and sat upright in his chair. Beneath the table, one of his legs began to pounce nervously. He raised his eyebrows at Jovita, who reclined in her chair with her hands together on her lap.

97   The door cracked open, then slammed shut. Señor Izquierdo wore an Alpine hat on his frizzy head and carried a brown grocery bag in his arms. He was a short man in his sixties. His sharp, restless eyes alighted upon Américo and Jovita. He ignored Señora Izquierdo at the sink.

98   "Hello, Américo" he said in a level voice.

99   "Hello, Pop."

100   "*Buenas tardes,*" Señor Izquierdo said to Jovita.

101   "*Buenas tardes.*"

102   Señor Izquierdo's muscular arms reached, one at a time, inside the grocery bag and retrieved two fistfulls of apples and oranges. "I brought you these," he said to Américo, a boyish smile parting his mustachioed mouth.

103   "Thanks Pop."

104   "Do you want one?"

105   "No, thank you."

106   Jovita declined too.

107   Señor Izquierdo, his eyes momentarily unsettled, put the fruit inside the bag and removed it to the kitchen counter. Without looking at his wife, he strolled to the stove where he poured himself some coffee. His squatty, rural hands were unsteady as he stirred the cream and sugar into it. He wore an old, unfashionable shirt and once dressy pants exhausted by repeated laundering and daily usage. It was part of his refusal to waste his "children's money" on new clothes for himself, though he needed them for his public image as a furniture salesman. He stood in shoes swollen by his vigilance at work.

108   "I understand you are leaving tomorrow," said Señor Izquierdo.

109   "Yes, sir," replied Américo.

110   "Do you need any money?"

111   "No, sir. Thank you very much."

112   "You know that you can always count on me if you need anything."

113   "Yes—I understand."

114   Señor Izquierdo's eyes wandered towards Jovita, who sat quietly next to Américo. Américo knew she wouldn't speak to his father if she could avoid it, but Señor Izquierdo thought he had gotten her attention.

115   "My children," he said to her, "come before anything else in the world. They are not like so many children I see in the streets—filthy, hungry, no one to tell them what's wrong or right. My children have a man for a father. As long as I am alive, they have nothing to fear."

116   Américo hated what his father said and the manner in which he said it, the tone of his voice as impudent as the ridiculous Alpine hat askew on his head.

117   "Have you eaten?" Señor Izquierdo's attention returned to Américo.

118   "No sir. We are going out to eat."

119   "Oh, I see."

120   "We were going to have a *carne asada*," Américo explained, "but everybody left, and we didn't know when you'd get back."

121   "You can have *carne asada* without me."

122   "We want the family together."

NOTES

Buenas tardes (par. 100): good afternoon
vigilance (par. 107): diligence
impudent (par. 116): cocky
askew (par. 116): crooked

123   "Yes." He sipped his coffee, nodded his head thoughtfully. "A family should always be together, should always work together. A family is a source of strength. Of course," he raised his eyebrows, "it's not easy. There are always people in the family who oppose the family's unity, people who plot against the father, who refuse to serve him a decent meal. . . ."

124   Américo tensed. His father had flung an insult at his mother. It was an old conflict, this business of the food, and it turned his stomach.

125   "Have you died of hunger?" shouted Señora Izquierdo. She kept her back towards them.

126   "Do you know, Américo," he continued, "that half the food in this house is wasted because it is not cooked properly? Do you think that is right?"

127   Señora Izquierdo turned and glared angrily at the back of the old man's head.

128   "If you don't eat," she shouted, "it's because you are an old man who cannot eat with your false teeth!"

129   Américo glanced at Jovita. She swallowed a smile. He focused his eyes on the clock on the wall.

130   "Américo," his mother said, taking a position at Señor Izquierdo's side, her face drawn and piqued, "ask your father who showed him how to use a bathroom. Ask him who told him he could sit on a toilet bowl, that he didn't have to crouch on it as if he were in some outhouse in Puerto Rico. You should have seen him. For years he perched like a *gallo* on the toilet bowl. When your father arrived in El Paso, he was nothing but a *jíbaro* and it was me"—she pointed the knife at herself, "who educated him"—she pointed to her husband.

131   She remained where she stood, eyes, ears, and mouth alert for whatever else he might say.

132   "All my life," Señor Izquierdo said to Américo, "I have worked to provide this house with everything it needs. My children have had everything they needed. Your mother has never had to work."

133   "And who has washed your filthy underwear?" Señora Izquierdo eyed her husband with the tusk-keenness of an embattled *javelina*.

134   "Yes, this is all I get," said Señor Izquierdo, regarding his wife with contempt. "A filthy mouth, ingratitude, disrespect."

135   "You are a sick man, Izquierdo," Señora Izquierdo said

136   "Shut up," he replied.

137   "Go to your room and watch television!" she exploded.

138   Señor Izquierdo shook his head. He turned to Américo and in a confidential tone said, "I'll be in my room. Maybe we can talk in peace before you leave. I am working on some big plans I'd like for you to know about. I am thinking about opening a big store. But I can't discuss these things in the presence of small minds."

139   He prepared himself another cup of coffee and then disappeared as abruptly as he had arrived, sliding the kitchen door shut behind him.

140   "Good," said Señora Izquierdo, relaxing by the sink. "He's gone."

141   Américo's legs stopped bouncing beneath the table, and he felt he could breathe at last. Jovita leaned forward, put her arm on the table, and smiled at Américo, though it was a smile contrived out of bewilderment.

NOTES

piqued (par. 130): resentful
gallo (par. 130): rooster
jíbaro (par. 130): buzzard
javelina (par. 133): wild boar
contrived (par. 141): created
bewilderment (par. 141): confusion

142   "Every day he comes home like that," Señora Izquierdo said, her face engrossed in the knife's slightly erratic movement through the potato in her hand. "I never do anything right. He says he has never been able to eat a decent meal since he left Puerto Rico. There was a time I made Puerto Rican food for him, but I stopped when I saw that he soon found something else to complain about. Your father is a very hard man to live with."

143   "Is it true he's thinking about opening a store?" Américo asked.

144   "When hasn't your father been up to something that was going to make him a millionaire? I let him talk about his big plans; I don't pay attention. What you don't do when you are young, you won't do when you are old. It won't be long before both of us are dead."

145   "*Ay, señora,*" said Jovita, "you are just like my grandmother. Every Christmas she says farewell to everybody because she thinks she has less than a year to live. She's been saying that since I was a little girl. Look at her. She's buried my grandfather and is in her eighties. You're very young."

146   Señora Izquierdo's eyes flashed with delight. "Thank you, thank you." She glanced at Américo. "I've been told I look like your father's daughter."

147   Jovita laughed. "*Ay,* Señora Izquierdo."

148   Américo looked at the clock again. "We have to go," he said.

149   "So soon?" Señora Izquierdo said. "We didn't even have a chance to talk."

150   "Why don't you go with us?" asked Jovita.

151   "Yeah, why don't you come with us?" said Américo with a smile. "You could give us a guided tour of Smeltertown. After that, you could eat all you wanted at the Hacienda Restaurant."

152   Señora Izquierdo liked the idea. She went "Mmmmm" and then acted as if she were gobbling food. She laughed loudly and warmly, her white teeth beaming in her round face, an old and weathered version of Américo's own. She followed Américo and Jovita to the door.

153   "No," she said. She whirled her forefinger about her temple, an allusion to her husband's mental condition. "I have to stay here and feed the *deschavetado.*"

II

154   Américo drove up the sloped street away from his parents' white stuccoed house which had been built on the escarpment at the foot of the Franklin Mountains.

155   "I'm glad we were able to get away," said Américo, glancing at Jovita, who reclined comfortably in her seat, the elegant contour of her face doused by sunlight. "I can't breathe in that house."

156   He turned onto the street that would take them downtown.

157   "Your mother is so funny," said Jovita.

158   Curious and agitated, he glanced at her. "What do you mean?" he said.

159   She sat there with a smile, shaking her head at the thought of his mother.

NOTES

engrossed (par. 142): absorbed
erratic (par. 142): irregular
allusion (par. 153): reference
deschavetado (par. 153): insane one
escarpment (par. 154): slope
contour (par. 155): outline
doused (par. 155): covered
agitated (par. 158): irritated

160   "I don't know," she said. "She's a real character. One minute she's laughing and joking, the next minute she's battling your father, then she is laughing again as if everything had been one big joke."

161   "Well, it hasn't always been one big joke," said Américo, staring morosely out the window. "There was a time when I had to put up with that nonsense every day. I mean every day. Just to think about those days gives me chills."

162   Américo stopped at an intersection by a lush green park.

163   "Let's take the mountain road," said Jovita.

164   "Okay," he said.

165   He veered onto Scenic Drive, the popular mountain road that zigzagged across the southernmost extension of the Franklin Mountains. Its curves snaked in and out of the crevasses. As they gained altitude, the vast cityscape spread out below, offering them a breathtaking view of a sophisticated American metropolis glittering in the desert sun of an immense sky. Jovita beheld the sight with wonder.

166   "El Paso is such a beautiful city," she said. "It is so different from Escandon."

167   "It is beautiful," Américo agreed, "but I could never live here again."

168   "My mother came here to visit many years ago. She fell in love with it. She even wanted to come and live here."

169   "I'm glad she didn't."

170   "Why?"

171   "I would never have met you."

172   They exchanged smiles.

173   Américo reached the "look-out" area, the highest point on the road. Atop a pole an American flag flapped sporadically. Beyond the urban valley rose the Mexican mountains, dark and remote. In the west appeared the smokestacks. The road curved sharply into the mountain, and the descent to the valley began.

174   "I used to come this way every day when I was at the university," said Américo. "In the morning it was very beautiful, except for the smog."

175   "Have people ever driven off the mountain?"

176   "Rarely. I don't remember anyone having done that, though I once heard of a girl who committed suicide by driving off the mountain."

177   "What a horrible way to die."

178   Américo shifted into low gear and stopped riding the brake pedal. He maneuvered through the familiar curves gracefully.

179   "Your family is strange," said Jovita thoughtfully. "They treat us well. The refrigerator is full of food. Your father brings sacks of fruit and offers you money. Compared to my family, they have everything, but they cannot eat a meal together. Your family seems like a family of strangers."

180   Américo sighed. "That's the way we were brought up. My father has always said that you don't have any friends but your own family. Yet he has never been a friend to any of us. It's impossible to talk to him. As for my brothers and sisters, I don't know what to talk to them about. I used to think *I* was different, Jovita, but I'm not. At first I thought the problem was my parents' lack of education. I have always seen them as peasants despite the money my father has managed to make. But in Escandon, I've seen families with absolutely nothing, neither money nor education, surviving together successfully. In my family we are all lonely wretches."

NOTES

morosely (par. 161): gloomily
crevasses (par. 165): deep cracks in mountains
sporadically (par. 173): occasionally

181   "They are good people, Américo."

182   "People may be good," he looked at her a bit peevishly, "but sick."

183   She shifted in her seat. He felt her eyes settle on the side of his face. "What I meant to say," she said, "is that they're good people, despite everything. You can't go on hating them all your life."

184   He kept his eyes on the winding road. "It was here in El Paso that I learned to live with the assumption that I have no family."

185   "That's what's so frightening about you sometimes," said Jovita softly. "Sometimes I feel you owe allegiance to nothing, to no one, perhaps not even to me one day."

186   He looked over at her poignant brown eyes. "Don't say that. I've never loved anybody as much as I love you, and I never will. You're the only valuable thing I've had in my life.

187   "I would hate to see us become," he added slowly, "what my parents are. But then you never know. This business of living is so tricky. Some families are cursed for generations."

188   "Still, curses can be lifted, no?" Jovita smiled.

189   "No," Américo said, returning the smile.

190   They came off the mountain road. They took the avenue that sloped to the heart of El Paso. Cars glittered like luminous insects in the bright sunlight. They idled past San Jacinto Plaza, once a station on the Spanish King's highway, now the city's main plaza where city buses disgorged pedestrians from all parts of the metropolis. Clusters of people, most of them Mexicans, walked in the shadows of the tall buildings enclosing the downtown area. When he reached Paisano Drive, Américo turned west.

191   "Paisano connects with the old highway at the train depot," said Américo. "I like this route because it runs along the Rio Grande."

192   "I'd get lost," said Jovita, "if I had to drive here."

193   "You get used to it."

194   They drove past the train depot, which resembled a Spanish cathedral, and onto the old highway.

195   "There's Mexico," said Américo, nodding at the low-lying hills clustered with adobe huts beyond the sandy river bottom. As usual, the stark contrast between the two sides of the river struck him, and it reminded him that his mother and her family were originally from Mexico, despite his mother's denials.

196   "You can walk across," said Jovita.

197   "I know. The river isn't very deep here."

198   "What river?" joked Jovita. "The *arroyos* in Escandon have more water in them than that."

199   Américo smiled. Jovita loved to tease him about the Rio Grande. It was not as large in El Paso as it was in Escandon, but it linked him to her nonetheless. He drove on, passed under a concrete bridge, beyond which appeared the Hacienda Restaurant against a mountain backdrop.

200   "Look, there's Mount Cristo Rey!" cried Américo, pointing to a small basalt peak in the distance, a tiny cross at its pinnacle. It looked like a small,

NOTES

peevishly (par. 182): irritably

poignant (par. 186): penetrating

luminous (par. 190): shiny

disgorged (par. 190): released

arroyos (par. 198): gullies

Mount Cristo Rey (par. 200): literally translated, Christ King Mountain

basalt (par. 200): dark, shiny volcanic rock

pinnacle (par. 200): highest point

perfectly shaped volcano set against the enormous Texas sky. "Every time I see Mount Cristo Rey, I feel something special. I feel a tenderness a pilgrim might feel for the Holy Land. It is as I imagine the Holy Land. My mother once told me she and *la abuela* made annual pilgrimages to the top of Mount Cristo Rey. When I lived in El Paso, there were times I felt so deperate and full of hatred that I drove out here, along this highway, just to see all this. It calmed me. There were also times I felt I didn't belong among the *gringos*, that I didn't belong in El Paso, period. Then I remembered that my mother was part of all this, the river, the mountians, and I felt that I did belong here, no matter what the *gringos* thought."

201   They were approaching Smeltertown. To the right of the highway, Américo saw the ASARCO smokestacks—the short one and the two long thin ones.

202   "Smeltertown is across the highway from the smelter," said Américo. "It should be somewhere around here."

203   They looked around as they passed a slag-covered ridge beyond which rose the complex of metal buildings overshadowed by smokestacks. They did not see anything. No wooden shacks, no grocery stores, no cars or people, no church.

204   As they drove on, they passed under a black metal bridge where the trains from the smelter crossed over the highway. "Jovita, I'm sure it's not past this bridge. We missed it."

205   Américo turned back. As they approached the smelter again, they slowed down and pulled off the highway, stopping in front of a bright sign: "For Sale, Coronado Realty 566-3965." They got out of the car.

206   "The smokestacks are there, so Smeltertown should be here," he said, standing at the edge of an empty field.

207   "Look, across the field, isn't that a church?"

208   Seeing the remains—white walls, no roof, debris—he asked, "So this is it?"

209   "Your mother was right," said Jovita. "There's nothing here."

210   "She meant something else," said Américo, stopping next to Jovita. "If she had known it had been torn down, she would have told us."

211   He gazed at the empty field. Though he had driven along this highway several times before he left El Paso and later when he took Jovita to New Mexico on one of their honeymoons, Américo had never paid much attention to Smeltertown. It had merely been the wretched town where his mother had grown up with *la abuela,* his great-grandmother, and Tía Rosaura, his great-aunt. When was the last time he had been there? A long time ago as a child, perhaps twenty years.

212   "I want to look around," said Américo. "Do you mind?"

213   "No, its early. I'll join you later. I want to look at the church."

214   "Okay." He wandered across the field.

215   There was none of the billowy sand he remembered trudging through every time his mother brought him and his brothers and sisters to visit *la abeula* and Tía Rosaura. The dirt felt compact; severed roots showed that it had been planed recently.

NOTES

a pilgrim (par. 200): a person who travels to a sacred place

gringos (par. 200): a scornful term for white Americans

smelter (par. 202): Smelting is a process in which ore is melted to separate the metals contained in it. The non-metallic part of the ore is called *slag* (par. 203).

billowy (par. 215): loose

compact (par. 215): solid

planed (par. 215): scraped

216   There had been candles burning inside *la abuela*'s wood frame house. Sulfur and incense mingled with the smell of Mexican food. She was a very old woman, short and frail, with a wrinkled face and green eyes. She wore a *chongo* at the back of her head, gold-rimmed glasses, and a black shawl wrapped around her shoulders. He could recall nothing of her temperament. He remembered the other woman, Tía Rosaura, a short Mexican woman with a square head on her neckless shoulders, a woman who seemed to have been smelted from the igneous rock of this land. Their hearts lay buried somewhere in this soil that had poisoned his, and he felt like a ghost crossing an immense desert in search of their blessings.

217   Not able to find where *la abuela*'s house had been, he attempted to reconstruct the original scene from memory—a picket fence; an outhouse which smelled and whose spiders had scared him; a lanky, yellow-eyed dog in the dirt yard; and a dark wooden house with a corrugated aluminum roof. Once on a visit to Smeltertown, his mother had sent him to the store a block away. It had been a short walk; the store had been on a street facing the highway. If he could locate where the store had been, he might find *la abuela*'s property. To his left Américo spotted a curbstone, a few yards from the highway, where there had once been a street corner. As he walked towards it, he came across a prominent mound of dirt and stopped.

218   When he stepped onto the mound, the dirt grated beneath his foot. He hit the ground with the heel of his shoe. It sounded hollow. He crouched down. Upon clearing some of the dirt, he found a slab of wood beneath, and when he lifted it, he saw the hole. It had been hastily and incompletely filled in; it looked as if it might have been a cesspool hole. He studied the distance between mound and curbstone and church. If his estimates were correct, he might be standing on top of *la abuela*'s cesspool.

219   He wanted to tell Jovita about his discovery, but she sat on a wooden beam in the shadow of the church walls. He crossed the field and sat down next to her.

220   "Did you see where I was standing?"

221   "Yes."

222   "There's a mound of dirt there. I think it's a cesspool. Several yards away, there used to be a store on the corner. *La abuela*'s house would have been where that mound of dirt is. I am almost certain it was her cesspool I was standing on."

223   They sat quietly for a moment.

224   "Where's the Rio Grande?" asked Jovita.

225   Américo glanced at the church walls.

226   "Oh, that's behind the church. We can't see it from here."

227   "Is Mexico on the other side?"

228   "I don't think so. Somewhere around here the river turns and ceases to be the Mexican-American border. I don't know exactly where in the river's bend that happens."

229   "What was *la abuela*'s name?"

230   "Just *la abuela*."

231   "Didn't your mother tell you her name?"

232   Américo paused. He sifted through the assortment of memories he had about his childhood: Smeltertown, his mother, the sulfur fumes—all the links

NOTES

chongo (par. 216): ponytail
igneous (par. 216): volcanic rock
prominent (par. 217): noticeable
cesspool (par. 218): sewage hole

to *la abuela*—but he could not remember her name. His mind seemed as empty as the field at his feet.

233   He shook his head. "My mother told me her name, but I cannot remember. It's all jumbled in my mind. Until *la abuela* died, she lived with Tía Rosaura. Their last name was Buenaventura. *La abuela* was not really my grandmother; she was really my mother's grandmother. I never got to know my real grandmother—my mother's mother. Her name was Guadalupe. Guadalupe gave my mother to *la abuela* to raise in Smeltertown. I never understood why. My mother often said she grew up like an orphan, alone. I suppose she meant she grew up without her mother and her brothers and sisters. Her father was murdered, so my mother says, somewhere in Mexico when she was very young, probably when she was already living here."

234   "Did you come to visit *la abuela* and Tía Rosaura often?"

235   "Maybe once or twice a year. Some years we didn't see them at all. Sometimes they came to visit us when my father wasn't home or when we were at school. My father objected to our seeing my mother's family. Whenever we came here, my mother would say, 'Shhhh, don't tell your father we're going to see *la abuela*.' We'd come on the bus frightened to death my father would find out, and there would be another fight. But there always was a fight—even when we didn't come."

236   "That's very sad," said Jovita. "We grew up with all of our relatives, and when our grandparents died, they died at our house. We remained by their side until their last moments."

237   "I've always envied that in you. I've always wanted to have a family like that. To have grown up with aunts and uncles, with cousins, big family get-togethers and *carne asadas*. To be able to speak to my father, to repect him."

238   "Well, my father isn't a saint. He's never laid a hand on my mother or any of us, but he's made my mother's life miserable. At least your father has provided well for your family. Your mother has never had to work. Compared to your father, my father is incompetent. But just because they're like that doesn't mean that I have to hate them the way you have hated your family."

239   "Haven't you had other members of your family to turn to, like your aunt and your grandmother? The simple fact that your grandparents died at your parents' home has counted for something, no? Hasn't that been a source of strength."

240   "Yes."

241   "When you talk about your grandmother singing the *Ave Maria* at church or about walking on Sunday morning to church with your aunt or about how you felt the morning your grandfather died, I feel envious. I feel like a stranger. So when we come to El Paso this is really all I have to show you—this empty field, these beautiful mountains that mean more to you than to me. When people find out I'm from El Paso and they say, 'Oh, El Paso is such a beautiful town. I wish I could live there,' my stomach goes into knots. If we have children," he said slowly, "I don't want them to grow up the way I did, without a solid sense of who they are." He stopped, breathed deeply, picked up a small stick, and drew an "X" in the dirt. "What time is it?"

242   Jovita looked at her watch. "Three o'clock."

243   "Are you hungry?"

244   "Not yet."

245   Américo looked at the church. He had not been inside a church for years. He wondered if this was where *la abuela* had been brought when she died. He got up and walked to the front of the church's entrance and found a doorless passageway through which he could see the blue walls inside. Piles of smashed wood, brick, and glass blocked his way to the front steps, but he saw a thin path.

246   "Let's climb inside," he said to Jovita.

247   "No, it's dangerous."

248   "I'm going inside," he said. "It won't be long before all of this is torn down."

249   "Be careful. There are nails all over the place."

250   Américo took the path and climbed the steps, where he sat on the door sill and stared inside at the blue walls smouldering in the sunlight. He pushed himself inside and landed on the dirt floor several feet below. Somehow he had expected to see some vestiges of the original church still intact—a pulpit, an altar, a cross, anything. All he saw were the marks on the walls where the floor had once been and piles of broken wood on the dirt floor. Up front, where the altar must have been, rose a stack of tattered linoleum-like roofing. Set high in the walls was a series of broken windows. Beyond the roofless walls was the sky.

251   He walked amid the debris to the center of the church floor which was bisected by shadow and sunlight. Finding a wooden box, which he pulled to a clearing, he sat down and lit a cigarette. He imagined two old women leading a young girl down the center aisle for communion and the people in the pews listening to the choir as a priest poised white wafers on the tongues of the communicants. He imagined an old woman lying dead in a coffin.

252   The images were interrupted by the memory of a story his mother had once told him. During the years of the war, it had been here, in Smeltertown, where his father, a soldier then, had come to look for his mother at *la abuela*'s house. It was one night, months after they had been married and Américo had been conceived. He had come drunk. She would not open the door even after he stopped beating on it and began to thrash about on the ground, crying and threatening to kill himself if she did not return to him. It had been *la abuela* who scolded her, telling her that she was now a woman, not a girl, a wife and mother-to-be, and that unless he abandoned her, she must never leave him, regardless of how unhappy she might be. His mother had opened the door.

253   Whatever else Américo may have detested in his father, he had always admired his father's capacity for hard work and making money. In a few years his father had moved the family from a decrepit barrio in south El Paso to a nice neighborhood near Five Points and then to the suburb at the foot of the mountains. In his prosperity he thought he could return to Puerto Rico and change everything he had left. The thatched-roof hut he grew up in with his ten brothers and sisters, the poverty and misery of his saintly mother, and tyranny of his tall, red-headed, machete-wielding drunken father. He sent money instead. The times he visited his family in Puerto Rico, he went with his wife's blessing and the knowledge that he didn't have to return. But to the family's relief, he always came back. In his drunken rages he cursed the desert, the mountains, his wife, the Mexicans, and his fate.

254   Américo could never forgive, then or now, his father's humiliation of his mother and rejection of her family. In his isolation, Américo turned to books. And, when they weren't enough, Mexican *cantinas* and abandoned women. When his long pent-up desire to leave El Paso forever, to destroy it by his absence, was satisfied by an opportunity to teach in Escandon, he found refuge. He found Jovita.

NOTES

vestiges (par. 250): traces
bisected (par. 251): divided in halves
decrepit barrio (par. 253): run-down neighborhood
machete (par. 253): a long, broad knife
refuge (par. 254): escape, protection

255   And every time he returned to El Paso, zipping along the elaborate highway from the south, he felt an immense weight settle upon his shoulders. At first gently. Then it would begin to push down upon him so hard that he felt the mountains were crushing him. At his parents' home and everywhere else he went, everything seem devastated until Jovita and he escaped to the other side of the Rio Grande, where he drank excessively at the Kentucky Club. That is where they had been the previous night and why he had gotten up so late. It had been a wonderful time, alive with Mexican music, polite waiters in white shirts, and superbly rendered Scotch and sodas. But this time, the Sunday after, he felt unusually weak, as if something that had driven him along all those years was beginning to fail him. The sensation frightened him. Was it Jovita's and his desire to have a child and settle down? Perhaps Jovita's wish to get away from the nightlife whose warmth and charm had sustained him for so long among strangers? Whatever change was afoot, he was certain of one thing though—he would still have to travel a long distance, years, before he could turn around, look at El Paso, and feel free of it.

256   When he finished his cigarette, Américo stood up and looked around, wondering if he had missed something. No. All of it was dead—Smeltertown, *la abuela*, Tía Rosaura, and even his mother, the little girl who, with *la abuela*, had washed clothes in the Rio Grande and climbed Mount Cristo Rey in the religious processions there. He stood in the graveyard of a past, his Mexican past. Then, as his eyes scaled the church walls, a glint of yellow caught his attention. It was a window, stained blue and yellow, resting high on the church walls, still intact.

257   He picked up several pieces of brick and tossed them. He missed several times. At last he lobbed a chunk squarely at the base of the window so the pieces cascaded backwards into the church and landed on a pile of wood armed with splinters and nails. The face of a madonna, with drooping eyes and a silver halo around her head, survived in a triangle of glass. Américo got as close as he could. He did not see the nail when he reached for the madonna, just felt it. A thin, rusted nail like a rattlesnake fang curved out of the stick of wood, striking the side of his hand. He cried out, and his feet blundered in the pile of wood, upsetting the madonna. She fell and burst. Was this what he was destined to take back home, to South Texas, a relic of Smeltertown engraved upon his hand?

258   He heard Jovita's desperate voice, "Américo! Américo!" flying over the church walls.

259   Without hesitation, he climbed to the sunlight outside. He paused and caught his breath. He turned to run back around to the front of the church. He stopped, gasped. A black man leaned against the church wall, his black arms rigidly outstretched. A smuggler or wetback scorched by the desert sun, poised to assault him? But it wasn't a man at all. It was a cross.

260   It was unlike any other cross he had seen before, not gold, not silver, not even marble-white like the cross atop Mount Cristo Rey. It was plain, the kind of cross that might have been smelted from the igneous stone of the region, the stone transfixed by iron rods whose protruding ends had rusted.

NOTES

a madonna (par. 257): a depiction of Jesus' mother, the Virgin Mary
relic (par. 257): something considered important because of its connection with a person or place
wetback (par. 259): scornful term for a Mexican
poised (par. 259): positioned

261   "Américo!" Jovita called.

262   "I'm back here," answered Américo.

263   As Jovita dashed around the corner of the church, she halted, abruptly startled by the sight of the cross.

264   "Wha . . . " she said, awed.

265   "I just found this cross," Américo said, stepping next to her. "It scared the hell out of me."

266   "It's so big."

267   "They probably removed it from inside the church. I wonder what they're going to do with it."

268   Jovita saw the handkerchief wrapped around his hand.

269   "What happened to you? I heard a window crash."

270   "I just wanted something to take home with us. It was a piece of glass with the face of a madonna. It was beautiful, but it broke."

271   "Your mother would have treasured it."

272   His eyes embraced the cross. He imagined it hanging inside the church. It was very old; *la abuela* and his mother must have seen it years ago. He stepped forward and ran his hand along its upright post. He marvelled. It was so simple yet so strong.

273   "Do you think we could take it home?" he said.

274   "What?"

275   "The cross."

276   "It's a long way to Escandon. How are we going to carry it? On top of our Volkswagen?"

277   Américo laughed.

278   "You're right," he said, running his fingers delicately along the stone's rough surface. "Come on. We'd better go."

279   Together they crossed the field.

280   "How does your hand feel?" asked Jovita.

281   "All right."

282   "Maybe you should get a shot."

283   "It'll be too much trouble. I'd have to go to a hospital."

284   "I'd feel better if you got a shot," she insisted. "Then we could go to eat."

285   "Okay."

286   They stopped between their car and the elongated shadow of the real estate sign. Américo looked at everything once more—the ASARCO smelter and its smokestacks across the highway, the curbstone, the empty field, the church walls and Mount Cristo Rey.

287   "There will be nothing left," he said.

288   Jovita, who had been gazing thoughtfully at the church walls, turned to Américo and said, "There will be your father and your mother."

NOTE
awed (par. 264): astonished

3

Essays

Shame

Dick Gregory

1   I never learned hate at home, or shame. I had to go to school for that. I was about seven years old when I got my first big lesson. I was in love with a little girl named Helene Tucker, a light-complexioned little girl with pig-tails and nice manners. She was always clean and she was smart in school. I think I went to school mostly to look at her. I brushed my hair and even got me a little old handkerchief. It was a lady's handkerchief, but I didn't want Helene to see me wipe my nose on my hand. The pipes were frozen again, there was no water in the house, but I washed my socks and shirt every night. I'd get a pot, and go over to Mr. Ben's grocery store, and stick my pot down into his soda machine. Scoop out some chopped ice. By evening the ice melted to water for washing. I got sick a lot that winter because the fire would go out at night before the clothes were dry. In the morning I'd put them on, wet or dry, because they were the only clothes I had.

2   Everybody's got a Helene Tucker, a symbol of everything you want. I loved her for her goodness, her cleanness, her popularity. She'd walk down my street and my brothers and sisters would yell, "Here comes Helene," and I'd rub my tennis sneakers on the back of my pants and wish my hair wasn't so nappy and the white folk's shirt fit me better. I'd run out on the street. If I knew my place and didn't come too close, she'd wink at me and say hello. That was a good feeling. Sometimes I'd follow her all the way home, and shovel the snow off her walk and try to make friends with her Momma and her aunts. I'd drop money on her stoop late at night on my way back from shining shoes in the taverns. And she had a Daddy, and he had a good job. He was a paper hanger.

3   I guess I would have gotten over Helene by summertime, but something happened in that classroom that made her face hang in front of me for the next twenty-two years. When I played the drums in high school it was for Helene and when I broke track records in college it was for Helene and when I started standing behind microphones and heard applause I wished Helene could hear it, too. It wasn't until I was twenty-nine years old and married and making money that I really got her out of my system. Helene was sitting in that classroom when I learned to be ashamed of myself.

4   It was on a Thursday. I was sitting in the back of the room, in a seat with a chalk circle drawn around it. The idiot's seat, the troublemaker's seat.

5   The teacher thought I was stupid. Couldn't spell, couldn't read, couldn't do arithmetic. Just stupid. Teachers were never interested in finding out that you couldn't concentrate because you were so hungry, because you hadn't had any breakfast. All you could think about was noontime, would it ever come? Maybe you could sneak in to the cloakroom and steal a bite of some kid's lunch out of a coat pocket. A bite of something. Paste. You can't really make a meal of paste, or put it on bread for a sandwich, but sometimes I'd scoop a few spoonfuls out of the paste jar in the back of the room. Pregnant people get strange tastes. I was pregnant with poverty. Pregnant with dirt and preg-nant with smells that made people turn away, pregnant with cold and

pregnant with shoes that were never bought for me, pregnant with five other people in my bed and no Daddy in the next room, and pregnant with hunger. Paste doesn't taste too bad when you're hungry.

6   The teacher thought I was a troublemaker. All she saw from the front of the room was a little black boy who squirmed in his idiot's seat and made noises and poked the kids around him. I guess she couldn't see a kid who made noises because he wanted someone to know he was there.

7   It was on a Thursday, the day before the Negro payday. The eagle always flew on Friday. The teacher was asking each student how much his father would give to the Community Chest. On Friday night, each kid would get the money from his father, and on Monday he would bring it to the school. I decided I was going to buy me a Daddy right then. I had money in my pocket from shining shoes and selling papers, and whatever Helene Tucker pledged for her Daddy I was going to top it. And I'd hand the money right in. I wasn't going to wait until Monday to buy me a Daddy.

8   I was shaking, scared to death. The teacher opened her book and started calling out names alphabetically.

9   "Helene Tucker?"

10 "My Daddy said he'd give two dollars and fifty cents."

11 "That's very nice, Helene. Very, very nice indeed."

12 That made me feel pretty good. It wouldn't take too much to top that. I had almost three dollars in dimes and quarters in my pocket. I stuck my hand in my pocket and held onto the money, waiting for her to call my name. But the teacher closed her book after she called everybody else in the class.

13 I stood up and raised my hand.

14 "What is it now?"

15 "You forgot me."

16 She turned toward the blackboard. "I don't have time to be playing with you, Richard."

17 "My Daddy said he'd ... "

18 "Sit down, Richard, you're disturbing the class."

19 "My Daddy said he'd give ... fifteen dollars."

20 She turned and looked mad. "We are collecting this money for you and your kind, Richard Gregory. If your Daddy can give fifteen dollars you have no business being on relief."

21 "I got it right now, I got it right now, my Daddy gave it to me to turn in today, my Daddy said ... "

22 "And furthermore," she said, looking right at me, her nostrils getting big and her lips getting thin and her eyes opening wide, "we know you don't have a Daddy."

23 Helene Tucker turned around, her eyes full of tears. She felt sorry for me. Then I couldn't see her too well because I was crying, too.

24 "Sit down, Richard."

25 And I always thought the teacher kind of liked me. She always picked me to wash the blackboard on Friday, after school. That was a big thrill, it made me feel important. If I didn't wash it, come Monday the school might not function right.

26 "Where are you going, Richard?"

27 I walked out of school that day, and for a long time I didn't go back very often. There was shame there.

NOTES

The eagle always flew on Friday (par. 7): Ten dollar gold coins and, later, ten dollar bills were called "eagles"; Friday was payday.

being on relief (par. 20): getting welfare

28   Now there was shame everywhere. It seemed like the whole world had been inside that classroom, everyone had heard what the teacher had said, everyone had turned around and felt sorry for me. There was shame in going to the Worthy Boys Annual Christmas Dinner for you and your kind, because everybody knew what a worthy boy was. Why couldn't they just call it the Boys Annual Dinner, why'd they have to give it a name? There was shame in wearing the brown and orange and white plaid mackinaw the welfare gave to three thousand boys. Why'd it have to be the same for everybody so when you walked down the street the people could see you were on relief? It was a nice warm mackinaw and it had a hood, and my Momma beat me and called me a little rat when she found out I stuffed it in the bottom of a pail full of garbage way over on Cottage Street. There was shame in running over to Mister Ben's at the end of the day and asking for his rotten peaches, there was shame in asking Mrs. Simmons for a spoonful of sugar, there was shame in running out to meet the relief truck. I hated that truck, full of food for you and your kind. I ran into the house and hid when it came. And then I started to sneak through alleys, to take the long way home so the people going into White's Eat Shop wouldn't see me. Yeah, the whole world heard the teacher that day, we all know you don't have a Daddy.

Daddy Tucked the Blanket

Randall Williams

1   About the time I turned 16, my folks began to wonder why I didn't stay home any more. I always had an excuse for them, but what I didn't say was that I had found my freedom and I was getting out.

2   I went through four years of high school in semi-rural Alabama and became active in clubs and sports; I made a lot of friends and became a regular guy, if you know what I mean. But one thing was irregular about me: I managed those four years without ever having a friend visit at my house.

3   I was ashamed of where I lived. I had been ashamed for as long as I had been conscious of class.

4   We had a big family. There were several of us sleeping in one room, but that's not so bad if you get along, and we always did. As you get older, though, it gets worse.

5   Being poor is a humiliating experience for a young person trying hard to be accepted. Even now—several years removed—it is hard to talk about. And I resent the weakness of these words to make you feel what it was really like.

6   We lived in a lot of old houses. We moved a lot because we were always looking for something just a little better than what we had. You have to understand that my folks worked harder than most people. My mother was always at home, but for her that was a full-time job—and no fun, either. But my father worked his head off from the time I can remember in construction and shops. It was hard, physical work.

7   I tell you this to show that we weren't shiftless. No matter how much money Daddy made, we never made much progress up the social ladder. I got out thanks to a college scholarship and because I was a little more articulate than the average.

NOTE

shiftless (par. 7): lazy, irresponsible

8   I have seen my Daddy wrap copper wire through the soles of his boots to keep them together in the wintertime. He couldn't buy new boots because he had used the money for food and shoes for us. We lived like hell, but we went to school well-clothed and with a full stomach.

9   It really is hell to live in a house that was in bad shape 10 years before you moved in. And a big family puts a lot of wear and tear on a new house, too, so you can imagine how one goes downhill if it is teetering when you move in. But we lived in houses that were sweltering in summer and freezing in winter. I woke up every morning for a year and a half with plaster on my face where it had fallen out of the ceiling during the night.

10   This wasn't during the Depression; this was in the late '60s and early '70s.

11   When we boys got old enough to learn trades in school, we would try to fix up the old houses we lived in. But have you ever tried to paint a wall that crumbled when the roller went across it. And bright paint emphasized the holes in the wall. You end up more frustrated than when you began, especially when you know that at best you might come up with only enough money to improve one of the six rooms in the house. And we might move out soon after, anyway.

12   The same goes for keeping a house like that clean. If you have a house full of kids and the house is deteriorating, you'll never keep it clean. Daddy used to yell at Mama about that, but she couldn't do anything. I think Daddy knew it inside, but he had to have an outlet for his rage somewhere, and at least yelling isn't as bad as hitting, which they never did to each other.

13   But you have a kitchen which has no counter space and no hot water, and you will have dirty dishes stacked up. That sounds like an excuse, but try it. You'll go mad from the sheer sense of futility. It's the same thing in a house with no closets. You can't keep clothes clean and rooms in order if they have to be stacked up with things.

14   Living in a bad house is generally worse on girls. For one thing, they traditionally help their mother with the housework. We boys could get outside and work in the field or cut wood or even play ball and forget about living conditions. The sky was still pretty.

15   But the girls got the pressure, and as they got older it became worse. Would they accept dates knowing they had to "receive" the young man in a dirty hallway with broken windows, peeling wallpaper and a cracked ceiling? You have to live it to understand it, but it creates a shame which drives the soul of a young person inward.

16   I'm thankful none of us ever blamed our parents for this, because it would have crippled our relationships. As it worked out, only the relationship between our parents was damaged. And I think the harshness which they expressed to each other was just an outlet to get rid of their anger at the trap their lives were in. It ruined their marriage because they had no one to yell at but each other. I knew other families where the kids got the abuse, but we were too much loved for that.

17   Once I was about 16 and Mama and Daddy had a particularly violent argument about the washing machine, which had broken down. Daddy was on the back porch—that's where the only water faucet was—trying to fix it

NOTES

teetering (par. 9): on the brink of going downhill

the Depression (par. 10): a time of terrible economic conditions, beginning with the great Stock Market crash of 1929 and lasting until about 1940.

deteriorating (par. 12): decaying, falling apart

futility (par. 13): uselessness

Old House, Clayton, Alabama.

–Leah McCraney.

and Mama had a washtub out there washing school clothes for the next day and they were screaming at each other.

18   Later that night everyone was in bed and I heard Daddy get up from the couch where he was reading. I looked out from my bed across the hall into their room. He was standing right over Mama and she was already asleep. He pulled the blanket up and tucked it around her shoulders and just stood there and tears were dropping off his cheeks and I thought I could faintly hear them splashing against the linoleum rug.

19   Now they're divorced.

20   I had courses in college where housing was discussed, but the sociologists never put enough emphasis on the impact living in substandard housing has on a person's psyche. Especially children's.

21   Small children have a hard time understanding poverty. They want the same things children from more affluent families have. They want the same things they see advertised on television, and they don't understand why they can't have them.

22   Other children can be incredibly cruel. I was in elementary school in Georgia—and this is interesting because it is the only thing I remember about that particular school—when I was about eight or nine.

23   After Christmas vacation had ended, my teacher made each student describe all his or her Christmas presents. I became more and more uncomfortable as the privilege passed around the room towards me. Other children were reciting the names of the dolls they had been given, the kinds of bicycles and the grandeur of their games and toys. Some had lists which seemed to go on and on for hours.

24   It took me only a few seconds to tell the class that I had gotten for Christmas a belt and a pair of gloves. And then I was laughed at—because I cried—by a roomful of children and a teacher. I never forgave them, and that night I made my mother cry when I told her about it.

25   In retrospect, I am grateful for that moment, but I remember wanting to die at the time.

NOTES
psyche (par. 20): soul, spirit
affluent (par. 21): wealthy
grandeur (par. 23): greatness

A Hanging

George Orwell

1   It was in Burma, a sodden morning of the rains. A sickly light, like yellow tinfoil, was slanting over the high walls into the jail yard. We were waiting outside the condemned cells, a row of sheds fronted with double bars, like small animal cages. Each cell measured about ten feet by ten and was quite bare within except for a plank bed and a pot for drinking water. In some of them brown silent men were squatting at the inner bars, with their blankets draped round them. These were the condemned men, due to be hanged within the next week or two.

NOTE
sodden (par. 1): soaked

2   One prisoner had been brought out of his cell. He was a Hindu, a puny wisp of a man, with a shaven head and vague liquid eyes. He had a thick, sprouting moustache, absurdly too big for his body, rather like the moustache of a comic man of the films. Six tall Indian warders were guarding him and getting him ready for the gallows. Two of them stood by with rifles with fixed bayonets, while the other handcuffed him, passed a chain through his handcuffs and fixed it to their belts, and lashed his arms tight to his sides. They crowded very close about him, with their hands always on him in a careful, caressing grip, as though all the while feeling him to make sure he was there. It was like men handling a fish which is still alive and may jump back into the water. But he stood quite unresisting, yielding his arms limply to the ropes, as though he hardly noticed what was happening.

3   Eight o'clock struck and a bugle call, desolately thin in the wet air, floated from the distant barracks. The superintendent of the jail, who was standing apart from the rest of us, moodily prodding the gravel with his stick, raised his head at the sound. He was an army doctor, with a grey toothbrush moustache and a gruff voice. "For God's sake hurry up, Francis," he said irritably. "The man ought to have been dead by this time. Aren't you ready yet?"

4   Francis, the head jailer, a fat Dravidian in a white drill suit and gold spectacles, waved his black hand. "Yes sir, yes sir," he bubbled. "All iss satisfactorily prepared. The hangman iss waiting. We shall proceed."

5   "Well, quick march, then. The prisoners can't get their breakfast till this job's over."

6   We set out for the gallows. Two warders marched on either side of the prisoner, with their rifles at the slope; two others marched close against him, gripping him by arm and shoulder, as though at once pushing and supporting him. The rest of us, magistrates and the like, followed behind. Suddenly, when we had gone ten yards, the procession stopped short without any order or warning. A dreadful thing had happened—a dog, come goodness knows whence, had appeared in the yard. It came bounding among us with a loud volley of barks, and leapt round us wagging its whole body, wild with glee at finding so many human beings together. It was a large wooly dog, half Airedale, half pariah. For a moment it pranced round us, and then, before anyone could stop it, it had made a dash for the prisoner, and jumping up, tried to lick his face. Everyone stood aghast, too taken aback even to grab at the dog.

7   "Who let that bloody brute in here?" said the superintendent angrily. "Catch it, someone!"

8   A warder, detached from the escort, charged clumsily after the dog, but it danced and gambolled just out of his reach, taking everything as part of the game. A young Eurasian jailer picked up a handful of gravel and tried to stone the dog away, but it dodged the stones and came after us again. Its yaps echoed from the jail walls. The prisoner, in the grasp of the two warders, looked on incuriously, as though this was another formality of the hanging. It was several minutes before someone managed to catch the dog. Then we put my handkerchief through its collar and moved off once more, with the dog still straining and whimpering.

NOTES
desolately (par. 3): gloomily
Dravidian (par. 4): a member of the original native population of Southern India
magistrates (par. 6): officials who have the authority to enforce the law
pariah (par. 6): literally, an outcast
aghast (par. 6): shocked
gambolled (par. 8): leaped playfully
Eurasian (par. 8): one who is of European and Asian descent

9   It was about forty yards to the gallows. I watched the bare brown back of the prisoner marching in front of me. He walked clumsily with his bound arms, but quite steadily, with the bobbing gait of the Indian who never straightens his knees. At each step his muscles slid neatly into place, the lock of hair on his scalp danced up and down, his feet printed themselves on the wet gravel. And once, in spite of the men who gripped him by each shoulder, he stepped slightly aside to avoid a puddle on the path.

10   It is curious, but till that moment I had never realized what it means to destroy a healthy, conscious man. When I saw the prisoner step aside to avoid the puddle, I saw the mystery, the unspeakable wrongness, of cutting a life short when it is in full tide. This man was not dying, he was alive just as we are alive. All the organs of his body were working—bowels digesting food, skin renewing itself, nails growing, tissues forming—all toiling away in solemn foolery. His nails would still be growing when he stood on the drop, when he was falling through the air with a tenth-of-a-second to live. His eyes saw the yellow gravel and the grey walls, and his brain still remembered, foresaw, reasoned—reasoned even about puddles. He and we were a party of men walking together, seeing, hearing, feeling, understanding the same world; and in two minutes, with a sudden snap, one of us would be gone—one mind less, one world less.

11   The gallows stood in a small yard, separate from the main grounds of the prison, and overgrown with tall prickly weeds. It was a brick erection like three sides of a shed, with planking on top, and above that two beams and a crossbar with the rope dangling. The hangman, a grey-haired convict in the white uniform of the prison, was waiting beside his machine. He greeted us with a servile crouch as we entered. At a word from Francis the two warders, gripping the prisoner more closely than ever, half led, half pushed him to the gallows and helped him clumsily up the ladder. Then the hangman climbed up and fixed the rope round the prisoner's neck.

12   We stood waiting, five yards away. The warders had formed in a rough circle round the gallows. And then, when the noose was fixed, the prisoner began crying out to his god. It was a high, reiterated cry of "Ram! Ram! Ram! Ram!" not urgent and fearful like a prayer or cry for help, but steady, rhythmical, almost like the tolling of a bell. The dog answered the sound with a whine. The hangman, still standing on the gallows, produced a small cotton bag like a flour bag and drew it down over the prisoner's face. But the sound, muffled by the cloth, still persisted, over and over again: "Ram! Ram! Ram! Ram! Ram!"

13   The hangman climbed down and stood ready, holding the lever. Minutes seemed to pass. The steady, muffled crying from the prisoner went on and on "Ram! Ram! Ram!" never faltering for an instant. The superintendent, his head on his chest, was slowly poking the ground with his stick; perhaps he was counting the cries, allowing the prisoner a fixed number—fifty, perhaps, or a hundred. Everyone had changed color. The Indians had gone grey like bad coffee, and one or two of the bayonets were wavering. We looked at the lashed, hooded man on the drop, and listened to his cries—each cry another second of life; the same thought was in all our minds: oh, kill him quickly, get it over, stop that abominable noise!

NOTES
gait (par. 9): walk
servile crouch (par. 11): bending like an obedient servant
reiterated (par. 12): repeated
abominable (par. 13): awful

14   Suddenly the superintendent made up his mind. Throwing up his head he made a swift motion with his stick. "Chalo!" he shouted almost fiercely.

15   There was a clanking noise, and then dead silence. The prisoner had vanished, and the rope was twisted on itself. I let go of the dog, and it galloped immediately to the back of the gallows; but when it got there it stopped short, barked, and then retreated into a corner of the yard, where it stood among the weeds, looking timorously out at us. We went round the gallows to inspect the prisoner's body. He was dangling with his toes pointed straight downwards, very slowly revolving, as dead as a stone.

16   The superintendent reached out with his stick and poked the bare body; it oscillated, slightly. "*He's* all right," said the superintendent. He backed out from under the gallows, and blew out a deep breath. The moody look had gone out of his face quite suddenly. He glanced at his wrist-watch. "Eight minutes past eight. Well, that's all for this morning, thank God."

17   The warders unfixed bayonets and marched away. The dog, sobered and conscious of having misbehaved itself, slipped after them. We walked out of the gallows yard, past the condemned cells with their waiting prisoners, into the big central yard of the prison. The convicts, under the command of warders armed with lathis, were already receiving their breakfast. They squatted in long rows, each man holding a tin pannikin, while two warders with buckets marched round ladling out rice; it seemed quite a homely, jolly scene, after the hanging. An enormous relief had come upon us now that the job was done. One felt an impulse to sing, to break into a run, to snigger. All at once everyone began chattering gaily.

18   The Eurasian boy walking beside me nodded towards the way we had come, with a knowing smile: "Do you know, sir, our friend (he meant the dead man), when he heard his appeal had been dismissed, he pissed on the floor of his cell. From fright. Kindly take one of my cigarettes, sir. Do you not admire my new silver case, sir? From the boxwallah, two rupees eight annas. Classy European style."

19   Several people laughed—at what, nobody seemed certain.

20   Francis was walking by the superintendent, talking garrulously: "Well, sir, all hass passed off with the utmost satisfactoriness. It wass all finished—flick! like that. It iss not always so—oah, no! I have known cases where the doctor wass obliged to go beneath the gallows and pull the prisoner's legs to ensure decease. Most disagreeable!"

21   "Wriggling about, eh? That's bad," said the superintendent.

22   "Ach, sir, it iss worse when they become refractory! One man, I recall, clung to the bars of hiss cage when we went to take him out. You will scarcely credit, sir, that it took six warders to dislodge him, three pulling at each leg. We reasoned with him. 'My dear fellow,' we said, 'think of all the pain and trouble you are causing to us!' But no, he would not listen! Ach, he was very troublesome!"

NOTES

"Chalo" (par. 14): start

timorously (par. 15): timidly, shyly

oscillated (par. 16): moved back and forth

lathis (par. 17): clubs

pannikin (par. 17): cup

boxwallah (par. 18): peddler

rupees and *annas* (par. 18): Rupees are the basic monetary unit of India; annas are equal to one-sixteenth of a rupee.

talking garrulously (par. 20): talking in a rambling manner, babbling

refractory (par. 22): stubborn

23   I found that I was laughing quite loudly. Everyone was laughing. Even the superintendent grinned in a tolerant way. "You'd better all come out and have a drink," he said quite genially. "I've got a bottle of whisky in the car. We could do with it."

24   We went through the big double gates of the prison, into the road. "Pulling at his legs!" exclaimed a Burmese magistrate suddenly, and burst into a loud chuckling. We all began laughing again. At that moment Francis's anecdote seemed extraordinarily funny. We all had a drink together, native and European alike, quite amicably. The dead man was a hundred yards away.

NOTES
genially (par. 23): pleasantly
amicably (par. 24): friendly

Death and Justice

Edward Koch

1   Last December a man named Robert Lee Willie, who had been convicted of raping and murdering an 18-year-old woman, was executed in a Louisiana state prison. In a statement issued several minutes before his death, Mr. Willie said: "Killing people is wrong . . . . It makes no difference whether it's citizens, countries, or governments. Killing is wrong." Two weeks later in South Carolina, an admitted killer named Joseph Carl Shaw was put to death for murdering two teenagers. In an appeal to the governor for clemency, Mr. Shaw wrote: "Killing was wrong when I did it. Killing is wrong when you do it. I hope you have the courage and the moral strength to stop the killing."

2   It is a curiosity of modern life that we find ourselves being lectured on morality by cold-blooded killers. Mr. Willie previously had been convicted of aggravated rape, aggravated kidnapping, and the murders of a Louisiana deputy and a man from Missouri. Mr. Shaw committed another murder a week before the two for which he was executed, and admitted mutilating the body of a 14-year-old girl he killed. I can't help wondering what prompted these murderers to speak out against killing as they entered the death-house door. Did their newfound reverence for life stem from the realization that they were about to lose their own?

3   Life is indeed precious, and I believe the death penalty helps to affirm this fact. Had the death penalty been a real possibility in the minds of these murderers, they might well have stayed their hand. They might have shown moral awareness before their victims died, and not after. Consider the tragic death of Rosa Velez, who happened to be home when a man named Luis Vera burglarized her apartment in Brooklyn. "Yeah, I shot her," Vera admitted. "She knew me, and I knew I wouldn't go to the chair."

4   During my 22 years in public service, I have heard the pros and cons of capital punishment expressed with special intensity. As a district leader,

NOTES
clemency (par. 1): a reduction of the sentence given a criminal
affirm (par. 3): confirm, support
stayed (par. 3): stopped
the chair (par. 3): that is, the electric chair

councilman, congressman, and mayor, I have represented constituencies generally thought of as liberal. Because I support the death penalty for heinous crimes of murder, I have sometimes been the subject of emotional and outraged attacks by voters who find my position reprehensible or worse. I have listened to their ideas. I have weighed their objections carefully. I still support the death penalty. The reasons I maintain my position can be best understood by examining the arguments most frequently heard in opposition.

5 1. *The death penalty is "barbaric."* Sometimes opponents of capital punishment horrify with tales of lingering death on the gallows, of faulty electric chairs, or of agony in the gas chamber. Partly in response to such protests, several states such as North Carolina and Texas switched to death by lethal injection. The condemned person is put to death painlessly, without ropes, voltage, bullets, or gas. Did this answer the objections of death penalty opponents? Of course not. On June 22, 1984, *The New York Times* published an editorial that sarcastically attacked the new "hygienic" method of death by injection, and stated that "execution can never be made humane through science." So it's not the method that really troubles opponents. It's the death itself they consider barbaric.

6 Admittedly, capital punishment is not a pleasant topic. However, one does not have to like the death penalty in order to support it any more than one must like radical surgery, radiation, or chemotherapy in order to find necessary these attempts at curing cancer. Ultimately we may learn how to cure cancer with a simple pill. Unfortunately, that day has not yet arrived. Today we are faced with the choice of letting the cancer spread or trying to cure it with the methods available, methods that one day will almost certainly be considered barbaric. But to give up and do nothing would be far more barbaric and would certainly delay the discovery of an eventual cure. The analogy between cancer and murder is imperfect, because murder is not the "disease" we are trying to cure. The disease is injustice. We may not like the death penalty, but it must be available to punish crimes of cold-blooded murder, cases in which any other form of punishment would be inadequate and, therefore, unjust. If we create a society in which injustice is not tolerated, incidents of murder—the most flagrant form of injustice—will diminish.

7 2. *No other major democracy uses the death penalty.* No other major democracy—in fact, few other countries of any description—is plagued by a murder rate such as that in the United States. Fewer and fewer Americans can remember the days when unlocked doors were the norm and murder was a rare and terrible offense. In America the murder rate climbed 122 percent between 1963 and 1980. During that same period, the murder rate in New York City increased by almost 400 percent, and the statistics are even worse

NOTES
constituencies (par. 4): groups of voters
liberal (par. 4): one who tends to favor social or political reform; A conservative is one who tends to favor the preservation of existing social or political systems.
heinous (par. 4): horribly evil
reprehensible (par. 4): deserving strong criticism
"barbaric" (par. 5): brutal, uncivilized
lethal (par. 5): deadly
"hygienic" (par. 5): clean, neat
humane (par. 5): compassionate
analogy (par. 6): comparison
flagrant (par. 6): obvious

in many other cities. A study at M.I.T. showed that based on 1970 homicide rates a person who lived in a large American city ran a greater risk of being murdered than an American soldier in World War II ran of being killed in combat. It is not surprising that the laws of each country differ according to differing conditions and traditions. If other countries had our murder problem, the cry for capital punishment would be just as loud as it is here. And I dare say that any other major democracy where 75 percent of the people supported the death penalty would soon enact it into law.

8   3. *An innocent person might be executed by mistake.* Consider the work of Adam Bedau, one of the most implacable foes of capital punishment in this country. According to Mr. Bedau, it is "false sentimentality to argue that the death penalty should be abolished because of the abstract possibility that an innocent person might be executed." He cites a study of the 7,000 executions in this country from 1893 to 1971, and concludes that the record fails to show that such cases occur. The main point, however, is this. If government functioned only when the possibility of error didn't exist, government wouldn't function at all. Human life deserves special protection, and one of the best ways to guarantee that protection is to assure that convicted murderers do not kill again. Only the death penalty can accomplish this end. In a recent case in New Jersey, a man named Richard Biegenwald was freed from prison after serving 18 years for murder; since his release he has been convicted of committing four murders. A prisoner named Lemuel Smith, who, while serving four life sentences for murder (plus two life sentences for kidnapping and robbery) in New York's Green Haven Prison, lured a woman corrections officer into the chaplain's office and strangled her. He then mutilated and dismembered her body. An additional life sentence for Smith is meaningless. Because New York has no death penalty statute, Smith has effectively been given a license to kill.

9   But the problem of multiple murder is not confined to the nation's penitentiaries. In 1981, 91 police officers were killed in the line of duty in this country. Seven percent of those arrested in the cases that have been solved had a previous arrest for murder. In New York City in 1976 and 1977, 85 persons arrested for homicide had a previous arrest for murder. Six of these individuals had two previous arrests for murder, and one had four previous murder arrests. During those two years the New York police were arresting for murder persons with a previous arrest for murder on the average of one every 8.5 days. This is not surprising when we learn that in 1975, for example, the median time served in Massachusetts for homicide was less than two-and-a-half years. In 1976 a study sponsored by the Twentieth Century Fund found the average time served in the United States for first degree murder is ten years. The median time served may be considerably lower.

10   4. *Capital punishment cheapens the value of human life.* On the contrary, it can be easily demonstrated that the death penalty strengthens the value of human life. If the penalty for rape were lowered, clearly it would signal a lessened regard for the victims' suffering, humiliation, and personal integrity. It would cheapen their horrible experience, and expose them to an increased danger of recurrence. When we lower the penalty for murder, it signals a lessened regard for the value of the victim's life. Some critics of capital punish-

NOTES
M.I.T. (par. 7): Massachusetts Institute of Technology
implacable (par. 8): unchanging
dismembered (par. 8): cut the limbs off
statute (par. 8): law

ment, such as columnist Jimmy Breslin, have suggested that a life sentence is actually a harsher penalty for murder than death. This is sophistic nonsense. A few killers may decide not to appeal a death sentence, but the overwhelming majority make every effort to stay alive. It is by exacting the highest penalty for the taking of human life that we affirm the highest value of human life.

11   5. *The death penalty is applied in a discriminatory manner.* This factor no longer seems to be the problem it once was. The appeals process for a condemned prisoner is lengthy and painstaking. Every effort is made to see that the verdict and sentence were fairly arrived at. However, assertions of discrimination are not an argument for ending the death penalty but for extending it. It is not justice to exclude everyone from the penalty of the law if a few are found to be so favored. Justice requires that the law be applied equally to all.

12   6. *Thou Shalt Not Kill.* The Bible is our greatest source of moral inspiration. Opponents of the death penalty frequently cite the sixth of the Ten Commandments in an attempt to prove that capital punishment is divinely proscribed. In the original Hebrew, however, the Sixth Commandment reads, "Thou Shall Not Commit Murder," and the Torah specifies capital punishment for a variety of offenses. The biblical viewpoint has been upheld by philosophers throughout history. The greatest thinkers of the 19th century— Kant, Locke, Hobbes, Rousseau, Montesquieu, and Mill—agreed that natural law properly authorizes the sovereign to take life in order to vindicate justice. Only Jeremy Bentham was ambivalent. Washington, Jefferson, and Franklin endorsed it. Abraham Lincoln authorized executions for deserters in wartime. Alexis de Tocqueville, who expressed profound respect for American institutions, believed that the death penalty was indispensable to the support of social order. The United States Constitution, widely admired as one of the seminal achievements in the history of humanity, condemns cruel and inhuman punishment, but does not condemn capital punishment.

13   7. *The death penalty is state-sanctioned murder.* This is the defense with which Messrs. Willie and Shaw hoped to soften the resolve of those who sentenced them to death. By saying in effect, "You're no better than I am," the murderer seeks to bring his accusers down to his own level. It is also a popular argument among opponents of capital punishment, but a transparently false one. Simply put, the state has rights that the private individual does not. In a democracy, those rights are given to the state by the electorate. The execution of a lawfully condemned killer is no more an act of murder than is legal imprisonment an act of kidnapping. If an individual forces a neighbor to pay him money under a threat of punishment, it's called extortion. If the state

NOTES
sophistic (par. 10): clever
assertions (par. 11): claims
proscribed (par. 12): forbidden
Torah (par. 12): sacred law of Judaism; first five books of the Old Testament
sovereign (par. 12): ruler
vindicate (par. 12): defend
ambivalent (par. 12): unsure
indispensable (par. 12): necessary
seminal (par. 12): creative
sanctioned (par. 13): approved
resolve (par. 13): determination
transparently (par. 13): obviously
electorate (par. 13): voters

does it, it's called taxation. Rights and responsibilities surrendered by the individual are what give the state its power to govern. This contract is the foundation of civilization itself.

14   Everyone wants his or her rights, and will defend them zealously. Not everyone, however, wants responsibilities, especially the painful responsibilities that come with law enforcement. Twenty-one years ago a woman named Kitty Genovese was assaulted and murdered on a street in New York. Dozens of neighbors heard her cries for help but did nothing to assist her. They didn't even call the police. In such a climate the criminal understandably grows bolder. In the presence of moral cowardice, he lectures us on our supposed failings and tries to equate his crimes with our quest for justice.

15   The death of anyone—even a convicted killer—diminishes us all. But we are diminished even more by a justice system that fails to function. It is an illusion to let ourselves believe that doing away with capital punishment removes the murderer's deed from our conscience. The rights of society are paramount. When we protect guilty lives, we give up innocent lives in exchange. When opponents of capital punishment say to the state: "I will not let you kill in my name," they are also saying to murderers: "You can kill in your *own* name as long as I have an excuse for not getting involved."

16   It is hard to imagine anything worse than being murdered while neighbors do nothing. But something worse exists. When those neighbors shrink back from justly punishing the murderer, the victim dies twice.

NOTES
zealously (par. 14): passionately
diminishes (par. 15): lessens
paramount (par. 15): most important

A Question of Values

Andrew Pate

1   In a recent literature class, I was trying to interest my students in questions raised in the two stories assigned for the day's discussion. As powerful literature does, these stories concern our place in the world: What kind of world is it? How can we make sense of it? Specifically, they raise questions about human suffering and how we are to understand it, questions people have been struggling with at least since the writing of the Book of Job.

2   Such works don't presume to offer rigid answers; rather, they try to show us something of life, and so encourage us to look again at our own experience of the world and ourselves. If we are able to look at life with a fresh eye, to deepen or broaden our vision of it, what a wonderful thing. We are changed. In my opinion, education has—or should have—this as its end.

3   Perhaps I was too heavy-handed in my presentation of the questions: How are we to understand seemingly accidental suffering? Does it have meaning? What role does God play in this? Perhaps I didn't give the students time to come upon the questions for themselves. In any event, the response was

NOTES
Book of Job (par. 1): book from the Old Testament that focuses on human suffering
presume (par. 2): claim, attempt
rigid (par. 2): definite

disturbing. After some heatedly voiced opinions, several students said in effect that we had no business concerning ourselves with such matters. Their reasons: "We cannot decide the answer in class, so why bother to discuss it?" And, "there are some things we simply are not meant to question."

4   I wouldn't want to give the impression that the class as a whole—or even many of its members—felt that way. But a sizable minority seemed to, enough to set the tone. It was not the first time I have been struck by the attitudes people bring to learning, but each time it is like an unexpected slap in the face. All I could think was, "These people don't know what education is." The two attitudes most troubling to me were neatly expressed in class that day. One is the idea that some questions are off limits; for those, we should merely accept whatever the authorities tell us. The other, I think closely related to the first, is a deep apathy: "Why bother to ask questions anyway? What good does it do?"

5   Yet, people attend college "to receive an education," or rather to continue one they have been receiving for a dozen years. What do they—what do we—mean by that phrase? I think we, as individuals and as a society, need to ask ourselves some important questions. What do we believe education to be? What is its purpose? Why bother, anyway?

6   I thought a great deal about such concerns in the three years I spent teaching English literature in China. As I watched people to whom I had grown very close courageously ask hard questions of themselves and their society, as I listened to many of them complain of the hopelessness of their efforts, I had to ask myself what my place was in all this. With the turmoil and oppression in Chinese society, what is the role of education?

7   I was struck by the extremes of response I drew, in my role as foreign teacher. The students were overwhelmingly enthusiastic; they were hungry for information about the outside world. The teachers were more reserved, perhaps because of their greater familiarity with the government's attitude. And the authorities were torn between need and fear. They need new ideas, but are terribly threatened by them. On the one hand, they know that if China is to raise its standard of living the people must learn to incorporate Western technology. To do this, they need English language skills, among others. In order to interact productively with the outside world, they must have some understanding of it, so the authorities can accept the study of foreign literature. On the other hand, there has been ample evidence in the past decade that such learning produces by-products which are not at all to the liking of those in power.

8   As people learn, they question. As the Chinese learn more about the outside world, they ask questions about their own society. They can never see it again as they did before China's opening to the West, and the leadership surely realizes that the change taking place now cannot be erased. Who knows what direction it will take? But the people, having learned something, cannot lose it. They have been changed; they cannot be what they once were.

9   This is the power of education. Real education, that opens people's minds to new ideas, that helps them to see themselves and their world in a new way, that teaches them not what to think but how to think well, is a force to be reckoned with. Witness the demonstrations in Beijing's Tiananmen Square three years ago last week, led by students.

NOTES

apathy (par. 4): lack of concern

to incorporate (par. 7): to make use of

Beijing's Tiananmen Square (par. 9): the site of a 1989 uprising led primarily by students demanding democratic reform; The uprising was brutally put down by Chinese authorities.

10   This is not to say that real education is restricted to the classroom (if only it were more often found there). On the contrary, most of each person's learning takes place informally. And it is important to realize that there is a connection between the informal education we each receive from our families and society and the formal education we receive in schools. The roots of education reach much deeper than the classroom. They must absorb nutrients from the surrounding culture. So it seems clear that the values by which we live our lives in the "real" world will be reflected in the attitudes we bring to the classroom.

11   Among Chinese youth cynicism runs deep. Student cheating is epidemic. I remember debating with a group of close friends and students the justifiability of cheating on exams. Many found it difficult to understand my qualms. Their reaction: "The system cheats us all the time, why shouldn't we cheat it? They lie to us, why shouldn't we lie to them?" When I responded that some actions are simply wrong, they smiled and said, "We understand what you are saying, but this is the real world." When people have such attitudes—and they are not limited to cheating on school exams—then what is suggested about the society which has nurtured them?

12   In the spring of 1990, the Chinese government initiated one of its periodic campaigns toward moral reform. Most people I knew played along, doing what was expected of them, attending meetings, not believing a word of it. They were so angry at the irony they had to laugh that the men who had brutally put down the students in Tiananmen Square were now presuming to play the role of moral authority. Besides, they said, ideals of charity, of devotion to duty, are nice to talk about, but "you cannot live like that in China today; if you were to try, you would not survive."

13   The youth were learning to separate what their society claims as its values from those values it actually holds. No wonder they were so cynical. Their cynicism, to me, seemed an expression of frustration and almost-lost hope. The events in Tiananmen in 1989 were in part a product of those hopes and frustrations.

14   But China is not alone in having frustrated and cynical youth. I recently had a student to write an essay defining "success." It is measured, he wrote, by money and power. I tried to persuade him that this was but one type of success, and that there might be others. I wanted him to consider his topic from various angles, to see it more broadly and, I hoped, more deeply.

15   "How do different types of people measure success?" I asked him. He explained, in his revision, that doctors and drug dealers are no different, really: They both are motivated by money and power; one had the chance to go to medical school, the other didn't. I asked him about people of deep religious faith: "What is success to them?" He told me that he has a strong faith himself, that he was raised in a church-going family, that such ideas are well and good, but that "this is the real world."

16   So I am not surprised when a student, so innocently, and yet with such tired, if unconscious, cynicism, says, "Why bother to ask questions about our beliefs and values?" Why bother, indeed. After all, what do such questions have to do with the "real" world in which we must live? But I am saddened.

NOTES

cynicism (par. 11): an attitude of distrust or suspicion
epidemic (par. 11): widespread
qualms (par. 11): concerns
nurtured (par. 11): developed
periodic (par. 12): occasional
irony (par. 12): contradiction

I am saddened by what that person has shown me about the attitude our society has taught him to bring to his education. We have given him little sense of its power or his responsibility. We have given him little sense of wonder at this opportunity to question, this freedom that many Chinese would die for, and have.

17   Thomas Jefferson wrote 200 years ago of the fundamental importance of "the diffusion of knowledge among the people. No other sure foundation can be devised, for the preservation of freedom and happiness." A half-century later, Ralph Waldo Emerson wrote: "Education should be commensurate with the object of life. It should be a moral one; to teach self-trust; to inspire the youthful man with an interest in himself; with a curiosity touching his own nature; to acquaint him with the resources of his mind, and to teach him that there is all his strength, and to inflame him with a piety towards the Grand Mind in which he lives."

18   Each of these men was greatly concerned with the role of education in a society of free individuals. Each of them foresaw the sorts of dangers we are facing, but they remained hopeful. I hope that our students may learn to respect themselves and others enough to listen to what Jefferson and Emerson have to say to us today. The role of real education, real thinking and real questioning is crucial in a healthy, free society.

NOTES
diffusion (par. 17): spreading
commensurate with (par. 17): directly related to
piety (par. 17): devotion, great respect

Mother Tongue

Amy Tan

1   I am not a scholar of English or literature. I cannot give you much more than personal opinions on the English language and its variations in this country or others.

2   I am a writer. And by that definition, I am someone who has always loved language. I am fascinated by language in daily life. I spend a great deal of my time thinking about the power of language—the way it can evoke an emotion, a visual image, a complex idea, or a simple truth. Language is the tool of my trade. And I use them all—all the Englishes I grew up with.

3   Recently, I was made keenly aware of the different Englishes I do use. I was giving a talk to a large group of people, the same talk I had already given to half a dozen other groups. The nature of the talk was about my writing, my life, and my book, *The Joy Luck Club*. The talk was going along well enough, until I remembered one major difference that made the whole talk sound wrong. My mother was in the room. And it was perhaps the first time she had heard me give a lengthy speech, using the kind of English I have never used with her. I was saying things like, "The intersection of memory upon imagination" and "There is an aspect of my fiction that relates to

NOTE
evoke (par. 2): call forth

thus-and-thus"—a speech filled with carefully wrought grammatical phrases, burdened, it suddenly seemed to me, with nominalized forms, past perfect tenses, conditional phrases, all the forms of standard English that I had learned in school and through books, the forms of English I did not use at home with my mother.

4   Just last week, I was walking down the street with my mother, and I again found myself conscious of the English I was using, the English I do use with her. We were talking about the price of new and used furniture and I heard myself saying this: "Not waste money that way." My husband was with us as well, and he didn't notice any switch in my English. And then I realized why. It's because over the twenty years we've been together I've often used that same kind of English with him, and sometimes he even uses it with me. It has become our language of intimacy, a different sort of English that relates to family talk, the language I grew up with.

5   So you'll have some idea of what this family talk I heard sounds like, I'll quote what my mother said during a recent conversation which I videotaped and than transcribed. During this conversation, my mother was talking about a political gangster in Shanghai who had the same last name as her family's, Du, and how the gangster in his early years wanted to be adopted by her family, which was rich by comparison. Later, the gangster became more powerful, far richer than my mother's family, and one day showed up at my mother's wedding to pay his respects. Here's what she said in part:

6   "Du Yusong having business like fruit stand. Like off the street kind. He is Du like Du Zong—but not Tsung-ming Island people. The local people call putong, the river east side, he belong to that side local people. That man want to ask Du Zong father take him in like become own family. Du Zong father wasn't look down on him, but didn't take seriously, until that man big like become a mafia. Now important person, very hard to inviting him. Chinese way, came only to show respect, don't stay for dinner. Respect for making big celebration, he shows up. Mean gives lots of respect. Chinese custom. Chinese social life that way. If too important won't have to stay too long. He come to my wedding. I didn't see, I heard it. I gone to boy's side, they have YMCA dinner. Chinese age I was nineteen."

7   You should know that my mother's expressive command of English belies how much she actually understands. She reads the *Forbes* report, listens to *Wall Street Week,* converses daily with her stockbroker, reads all of Shirley MacLaine's books with ease—all kinds of things I can't begin to understand. Yet some of my friends tell me they understand 50 percent of what my mother says. Some say they understand 80 to 90 percent. Some say they understand none of it, as if she were speaking pure Chinese. But to me, my mother's English is perfectly clear, perfectly natural. It's my mother tongue. Her language, as I hear it, is vivid, direct, full of observation and imagery. That was the language that helped shape the way I saw things, expressed things, made sense of the world.

8   Lately, I've been giving more thought to the kind of English my mother speaks. Like others, I have described it to people as "broken" or "fractured" English. But I wince when I say that. It has always bothered me that I can

NOTES
wrought (par. 3): constructed
nominalized (par. 3): referring to nouns
intimacy (par. 4): personal communication
belies (par. 7): disguises
vivid (par. 7): lively
wince (par. 8): react with discomfort

think of no way to describe it other than "broken," as if it were damaged and needed to be fixed, as if it lacked a certain wholeness and soundness. I've heard other terms used, "limited English," for example. But they seem just as bad, as if everything is limited, including people's perceptions of the limited English speaker.

9   I know this for a fact, because when I was growing up, my mother's "limited" English limited *my* perception of her. I was ashamed of her English. I believed that her English reflected the quality of what she had to say. That is, because she expressed them imperfectly her thoughts were imperfect. And I had plenty of empirical evidence to support me: the fact that people in department stores, at banks, and at restaurants did not take her seriously, did not give her good service, pretended not to understand her, or even acted as if they did not hear her.

10   My mother has long realized the limitations of her English as well. When I was fifteen, she used to have me call people on the phone to pretend I was she. In this guise, I was forced to ask for information or even to complain and yell at people who had been rude to her. One time it was a call to her stockbroker in New York. She had cashed out her small portfolio and it just so happened we were going to go to New York the next week, our very first trip outside California. I had to get on the phone and say in an adolescent voice that was not very convincing, "This is Mrs. Tan."

11   And my mother was standing in the back whispering loudly, "Why he don't send me check, already two weeks late. So mad he lie to me, losing me money."

12   And then I said in perfect English, "Yes, I'm getting rather concerned. You had agreed to send the check two weeks ago, but it hasn't arrived."

13   Then she began to talk more loudly. "What he want, I come to New York tell him front of his boss, you cheating me?" And I was trying to calm her down, make her be quiet, while telling the stockbroker, "I can't tolerate any more excuses. If I don't receive the check immediately, I am going to have to speak to your manager when I'm in New York next week." And sure enough, the following week there we were in front of this astonished stockbroker, and I was sitting there red-faced and quiet, and my mother, the real Mrs. Tan, was shouting at his boss in her impeccable broken English.

14   We used a similar routine just five days ago, for a situation that was far less humorous. My mother had gone to the hospital for an appointment, to find out about a benign brain tumor a CAT scan had revealed a month ago. She said she had spoken very good English, her best English, no mistakes. Still, she said, the hospital did not apologize when they said they had lost the CAT scan and she had come for nothing. She said they did not seem to have any sympathy when she told them she was anxious to know the exact diagnosis, since her husband and son had both died of brain tumors. She said they would not give her any more information until the next time and she would have to make another appointment for that. So she said she would not leave until the doctor called her daughter. She wouldn't budge. And when the doctor finally called her daughter, me, who spoke in perfect English—lo and behold—we had assurances the CAT scan would be found, promises that a conference call on Monday would be held, and apologies for any suffering my mother had gone through for a most regrettable mistake.

NOTES

empirical evidence (par. 9): evidence gathered from one's observations
portfolio (par. 10): collection of stocks
impeccable (par. 13): flawless
benign (par. 14): non-cancerous

15   I think my mother's English almost had an effect on limiting my possibilities in life as well. Sociologists and linguists probably will tell you that a person's developing language skills are more influenced by peers. But I do think that the language spoken in the family, especially in immigrant families which are more insular, plays a large role in shaping the language of the child. And I believe that it affected my results on achievement tests, IQ tests, and the SAT. While my English skills were never judged as poor, compared to math, English could not be considered my strong suit. In grade school I did moderately well, getting perhaps B's, sometimes B-pluses, in English and scoring perhaps in the sixtieth or seventieth percentile on achievement tests. But those scores were not good enough to override the opinion that my true abilities lay in math and science, because in those areas I achieved A's and scored in the ninetieth percentile or higher.

16   This was understandable. Math is precise; there is only one correct answer. Whereas, for me at least, the answers on English tests were always a judgment call, a matter of opinion and personal experience. Those tests were constructed around items like fill-in-the-blank sentence completion, such as, "Even though Tom was_____, Mary thought he was_____." And the correct answer always seemed to be the most bland combinations of thoughts, for example, "Even though Tom was shy, Mary thought he was charming," with the grammatical structure "even though" limiting the correct answer to some sort of semantic opposites, so you wouldn't get answers like, "Even though Tom was foolish, Mary thought he was ridiculous." Well, according to my mother, there were very few limitations as to what Tom could have been and what Mary might have thought of him. So I never did well on tests like that.

17   The same was true with word analogies, pairs of words in which you were supposed to find some sort of logical, semantic relationship—for example, "*Sunset* is to *nightfall* as_____ is to_____." And here you would be presented with a list of four possible pairs, one of which showed the same kind of relationship: *red* is to *stoplight, bus* is to *arrival, chills* is to *fever, yawn* is to *boring.* Well, I could never think that way. I knew what the tests were asking, but I could not block out of my mind the images already created by the first pair, "*sunset* is to *nightfall*"—and I would see a burst of colors against a darkening sky, the moon rising, the lowering of a curtain of stars. And all the other pairs of words—red, bus, stoplight, boring—just threw up a mass of confusing images, making it impossible for me to sort out something as logical as saying: "A sunset precedes nightfall" is the same as "a chill precedes a fever." The only way I would have gotten that answer right would have been to imagine an associative situation, for example, my being disobedient and staying out past sunset, catching a chill at night, which turns into feverish pneumonia as punishment, which indeed did happen to me.

18   I have been thinking about all this lately, about my mother's English, about achievement tests. Because lately I've been asked, as a writer, why there are not more Asian-Americans represented in American literature. Why are there few Asian-Americans enrolled in creative writing programs? Why do so many Chinese students go into engineering? Well, these are broad sociological questions I can't begin to answer. But I have noticed in surveys—in fact, just last week—that Asian students, as a whole, always do significantly better on math achievement tests than in English. And this makes me think that

NOTES
linguists (par. 15): specialists in language studies
insular (par. 15): isolated
semantic opposites (par. 16): terms opposite in meaning

there are other Asian-American students whose English spoken in the home might also be described as "broken" or "limited." And perhaps they also have teachers who are steering them away from writing and into math and science, which is what happened to me.

19   Fortunately, I happen to be rebellious in nature and enjoy the challenge of disproving assumptions made about me. I became an English major my first year in college, after being enrolled as pre-med. I started writing nonfiction as a freelancer the week after I was told by my former boss that writing was my worst skill and I should hone my talents toward account management.

20   But it wasn't until 1985 that I finally began to write fiction. And at first I wrote using what I thought to be wittily crafted sentences, sentences that would finally prove I had mastery over the English language. Here's an example from the first draft of a story that later made its way into *The Joy Luck Club*, but without this line: "That was my mental quandary in its nascent state." A terrible line, which I can barely pronounce.

21   Fortunately, for reasons I won't get into today, I later decided I should envision a reader for the stories I would write. And the reader I decided upon was my mother, because these were stories about mothers. So with this reader in mind—and in fact she did read my early drafts—I began to write stories using all the Englishes I grew up with: the English I spoke to my mother, which for lack of a better term might be described as "simple"; the English she used with me, which for lack of a better term might be described as "broken"; my translation of her Chinese, which could certainly be described as "watered down"; and what I imagined to be her translation of her Chinese if she could speak in perfect English, her internal language, and for that I sought to preserve the essence, but neither an English nor a Chinese structure. I wanted to capture what language ability tests can never reveal: her intent, her passion, her imagery, the rhythms of her speech and the nature of her thoughts.

22   Apart from what any critic had to say about my writing, I knew I had succeeded where it counted when my mother finished reading my book and gave me her verdict: "So easy to read."

NOTES
freelancer (par. 19): a self-employed writer
hone (par. 19): develop
quandary (par. 20): dilemma
nascent (par. 20): beginning
envision (par. 21): imagine
essence (par. 21): essential and distinct qualities

Confession of a Female Chauvinist Sow

Anne Richardson Roiphe

1   I once married a man I thought was totally unlike my father and I imagined a whole new world of freedom emerging. Five years later it was clear even to me—floating face down in a wash of despair—that I had simply

NOTES
chauvinist (title): one who believes in the superiority of one's own group
sow (title): female pig

chosen a replica of my handsome daddy-true. The updated version spoke English like an angel but—good God!—underneath he was my father exactly: wonderful, but not the right man for me.

2   Most people I know have at one time or another been fouled up by their childhood experiences. Patterns tend to sink into the unconscious only to reappear, disguised, unseen, like marionettes' strings, pulling us this way or that. Whatever ails people—keeps them up at night, tossing and turning—also ails movements no matter how historically huge or politically important. The women's movement cannot remake consciousness, or reshape the future, without acknowledging and shedding all the unnecessary and ugly baggage of the past. It's easy enough to recognize the hidden directions that limit Sis to cake-baking and Junior to bridge-building; it's now possible for even Miss America herself to identify what *they* have done to us, and, of course, *they* have and *they* did and *they* are. . . . But along the way we also developed our own hidden prejudices, class assumptions and an anti-male humor and collection of expectations that gave us, like all oppressed groups, *a secret sense of superiority (co-existing with a poor self-image*—it's not news that people can believe two contradictory things at once).

3   Listen to any group that suffers materially and socially. They have a lexicon with which they tease the enemy: ofay, goy, honky, gringo. "Poor pale devils," said Malcolm X loud enough for us to hear, although blacks had joked about that to each other for years. Behind some of the women's liberation thinking lurk the rumors, the prejudices, the defense systems of generations of oppressed women whispering in the kitchen together, presenting one face to their menfolk and another to their card clubs, their mothers and sisters. All this is natural enough but potentially dangerous in a revolutionary situation in which you hope to create *a future that does not mirror the past.* The hidden anti-male feelings, a result of the old system, will foul us up if they are allowed to persist.

4   During my teen years I never left the house on Saturday night dates without my mother slipping me a few extra dollars—mad money, it was called. I'll explain what it was for the benefit of the new generation in which people just sleep with each other: the fellow was supposed to bring me home, *lead me safely through the asphalt jungle, protect me from slithering snakes, rapists and the like.* But my mother and I knew young men were apt to drink too much, to slosh down so many rye-and-gingers that some hero might well lead me in front of an oncoming bus, smash his daddy's car into Tiffany's window or, less gallantly, throw up on my new dress. Mad money was for getting home on your own, no matter what form of insanity your date happened to evidence. Mad money was also a wallflower's rope ladder; if the guy you came with suddenly fancied someone else, well, you didn't have to stay there and

NOTES

marionettes' (par. 2): puppets'
consciousness (par. 2): awareness
baggage of the past (par. 2): theories or practices that are outdated
oppressed (par. 2): mistreated, subjected to prejudice
contradictory (par. 2): opposite
lexicon (par. 3): vocabulary
Malcolm X (par. 3): civil rights activist; assassinated in 1965
Tiffany's (par. 4): famous jewelry store in New York City
gallantly (par. 4): nobly
to evidence (par. 4): to reveal
fancied (par. 4): took a liking to

suffer, you could go home. Boys were fickle and likely to be unkind; my mother and I knew that, as surely as we knew they tried to make you do things in the dark they wouldn't respect you for afterwards, and in fact would spread the word and spoil your rep. Boys liked to be flattered; if you made them feel important they would eat out of your hand. So talk to them about their interests, don't alarm them with displays of intelligence—we all knew that, we groups of girls talking into the wee hours of the night in a kind of easy companionship we thought impossible with boys. Boys were prone to have a good time, get you pregnant, and then pretend they didn't know your name when you came knocking on their door for finances or comfort. In short, we believed boys were less moral than we were. They appeared to be hypocritical, self-seeking, exploitative, untrustworthy and very likely to be showing off their precious masculinity. I never had a girl friend I thought would be unkind or embarrass me in public. I never expected a girl to lie to me about her marks or sports skill or how good she was in bed. Altogether—without anyone's directly coming out and saying so—I gathered that men were sexy, powerful, very interesting, but not very nice, not very moral, humane and tender, like us. Girls played fairly while men, unfortunately, reserved their honor for the battlefield.

5   Why are there laws insisting on alimony and child support? Well, everyone knows that men don't have an instinct to protect their young and, given half a chance, with the moon in the right phase, they will run off and disappear. Everyone assumes a mother will not let her child starve, yet it is necessary to legislate that a father must not do so. We are taught to accept the idea that men are less than decent; their charms may be manifold but their characters are riddled with faults. To this day I never blink if I hear that a man has gone to find his fortune in South America, having left his pregnant wife, his blind mother and taken the family car. I still gasp in horror when I hear of a woman leaving her asthmatic infant for a rock group in Taos because I can't seem to avoid the assumption that men are naturally heels and women the ordained carriers of what little is moral in our dubious civilization.

6   My mother never gave me mad money thinking I would ditch a fellow for some other guy or that I would pass out drunk on the floor. She knew I would be considerate of my companion because, after all, I was more mature than the boys that gathered about. Why was I more mature? Women just are people-oriented; they learn to be empathetic at an early age. Most English students (students interested in humanity, not artifacts) are women. Men and boys—so the myth goes—conceal their feelings and lose interest in anybody else's. Everyone knows that even little boys can tell the difference between one kind of a car and another—proof that their souls are mechanical, their attention directed to the nonhuman.

7   I remember shivering in the cold vestibule of a famous men's athletic club. Women and girls are not permitted inside the club's door. What are they doing in there? I asked. They're naked, said my mother, they're sweating,

NOTES
fickle (par. 4): unreliable
prone (par. 4): inclined
exploitative (par. 4): To exploit is to use or take advantage of someone.
manifold (par. 5): many
ordained (par. 5): chosen
dubious (par. 5): uncertain
empathetic (par. 6): compassionate
artifacts (par. 6): objects
vestibule (par. 7): entryway

jumping up and down a lot, telling each other dirty jokes and bragging about their stock market exploits. Why can't we go in? I asked. Well, my mother told me, they're afraid we'd laugh at them.

8   The prejudices of childhood are hard to outgrow. I confess that every time my business takes me past that club, I shudder. Images of large bellies resting on massage tables and flaccid penises rising and falling with the Dow Jones average flash through my head. There it is, chauvinism waving its cancerous tentacles from the depths of my psyche.

9   Minorities automatically feel superior to the oppressor because, after all, they are not hurting anybody. In fact, they feel morally better. The old canard that women need love, men need sex—believed for too long by both sexes—attributes moral and spiritual superiority to women and makes of men beasts whose urges send them prowling into the night. This false division of good and bad, placing deforming pressure on everyone, doesn't have to contaminate the future. We know that the assumptions we have about each other become a part of the cultural air we breathe and, in fact, become social truths. Women who want equality must be prepared to give it and to believe in it, and in order to do that it is not enough to state that you are as good as any man, but also it must be stated that he is as good as you and both will be humans together. If we want men to share in the care of the family in a new way, we must assume them as capable of consistent loving tenderness as we.

10   I rummage about and find in my thinking all kinds of anti-male prejudices. Some are just jokes and others I will have a hard time abandoning. First, I share an emotional conviction with many sisters that women given power would not create wars. Intellectually I know that's ridiculous; great queens have waged war before; the likes of Lurleen Wallace, Pat Nixon and Mrs. General Lavelle can be depended upon in the future to guiltlessly condemn to death other people's children in the name of some ideal of their own. Little girls, of course, don't take toy guns out of their hip pockets and say "Pow, pow" to all their neighbors and friends like the average well-adjusted little boy. However, if we gave little girls the six-shooters, we would soon have double the pretend body count.

11   *Aggression is not, as I secretly think, a male-sex-linked characteristic: brutality is masculine only by virtue of opportunity.* True, there are 1,000 Jack the Rippers for every Lizzie Borden, but that surely is the result of social norms. Women as a group are indeed more masochistic than men. The practical result of this division is that women seem nicer and kinder, but when

NOTES

flaccid (par. 8): limp
tentacles (par. 8): literally, a long, flexible growth projecting from the mouth or head of some animals
psyche (par. 8): soul
canard (par. 9): a false story
conviction (par. 10): strong belief
Lurleen Wallace (par. 10): governor of Alabama from 1967–1968; wife of George Wallace, governor of Alabama (1963–1967; 1971–1979; 1983–1987)
Pat Nixon (par. 10): wife of Richard M. Nixon, President of the United States (1969–1974, resigned)
Mrs. General Lavelle (par. 10): wife of General Lavelle, one of the early commanders in Vietnam
Jack the Ripper (par. 11): the name used by an unknown mass murderer in nineteenth-century London
Lizzy Borden (par. 11): woman tried and found not guilty of murdering her parents with an axe (1892)
masochistic (par. 11): enjoying suffering

the world changes, women will have a fuller opportunity to be just as rotten as men and there will be fewer claims of female moral superiority.

12   Now that I am entering early middle age, I hear many women complaining of husbands and ex-husbands who are attracted to younger females. This strikes the older woman as unfair, of course. But I remember a time when I thought all boys around my age and grade were creeps and bores. I wanted to go out with an older man: a senior or, miraculously, a college man. I had a certain contempt for my *coevals,* not realizing that the freshman in college I thought so desirable was some older girl's creep. Some women never lose that contempt for men of their own age. That isn't fair either and may be one reason why some sensible men of middle years find solace in young women.

13   I remember coming home from school one day to find my mother's card game dissolved in hysterical laughter. The cards were floating in black rivers of running mascara. What was so funny? A woman named Helen was lying on a couch pretending to be her husband with a cold. She was issuing demands for orange juice, aspirin, suggesting a call to a specialist, complaining of neglect, of fate's cruel finger, of heat, of cold, of sharp pains on the bridge of the nose that might indicate brain involvement. What was so funny? The ladies explained to me that all men behave just like that with colds, they are reduced to temper tantrums by simple nasal congestion, men cannot stand any little physical discomfort—on and on the laughter went.

14   The point of this vignette is the nature of the laughter—*us laughing at them, us feeling superior to them, us ridiculing them behind their backs.* If they were doing it to us, we'd call it male chauvinist pigness; if we do it to them, it is inescapably female chauvinist sowness and, whatever its roots, it leads to the same isolation. Boys are messy, boys are mean, boys are rough, boys are stupid and have sloppy handwriting. A cacophony of childhood memories rushes through my head, balanced, of course, by all the well-documented feelings of inferiority and envy. But the important thing, the hard thing, is to wipe the slate clean, to start again without the meanness of the past. That's why it's so important that the women's movement not become anti-male and allow its most prejudiced spokesmen total leadership. The much-chewed-over abortion issue illustrates this. The women's liberation position, insisting on a woman's right to determine her own body's destiny, leads in fanatical extreme to a kind of *emotional immaculate conception in which the father is not judged even half-responsible*—he has no rights, and no consideration is to be given to his concern for either the woman or the fetus.

15   Woman, who once was abandoned and disgraced by an unwanted pregnancy, has recently arrived at a new pride of ownership or disposal. She has traveled in a straight line that still excludes her sexual partner from an equal share in the wanted or unwanted pregnancy. A better style of life may develop from an assumption that men are as human as we. Why not ask the child's father if he would like to bring up the child? Why not share the decisions, when possible, with the male? If we cut them out, assuming an old-style

NOTES

coevals (par. 12): of equal age
solace (par. 12): comfort
vignette (par. 14): short description
cacophony (par. 14): literally, harsh sounds
fanatical (par. 14): unreasonable
immaculate conception (par. 14): Actually, the writer is referring to the virgin birth, the belief that Mary became pregnant with Jesus without having sexual intercourse. The Immaculate Conception is the Roman Catholic belief that Mary herself was kept free from the stain of original sin from the moment of her conception.

indifference on their part, we perpetrate the ugly divisiveness that has characterized relations between the sexes so far.

16   Hard as it is for many of us to believe, women are not really superior to
men in intelligence or humanity—they are only equal.

NOTES
perpetrate (par. 15): continue
divisiveness (par. 15): conflict

Friendships among Men

Marc Feigen Fasteau

1   There is a long-standing myth in our society that the great friendships are
between men. Forged through shared experience, male friendship is portrayed
as the most unselfish, if not the highest form, of human relationship. The
more traditionally masculine the shared experience from which it springs, the
stronger and more profound the friendship is supposed to be. Going to war,
weathering crises together at school or work, playing on the same athletic
team are some of the classic experiences out of which friendships between
men are believed to grow.

2   By and large, men do prefer the company of other men, not only in their
structured time but in the time they fill with optional, nonobligatory activity. They prefer to play games, drink, and talk, as well as work and fight
together. Yet something is missing. Despite the time men spend together, their
contact rarely goes beyond the external, a limitation which tends to make
their friendships shallow and unsatisfying.

3   My own childhood memories are of doing things with my friends—playing games or sports, building walkie-talkies, going camping. Other people and
my relationships to them were never legitimate subjects for attention. If someone liked me, it was an opaque, mysterious occurrence that bore no analysis.
When I was slighted, I felt hurt. But relationships with people just happened.
I certainly had feelings about my friends, but I can't remember a single
instance of trying consciously to sort them out until I was well into college.

4   For most men this kind of shying away from the personal continues into
adult life. In conversations with each other, we hardly ever use ourselves as
reference points. We talk about almost everything except how we ourselves
are affected by people and events. Everything is discussed as though it were
taking place out there somewhere, as though we had no more felt response to
it than to the weather. Topics that can be treated in this detached, objective

NOTES
myth (par. 1): widely held belief not based on fact
forged (par. 1): formed
profound (par. 1): significant
structured time (par. 2): time that is devoted to necessary activities, such as work
legitimate (par. 3): acceptable, proper
opaque (par. 3): unclear
detached (par. 4): impersonal

way become conversational mainstays. The few subjects which are fundamentally personal are shaped into discussions of abstract general questions. Even in an exchange about their reactions to liberated women—a topic of intensely personal interest—the tendency will be to talk in general, theoretical terms. Work, at least its objective aspects, is always a safe subject. Men also spend an incredible amount of time rehashing the great public issues of the day. Until early 1973, Vietnam was the work-horse topic. Then came Watergate. It doesn't seem to matter that we've all had a hundred similar conversations. We plunge in for another round, trying to come up with a new angle as much as to impress the others with what we know as to keep from being bored stiff.

5   Games play a central role in situations organized by men. I remember a weekend some years ago at the country house of a law-school classmate as a blur of softball, football, croquet, poker, and a dice-and-board game called Combat, with swimming thrown in on the side. As soon as one game ended, another began. Taken one at a time, these "activities" were fun, but the impression was inescapable that the host, and most of his guests, would do anything to stave off a lull in which they would be together without some impersonal focus for their attention. A snapshot of almost any men's club would show the same thing, 90 percent of the men engaged in some activity—ranging from backgammon to watching the tube—other than, or at least as an aid to, conversaton.*

6   My composite memory of evenings spent with a friend at college and later when we shared an apartment in Washington is of conversations punctuated by silences during which we would internally pass over any personal or emotional thoughts which had arisen and come back to the permitted track. When I couldn't get my mind off personal matters, I said very little. Talks with my father have always had the same tone. Respect for privacy was the rationale for our diffidence. His questions to me about how things were going at school or at work were asked as discreetly as he would have asked a friend about someone's commitment to a hospital for the criminally insane. Our conversations, when they touched these matters at all, to say nothing of more sensitive matters, would veer quickly back to safe topics of general interest.

7   In our popular literature, the archetypal male hero embodying this personal muteness is the cowboy. The classic mold for the character was set in

---

*Women may use games as a reason for getting together—bridge clubs, for example. But the show is more for the rest of the world—to indicate that they are doing *something*—and games themselves are not the only means of communication.

NOTES

mainstays (par. 4): supports
fundamentally (par. 4): basically
abstract (par. 4): vague, impersonal
theoretical (par. 4): based on theory or speculation, rather than personal feelings
work-horse topic (par. 4): frequently discussed topic
stave off (par. 5): prevent
composite (par. 6): total
punctuated (par. 6): interrupted
rationale (par. 6): reason, excuse
diffidence (par. 6): hesitance
veer (par. 6): turn
archetypal (par. 7): model

1902 by Owen Wister's novel *The Virginian* where the author spelled out, with an explicitness that was never again necessary, the characteristics of his protagonist. Here's how it goes when two close friends the Virginian hasn't seen in some time take him out for a drink:

> All of them had seen rough days together, and they felt guilty with emotion. "It's hot weather," said Wiggin.
> "Hotter in Box Elder," said McLean. "My kid has started teething." Words ran dry again. They shifted their positions, looked in their glasses, read the labels on the bottles. They dropped a word now and then to the proprietor about his trade, and his ornaments.

One of the Virginian's duties is to assist at the hanging of an old friend as a horse thief. Afterward, for the first time in the book, he is visibly upset. The narrator puts his arm around the hero's shoulders and describes the Virginian's reaction:

> I had the sense to keep silent, and presently he shook my hand, not looking at me as he did so. He was always very shy of demonstration.

And, for explanation of such reticence, "As all men know, he also knew that many things should be done in this world in silence, and that talking about them is a mistake."

8   There are exceptions, but they only prove the rule.

9   One is the drunken confidence: "Bob, ole boy, I gotta tell ya—being divorced isn't so hot.... [and see, I'm too drunk to be held responsible for blurting it out]." Here, drink becomes an excuse for exchanging confidences and a device for periodically loosening the restraint against expressing a need for sympathy and support from other men—which may explain its importance as a male ritual. Marijuana fills a similar need.

10   Another exception is talking to a stranger—who may be either someone the speaker doesn't know or someone who isn't in the same social or business world. (Several black friends told me that they have been on the receiving end of personal confidences from white acquaintances that they were sure had not been shared with white friends.) In either case, men are willing to talk about themselves only to other men with whom they do not have to compete or whom they will not have to confront socially later.

11   Finally, there is the way men depend on women to facilitate certain conversations. The women in a mixed group are usually the ones who make the first personal reference, about themselves or others present. The men can then join in without having the onus for initiating a discussion of "personalities." Collectively, the men can "blame" the conversation on the women. They can also feel in these conversations that since they are talking "to" the women instead of "to" the men, they can be excused for deviating from the masculine norm. When the women leave, the tone and subject invariably shift away from the personal.

NOTES

protagonist (par. 7): main character
proprietor (par. 7): owner
reticence (par. 7): shyness
confront (par. 10): face, meet
facilitate (par. 11): to make easier
onus (par. 11): responsibility, blame
deviating (par. 11): departing from

12   The effect of these constraints is to make it extraordinarily difficult for men to really get to know each other. A psychotherapist who has conducted a lengthy series of encounter groups for men summed it up:

> With saddening regularity [the members of these groups] described how much they wanted to have closer, more satisfying relationships with other men: "I'd settle for having one really close man friend. I supposedly have some close men friends now. We play golf or go for a drink. We complain about our jobs and our wives. I care about them and they care about me. We even have some physical contact—I mean we may even give a hug on a big occasion. But it's not enough."

The sources of this stifling ban on self-disclosure, the reasons why men hide from each other, lie in the taboos and imperatives of the masculine stereotype.

13   To begin with, men are supposed to be functional, to spend their time working or otherwise solving or thinking about how to solve problems. Personal reaction, how one feels about something, is considered dysfunctional, at best an irrelevant distraction from the expected objectivity. Only weak men, and women, talk about—i.e., "give in" to—their feelings. "I group my friends in two ways," said a business executive:

> those who have made it and don't complain and those who haven't made it. And only the latter spend time talking to their wives about their problems and how bad their boss is and all that. The ones who concentrate more on communicating . . . are those who have realized that they aren't going to make it and therefore they have changed the focus of attention.

In a world which tells men they have to choose between expressiveness and manly strength, this characterization may be accurate. Most of the men who talk personally to other men *are* those whose problems have gotten the best of them, who simply can't help it. Men not driven to despair don't talk about themselves, so the idea that self-disclosure and expressiveness are associated with problems and weakness becomes a self-fulfilling prophecy.

14   Obsessive competitiveness also limits the range of communication in male friendships. Competition is the principal mode by which men relate to each other—at one level because they don't know how else to make contact, but more basically because it is the way to demonstrate, to themselves and others, the key masculine qualities of unwavering toughness and the ability to dominate and control. The result is that they inject competition into situations which don't call for it.

15   In conversations, you must show that you know more about the subject than the other man, or at least as much as he does. For example, I have often engaged in a contest that could be called My Theory Tops Yours, disguised as a serious exchange of ideas. The proof that it wasn't serious was that I was willing to participate even when I was sure that the participants, including myself, had nothing fresh to say. Convincing the other person—victory—is

NOTES
stifling (par. 12): restrictive
self-disclosure (par. 12): revealing one's feelings and thoughts
taboos (par. 12): things forbidden by society
imperatives (par. 12): requirements
dysfunctional (par. 13): not functioning properly
self-fulfilling prophecy (par. 13): a prediction that comes true because people unconsciously act in such a way as to make it come true
obsessive (par. 14): extreme
mode (par. 14): method

the main objective, with control of the floor an important tactic. Men tend to lecture at each other, insist that the discussion follow their train of thought, and are often unwilling to listen. As one member of a men's rap group said,

> When I was talking I used to feel that I had to be driving to a point, that it had to be rational and organized, that I had to persuade at all times, rather than exchange thoughts and ideas.

Even in casual conversation some men hold back unless they are absolutely sure of what they are saying. They don't want to have to change a position once they have taken it. It's "just like a woman" to change your mind, and, more important, it is inconsistent with the approved masculine posture of total independence.

16   Competition was at the heart of one of my closest friendships, now defunct. There was a good deal of mutual liking and respect. We went out of our way to spend time with each other and wanted to work together. We both had "prospects" as "bright young men" and the same "liberal but tough" point of view. We recognized this about each other, and this recognition was the basis of our respect and of our sense of equality. That we saw each other as equals was important—our friendship was confirmed by the reflection of one in the other. But our constant and all-encompassing competion made this equality precarious and fragile. One way or another, everything counted in the measuring process. We fought out our tennis matches as though our lives depended on it. At poker, the two of us would often play on for hours after the others had left. These *mano-a-mano* poker marathons seem in retrospect especially revealing of the competitiveness of the relationship: playing for small stakes, the essence of the game is in outwitting, psychologically beating down the other player—the other skills involved are negligible. Winning is the only pleasure, one that evaporates quickly, a truth that struck me in inchoate form every time our game broke up at four A.M. and I walked out the door with my five-dollar winnings, a headache, and a sense of time wasted. Still, I did the same thing the next time. It was what we did together, and somehow it counted. Losing at tennis could be balanced by winning at poker; at another level, his moving up in the federal government by my getting on the *Harvard Law Review.*

17   This competitiveness feeds the most basic obstacle to openness between men, the inability to admit to being vulnerable. Real men, we learn early, are not supposed to have doubts, hopes and ambitions which may not be realized, things they don't (or even especially do) like about themselves, fears and disappointments. Such feelings and concerns, of course, are part of everyone's inner life, but a man must keep quiet about them. If others know how you really feel you can be hurt, and that in itself is incompatible with manhood. The inhibiting effect of this imperative is not limited to disclosures of major personal problems. Often men do not share even ordinary uncertainties and

NOTES

defunct (par. 16): ended
mutual (par. 16): applying to both sides
precarious (par. 16): uncertain
mano-a-mano (par. 16): hand to hand
marathons (par. 16): long and tiring activity
retrospect (par. 16): looking back
essence (par. 16): the essential quality
negligible (par. 16): unimportant, insignificant
evaporates (par. 16): disappears
inchoate (par. 16): vague
inhibiting (par. 17): restricting

half-formulated plans of daily life with their friends. And when they do, they are careful to suggest that they already know how to proceed—that they are not really asking for help or understanding but simply for particular bits of information. Either way, any doubts they have are presented as external, carefully characterized as having to do with the issue as distinct from the speaker. They are especially guarded about expressing concern or asking a question that would invite personal comment. It is almost impossible for men to simply exchange thoughts about matters involving them personally in a comfortable, non-crisis atmosphere. If a friend tells you of his concern that he and a colleague are always disagreeing, for example, he is likely to quickly supply his own explanation—something like "different professional backgrounds." The effect is to rule out observations or suggestions that do not fit within this already reconnoitered protective structure. You don't suggest, even if you believe it is true, that in fact the disagreements arise because he presents his ideas in a way which tends to provoke a hostile reaction. It would catch him off guard; it would be something he hadn't already thought of and accepted about himself and, for that reason, no matter how constructive and well-intentioned you might be, it would put you in control for the moment. He doesn't want that; he is afraid of losing your respect. So, sensing he feels that way, because you would yourself, you say something else. There is no real give-and-take.

18   It is hard for men to get angry at each other honestly. Anger between friends often means that one has hurt the other. Since the straightforward expression of anger in these situations involves an admission of vulnerability, it is safer to stew silently or find an "objective" excuse for retaliation. Either way, trust is not fully restored.

19   Men even try not to let it show when they feel good. We may report the reasons for our happiness, if they have to do with concrete accomplishments, but we try to do it with a straight face, as if to say, "Here's what happened, but it hasn't affected my grown-up unemotional equilibrium, and I am not asking for any kind of response." Happiness is a precarious, "childish" feeling, easy to shoot down. Others may find the event that triggers it trivial or incomprehensible, or even threatening to their own self-esteem—in the sense that if one man is up, another man is down. So we tend not to take the risk of expressing it.

20   What is particularly difficult for men is seeking or accepting help from friends. I, for one, learned early that dependence was unacceptable. When I was eight, I went to a summer camp I disliked. My parents visited me in the middle of the summer and, when it was time for them to leave, I wanted to go with them. They refused, and I yelled and screamed and was miserably unhappy for the rest of the day. That evening an older camper comforted me, sitting by my bed as I cried, patting me on the back soothingly and saying whatever it is that one says at times like that. He was in some way clumsy or funny-looking, and a few days later I joined a group of kids in cruelly making fun of him, an act which upset me, when I thought about it, for years. I can only explain it in terms of my feeling, as early as the age of eight, that

NOTES
reconnoitered (par. 17): examined, established
retaliation (par. 18): revenge
equilibrium (par. 19): balance
precarious (par. 19): delicate
trivial (par. 19): unimportant
incomprehensible (par. 19): not understandable
self-esteem (par. 19): pride

by needing and accepting his help and comfort I had compromised myself, and took it out on him.

21   "You can't express dependence when you feel it," a corporate executive said, "because it's a kind of absolute. If you are loyal 90 percent of the time and disloyal 10 percent, would you be considered loyal? Well, the same happens with independence: you are either dependent or independent; you can't be both." "Feelings of dependence," another explained, "are identified with weakness or 'untoughness' and our culture doesn't accept those things in men." The result is that we either go it alone or "act out certain games or rituals to provoke the desired reaction in the other and have our needs satisfied without having to ask for anything."

22   Somewhat less obviously, the expression of affection also runs into emotional barriers growing out of the masculine stereotype. When I was in college, I was suddenly quite moved while attending a friend's wedding. The surge of feeling made me uncomfortable and self-concious. There was nothing inherently difficult or, apart from the fact of being moved by a moment of tenderness, "unmasculine" about my reaction. I just did not know how to deal with or communicate what I felt. "I consider myself a sentimentalist," one man said, "and I think I am quite able to express my feelings. But the other day my wife described a friend of mine to some people as my best friend and I felt embarrassed when I heard her say it."

23   A major source of these inhibitions is the fear of being, of being thought, homosexual. Nothing is more frightening to a heterosexual man in our society. It threatens, at one stroke, to take away every vestige of his claim to a masculine identity—something like knocking out the foundations of a building—and to expose him to the ostracism, ranging from polite tolerance to violent revulsion, of his friends and colleagues. A man can be labeled as homosexual not just because of an overt sexual act but because of almost any sign of behavior which does not fit the masculine stereotype. The touching of another man, other than shaking hands or, under emotional stress, an arm around the shoulder, is taboo. Women may kiss each other when they meet; men are uncomfortable when hugged even by close friends. Onlookers might misinterpret what they saw, and more important, what would we think of ourselves if we felt a twinge of sensual pleasure from the embrace.

24   Direct verbal expressions of affection or tenderness are also something that only homosexuals and women engage in. Between "real" men affection has to be disguised in gruff, "you old son-of-a-bitch" style. Paradoxically, in some instances, terms of endearment between men can be used as a ritual badge of manhood, dangerous medicine safe only for the strong. The flirting with homosexuality that characterizes the initiation rites of many fraternities and men's clubs serves this purpose. Claude Brown wrote about black life in New York City in the 1950s:

> The term ["baby"] had a hip ring to it. . . . It was like saying, "Man, look at me. I've got masculinity to spare. . . . I can say 'baby' to another cat and he can say 'baby' to me, and we can say it with strength in our voices." If you could say it, this meant that you really had to be sure of yourself, sure of your masculinity.

NOTES

compromised (par. 20): exposed to danger or ridicule
surge (par. 22): flood
inherently (par. 22): basically
vestige (par. 23): trace, part
ostracism (par. 23): disgraceful exclusion
revulsion (par. 23): disgust
overt (par. 23): open to view
paradoxically (par. 24): seemingly contradictory

Fear of homosexuality does more than inhibit the physical display of affection. One of the major recurring themes in the men's groups led by psychotherapist Don Clark was:

> "A large segment of my feelings about other men are unknown or distorted because I am afraid they might have something to do with homosexuality. Now I'm lonely for other men and don't know how to find what I want with them."

As Clark observes, "The specter of homosexuality seems to be the dragon at the gateway to self-awareness, understanding, and acceptance of male-male needs. If a man tries to pretend the dragon is not there by turning a blind eye to erotic feeling for all other males, he also blinds himself to the rich variety of feelings that are related."

25   The few situations in which men do acknowledge strong feelings of affection and dependence toward other men are exceptions which prove the rule. With "cop couples," for example, or combat soldier "buddies," intimacy and dependence are forced on the men by their work—they have to ride in the patrol car or be in the same foxhole with somebody—and the jobs themselves have such highly masculine images that men can get away with behavior that would be suspect under any other conditions.

26   Furthermore, even these combat-buddy relationships, when looked at closely, turn out not to be particularly intimate or personal. Margaret Mead has written:

> During the last war English observers were confused by the apparent contradiction between American soldiers' emphasis on the buddy, so grievously exemplified in the break-downs that followed a buddy's death, and the results of detailed inquiry which showed how transitory these buddy relationships were. It was found that men actually accepted their buddies a derivatives from their outfit, and from accidents of association, rather than because of any special personality characteristics capable of ripening into friendship.

One effect of the fear of appearing to be homosexual is to reinforce the practice that two men rarely get together alone without a reason. I once called a friend to suggest that we have dinner together. "O.K.," he said. "What's up?" I felt uncomfortable telling him that I just wanted to talk, that there was no other reason for the invitation.

27   Men get together to conduct business, to drink, to play games and sports, to re-establish contact after long absences, to participate in heterosexual social occasions—circumstances in which neither person is responsible for actually wanting to see the other. Men are particularly comfortable seeing each other in groups. The group situation defuses any possible assumptions about the intensity of feeling between particular men and provides the safety of numbers—"All the guys are here." It makes personal communication, which requires a level of trust and mutual understanding not generally shared by all members of a group, more difficult and offers an excuse for avoiding this dangerous territory. And it provides what is most sought after in men's friendships: mutual reassurance of masculinity.

NOTES

specter (par. 24): literally, a ghost or spirit; here, a fear
grievously (par. 26): sadly
exemplified (par. 26): shown
transitory (par. 26): temporary, short-lived
derivatives from (par. 26): parts of
ripening (par. 26): developing
reinforce (par. 26): strengthen, encourage
defuses (par. 27): decreases

Seven Doomsday Myths about the Environment

Ronald Bailey

1   As the author of *Eco-Scam: The False Prophets of Ecological Apocalypse*, I know by surprising experience that what I am about to say is going to make many people angry. But here goes.

2   THE END IS NOT NIGH! That's right—the Apocalypse has been postponed for the foreseeable future, despite the gloomy prognostications by the likes of Paul Ehrlich, Lester Brown, Al Gore, Stephen Schneider, and Carl Sagan. There is no scientific evidence to support the often heard claim that there is a global ecological crisis threatening humanity and life on the entire Planet Earth.

3   There are local environmental problems, of course, but no global threats. Instead, there is a record of enormous environmental progress and much to be optimistic about. As far as the global environment is concerned, there is a brilliant future for humanity and Planet Earth.

4   Of course, millions of people believe that we have only a few more years before the end, and no doubt some such doomsters are among the readers of this article. But I would like to remind them of seven false doomsday predictions—many of which are still being peddled by unscrupulous activists—and take a hard look at what actually happened.

False Doomsday Prediction No. 1:

Global Famine

5   "The battle to feed all of humanity is over. In the 1970s the world will undergo famines—hundreds of millions of people are going to starve to death in spite of any crash programs embarked upon now," predicted population alarmist Paul Ehrlich in his book *The Population Bomb* (1968).

6   Two years later Ehrlich upped the ante by also painting a gruesome scenario in the Earth Day 1970 issue of *The Progressive*, in which *65 million* Americans would die of famine and a total of *4 billion* people worldwide would perish in "the Great Die-Off" between the years 1980 and 1989.

What Really Happened?

7   While the world's population *doubled* since World War II, food production *tripled*. The real price of wheat and corn dropped by 60%, while the price of rice was cut in half. Worldwide life expectancy rose from 47.5 years in 1950 to 63.9 years in 1990, while the world infant mortality rate dropped from 155 to 70 per 1,000 live births. Even in the poorest countries, those with per capita incomes under $400, average life expectancy rose spectacularly from 35 years in 1960 to 60 years in 1990.

NOTES

Apocalypse (par. 1): doomsday, catastrophe
prognostications (par. 2): predictions
embarked upon (par. 5): begun
ante (par. 6): Literally, an ante is the stake that a poker player places in the pool before receiving his or her cards.
scenario (par. 6): outline of expected events
per capita (par. 7): per person

8   And there's even more good news—for the last decade, grain output rose 5% per year in the developing world, while population growth has slowed from 2.3% to 1.9% and continues to fall. These figures strongly bolster University of Chicago agricultural economist Gale Johnson when he claims, "The scourge of famine due to natural causes has been almost conquered and could be entirely eliminated by the end of the century."

False Doomsday Prediction No. 2:

Exhaustion of Nonrenewable Resources

9   In 1972, the Club of Rome's notorious report, *The Limits to Growth*, predicted that at exponential growth rates the world would run out of raw materials—gold by 1981, mercury by 1985, tin by 1987, zinc by 1990, oil by 1992, and copper, lead, and natural gas by 1993.

What Really Happened?

10   Humanity hasn't come close to running out of any mineral resource. Even the World Resources Institute estimates that the average price of all metals and minerals *fell* by more than 40% between 1970 and 1988. As we all know, falling prices mean that goods are becoming more abundant, not more scarce. The U.S. Bureau of Mines estimates that, at 1990 production rates, world reserves of gold will last 24 years, mercury 40 years, tin 28 years, zinc 40 years, copper 65 years, and lead 35 years. Proven reserves of petroleum will last 44 years and natural gas 63 years.

11   Now don't worry about the number of years left for any of these reserves. Just as a family replenishes its larder when it begins to empty, so, too, does humanity look for new mineral reserves only when supplies begin to run low. Even the alarmist Worldwatch Institute admits that "recent trends in price and availability suggest that for most minerals we are a long way from running out."

False Doomsday Prediction No. 3:

Skyrocketing Pollution

12   In 1972, *The Limits to Growth* also predicted that pollution would skyrocket as population and industry increased: "Virtually every pollutant that has been measured as a function of time appears to be increasing exponentially."

13   In 1969, Paul Ehrlich outlined a future "eco-catastrophe" in which he prophesied that 200,000 people would die in 1973 in "smog disasters" in New York and Los Angeles.

What Really Happened?

14   Since the publication of *The Limits to Growth*, U.S. population has risen 22% and the economy has grown by more than 58%. Yet, instead of increasing as predicted, air pollutants have dramatically declined.

NOTES

bolster (par. 8): support
scourge (par. 8): devastation
exponential growth (par. 9): growth that is progressively more rapid
larder (par. 11): pantry
alarmist (par. 11): a person or group who needlessly alarms others
eco-catastrophe (par. 13): ecological catastrophe
prophesied (par. 13): predicted

15 Sulfur-dioxide emissions are down 25% and carbon monoxide down 41%. Volatile organic compounds—chief contributors to smog formation—have been reduced by 31%, and total particulates like smoke, soot, and dust have fallen by 59%. Smog dropped by 50% in Los Angeles over the last decade.

16 Water quality deteriorated until the 1960s; now, water pollution is abating. Experts estimate that up to 95% of America's rivers, 92% of its lakes, and 86% of its estuaries are fishable and swimmable. These favorable pollution trends are being mirrored in both western Europe and Japan.

17 But what about the developing countries and former communist countries? It is true that industrial pollution continues to rise in some poorer countries. But a recent study by two Princeton University economists, Gene Grossman and Alan Krueger, using World Health Organization data, concluded that air pollution typically increases in a city until the average per capita income of its citizens reaches $4,000–$5,000, at which point pollution levels begin to fall. This is what happened in the developed nations and will happen as developing nations cross that threshold. In other words, economic growth leads to less pollution—not more, as asserted by the doomsters.

False Doomsday Prediction No. 4:

The Coming Ice Age

18 The public has forgotten that the chief climatological threat being hyped by the eco-doomsters in the 1970s was the beginning of a new ice age. The new ice age was allegedly the result of mankind's polluting haze, which was blocking sunlight. "The threat of a new ice age must now stand alongside nuclear war as a likely source of wholesale death and misery for mankind," declared Nigel Calder, former editor of *New Scientist*, in 1975.

What Really Happened?

19 Global temperatures, after declining for 40 years, rebounded in the late 1970s, averting the feared new ice age. But was this cause for rejoicing? NO! Now we are supposed to fear global warming. Freeze or fry, the problem is always viewed as industrial capitalism, and the solution, international socialism.

False Doomsday Prediction No. 5:

The Antarctic Ozone Hole

20 There have been widespread fears that the hole in the ozone layer of the earth's atmosphere will wipe out life all over the world. John Lynch, program

NOTES

sulfur-dioxide (par. 15): an irritating, poisonous gas used in many industrial processes
carbon monoxide (par. 15): an odorless, poisonous gas formed by the burning of carbon or substances containing carbon, such as gasoline
volatile (par. 15): rapidly evaporating
particulates (par. 15): substances formed of separate particles
abating (par. 16): being reduced
estuaries (par. 16): the area where the mouth of a river meets the sea
averting (par. 19): preventing
capitalism (par. 19): an economic system in which private or corporate owners produce and distribute goods in order to make a profit
socialism (par. 19): a social system in which the whole community possesses political power and owns the means of producing and distributing goods
ozone layer (par. 20): a layer of the earth's upper atmosphere which contains a high concentration of ozone, a substance that absorbs ultraviolet radiation

manager of polar aeronomy at the National Science Foundation, declared in 1989, "It's terrifying. If these ozone holes keep growing like this, they'll eventually eat the world."

What Really Happened?

21   In 1985, British scientists detected reduced levels of stratospheric ozone over Antarctica. Could the Antarctic ozone hole "eventually eat the world"? No. "It is a purely localized phenomenon," according to Guy Brasseur at the National Center for Atmospheric Research. It is thought that the "ozone hole" results from catalytic reactions of some chlorine-based chemicals, which can take place only in high, very cold (below −80° C, or −176° F) clouds in the presence of sunlight. It is a transitory phenomenon enduring only a bit more than a month in the austral spring. The polar vortex—that is, the constant winds that swirl around the margins of the ice continent—tightly confine the hole over Antarctica.

22   What about the southern ecosystems? Isn't the increased ultraviolet light threatening plants and animals there? U.S. Vice President Albert Gore credulously reports in his book that hunters are finding rabbits and fish blinded by ultraviolet light in Patagonia.

23   This is sheer nonsense. Scientists have found not one example of animals being blinded by excess ultraviolet light in the Southern Hemisphere.

24   What about the phytoplankton in the seas around Antarctica? Osmond Holm-Hansen, a marine ecologist at Scripps Institute of Oceanography, has been studying the effects of ultraviolet light on Antarctica's ecosystems since 1988. He found that the extra ultraviolet-B light reduces phytoplankton by less than 4%–5%, which is well within the natural variations for the region. Holm-Hansen concludes, "Unlike the scare stories you hear some scientists spreading, the Antarctic ecosystem is absolutely not on the verge of collapse due to increased ultraviolet light."

False Doomsday Prediction No. 6:

Ozone Hole Over America

25   In 1992, NASA spooked Americans by declaring that an ozone hole like the one over Antarctica could open up over the United States. *Time* magazine showcased the story on its front cover (February 16, 1992), warning that "danger is shining through the sky. . . . No longer is the threat just to our future; the threat is here and now." Then-Senator Albert Gore thundered in Congress: "We have to tell our children that they must redefine their relationship to the sky, and they must begin to think of the sky as a threatening part of their environment."

NOTES

aeronomy (par. 20): study of the upper atmosphere

stratospheric (par. 21): The stratosphere is part of the atmosphere that begins five miles above the earth at the poles and 10 miles above it at the equator; it extends about 30 miles above the earth's surface.

catalytic reactions (par. 21): reactions that involve a catalyst, a substance that increases the rate of a chemical reaction without itself being permanently changed

transitory (par. 21): short-lived

austral spring (par. 21): spring in the southern half of the earth

credulously (par. 22): gullibly, naively

phytoplankton (par. 24): tiny, free-floating water plants

marine (par. 24): sea

What Really Happened?

26   On April 30, 1992, NASA sheepishly admitted that no ozone hole had opened up over the United States. *Time,* far from trumpeting the news on its cover, buried the admission in four lines of text in its May 11 issue. It's no wonder the American public is frightened.

27   But let's stipulate that there have been minor reductions in ozone over the United States due to chlorofluorocarbons in the stratosphere. So what?

28   Reduced stratospheric ozone over the United States was never going to be a disaster or a catastrophe. At most, it might have become an environmental nuisance in the next century.

29   But doesn't reduced stratospheric ozone severely injure crops and natural ecosystems? The answer is no. Ultraviolet levels vary naturally by as much as 50% over the United States. The farther south you go, the higher the ultraviolet exposure a person or plant receives. For example, an average 5% reduction in the ozone layer over the United States would increase ultraviolet exposure by about as much as moving a mere 60 miles south—the distance from Palm Beach to Miami. How many people worry about getting skin cancer as a result of moving 60 miles? Not many, I bet.

30   Alan Teramura, who is perhaps the world's leading expert on the effects of ultraviolet light on plants, says, "There is no question that terrestrial life is adapted to ultraviolet." His experiments have shown that many varieties of crops would be unaffected by reductions in the ozone layer. In fact, corn, wheat, rice, and oats all grow in a wide variety of ultraviolet environments now.

False Doomsday Prediction No. 7:

Global Warming

31   Global warming is "the Mother of all environmental scares," according to the late political scientist Aaron Wildavsky. Based on climate computer models, eco-doomsters predict that the earth's average temperature will increase by 4°–9° F over the next century due to the "greenhouse effect": Burning fossil fuels boosts atmospheric carbon dioxide, which traps the sun's heat.

What Is Really Happening?

32   The earth's average temperature has apparently increased by less than a degree (0.9) Fahrenheit in the last century. Unfortunately for the global-warming alarmists, most of that temperature rise occurred before World War II, when greenhouse gases had not yet accumulated to any great extent in the atmosphere.

33   And here's more bad news for doomsters: Fifteen years of very precise satellite data show that the planet has actually cooled by 0.13° C. Some years are warmer while others are cooler, according to NASA space scientist Roy Spencer, but the global temperature trend has been slightly downward. The satellites can measure temperature differences as small as 0.01° C. By contrast, the computer models of the doomsters predict that temperatures should have risen by an easily detectable 0.3° C per decade. They have not.

NOTES

chlorofluorocarbons (par. 27): compounds of carbon, hydrogen, chlorine, and fluorine which have been used in aerosol sprays and refrigerants
terrestrial (par. 30): earthly
fossil fuels (par. 31): a natural fuel such as petroleum, coal, or natural gas, formed in the earth from the remains of organisms that lived in the distant past

34   Even more bad news for the global-warming doomsters: One of the more robust predictions of the climate computer models is that global warming should be strongest and start first in the Arctic. Indeed, Albert Gore says in his book: "Global warming is expected to push temperatures up much more rapidly in the polar regions than in the rest of the world."

35   However, scientists did a recent comprehensive analysis of 40 years of arctic temperature data from the United States and the former Soviet Union. In an article in the prestigious scientific journal *Nature,* the scientists reported, "We do not observe the large surface warming trends predicted by the models; indeed, we detect significant surface cooling trends over the western Arctic Ocean during the winter and autumn." This is the exact opposite of what the doomsters are predicting is happening; the Arctic is becoming *cooler.*

36   Climate doomsters also predict that the ice caps of Antarctica and Greenland will melt, drastically raising sea levels and inundating New York, London, Bangladesh, and Washington, D.C. Recent scientific evidence shows that in fact the glaciers in both Antarctica and Greenland are accumulating ice, which means that sea levels will drop, not rise. Another false apocalypse averted.

37   Furthermore, over the past 100 years, winters in the Northern Hemisphere have become warmer. Why? Because the world is becoming cloudier. Cloud blankets warm long winter nights while long summer days are shaded by their cloud shields. This means longer growing seasons and fewer droughts for crops. This is decidedly not a recipe for a climate disaster.

Conclusion

38   Given the dismal record of the environmental doomsayers, why do so many people think the world is coming to an end? I think it's pretty clear. People are afraid because so many interest groups have a stake in making them afraid. "Global emergencies" and "worldwide crises" keep hundreds of millions of dollars in donations flowing into the coffers of environmental organizations. As environmental writer Bill McKibben admitted in *The End of Nature,* "The ecological movement has always had its greatest success in convincing people that we are threatened by some looming problem." That success is now measured at the cash register for many leading environmental groups. For example, in 1990, the 10 largest environmental organizations raised $400 million from donors. That pays for a lot of trips to international environmental conferences, furnishes some nice headquarters, and buys a lot of influence on Capitol Hill.

39   Crises also advance the careers of certain politicians and bureaucrats, attract funds to scientists' laboratories, and sell newspapers and TV air time. The approach of inevitable doom is now the conventional wisdom of the late twentieth century.

40   But despite the relentless drumbeat of environmental doomsaying, people have to want to believe that the end is nigh. How do we account for the acquiescence of such a large part of the public to a gloomy view of the future?

41   I conclude that the psychological attraction of the apocalyptic imagination is strong. Eric Zencey, a self-described survivor of apocalyptic environmentalism, wrote about his experience in the *North American Review* (June 1988): "There is a seduction in apocalyptic thinking. If one lives in the Last Days, one's actions, one's very life, take on historical meaning and no small

NOTES
robust (par. 34): energetic
coffers (par. 38): treasuries
acquiescence (par. 40): passive acceptance

measure of poignance.... Apocalypticism fulfills a desire to escape the flow of real and ordinary time, to fix the flow of history into a single moment of overwhelming importance."

42   To counteract the seduction of the apocalypse, scientists, policy makers, intellectuals, and businessmen must work to restore people's faith in themselves and in the fact of human progress. History clearly shows that our energy and creativity will surmount whatever difficulties we encounter. Life and progress will always be a struggle and humanity will never lack for new challenges, but as the last 50 years of solid achievement show, there is nothing out there that we cannot handle.

43   So what's the moral of the story? Please don't listen to the doomsters' urgent siren calls to drastically reorganize society and radically transform the world's economy to counter imaginary ecological apocalypses. The relevant motto is not "He who hesitates is lost," but rather, "Look before you leap."

NOTES
poignance (par. 41): deeply felt emotion
surmount (par. 42): overcome

A Planet in Jeopardy

Lester R. Brown,
Christopher Flavin,
and Sandra Postel

1   Bruce Wallace, a biology professor at Virginia Polytechnic Institute and State University, offers this story from the past that reflects on our own times: "Five days after departing from Southhampton, England, the *Titanic* grazed an iceberg in the North Atlantic. The incident passed unnoticed by most passengers—a mere trembling, according to one.

2   "Having heard reports of water entering the hold, Captain Edward J. Smith and Mr. Thomas Andrews, a ship designer who was aboard representing the *Titanic*'s builders, went below to conduct an inspection. Upon returning to the bridge, Mr. Andrews made some rapid calculations, then broke the news to the captain: 'The ship is doomed; at best you have one and a half hours before she goes down.' An immediate order was issued: Uncover the lifeboats!

3   "The *Titanic*'s passengers were not seasoned sailors. The ship was large and reassuring; it had been their home for the better part of a week. Bankers still intent upon returning to their New York offices continued to plan upcoming business deals. Professors returning from sabbatical leaves still mulled over lesson plans. Eventually, many preferred to stay on board rather than disembark on a tiny lifeboat.

4   "Grasp of an altered reality comes slowly, not as much the result of denial as of not comprehending. When the truth could no longer be denied, the passengers exhibited the entire range of human qualities—from bravery

NOTES
sabbatical leave (par. 3): leave that is periodically taken by college professors to travel and study
mulled over (par. 3): thought about
disembark (par. 3): leave

and heroism to cowardice. Some panicked and gave up hope entirely. Others achieved comfort by maintaining the status quo: Third-class passengers were prevented by many crew members from leaving the flooded steerage quarters for the temporary haven of the upper, higher-priced decks.

5   "In the end, reality could not be denied. Early on the morning of April 15, 1912, the *Titanic* sank with a loss of over 1,500 lives."

6   As the twentieth century nears a close, the tale of the *Titanic* comes uncomfortably close to describing the perceptual gap we now face: our inability to comprehend the scale of the ongoing degradation of the planet and how it will affect our future. Few understand the magnitude of the potential tragedy; fewer still have a good idea of what to do about it.

7   The *Titanic*'s passengers were mainly innocent victims, but the dilemma now facing society is largely of our own making. And for us, there is still hope. But saving Planet Earth—and its human passengers—will require going beyond the denial of reality that still characterizes many of our political and business leaders. It also hinges on the collective capacity and will to quickly make the transition from perception to policy change—an unprecedented challenge.

Success Stories Are Few

8   The first step—waking up to the dimensions of the world's environmental problems—has in a sense been under way for more than two decades. At the global level, a milestone was the U.N. Conference on the Human Environment held in Stockholm, Sweden, in 1972. The 20 years since that meeting have seen the birth of a worldwide environmental movement, the emergence of thousands of grass-roots environmental organizations, and the proliferation of environmental laws and regulations in nations around the world.

9   Now, as the world prepares for another global environmental summit, this time in Rio de Janeiro, Brazil, major speeches of prime ministers and presidents are incomplete without mention of the environment. Dozens of corporate executives have declared themselves committed environmentalists. And more than 115 nations have established environment agencies or ministries since 1972.

10   Laws and ministries are one thing. Real environmental progress is another. The two decades since the Stockholm conference have seen only scattered success stories. The Cuyahoga River in Cleveland, Ohio, no longer catches fire, and swimming has resumed in some of the Great Lakes. Air quality has improved in Tokyo and in many northern European cities as well. Soil erosion has slowed on U.S. cropland.

11   But outside of the "post-industrial" North, progress is rarer: Some regions of eastern Europe now face virtual epidemics of environmental disease, misuse of water resources is reducing the agricultural potential of wide sections of South Asia, and soil erosion is undermining the food prospects of much of

NOTES
status quo (par. 4): usual state of affairs
steerage (par. 4): lower, least expensive
haven (par. 4): safety
degradation (par. 6): corruption
grass-roots environmental organizations (par. 8): environmental organizations founded and maintained by ordinary citizens
proliferation of (par. 8): rapid increase in
Cuyahoga River in Cleveland, Ohio (par. 10): This river was so polluted with chemicals that it caught fire in the late 1960s.
Soil erosion (par. 10): the wearing away of topsoil by wind and water

Africa. Peru's inability to provide clean water for its people became evident when it was struck in 1991 by the world's worst cholera epidemic in decades. In Mexico City, coin-operated oxygen stations are being planned to help people cope with air pollution that has become life threatening.

12   At the global level, almost all of the indicators are negative. Each year now, the level of greenhouse gases in the atmosphere reaches a new high, and the ozone layer grows thinner. These fundamental assaults on the atmosphere are caused almost entirely by rich nations that use most of the fossil fuels and ozone-depleting chemicals. Yet, the long-term costs will be borne by humanity as a whole. Ozone depletion may cause skin cancer among Andean peasants who never used aerosol spray cans, while global warming could flood the homelands of Bangladeshis who have never used electricity.

13   Environmental concerns were viewed by many Third World leaders in 1972 as "luxury problems" that only rich nations could afford to deal with. Although this view is still espoused by some, it has a thoroughly unconvincing ring. In the wattle-and-daub villages and urban shantytowns where most Third World people live, environmental quality is more than a question of the quality of life; it is often a matter of life or death. In many nations, environmental degradation is now recognized as a key barrier to governments' ability to meet basic needs and sustain living standards.

Winning Battles, but Losing the War?

14   But despite increased awareness, the health of the planet has deteriorated at an unprecedented rate. Since 1972, the world has lost nearly 200 million hectares of trees, an area the size of the United States east of the Mississippi. Deserts have expanded by 120 million hectares, claiming more land than is planted to crops in China and Nigeria combined. The world's farmers lost about 480 million tons of topsoil, roughly equal to that which covers the agricultural land of India and France. And thousands of plant and animal species with which we shared the planet in 1972 no longer exist.

15   In the past 20 years, human numbers have grown by 1.6 billion—the same number of people that inhabited the planet in 1900. Each year now, the annual addition of more than 90 million people is equivalent to the combined populations of Denmark, Finland, the Netherlands, Norway, Sweden, and the United Kingdom. Meanwhile, world economic output, which historically has

NOTES

greenhouse gases (par. 12): Gases such as carbon dioxide, water vapor, and methane are believed to contribute to the "greenhouse effect." The sun's radiation passes through the atmosphere and warms the earth. The greenhouse gases in the atmosphere prevent this heat from escaping from the earth in much the same way that glass prevents the heat in a greenhouse from escaping. The heat trapped by the greenhouse gases causes the earth's temperature to rise, a phenomenon known as *global warming* (par. 12).

ozone layer (par. 12): a layer of the earth's upper atmosphere which contains a high concentration of ozone, a substance that absorbs ultraviolet radiation

fossil fuels (par. 12): natural fuels such as petroleum, coal, or natural gas, formed in the earth from the remains of organisms that lived in the distant past

espoused (par. 13): supported

wattle-and-daub villages (par. 13): The structures in these villages are built with a framework of rods and twigs that is plastered with mud or clay.

shantytowns (par. 13): impoverished parts of towns where people live in shacks

hectares (par. 14): A *hectare* is a metric unit equal to 100 ares (2.471 acres); an *are* is a metric unit equal to 100 square meters (119.6 square yards).

paralleled demands on the earth's resources, has increased by nearly 75% over the same two decades.

16   Denis Hayes, chairman of Earth Day 1990, raised the essential paradox when he asked, "How could we have fought so hard, and won so many battles, only to find ourselves now on the verge of losing the war?" Part of the answer lies in the failure to alter the basic patterns of human activity that cause environmental deterioration—from our reproductive behavior to our dependence on fossil fuels. Like the *Titanic*'s passengers, most of whom were unable to grasp the fundamental nature of their predicament, we are still struggling to understand the dimensions of the changes we are causing.

17   National governments have focused on building water-treatment facilities, controlling air pollutants from power plants, cleaning up toxic-waste sites, and trying to find new places to put their garbage. While much of this is necessary, such efforts cannot by themselves restore the planet's environmental health. Stabilizing the climate, for example, depends on restructuring national energy policies. Getting the brakes on population growth requires fundamental changes in social values and services. So far, only a handful of countries have undertaken such initiatives.

Economists versus Ecologists

18   The still widely held belief that the global economy can continue along the path it has been following stems in part from a narrow economic view of the world. Anyone who regularly reads the financial papers or business weeklies would conclude that the world is in reasonably good shape and that long-term economic prospects are promising. Even the apparent problems—the U.S. budget deficit, Third World debt, and gyrating oil prices—are considered minor by most economic planners. They call for marginal course corrections as they pursue business as usual. To the extent that constraints on economic expansion are discussed on the business pages, it is in terms of inadequate demand growth rather than limits imposed by the earth's resources.

19   Lacking an understanding of the carrying capacity of ecological systems, economic planners are unable to relate demand levels to the health of the natural world. If they regularly read the leading scientific journals, their faith might be shaken. Every major indicator shows deterioration in natural systems.

20   These different views of the world have their roots in economics and ecology—disciplines with intellectual frameworks that contrast starkly. From an economist's perspective, ecological concerns are but a minor subdiscipline of economics—to be "internalized" in economic models and dealt with at the margins of economic planning. But to an ecologist, the economy is a narrow subset of the global ecosystem. Humanity's expanding economic activities cannot be separated from the natural systems and resources from which they ultimately derive, and any activity that undermines the global ecosystem cannot continue indefinitely. Modern societies, even with their technological sophistication, ignore dependence on nature at their own peril.

NOTES

paradox (par. 16): a statement that seems to be contradictory but may nonetheless be true

gyrating (par. 18): spiraling

marginal (par. 18): slight

constraints (par. 18): restrictions

subdiscipline (par. 20): specialized field of study within a broader field

internalized (par. 20): absorbed

peril (par. 20): risk

Environment and Development

21   The health of the planet is ultimately about the health of its people, and from this perspective as well, disturbing trends emerged during the past two decades. Despite soaring economic output, the ranks of the world's poor have increased. Some 1.2 billion people now meet former World Bank President Robert McNamara's 1978 definition of absolute poverty: "a condition of life so limited by malnutrition, illiteracy, disease, squalid surroundings, high infant mortality, and low life expectancy as to be beneath any reasonable definition of human decency."

22   In the 1980s, average incomes fell by 10% in most of Latin America; in sub-Saharan Africa, they were down by 20%. Economic "development" is simply not occurring in many countries. And even a large portion of the industrial world is no longer moving forward. In the former Soviet Union, the economy is in a state that economists describe as "free fall." Real income dropped 2% in 1990 and an estimated 10%–15% in 1991.

23   The ranks of the poor are concentrated among the rapidly growing populations of sub-Saharan Africa, Latin America, the Middle East, and South Asia. The growth in Third World jobs has fallen short of population growth, leaving tens of millions unemployed and hundreds of millions underemployed. Even more people lack access to clean water, adequate health care, and a full and balanced diet.

24   The rising tide of world poverty has many roots. Rapid population growth is one; another is the failure of many governments to reform their economic and political systems. Meanwhile, foreign-aid donations have stagnated since the mid-1980s, and $1.2 trillion worth of foreign debt has accumulated, sapping financial earnings and undermining the credit-worthiness of low-income countries. The $950 billion spent on the military in 1990 was the biggest drain on resources of all.

25   ·The once separate issues of environment and development are now inextricably linked. Environmental degradation is driving a growing number of people into poverty. And poverty itself has become an agent of ecological degradation, as desperate people consume the resource bases on which they depend. Rather than a choice between the alleviation of poverty and the reversal of environmental decline, world leaders now face the reality that neither goal is achievable unless the other is pursued as well.

Unsustainable Economies

26   Our economies are engaged in a disguised form of deficit financing: Processes such as deforestation and overpumping of groundwater inflate current output at the expense of long-term productivity. In sector after sector, we violate fundamental principles of environmental sustainability. Relying on an incomplete accounting system, one that does not measure the destruction of natural capital associated with gains in economic output, we deplete our

NOTES
squalid (par. 21): unsanitary
stagnated (par. 24): have lagged or come to a lull
inextricably (par. 25): inseparably
alleviation (par. 25): relief
deforestation (par. 26): the destruction of forests
sector (par. 26): area
capital (par. 26): assets, wealth

productive assets, satisfying our needs today at the expense of our children. As economist Herman Daly puts it, "there is something fundamentally wrong in treating the earth as if it were a business in liquidation."

27   To extend the analogy, it is as though a vast industrial corporation quietly sold off a few of its factories each year, using an accounting system that did not reflect these sales. As a result, its cash flow would be strong and profits would rise. Stockholders would be pleased with the annual reports, not realizing that the profits were coming at the expense of the corporation's assets. But once all the factories were sold off, corporate officers would have to inform stockholders that their shares were worthless.

28   To reverse this process, industries and governments will need to alter their world views—focusing less on the short-term financial bottom line and more on the long-term sustainability of the economies they invest in. If we do not change our ways, we may find that the lifeboats are rapidly filling up and that it is too late for many to get aboard. While the rich may congregate on the upper decks and protect themselves for a while, they too are ultimately threatened.

29   The effort required to create a sustainable society is more like mobilizing for war than any other human experience. Time itself is the scarcest resource as we begin preparing for the struggle that will unfold in this decade and beyond. Indeed, we have only a few short years to overcome the political, social, and economic impediments to real progress—to lay the foundations for a fundamentally improved society. Once the self-reinforcing trends of environmental degradation and deepening poverty are too deeply established, only a superhuman effort could break the cycle and reverse the trend.

30   If the struggle for a sustainable society is to succeed, we must have some vision of what we are aiming for. If not fossil fuels to power society, then what? If forests are no longer to be cleared to grow food, then how is a larger population to be fed? If a throwaway culture leads inevitably to pollution and resource depletion, how can we satisfy our material needs? In sum, if the present path is so obviously unsound, what vision of the future can we use to guide our actions toward a global community that can endure?

31   A sustainable society is one that satisfies its needs without jeopardizing the prospects of future generations. Just as any technology of flight, no matter how primitive or advanced, must abide by the basic principles of aerodynamics, so must a lasting society satisfy basic ecological principles. At least two preconditions are undeniable: If population growth is not slowed and climate stabilized, there may not be an ecosystem on Earth we can save.

32   The 1990s will be the environmental decade—whether we want it to be or not. Already, it is a lost decade for many ecosystems and people, but it is also a last chance to begin turning things around.

NOTES

liquidation (par. 26): the selling of assets in order to raise money
analogy (par. 27): comparison
congregate (par. 28): gather
impediments (par. 29): obstacles
aerodynamics (par. 31): the relationship between air and objects moving through it

The Prisoner's Dilemma

Stephen Chapman

1   If the punitive laws of Islam were applied for only one year, all the devastating injustices would be uprooted. Misdeeds must be punished by the law of retaliation: cut off the hands of the thief; kill the murderers; flog the adulterous woman or man. Your concerns, your 'humanitarian' scruples are more childish than reasonable. Under the terms of Koranic law, any judge fulfilling the seven requirements (that he have reached puberty, be a believer, know the Koranic laws perfectly, be just, and not be affected by amnesia, or be a bastard, or be of the female sex) is qualified to be a judge in any type of case. He can thus judge and dispose of twenty trials in a single day, whereas the Occidental justice might take years to argue them out.

—from *Sayings of the Ayatollah Khomeini* (Bantam Books)

2   One of the amusements of life in the modern West is the opportunity to observe the barbaric rituals of countries that are attached to the customs of the dark ages. Take Pakistan, for example, our newest ally and client state in Asia. Last October President Zia, in harmony with the Islamic fervor that is sweeping this part of the world, revived the traditional Moslem practice of flogging lawbreakers in public. In Pakistan, this qualified as mass entertainment, and no fewer than 10,000 law-abiding Pakistanis turned out to see justice done to 26 convicts. To Western sensibilities the spectacle seemed barbaric—both in the sense of cruel and in the sense of pre-civilized. In keeping with Islamic custom each of the unfortunates—who had been caught in prostitution raids the previous night and summarily convicted and sentenced—was stripped down to a pair of white shorts, which were painted with a red stripe across the buttocks (the target). Then he was shackled against an easel, with pads thoughtfully placed over the kidneys to prevent injury. The floggers were muscular, fierce-looking sorts—convicted murderers, as it happens—who paraded around the flogging platform in colorful loincloths. When the time for the ceremony began, one of the floggers took a running start and brought a five-foot stave down across the first victim's buttocks, eliciting screams from the convict and murmurs from the audience. Each of the 26 received from five to 15 lashes. One had to be carried from the stage unconscious.

3   Flogging is one of the punishments stipulated by Koranic law, which has made it a popular penological device in several Moslem countries, including

NOTES

punitive laws (par. 1): laws relating to punishment
Islam (par. 1): a religion founded by the prophet Mohammed (570?–632 A.D.)
retaliation (par. 1): revenge
flog (par. 1): whip
Koranic (par. 1): pertaining to the Koran, the sacred book of Islam
Occidental (par. 1): western
barbaric (par. 2): brutal, uncivilized
client state (par. 2): a country dependent on the economic support of another country
sensibilities (par. 2): emotions, reasoning
spectacle (par. 2): public display
summarily (par. 2): quickly and without formality
shackled (par. 2): chained
stave (par. 2): stick
eliciting (par. 2): causing
stipulated (par. 3): specified
penological (par. 3): relating to prisoners

Pakistan, Saudi Arabia, and, most recently, the Ayatollah's Iran. Flogging, or *tázir*, is the general punishment prescribed for offenses that don't carry an explicit Koranic penalty. Some crimes carry automatic *hadd* punishments—stoning or scourging (a severe whipping) for illicit sex, scourging for drinking alcoholic beverages, amputation of the hands for theft. Other crimes—as varied as murder and abandoning Islam—carry the death penalty (usually carried out in public). Colorful practices like these have given the Islamic world an image in the West, as described by historian G. H. Jansen, "of blood dripping from the stumps of amputated hands and from the striped backs of malefactors, and piles of stones barely concealing the battered bodies of adulterous couples." Jansen, whose book *Militant Islam* is generally effusive in its praise of Islamic practices, grows squeamish when considering devices like flogging, amputation, and stoning. But they are given enthusiastic endorsement by the Koran itself.

4   Such traditions, we all must agree, are no sign of an advanced civilization. In the West, we have replaced these various punishments (including the death penalty in most cases) with a single device. Our custom is to confine criminals in prison for varying lengths of time. In Illinois, a reasonably typical state, grand theft carries a punishment of three to five years; armed robbery can get you from six to 30. The lowest form of felony theft is punishable by one to three years in prison. Most states impose longer sentences on habitual offenders. In Kentucky, for example, habitual offenders can be sentenced to life in prison. Other states are less brazen, preferring the more genteel sounding "indeterminate sentence," which allows parole boards to keep inmates locked up for as long as life. It was under an indeterminate sentence of one to 14 years that George Jackson served 12 years in California prisons for committing a $70 armed robbery. Under a Texas law imposing an automatic life sentence for a third felony conviction, a man was sent to jail for life last year because of three thefts adding up to less than $300 in property value. Texas also is famous for occasionally imposing extravagantly long sentences, often running into hundreds of thousands of years. This gives Texas a leg up on Maryland, which used to sentence some criminals to life plus a day—a distinctive if superfluous flourish.

5   The punishment *intended* by Western societies in sending their criminals to prison is the loss of freedom. But, as everyone knows, the actual punishment in most American prisons is of a wholly different order. The February 2 [1980] riot at New Mexico's state prison in Santa Fe, one of several bloody prison riots in the nine years since the Attica blood bath, once again dramatized the conditions of life in an American prison. Four hundred prisoners seized control of the prison before dawn. By sunset the next day 33 inmates had died at the hands of other convicts and another 40 people (including five guards) had been seriously hurt. Macabre stories came out [about] prisoners being hanged, murdered with blowtorches, decapitated, tortured, and mutilated in a variety of gruesome ways by drug-crazed rioters.

NOTES

malefactors (par. 3): law breakers
effusive (par. 3): excessive
endorsement (par. 3): approval
brazen (par. 4): excessively bold
genteel (par. 4): well-bred
indeterminate (par. 4): indefinite
superfluous flourish (par. 4): unnecessary addition
Attica (par. 5): prison in New York
Macabre (par. 5): horror
decapitated (par. 5): beheaded
gruesome (par. 5): horrible, brutal

6   The Santa Fe penitentiary was typical of most maximum-security facilities, with prisoners subject to overcrowding, filthy conditions, and routine violence. It also housed first-time, non-violent offenders, like check forgers and drug dealers, with murderers serving life sentences. In a recent lawsuit, the American Civil Liberties Union called the prison "totally unfit for human habitation." But the ACLU says New Mexico's penitentiary is far from the nation's worst.

7   That American prisons are a disgrace is taken for granted by experts of every ideological stripe. Conservative James Q. Wilson has criticized our "[c]rowded, antiquated prisons that require men and women to live in fear of one another and to suffer not only deprivation of liberty but a brutalizing regimen." Leftist Jessica Mitford has called our prisons "the ultimate expression of injustice and inhumanity." In 1973 a national commission concluded that "the American correctional system today appears to offer minimum protection to the public and maximum harm to the offender." Federal courts have ruled that confinement in prisons in 16 different states violates the constitutional ban on "cruel and unusual punishment."

8   What are the advantages of being a convicted criminal in an advanced culture? First there is the overcrowding in prisons. One Tennessee prison, for example, has a capacity of 806, according to accepted space standards, but it houses 2300 inmates. One Louisiana facility has confined four and five prisoners in a single six-foot-by-six-foot cell. Then there is the disease caused by overcrowding, unsanitary conditions, and poor or inadequate medical care. A federal appeals court noted that the Tennessee prison had suffered frequent outbreaks of infectious diseases like hepatitis and tuberculosis. But the most distinctive element of American prison life is its constant violence. In his book *Criminal Violence, Criminal Justice,* Charles Silberman noted that in one Louisiana prison, there were 211 stabbings in only three years, 11 of them fatal. There were 15 slayings in a prison in Massachusetts between 1972 and 1975. According to a federal court, in Alabama's penitentiaries (as in many others), "robbery, rape, extortion, theft and assault are everyday occurrences."

9   At least in regard to cruelty, it's not at all clear that the system of punishment that has evolved in the West is less barbaric than the grotesque practices of Islam. Skeptical? Ask yourself: would you rather be subjected to a few minutes of intense pain and considerable public humiliation, or be locked away for two or three years in a prison cell crowded with ill-tempered sociopaths? Would you rather lose a hand or spend 10 years or more in a typical state prison? I have taken my own survey on this matter. I have found no

NOTES
American Civil Liberties Union (par. 6): an organization that seeks to protect the civil rights of all Americans
habitation (par. 6): occupancy
ideological stripe (par. 7): political or philosophical position
Conservative (par. 7): one who tends to favor the preservation of existing social or political systems; considered a member of "the Right" (See "Leftist," below.)
antiquated (par. 7): outdated
deprivation (par. 7): loss
regimen (par. 7): system
Leftist (par. 7): a liberal, or one who tends to favor social or political reform
grotesque (par. 9): hideous, horrible
skeptical (par. 9): doubting
sociopaths (par. 9): people whose behavior is anti-social

one who does not find the Islamic system hideous. And I have found no one who, given the choices mentioned above, would not prefer its penalties to our own.

10   The great divergence between Western and Islamic fashions in punishment is relatively recent. Until roughly the end of the 18th century, criminals in Western countries rarely were sent to prison. Instead they were subject to an ingenious assortment of penalties. Many perpetrators of a variety of crimes simply were executed, usually by some imaginative and extremely unpleasant method involving prolonged torture, such as breaking on the wheel, burning at the stake, or drawing and quartering. Michael Foucault's book *Discipline and Punish: The Birth of the Prison* notes one form of capital punishment in which the condemned man's "belly was opened up, his entrails quickly ripped out, so that he had time to see them, with his own eyes, being thrown on the fire; in which he was finally decapitated and his body quartered." Some criminals were forced to serve on slave galleys. But in most cases various corporal measures such as pillorying, flogging, and branding sufficed.

11   In time, however, public sentiment recoiled against these measures. They were replaced by imprisonment, which was thought to have two advantages. First, it was considered to be more humane. Second, and more important, prison was supposed to hold out the possibility of rehabilitation—purging the criminal of his criminality—something that less civilized punishments did not even aspire to. An 1854 report by inspectors of the Pennsylvania prison system illustrates the hopes nurtured by humanitarian reformers:

> Depraved tendencies, characteristic of the convict, have been restrained by the absence of vicious association, and in the mild teaching of Christianity, the unhappy criminal finds a solace for an involuntary exile from the comforts of social life. If hungry, he is fed; if naked, he is clothed; if destitute of the first rudiments of education, he is taught to read and write; and if he has never been blessed with a means of livelihood, he is schooled in a mechanical art, which in after life may be to him the source of profit and respectability. Employment is not his toil nor labor, weariness. He embraces them with alacrity, as contributing to his moral and mental elevation.

12   Imprisonment is now the universal method of punishing criminals in the United States. It is thought to perform five functions, each of which has been given a label by criminologist. First, there is simple *retribution:* punishing the

NOTES

divergence (par. 10): difference
ingenious (par. 10): creative, clever
perpetrators (par. 10): those who are guilty
drawing and quartering (par. 10): the practice of tying each of a person's limbs to a different horse and having the four horses run in different directions so that the person was pulled into four pieces, or quartered
entrails (par. 10): intestines
galleys (par. 10): ships
pillorying (par. 10): a type of punishment in which one's hands and head are placed within the holes of a stock or wooden frame
recoiled (par. 11): turned
purging (par. 11): ridding
aspire to (par. 11): attempt
depraved (par. 11): morally corrupt
solace (par. 11): comfort
destitute (par. 11): lacking
rudiments (par. 11): basics
alacrity (par. 11): eagerness
elevation (par. 11): improvement

lawbreaker to serve society's sense of justice and to satisfy the victims' desire for revenge. Second, there is *specific deterrence:* discouraging the offender from misbehaving in the future. Third, *general deterrence:* using the offender as an example to discourage others from turning to crime. Fourth, *prevention:* at least during the time he is kept off the streets, the criminal cannot victimize other members of society. Finally, and most important, there is *rehabilitation:* reforming the criminal so that when he returns to society he will be inclined to obey the laws and able to make an honest living.

13   How satisfactorily do American prisons perform by these criteria? Well, of course, they do punish. But on the other scores they don't do so well. Their effect in discouraging future criminality by the prisoner or others is the subject of much debate, but the soaring rates of the last 20 years suggest that prisons are not a dramatically effective deterrent to criminal behavior. Prisons do isolate convicted criminals, but only to divert crime from ordinary citizens to prison guards and fellow inmates. Almost no one contends any more that prisons rehabilitate their inmates. If anything, they probably impede rehabilitation by forcing inmates into prolonged and almost exclusive association with other criminals. And prisons cost a lot of money. Housing a typical prisoner in a typical prison costs far more than a stint at a top university. This cost would be justified if prisons did the job they were intended for. But it is clear to all that prisons fail on the very grounds—humanity and hope of rehabilitation—that caused them to replace earlier, cheaper forms of punishment.

14   The universal acknowledgment that prisons do not rehabilitate criminals has produced two responses. The first is to retain the hope of rehabilitation but do away with imprisonment as much as possible and replace it with various forms of "alternative treatment," such as psychotherapy, supervised probation, and vocational training. Psychiatrist Karl Menninger, one of the principal critics of American penology, has suggested even more unconventional approaches, such as "a new job opportunity or a vacation trip, a course of reducing exercises, a cosmetic surgical operation or a herniotomy, some night school courses, a wedding in the family (even one for the patient!), an inspiring sermon." The starry-eyed approach naturally has produced a backlash from critics on the right, who think that it's time to abandon the goal of rehabilitation. They argue that prisons perform an important service just by keeping criminals off the streets, and thus should be used with that purpose alone in mind.

15   So the debate continues to rage in all the same old ruts. No one, of course, would think of copying the medieval practices of Islamic nations and experimenting with punishments such as flogging and amputation. But let us consider them anyway. How do they compare with our American prison system in achieving the ostensible objectives of punishment? First, do they punish? Obviously they do, and in a uniquely painful and memorable way. Of course any sensible person, given the choice, would prefer suffering these punishments to years of incarceration in a typical American prison. But presumably no Western penologist would criticize Islamic punishments on the grounds

NOTES

criteria (par. 13): a set of guidelines
contends (par. 13): argues
impede (par. 13): hinder
stint (par. 13): stay
herniotomy (par. 14): removal of a hernia
ostensible (par. 15): supposed
incarceration (par. 15): imprisonment

that they are not barbaric enough. Do they deter crime? Yes, and probably more effectively than sending convicts off to prison. Now we read about a prison sentence in the newspaper, then think no more about the criminal's payment for his crimes until, perhaps, years later we read a small item reporting his release. By contrast, one can easily imagine the vivid impression it would leave to be wandering through a local shopping center and to stumble onto the scene of some poor wretch being lustily flogged. And the occasional sight of an habitual offender walking around with a bloody stump at the end of his arm no doubt also would serve as a forceful reminder that crime does not pay.

16   Do flogging and amputation discourage recidivism? No one knows whether the scars on his back would dissuade a criminal from risking another crime, but it is hard to imagine that corporal measures could stimulate a higher rate of recidivism than already exists. Islamic forms of punishment do not serve the favorite new right goal of simply isolating criminals from the rest of society, but they may achieve the same purpose of making further crimes impossible. In the movie *Bonnie and Clyde*, Warren Beatty successfully robs a bank with his arm in a sling, but this must be dismissed as artistic license. It must be extraordinarily difficult, at the very least, to perform much violent crime with only one hand.

17   Do these medieval forms of punishment rehabilitate the criminal? Plainly not. But long prison terms do not rehabilitate either. And it is just as plain that typical Islamic punishments are no crueler to the convict than incarceration in the typical American state prison.

18   Of course there are other reasons besides its bizarre forms of punishment that the Islamic system of justice seems uncivilized to the Western mind. One is the absence of due process. Another is the long list of offenses—such as drinking, adultery, blasphemy, "profiteering," and so on—that can bring on conviction and punishment. A third is all the ritualistic mumbo-jumbo in pronouncements of Islamic law (like that talk about puberty and amnesia in the Ayatollah's quotation at the beginning of this article). Even in these matters, however, a little cultural modesty is called for. The vast majority of American criminals are convicted and sentenced as a result of plea bargaining, in which due process plays almost no role. It has been only half a century since a wave of religious fundamentalism stirred this country to outlaw the consumption of alcoholic beverages. Most states also still have laws imposing austere constraints on sexual conduct. Only two weeks ago the *Washington Post* reported that the FBI had spent two and a half years and untold amounts of money to break up a nationwide pornography ring. Flogging the clients of prostitutes, as the Pakistanis did, does seem silly. But only a few months ago Mayor Koch of New York was proposing that clients caught in his own city have their names broadcast by radio stations. We are not so far advanced on

NOTES

vivid (par. 15): sharp, lasting
recidivism (par. 16): return to criminal behavior
dissuade (par. 16): discourage
due process (par. 18): a set of procedures designed to protect the legal rights of citizens
blasphemy (par. 18): expressing lack of respect for God or anything considered sacred
profiteering (par. 18): making excessive profits
ritualistic (par. 18): ceremonial
pronouncements (par. 18): statements, declarations
plea bargaining (par. 18): a process in which a criminal agrees to plead guilty, thus avoiding a trial, in exchange for a reduced charge or sentence
austere (par. 18): severe

such matters as we often like to think. Finally, my lawyer friends assure me that the rules of jurisdiction for American courts contain plenty of petty requirements and bizarre distinctions that would sound silly enough to foreign ears.

19   Perhaps it sounds barbaric to talk of flogging and amputation, and perhaps it is. But our system of punishment also is barbaric, and probably more so. Only cultural smugness about their system and willful ignorance about our own make it easy to regard the one as cruel and the other as civilized. We inflict our cruelties away from public view, while nations like Pakistan stage them in front of 10,000 onlookers. Their outrages are visible; ours are not. Most Americans can live their lives for years without having their peace of mind disturbed by the knowledge of what goes on in our prisons. To choose imprisonment over flogging and amputation is not to choose human kindness over cruelty, but merely to prefer that our cruelties be kept out of sight, and out of mind.

20   Public flogging and amputation may be more barbaric forms of punishment than imprisonment, even if they are not more cruel. Society may pay a higher price for them, even if the particular criminal does not. Revulsion against officially sanctioned violence and infliction of pain derives from something deeply ingrained in the Western conscience, and clearly it is something admirable. Grotesque displays of the sort that occur in Islamic countries probably breed a greater tolerance for physical cruelty, for example, which prisons do not do precisely because they conceal their cruelties. In fact it is our admirable intolerance for calculated violence that makes it necessary for us to conceal what we have not been able to do away with. In a way this is a good thing, since it holds out the hope that we may eventually find a way to do away with it. But in another way it is a bad thing, since it permits us to congratulate ourselves on our civilized humanitarianism while violating its norms in this one area of our national life.

NOTES

petty (par. 18): unimportant
smugness (par. 19): feeling of superiority
revulsion (par. 20): disgust
sanctioned (par. 20): approved
ingrained (par. 20): rooted
calculated (par. 20): planned, intended
humanitarianism (par. 20): respect for the rights and life of human beings
norms (par. 20): standards of behavior

Violent Crime: Myths, Facts, and Solutions

The Conservative and Progressive Answers

D. Stanley Eitzen

Lecture delivered at the 1995 Symposium "The Shadow of Violence: Unconsidered Perspectives," Hastings College, Hastings, Nebraska, March 15, 1995

1   My remarks are limited to violent street crimes (assault, robbery, rape, and murder). We should not forget that there are other types of violent crimes

that are just as violent and actually greater in magnitude than street crimes: corporate, political, organized, and white collar. But that is another subject for another time. Our attention this morning is on violent street crime, which has made our cities unsafe and our citizens extremely fearful. What are the facts about violent crime and violent criminals and what do we, as a society, do about them?

2   I am going to critique the prevailing thought about violent crime and its control because our perceptions about violent crime and much of what our government officials do about it is wrong. My discipline—sociology—knows a lot about crime but what we know does not seem to affect public perceptions and public policies. Not all of the answers, however, are always crystal clear. There are disagreements among reasonable and thoughtful people, coming from different theoretical and ideological perspectives. You may, difficult as it seems to me, actually disagree with my analysis. That's all right. The key is for us to address this serious problem, determine the facts, engage in dialogue, and then work toward logical and just solutions.

3   What do criminologists know about violent crime? Much of what we know is counter intuitive; it flies in the face of the public's understanding. So, let me begin with some demythologizing.

4   *Myth 1: As a Christian nation with high moral principles, we rank relatively low in the amount of violent crime.* Compared with the other industrialized nations of the world, we rank number one in belief in God, "the importance of God in our lives," and church attendance. We also rank first in murder rates, robbery rates, and rape rates. Take homicide, for example: the U.S. rate of 10 per 100,000 is three times that of Finland, five times that of Canada, and nine times greater than found in Norway, the Netherlands, Germany, and Great Britain. In 1992, for example, Chicago, a city about one-fifth the population of the Netherlands had nine times more gun-related deaths than occurred in the Netherlands.

5   *Myth 2: We are in the midst of a crime wave.* When it comes to crime rates we are misled by our politicians, and the media. Government data indicate that between 1960 and 1970 crime rates doubled, then continued to climb through the 1970s. From 1970 to 1990 the rates remained about the same. The problem is with violent crime by youth, which has increased dramatically. Despite the rise in violent crime among youth, however, the *overall* violent crime rate actually has decreased in the 1990s.

6   Our perceptions are affected especially by the media. While crime rates have leveled and slightly declined during the 1990s, the media have given us a different picture. In 1993, for example, the three major networks doubled their crime stories and tripled their coverage of murders. This distortion of reality results, of course, in a general perception that we are in the midst of a crime wave.

7   *Myth 3: Serious violent crime is found throughout the age structure.* Crime is mainly a problem of male youths. Violent criminal behaviors peak at age 17 and by age 24 it is one-half the rate. Young males have always posed a special crime problem. There are some differences now, however. Most significant, young males and the gangs to which they often belong now have much greater firepower. Alienated and angry youth once used clubs, knives,

NOTES
magnitude (par. 1): extent
critique (par. 2): review critically
perspectives (par. 2): mental outlooks
is counter intuitive (par. 3): contradicts instinct

brass knuckles, and fists but now they use Uzis, AK47s, and "streetsweep-ers." The result is that since 1985, the murder rate for 18–24 year-olds has risen 65 percent while the rate for 14–17 year-olds has increased 165 percent.

8   The frightening demographic fact is that between now and the year 2005, the number of teenagers in the U.S. will grow by 23 percent. During the next ten years, black teenagers will increase by 28 percent and the Hispanic teenage population will grow by about 50 percent. The obvious prediction is that violent crime will increase dramatically over this period.

9   *Myth 4: The most dangerous place in America is in the streets where strangers threaten, hit, stab, or shoot each other.* The streets in our urban places are dangerous, as rival gangs fight, and drive-by shootings occur. But, statistically, the most dangerous place is in your own home, or when you are with a boyfriend or girlfriend, family member, or acquaintance.

10   *Myth 5: Violent criminals are born with certain predispositions toward violence.* Criminals are not born with a criminal gene. If crime were just a function of biology, then we would expect crime rates to be more or less the same for all social categories, times, and places. In fact, violent crime rates vary considerably by social class, race, unemployment, poverty, geographical place, and other social variables. Research on these variables is the special contribution of sociology to the understanding of criminal behavior.

11   Let's elaborate on these social variables because these have so much to do with solutions. Here is what we know about these social variables:

12   1. The more people in poverty, the higher the rate of street crime.

13   2. The higher the unemployment rate in an area, the higher the crime rate. Sociologist William J. Wilson says that black and white youths at age 11 are equally likely to commit violent crimes but by their late 20s, blacks are four times more likely to be violent offenders. However, when blacks and whites in their late 20s are employed, they differ hardly at all in violent behavior.

14   3. The greater the racial segregation in an area, the higher the crime rate. So-ciologist Doug Massey argues that urban poverty and urban crime are the con-sequences of extremely high levels of black residential segregation and racial discrimination. Massey says,

> "Take a group of people, segregate them, cut off their capital and guess what? The neighborhoods go downhill. There's no other outcome possible."

As these neighborhoods go downhill and economic opportunities evaporate, crime rates go up.

15   4. The greater the family instability, the higher the probability of crimes by juveniles. Research is sketchy, but it appears that the following conditions are related to delinquent behaviors: (a) intense parental conflict; (b) lack of parental supervision; (c) parental neglect and abuse; and (d) failure of parents to disci-pline their children.

16   5. The greater the inequality in a neighborhood, city, region, or society, the higher the crime rate. In other words, the greater the disparities between rich and poor, the greater the probability of crime. Of all the industrialized nations, the U.S. has the greatest degree of inequality. For example, one percent of Americans own 40 percent of all the wealth. At the other extreme, $14\frac{1}{2}$

NOTES

"streetsweepers" (par. 7): 12 gauge shotguns that can discharge the 12 rounds they hold in three seconds
demographic fact (par. 8): statistical fact about the population
predispositions (par. 10): tendencies
capital (par. 14): money for spending, lending, and investing
disparities (par. 16): differences

percent of all Americans live below the poverty line and 5 percent of all Americans live below *one-half* of the poverty line.

17   When these social variables coverge, they interact to increase crime rates. Thus, there is a relatively high probability of criminal behavior—violent criminal behavior—among young, black, impoverished males in inner cities where poverty, unemployment, and racial segregation are concentrated. There are about 5 million of these high-risk young men. In addition, we have other problem people. What do we do? How do we create a safer America?

18   To oversimplify a difficult and contentious debate, there are two answers—the conservative and progressive answers. The conservative answer has been to get tough with criminals. This involves mandatory sentences, longer sentences, putting more people in prison, and greater use of the death penalty. This strategy has accelerated with laws such as "three strikes and you're out (actually in)," and the passage of expensive prison building programs to house the new prisoners.

19   In my view, this approach is wrong-headed. Of course, some individuals must be put in prison to protect the members of society. Our policies, however, indiscriminately put too many people in prison at too high a cost. Here are some facts about prisons:

20   1. Our current incarceration rate is 455 per 100,000 (in 1971 it was 96 per 100,000). The rate in Japan and the Netherlands is one-tenth ours. Currently, there are 1.2 million Americans in prisons and jails (equivalent to the population of Philadelphia).

21   2. The cost is prohibitive, taking huge amounts of money that could be spent on other programs. It costs about $60,000 to build a prison cell and $20,000 to keep a prisoner for a year. Currently the overall cost of prisons and jails (federal, state, and local) is $29 billion annually. The willingness to spend for punishment reduces money that could be spent to alleviate other social problems. For example, eight years ago Texas spent $7 dollars on education for every dollar spent on prisons. Now the ratio is 4 to 1. Meanwhile, Texas ranks 37th among the states in per pupil spending.

22   3. As mentioned earlier, violent crimes tend to occur in the teenage years with a rapid drop off afterwards. Often, for example, imprisonment under "3 strikes and you're out" laws gives life imprisonment to many who are in the twilight of their criminal careers. We, and they, would be better off if we found alternatives to prison for them.

23   4. Prisons do not rehabilitate. Actually, prisons have the opposite effect. The prison experience tends to increase the likelihood of further criminal behavior. Prisons are overcrowded, mean, gloomy, brutal places that change people, but usually for the worse, not the better. Moreover, prisoners usually believe that their confinement is unjust because of the bias in the criminal justice system toward the poor and racial minorities. Finally, prisoners do not ever pay their debt to society. Rather they are forever stigmatized as "ex-cons" and, therefore, considered unreliable and dangerous by their neighbors, employers, fellow workers, and acquaintances. Also, they are harassed by the police as

NOTES

converge (par. 17): come together
contentious (par. 18): controversial
incarceration (par. 20): imprisonment
alleviate (par. 21): relieve
rehabilitate (par. 23): redirect prisoners so that they become law-abiding, productive citizens when they are released from prison
stigmatized (par. 23): labeled

"likely suspects." The result is that they are often driven into a deviant sub-culture and eventually caught—about two-thirds are arrested within three years of leaving prison.

24   Progressives argue that conservative crime control measures are funda-mentally flawed because they are "after the fact" solutions. Like a janitor mopping up the floor while the sink continues to overflow; he or she may even redouble the effort with some success but the source of the flooding has not been addressed. If I might mix metaphors here (although keeping with the aquatic theme), the obvious place to begin the attack on crime is *upstream*, before the criminal has been formed and the crimes have been committed.

25   We must concentrate our efforts on high-risk individuals before they become criminals (in particular, impoverished young inner city males). These prevention proposals take time, are very costly, and out-of-favor politically but they are the only realistic solutions to reduce violent street crime.

26   The problem with the conservative "after the fact" crime fighting pro-posals is that while promoting criminal justice, these programs dismantle social justice. Thus, they enhance a criminogenic climate. During the Reagan years, for example, $51 billion dollars were removed from various poverty pro-grams. Now, under the "Contract for America" the Republicans in Congress propose to reduce subsidized housing, to eliminate nutrition programs through WIC (Woman, Infants, and Children), to let the states take care of subsidized school lunches, and to eliminate welfare for unmarried mothers under 18 who do not live with their parents or a responsible guardian.

27   Progressives argue that we abandon these children at our own peril. The current Republican proposals forsake the 26 percent of American children under six who live in poverty including 54 percent of all African American children and 44 percent of all Latino children under the age of six. Will we be safer as these millions of children in poverty grow to physical maturity?

28   Before I address specific solutions, I want to emphasize that sociologists examine the structural reasons for crime. This focus on factors outside the individual does not excuse criminal behavior, it tries to understand how cer-tain structural factors *increase* the proportion of people who choose criminal options.

29   Knowing what we know about crime, the implications for policy are clear. These proposals, as you will note, are easy to suggest but they are very diffi-cult to implement. I will divide my proposals into immediate actions to deal with crime now and long-term preventive measure[s]:

Measures to protect society immediately:

30   1. The first step is to protect society from predatory sociopaths. This does not mean imprisoning more people. We should, rather, only imprison the truly dangerous. The criminal law should be redrawn so that the list of crimes reflects the real dangers that individuals pose to society. Since prison does more harm than good, we should provide reasonable alternatives such as house arrest, half-way houses, boot camps, electronic surveillance, job corps, and drug/alcohol treatment.

NOTES
deviant (par. 23): socially unacceptable
aquatic (par. 24): water related
criminogenic (par. 26): crime producing
subsidized housing (par. 26): housing that is partially or totally paid for by the government
peril (par. 27): risk
predatory sociopaths (par. 30): violent, aggressive antisocial individuals

31. 2. We must reduce the number of handguns and assault weapons by enacting and vigorously enforcing stringent gun controls at the federal level. The United States is an armed camp with 210 million guns in circulation. Jeffrey Reiman has put it this way:

> "Trying to fight crime while allowing such easy access to guns is like trying to teach a child to walk and tripping him each time he stands up. In its most charitable light, it is hypocrisy. Less charitably, it is complicity in murder."

32 3. We must make a special effort to get guns out of the hands of juveniles. Research by James Wright and his colleagues at Tulane University found that juveniles are much more likely to have guns for protection than for status and power. They suggest that we must restore order in the inner cities so that fewer young people do not feel the need to provide their own protection. They argue that a perceived sense of security by youth can be accomplished if there is a greater emphasis on community policing, more cooperation between police departments and inner city residents, and greater investment by businesses, banks, and cities in the inner city.

33 4. We must reinvent the criminal justice system so that it commands the respect of youth and adults. The obvious unfairness by race and social class must be addressed. Some laws are unfair. For example, the federal law requires a five-year, no-parole sentence for possession of five grams of crack cocaine, worth about $400. However, it takes 100 times as much powder cocaine—500 grams, worth $10,000—and a selling conviction to get the same sentence. Is this fair? Of course not. Is it racist? It is racist since crack is primarily used by African Americans while powder cocaine is more likely used by whites. There are also differences by race and social class in arrest patterns, plea bargain arrangements, sentencing, parole, and imposition of the death penalty. These differences provide convincing evidence that the poor and racial minorities are discriminated against in the criminal justice system. As long as the criminal justice system is perceived as unfair by the disadvantaged, that system will not exert any moral authority over them.

34 5. We must rehabilitate as many criminals as possible. Prisons should be more humane. Prisoners should leave prison with vocational skills useful in the real world. Prisoners should leave prison literate and with a high-school degree. And, society should formally adopt the concept of "forgiveness" saying to ex-prisoners, in effect, you have been punished for your crime, we want you to begin a new life with a "clean" record.

35 6. We must legalize the production and sale of "illicit drugs" and treat addiction as a medical problem rather than a criminal problem. If drugs were legalized or decriminalized, crimes would be reduced in several ways: (a) By eliminating drug use as a criminal problem, we would have 1.12 million *fewer* arrests each year. (b) There would be many *fewer* prisoners (currently about 60 percent of all federal prisoners and 25 percent of all state prisoners are incarcerated for drug offenses). (c) Money now spent on the drug war ($31 billion annually, not counting prison construction) could be spent for other crime control programs such as police patrols, treatment of drug users, and jobs programs. (d) Drugs could be regulated and taxed, generating revenues of about

NOTES

stringent (par. 31): rigorous, severe
hypocrisy (par. 31): saying one thing and doing the opposite
complicity (par. 31): criminal participation
vocational skills (par. 34): skills needed for occupations not requiring a college degree, such as plumbing and welding

$5 billion a year. (e) It would end the illicit drug trade that provides tremendous profits to organized crime, violent gangs, and other traffickers. (f) It would eliminate considerable corruption of the police and other authorities. (g) There would be many fewer homicides. Somewhere between one-fourth and one-half of the killings in the inner cities are drug-related. (h) The lower cost of purchasing drugs reduces the need to commit crimes to pay for drug habits.

Long-term preventive measures to reduce violent crime:

36   1. The link between poverty and street crime is indisputable. In the long run, reducing poverty will be the most effective crime fighting tool. Thus, as a society, we need to intensify our efforts to break the cycle of poverty. This means providing a universal and comprehensive health-care system, low-cost housing, job training, and decent compensation for work. There must be pay equity for women. And, there must be an unwavering commitment to eradicate institutional sexism and racism. Among other benefits, such a strategy will strengthen families and give children resources, positive role models, and hope.

37   2. Families must be strengthened. Single-parent families and the working poor need subsidized child care, flexible work schedules, and leave for maternity and family emergencies at a reasonable proportion of their wages. Adolescent parents need the resources to stay in school. They need job training. We need to increase the commitment to family planning. This means providing contraceptives and birth control counseling to adolescents. This means using federal funds to pay for legal abortions when they are requested by poor women.

38   3. There must be a societal commitment to full and decent employment. Meaningful work at decent pay integrates individuals into society. It is a source of positive identity. Employed parents are respected by their children. Good paying jobs provide hope for the future. They also are essential to keep families together.

39.   4. There must be a societal commitment to education. This requires two different programs. The first is to help at-risk children, beginning at an early age. As it is now, when poor children start school, they are already behind. As Sylvia Ann Hewlett has said:

> "At age five, poor children are often less alert, less curious, and less effective at interacting with their peers than are more privileged youngsters."

This means that they are doomed to be underachievers. To overcome this we need intervention programs that prepare children for school. Research shows that Head Start and other programs can raise IQ scores significantly. There are two problems with Head Start, however. First, the current funding only covers 40 percent of eligible youngsters. And second, the positive effects from the Head Start program are sometimes short-lived because the children then attend schools that are poorly staffed, overcrowded, and ill-equipped.

40   This brings us to the second education program to help at-risk children. The government must equalize the resources of school districts, rather than the current situation where the wealth of school districts determines the amount spent per pupil. Actually, equalization is not the answer. I believe that there should be special commitment to invest *extra* resources in at-risk children. If we do, we will have a safer society in the long run.

NOTES
illicit (par. 35): illegal
eradicate (par. 36): abolish
Head Start (par. 39): a federally funded program that provides preschool education for culturally and economically disadvantaged children

41   These proposals seem laughable in the current political climate, where politicians—Republicans *and* Democrats—try to outdo each other in their toughness on crime and their disdain for preventive programs. They are wrong, however, and society is going to pay in higher crime rates in the future. I am convinced that the political agenda of the conservatives is absolutely heading us in the wrong direction—toward more violent crime rather than less.

42   The proposals that I have suggested are based on what we sociologists know about crime. They should be taken seriously, but they are not. The proposals are also based on the assumption that if we can give at-risk young people hope, they will become a part of the community rather than alienated from it. My premise is this: Everyone needs a dream. Without a dream, we become apathetic. Without a dream, we become fatalistic. Without a dream, and the hope of attaining it, society becomes our enemy. Many young people act in antisocial ways because they have lost their dream. These troubled and troublesome people are society's creations because we have not given them the opportunity to achieve their dreams—instead society has structured the situation so that they will fail. Until they feel that they have a stake in society, they will fail, and so will we.

NOTES

disdain (par. 41): contempt
agenda (par. 41): program
apathetic (par. 42): indifferent
we become fatalistic (par. 42): the belief that we have no control over our lives

The False Promise of Gun Control

Daniel D. Polsby

1   During the 1960s and 1970s the robbery rate in the United States increased sixfold, and the murder rate doubled; the rate of handgun ownership nearly doubled in that period as well. Handguns and criminal violence grew together apace, and national opinion leaders did not fail to remark on the coincidence.

2   It has become a bipartisan article of faith that more handguns cause more violence. Such was the unequivocal conclusion of the National Commission on the Causes and Prevention of Violence in 1969, and such is now the editorial opinion of virtually every influential newspaper and magazine, from *The Washington Post* to *The Economist* to the *Chicago Tribune*. Members of the House and Senate who have not dared to confront the gun lobby concede the connection privately. Even if the National Rifle Association can produce blizzards of angry calls and letters to the Capitol virtually overnight, House members one by one have been going public, often after some new firearms atrocity at a fast-food restaurant or the like. And last November they passed the Brady bill.

NOTES

apace (par. 1): at a rapid pace
bipartisan article of faith (par. 2): a belief held by both Democrats and Republicans
unequivocal (par. 2): clear and straightforward
concede (par. 2): admit
National Rifle Association (par. 2): an organization whose members support, among other things, the private citizen's right to keep and bear arms
atrocity (par. 2): outrage

3   Alas, however well accepted, the conventional wisdom about guns and violence is mistaken. Guns don't increase national rates of crime and violence—but the continued proliferation of gun-control laws almost certainly does. Current rates of crime and violence are a bit below the peaks of the late 1970s, but because of a slight oncoming bulge in the at-risk population of males aged fifteen to thirty-four, the crime rate will soon worsen. The rising generation of criminals will have no more difficulty than their elders did in obtaining the tools of their trade. Growing violence will lead to calls for laws still more severe. Each fresh round of legislation will be followed by renewed frustration.

4   Gun-control laws don't work. What is worse, they act perversely. While legitimate users of firearms encounter intense regulation, scrutiny, and bureaucratic control, illicit markets easily adapt to whatever difficulties a free society throws in their way. Also, efforts to curtail the supply of firearms inflict collateral damage on freedom and privacy interests that have long been considered central to American public life. Thanks to the seemingly never-ending war on drugs and long experience attempting to suppress prostitution and pornography, we know a great deal about how illicit markets function and how costly to the public attempts to control them can be. It is essential that we make use of this experience in coming to grips with gun control.

5   The thousands of gun-control laws in the United States are of two general types. The older kind sought to regulate how, where, and by whom firearms could be carried. More recent laws have sought to make it more costly to buy, sell, or use firearms (or certain classes of firearms, such as assault rifles, Saturday-night specials, and so on) by imposing fees, special taxes, or surtaxes on them. The Brady bill is of both types: It has a background-check provision, and its five-day waiting period amounts to a "time tax" on acquiring handguns. All such laws can be called scarcity-inducing, because they seek to raise the cost of buying firearms, as figured in terms of money, time, nuisance, or stigmatization.

6   Despite the mounting number of scarcity-inducing laws, no one is very satisfied with them. Hobbyists want to get rid of them, and gun-control proponents don't think they go nearly far enough. Everyone seems to agree that gun-control laws have some effect on the distribution of firearms. But it has not been the dramatic and measurable effect their proponents desired.

7   Opponents of gun control have traditionally wrapped their arguments in the Second Amendment to the Constitution. Indeed, most modern scholarship affirms that so far as the drafters of the Bill of Rights were concerned, the right to bear arms was to be enjoyed by everyone, not just a militia, and that one of the principal justifications for an armed populace was to secure the tranquillity and good order of the community. But most people are not dedicated antiquitarians, and would not be impressed by the argument "I admit that my behavior is very dangerous to public safety, but the Second Amendment says I have a right to do it anyway." That would be a case for repealing the Second Amendment, not respecting it.

NOTES

proliferation (par. 3): rapid increase
perversely (par. 4): in opposition to what is right
illicit (par. 4): illegal
collateral (par. 4): accompanying
stigmatization (par. 5): disgrace
the Second Amendment to the Constitution (par. 7): "A well regulated Militia, being necessary to the security of a free State, the right of the people to keep and bear Arms, shall not be infringed."
antiquitarians (par. 7): scholars of ancient people and objects

Fighting the Demand Curve

8   Everyone knows that possessing a handgun makes it easier to intimidate, wound, or kill someone. But the implication of this point for social policy has not been so well understood. It is easy to count the bodies of those who have been killed or wounded with guns, but not easy to count the people who have avoided harm because they had access to weapons. Think about uniformed police officers, who carry handguns in plain view not in order to kill people but simply to daunt potential attackers. And it works. Criminals generally do not single out police officers for opportunistic attack. Though officers can expect to draw their guns from time to time, few even in big-city departments will actually fire a shot (except in target practice) in the course of a year. This observation points to an important truth: People who are armed make comparatively unattractive victims. A criminal might not know if any one civilian is armed, but if it becomes known that a large number of civilians do carry weapons, criminals will become warier.

9   Which weapons laws are the right kinds can be decided only after considering two related questions. First, what is the connection between civilian possession of firearms and social violence? Second, how can we expect gun-control laws to alter people's behavior? Most recent scholarship raises serious questions about the "weapons increase violence" hypothesis. The second question is emphasized here, because it is routinely overlooked and often mocked when noticed; yet it is crucial. Rational gun control requires understanding not only the relationship between weapons and violence but also the relationship between laws and people's behavior. Some things are very hard to accomplish with laws. The purpose of a law and its likely effects are not always the same thing. Many statutes are notorious for the way in which their unintended effects have swamped their intended ones.

10   In order to predict who will comply with gun-control laws, we should remember that guns are economic goods that are traded in markets. Consumers' interest in them varies. For religious, moral, aesthetic, or practical reasons, some people would refuse to buy firearms at any price. Other people willingly pay very high prices for them.

11   Handguns, so often the subject of gun-control laws, are desirable for one purpose—to allow a person tactically to dominate a hostile transaction with another person. The value of a weapon to a given person is a function of two factors: how much he or she wants to dominate a confrontation if one occurs, and how likely it is that he or she will actually be in a situation calling for a gun.

12   Dominating a transaction simply means getting what one wants without being hurt. Where people differ is in how likely it is that they will be involved in a situation in which a gun will be valuable. Someone who *intends* to engage in a transaction involving a gun—a criminal, for example—is obviously in the best possible position to predict that likelihood. Criminals should therefore be willing to pay more for a weapon than most other people would. Professors, politicians, and newspaper editors are, as a group, at

NOTES

daunt (par. 8): discourage
warier (par. 8): more cautious
mocked (par. 9): poked fun at
statutes (par. 9): laws
aesthetic (par. 10): philosophical
to allow a person tactically to dominate a hostile transaction with another person (par. 11): in other words, to allow a person to gain the tactic or strategic advantage over another person during a hostile encounter

very low risk of being involved in such transactions, and they thus systematically underrate the value of defensive handguns. (Correlative, perhaps, is their uncritical readiness to accept studies that debunk the utility of firearms for self-defense.) The class of people we wish to deprive of guns, then, is the very class with the most inelastic demand for them—criminals—whereas the people most likely to comply with gun-control laws don't value guns in the first place.

Do Guns Drive Up Crime Rates?

13   Which premise is true—that guns increase crime or that the fear of crime causes people to obtain guns? Most of the country's major newspapers apparently take this problem to have been solved by an article published by Arthur Kellermann and several associates in the October 7, 1993, *New England Journal of Medicine.* Kellermann is an emergency-room physician who has published a number of influential papers that he believes discredit the thesis that private ownership of firearms is a useful means of self-protection. (An indication of his wide influence is that within two months the study received almost 100 mentions in publications and broadcast transcripts indexed in the Nexis data base.) For this study Kellermann and his associates identified fifteen behavioral and fifteen environmental variables that applied to a 388-member set of homicide victims, found a "matching" control group of 388 non–homicide victims, and then ascertained how the two groups differed in gun ownership. In interviews Kellermann made clear his belief that owning a handgun markedly increases a person's risk of being murdered.

14   But the study does not prove that point at all. Indeed, as Kellermann explicitly conceded in the text of the article, the causal arrow may very well point in the other direction: the threat of being killed may make people more likely to arm themselves. Many people at risk of being killed, especially people involved in the drug trade or other illegal ventures, might well rationally buy a gun as a precaution, and be willing to pay a price driven up by gun-control laws. Crime, after all, is a dangerous business. Peter Reuter and Mark Kleiman, drug-policy researchers, calculated in 1987 that the average crack dealer's risk of being killed was far greater than his risk of being sent to prison. (Their data cannot, however, support the implication that ownership of a firearm causes or exacerbates the risk of being killed.)

15   Defending the validity of his work, Kellermann has emphasized that the link between lung cancer and smoking was initially established by studies methodologically no different from his. Gary Kleck, a criminology professor at Florida State University, has pointed out the flaw in this comparison. No one ever thought that lung cancer causes smoking, so when the association between the two was established the direction of the causal arrow was not in doubt. Kleck wrote that it is as though Kellermann, trying to discover how diabetics differ from other people, found that they are much more likely to

NOTES

Correlative (par. 12): also related (to the fact that they are "at very low risk of being involved in such transactions")
debunk (par. 12): expose the falseness of
premise (par. 13): concept
ascertained (par. 13): determined
exacerbates (par. 14): intensifies

possess insulin than nondiabetics, and concluded that insulin is a risk factor for diabetes.

16   *The New York Times,* the *Los Angeles Times, The Washington Post, The Boston Globe,* and the *Chicago Tribune* all gave prominent coverage to Kellermann's study as soon as it appeared, but none saw fit to discuss the study's limitations. A few, in order to introduce a hint of balance, mentioned that the NRA, or some member of its staff, disagreed with the study. But readers had no way of knowing that Kellermann himself had registered a disclaimer in his text. "It is possible," he conceded, "that reverse causation accounted for some of the association we observed between gun ownership and homicide." Indeed, the point is stronger than that: "Reverse causation" may account for *most* of the association between gun ownership and homicide. Kellermann's data simply do not allow one to draw any conclusion.

17   If firearms increased violence and crime, then rates of spousal homicide would have skyrocketed, because the stock of privately owned handguns has increased rapidly since the mid-1960s. But according to an authoritative study of spousal homicide in the *American Journal of Public Health,* by James Mercy and Linda Saltzman, rates of spousal homicide in the years 1976 to 1985 fell. If firearms increased violence and crime, the crime rate should have increased throughout the 1980s, while the national stock of privately owned handguns increased by more than a million units in every year of the decade. It did not. Nor should the rates of violence and crime in Switzerland, New Zealand, and Israel be as low as they are, since the number of firearms per civilian household is comparable to that in the United States. Conversely, gun-controlled Mexico and South Africa should be islands of peace instead of having murder rates more than twice as high as those here. The determinants of crime and law-abidingness are, of course, complex matters, which are not fully understood and certainly not explicable in terms of a country's laws. But gun-control enthusiasts, who have made capital out of the low murder rate in England, which is largely disarmed, simply ignore the counterexamples that don't fit their theory.

18   If firearms increased violence and crime, Florida's murder rate should not have been falling since the introduction, seven years ago, of a law that makes it easier for ordinary citizens to get permits to carry concealed handguns. Yet the murder rate has remained the same or fallen every year since the law was enacted, and it is now lower than the national murder rate (which has been rising). As of last November 183,561 permits had been issued, and only seventeen of the permits had been revoked because the holder was involved in a firearms offense. It would be precipitate to claim that the new law has "caused" the murder rate to subside. Yet here is a situation that doesn't fit the hypothesis that weapons increase violence.

19   If firearms increased violence and crime, programs of induced scarcity would suppress violence and crime. But—another anomaly—they don't. Why not? A theorem, which we could call the futility theorem, explains why gun-control laws must either be ineffectual or in the long term actually provoke more violence and crime. Any theorem depends on both observable fact and

NOTES

insulin (par. 15): Insulin is a hormone produced by the pancreas that enables sugar glucose to enter the tissues of the body. Insulin is a necessity. Diabetics produce no insulin or produce insulin that their body is unable to use.
Conversely (par. 17): on the other hand
precipitate (par. 18): rash
anomaly (par. 19): exception to the rule
theorem (par. 19): idea supposed to be true

assumption. An assumption that can be made with confidence is that the higher the number of victims a criminal assumes to be armed, the higher will be the risk—the price—of assaulting them. By definition, gun-control laws should make weapons scarcer and thus more expensive. By our prior reasoning about demand among various types of consumers, after the laws are enacted criminals should be better armed, compared with noncriminals, than they were before. Of course, plenty of noncriminals will remain armed. But even if many noncriminals will pay as high a price as criminals will to obtain firearms, a larger number will not.

20   Criminals will thus still take the same gamble they already take in assaulting a victim who might or might not be armed. But they may appreciate that the laws have given them a freer field, and that crime still pays—pays even better, in fact, than before. What will happen to the rate of violence? Only a relatively few gun-mediated transactions—currently, five percent of armed robberies committed with firearms—result in someone's actually being shot (the statistics are not broken down into encounters between armed assailants and unarmed victims, and encounters in which both parties are armed). It seems reasonable to fear that if the number of such transactions were to increase because criminals thought they faced fewer deterrents, there would be a corresponding increase in shootings. Conversely, if gun-mediated transactions declined—if criminals initiated fewer of them because they feared encountering an armed victim or an armed good Samaritan—the number of shootings would go down. The magnitude of these effects is, admittedly, uncertain. Yet it is hard to doubt the general tendency of a change in the law that imposes legal burdens on buying guns. The futility theorem suggests that gun-control laws, if effective at all, would unfavorably affect the rate of violent crime.

21   The futility theorem provides a lens through which to see much of the debate. It is undeniable that gun-control laws work—to an extent. Consider, for example, California's background-check law, which in the past two years has prevented about 12,000 people with a criminal record or a history of mental illness or drug abuse from buying handguns. In the same period Illinois's background-check law prevented the delivery of firearms to more than 2,000 people. Surely some of these people simply turned to an illegal market, but just as surely not all of them did. The laws of large numbers allow us to say that among the foiled thousands, some potential killers were prevented from getting a gun. We do not know whether the number is large or small, but it is implausible to think it is zero. And, as gun-control proponents are inclined to say, "If only one life is saved . . . ."

22   The hypothesis that firearms increase violence does predict that if we can slow down the diffusion of guns, there will be less violence; one life, or more, *will* be saved. But the futility theorem asks that we look not simply at the gross number of bad actors prevented from getting guns but at the effect the law has on *all* the people who want to buy a gun. Suppose we succeed in piling tax burdens on the acquisition of firearms. We can safely assume that a number of people who might use guns to kill will be sufficiently discouraged

NOTES

good Samaritan (par. 20): a person who unselfishly comes to the aid of others; The expression comes from the New Testament parable about the only man who helped a traveler who had been robbed, beaten, and left for dead by thieves (Luke 10:30–37).
foiled (par. 21): prevented
diffusion (par. 22): spread
gross (par. 22): total
acquisition (par. 22): purchasing

not to buy them. But we cannot assume this about people who feel that they must have guns in order to survive financially and physically. A few lives might indeed be saved. But the overall rate of violent crime might not go down at all. And if guns are owned predominantly by people who have good reason to think they will use them, the rate might even go up.

23   Are there empirical studies that can serve to help us choose between the futility theorem and the hypothesis that guns increase violence? Unfortunately, no: The best studies of the effects of gun-control laws are quite inconclusive. Our statistical tools are too weak to allow us to identify an effect clearly enough to persuade an open-minded skeptic. But it is precisely when we are dealing with undetectable statistical effects that we have to be certain we are using the best models available of human behavior.

Sealing the Border

24   Handguns are not legally for sale in the city of Chicago, and have not been since April of 1982. Rifles, shotguns, and ammunition are available, but only to people who possess an Illinois Firearm Owner's Identification card. It takes up to a month to get this card, which involves a background check. Even if one has a FOID card there is a waiting period for the delivery of a gun. In few places in America is it as difficult to get a firearm legally as in the city of Chicago.

25   Yet there are hundreds of thousands of unregistered guns in the city, and new ones arriving all the time. It is not difficult to get handguns—even legally. Chicago residents with FOID cards merely go to gun shops in the suburbs. Trying to establish a city as an island of prohibition in a sea of legal firearms seems an impossible project.

26   Is a state large enough to be an effective island, then? Suppose Illinois adopted Chicago's handgun ban. Same problem again. Some people could just get guns elsewhere: Indiana actually borders the city, and Wisconsin is only forty miles away. Though federal law prohibits the sale of handguns in one state to residents of another, thousands of Chicagoans with summer homes in other states could buy handguns there. And, of course, a black market would serve the needs of other customers.

27   When would the island be large enough to sustain a weapons-free environment? In the United States people and cargoes move across state lines without supervision or hindrance. Local shortages of goods are always transient, no matter whether the shortage is induced by natural disasters, prohibitory laws, or something else.

28   Even if many states outlawed sales of handguns, then, they would continue to be available, albeit at a somewhat higher price, reflecting the increased legal risk of selling them. Mindful of the way markets work to undermine their efforts, gun-control proponents press for federal regulation of firearms, because they believe that only Congress wields the authority to frustrate the interstate movement of firearms.

NOTES
empirical studies (par. 23): in other words, studies that rely on experiments or observations rather than theories
transient (par. 27): short-lived
induced (par. 27): caused
albeit (par. 28): although
wields (par. 28): exercises

29   Why, though, would one think that federal policing of illegal firearms would be better than local policing? The logic of that argument is far from clear. Cities, after all, are comparatively small places. Washington, D.C., for example, has an area of less than 45,000 acres. Yet local officers have had little luck repressing the illegal firearms trade there. Why should federal officers do any better watching the United States' 12,000 miles of coastline and millions of square miles of interior? Criminals should be able to frustrate federal police forces just as well as they can local ones. Ten years of increasingly stringent federal efforts to abate cocaine trafficking, for example, have not succeeded in raising the street price of the drug.

30   Consider the most drastic proposal currently in play, that of Senator John Chafee, of Rhode Island, who would ban the manufacture, sale, and home possession of handguns within the United States. This proposal goes far beyond even the Chicago law, because existing weapons would have to be surrendered. Handguns would become contraband, and selling counterfeit, stolen, and contraband goods is big business in the United States. The objective of law enforcement is to raise the costs of engaging in crime and so force criminals to take expensive precautions against becoming entangled with the legal system. Crimes of a given type will, in theory, decline as soon as the direct costs of engaging in them rise to the point at which criminals seek more profitable opportunities in other (not necessarily legal) lines of work.

31   In firearms regulation, translating theory into practice will continue to be difficult, at least if the objective is to lessen the practical availability of firearms to people who might abuse them. On the demand side, for defending oneself against predation there is no substitute for a firearm. Criminals, at least, can switch to varieties of law-breaking in which a gun confers little or no advantage (burglary, smash-and-grab), but people who are afraid of confrontations with criminals, whether rationally or (as an accountant might reckon it) irrationally, will be very highly motivated to acquire firearms. Long after the marijuana and cocaine wars of this century have been forgotten, people's demand for personal security and for the tools they believe provide it will remain strong.

32   On the supply side, firearms transactions can be consummated behind closed doors. Firearms buyers, unlike those who use drugs, pornography, or prostitution, need not recurrently expose themselves to legal jeopardy. One trip to the marketplace is enough to arm oneself for life. This could justify a consumer's taking even greater precautions to avoid apprehension, which would translate into even steeper enforcement costs for the police.

33   Don Kates Jr., a San Francisco lawyer and a much-published student of this problem, has pointed out that during the wars in Southeast and Southwest Asia local artisans were able to produce, from scratch, serviceable pot-metal counterfeits of AK-47 infantry rifles and similar weapons in makeshift backyard foundries. Although inferior weapons cannot discharge thousands of rounds without misfiring, they are more than deadly enough for light to medium service, especially by criminals and people defending themselves and their property, who ordinarily use firearms by threatening with them, not by

NOTES

stringent (par. 29): rigorous, severe
contraband (par. 30): illegal goods
predation (par. 31): acts of violence (such as robbery, car jacking, and kidnaping) in which a victim is personally confronted and threatened by a criminal
consummated (par. 32): completed
apprehension (par. 32): arrest

firing them. And the skills necessary to make them are certainly as widespread in America as in the villages of Pakistan or Vietnam. Effective policing of such a cottage industry is unthinkable. Indeed, as Charles Chandler has pointed out, crude but effective firearms have been manufactured in prisons—highly supervised environments, compared with the outside world.

34   Seeing that local firearms restrictions are easily defeated, gun-control proponents have latched onto national controls as a way of finally making gun control something more than a gesture. But the same forces that have defeated local regulation will defeat further national regulation. Imposing higher costs on weapons ownership will, of course, slow down the weapons trade to some extent. But planning to slow it down in such a way as to drive down crime and violence, or to prevent motivated purchasers from finding ample supplies of guns and ammunition, is an escape from reality. And like many another such, it entails a morning after.

Administering Prohibition

35   Assume for the sake of argument that to a reasonable degree of criminological certainty, guns are every bit the public-health hazard they are said to be. It follows, and many journalists and a few public officials have already said, that we ought to treat guns the same way we do smallpox viruses or other critical vectors of morbidity and mortality—namely, isolate them from potential hosts and destroy them as speedily as possible. Clearly, firearms have at least one characteristic that distinguishes them from smallpox viruses: Nobody wants to keep smallpox viruses in the nightstand drawer. Amazingly enough, gun-control literature seems never to have explored the problem of getting weapons away from people who very much want to keep them in the nightstand drawer.

36   Our existing gun-control laws are not uniformly permissive, and, indeed, in certain places are tough even by international standards. Advocacy groups seldom stress the considerable differences among American jurisdictions, and media reports regularly assert that firearms are readily available to anybody anywhere in the country. This is not the case. For example, handgun restrictions in Chicago and the District of Columbia are much less flexible than the ones in the United Kingdom. Several hundred thousand British subjects may legally buy and possess sidearms, and anyone who joins a target-shooting club is eligible to do so. But in Chicago and the District of Columbia, excepting peace officers and the like, only grandfathered registrants may legally possess handguns. Of course, tens or hundreds of thousands of people in both those cities—nobody can be sure how many—do in fact possess them illegally.

37   Although there is, undoubtedly, illegal handgun ownership in the United Kingdom, especially in Northern Ireland (where considerations of personal

---

NOTES

vectors of morbidity and mortality (par. 35): carriers of disease and death; *Vectors* are organisms, such as insects, that carry disease-causing microorganisms from one animal or plant to another.
hosts (par. 35): organisms in which or on which another organism lives
Advocacy groups (par. 36): groups that support specific causes; Here, the writer is referring to groups that support gun control.
jurisdictions (par. 36): the area over which a specific judicial system's authority extends

security and public safety are decidedly unlike those elsewhere in the British Isles), it is probable that Americans and Britons differ in their disposition to obey gun-control laws: There is reputed to be a marked national disparity in compliance behavior. This difference, if it exists, may have something to do with the comparatively marginal value of firearms to British consumers. Even before it had strict firearms regulation, Britain had very low rates of crimes involving guns; British criminals, unlike their American counterparts, prefer burglary (a crime of stealth) to robbery (a crime of intimidation).

38   Unless people are prepared to surrender their guns voluntarily, how can the U.S. government confiscate an appreciable fraction of our country's nearly 200 million privately owned firearms? We know that it is possible to set up weapons-free zones in certain locations—commercial airports and many courthouses and, lately, some troubled big-city high schools and housing projects. The sacrifices of privacy and convenience, and the costs of paying guards, have been thought worth the (perceived) gain in security. No doubt it would be possible, though it would probably not be easy, to make weapons-free zones of shopping centers, department stores, movie theaters, ball parks. But it is not obvious how one would cordon off the whole of an open society.

39   Voluntary programs have been ineffectual. From time to time community-action groups or police departments have sponsored "turn in your gun" days, which are nearly always disappointing. Sometimes the government offers to buy guns at some price. This approach has been endorsed by Senator Chafee and the *Los Angeles Times*. Jonathan Alter, of *Newsweek*, has suggested a variation on this theme: Youngsters could exchange their guns for a handshake with Michael Jordan or some other sports hero. If the price offered exceeds that at which a gun can be bought on the street, one can expect to see plans of this kind yield some sort of harvest—as indeed they have. But it is implausible that these schemes will actually result in a less-dangerous population. Government programs to buy up surplus cheese cause more cheese to be produced without affecting the availability of cheese to people who want to buy it. So it is with guns.

40   One could extend the concept of intermittent roadblocks of the sort approved by the Supreme Court for discouraging drunk driving. Metal detectors could be positioned on every street corner, or ambulatory metal-detector squads could check people randomly, or hidden magnetometers could be installed around towns, to detect concealed weapons. As for firearms kept in homes (about half of American households), warrantless searches might be rationalized on the well-established theory that probable cause is not required when authorities are trying to correct dangers to public safety rather than searching for evidence of a crime.

NOTES

disposition (par. 37): tendency
disparity (par. 37): difference
compliance (par. 37): obedience
stealth (par. 37): sneakiness
confiscate (par. 38): seize
appreciable (par. 38): measurable
cordon off (par. 38): seal off
intermittent (par. 40): periodic
warrantless searches (par. 40): A warrant is a document issued by a judge which permits police to search a specified area or arrest a specified person. The Fourth Amendment to the U.S. Constitution prohibits "warrantless searches." "The right of the people to be secure in their persons, houses, papers, and effects, against unreasonable searches and seizures, shall not be violated, and no Warrants shall issue, but upon probable cause, supported by Oath or affirmation, and particularly describing the place to be searched, and the persons or things to be seized."

41   In a recent "town hall" meeting in California, President Bill Clinton used the word "sweeps," which he did not define, to describe how he would confiscate firearms if it were up to him. During the past few years the Chicago Housing Authority chairman, Vincent Lane, has ordered "sweeps" of several gang-ridden public-housing projects, meaning warrantless searches of people's homes by uniformed police officers looking for contraband. Lane's ostensible premise was that possession of firearms by tenants constituted a lease violation that, as a conscientious landlord, he was obliged to do something about. The same logic could justify any administrative search. City health inspectors in Chicago were recently authorized to conduct warrantless searches for lead hazards in residential paint. Why not lead hazards in residential closets and nightstands? Someone has probably already thought of it.

Ignoring the Ultimate Sources of Crime and Violence

42   The American experience with prohibition has been that black marketeers—often professional criminals—move in to profit when legal markets are closed down or disturbed. In order to combat them, new laws and law-enforcement techniques are developed, which are circumvented almost as soon as they are put in place. New and yet more stringent laws are enacted, and greater sacrifices of civil liberties and privacy demanded and submitted to. But in this case the problem, crime and violence, will not go away, because guns and ammunition (which, of course, won't go away either) do not cause it. One cannot expect people to quit seeking new weapons as long as the tactical advantages of weapons are seen to outweigh the costs imposed by prohibition. Nor can one expect large numbers of people to surrender firearms they already own. The only way to make people give up their guns is to create a world in which guns are perceived as having little value. This world will come into being when criminals choose not to use guns because the penalties for being caught with them are too great, and when ordinary citizens don't think they need firearms because they aren't afraid of criminals anymore.

43   Neither of these eventualities seems very likely without substantial departures in law-enforcement policy. Politicians' nostrums—increasing the punishment for crime, slapping a few more death-penalty provisions into the code—are taken seriously by few students of the crime problem. The existing penalties for predatory crimes are quite severe enough. The problem is that they are rarely meted out in the real world. The penalties formally published by the code are in practice steeply discounted, and criminals recognize that the judicial and penal systems cannot function without bargaining in the vast majority of cases.

44   This problem is not obviously one that legislation could solve. Constitutional ideas about due process of law make the imposition of punishments extraordinarily expensive and difficult. Like the tax laws, the criminal laws are basically voluntary affairs. Our system isn't geared to a world of wholesale disobedience. Recalibrating the system simply by increasing its overall harshness would probably offend and then shock the public long before any of its benefits were felt.

NOTES
ostensible (par. 41): apparent
circumvented (par. 42): gotten around
nostrums (par. 43): unproven cures
meted out (par. 43): dispensed
Recalibrating (par. 44): readjusting

45   To illustrate, consider the prospect of getting serious about carrying out the death penalty. In recent years executions have been running at one or two dozen a year. As the late Supreme Court Justice Potter Stewart observed, those selected to die constitute a "capriciously selected random handful" taken from a much larger number of men and women who, just as deserving of death, receive prison sentences. It is not easy to be exact about that much larger number. But as an educated guess, taking into account only the most serious murders—the ones that were either premeditated or committed in the course of a dangerous felony—there are perhaps 5,000 prisoners a year who could plausibly be executed in the United States; say, 100,000 executions in the next twenty years. It is hard to think that the death penalty, if imposed on this scale, would not noticeably change the behavior of potential criminals. But what else in national life or citizens' character would have to change in order to make that many executions acceptable? Since 1930 executions in the United States have never exceeded 200 a year. At any such modest rate of imposition, rational criminals should consider the prospect of receiving the death penalty effectively nil. On the best current evidence, indeed, they do. Documentation of the deterrent effect of the death penalty, as compared with that of long prison sentences, has been notoriously hard to produce.

46   The problem is not simply that criminals pay little attention to the punishments in the books. Nor is it even that they also know that for the majority of crimes, their chances of being arrested are small. The most important reason for criminal behavior is this: The income that offenders can earn in the world of crime, as compared with the world of work, all too often makes crime appear to be the better choice.

47   Thus the crime bill that Bill Clinton introduced last year, which provides for more prisons and police officers, should be of only very limited help. More prisons means that fewer violent offenders will have to be released early in order to make space for new arrivals; perhaps fewer plea bargains will have to be struck—all to the good. Yet a moment's reflection should make clear that one more criminal locked up does not necessarily mean one less criminal on the street. The situation is very like one that conservationists and hunters have always understood. Populations of game animals readily recover from hunting seasons but not from loss of habitat. Mean streets, when there are few legitimate entry-level opportunities for young men, are a criminal habitat, so to speak, in the social ecology of modern American cities. Cull however much one will, the habitat will be reoccupied promptly after its previous occupant is sent away. So social science has found.

48   Similarly, whereas increasing the number of police officers cannot hurt, and may well increase people's subjective feelings of security, there is little evidence to suggest that doing so will diminish the rate of crime. Police forces are basically reactive institutions. At any realistically sustainable level of staffing they must remain so. Suppose 100,000 officers were added to police rosters nationwide, as proposed in the current crime bill. This would amount to an overall personnel increase of about 18 percent, which would be parceled

NOTES
capriciously (par. 45): arbitrarily
plausibly (par. 45): possibly
nil (par. 45): zero
conservationists (par. 47): people devoted to preserving natural resources
habitat (par. 47): natural environment
Cull (par. 47): remove

out according to the iron laws of democratic politics—distributed throughout states and congressional districts—rather than being sent to the areas that most need relief. Such an increase, though unprecedented in magnitude, is far short of what would be needed to pacify some of our country's worst urban precincts.

49   There is a challenge here that is quite beyond being met with tough talk. Most public officials can see the mismatch between their tax base and the social entropies they are being asked to repair. There simply isn't enough money; existing public resources, as they are now employed, cannot possibly solve the crime problem. But mayors and senators and police chiefs must not say so out loud; too-disquieting implications would follow. For if the authorities are incapable of restoring public safety and personal security under the existing ground rules, then obviously the ground rules must change, to give private initiative greater scope. Self-help is the last refuge of non-scoundrels.

50   Communities must, in short, organize more effectively to protect themselves against predators. No doubt this means encouraging properly qualified private citizens to possess and carry firearms legally. It is not morally tenable—nor, for that matter, is it even practical—to insist that police officers, few of whom are at a risk remotely as great as are the residents of many city neighborhoods, retain a monopoly on legal firearms. It is needless to fear giving honest men and women the training and equipment to make it possible for them to take back their own streets.

51   Over the long run, however, there is no substitute for addressing the root causes of crime—bad education and lack of job opportunities and the disintegration of families. Root causes are much out of fashion nowadays as explanations of criminal behavior, but fashionable or not, they are fundamental. *The root cause of crime is that for certain people, predation is a rational occupational choice.* Conventional crime-control measures, which by stiffening punishments or raising the probability of arrest aim to make crime pay less, cannot consistently affect the behavior of people who believe that their alternatives to crime will pay virtually nothing. Young men who did not learn basic literacy and numeracy skills before dropping out of their wretched public schools may not have been worth hiring at the minimum wage set by George Bush, let alone at the higher, indexed minimum wage that has recently been under discussion by the Clinton Administration. Most independent studies of the effects of raising minimum wages show a similar pattern of excluding the most vulnerable. This displacement, in turn, makes young men free, in the nihilistic, nothing-to-lose sense, to dedicate their lives to crime. Their legitimate opportunities, always precarious in a society where race and class still matter, often diminish to the point of being for all intents and purposes absent.

52   Unfortunately, many progressive policies work out in the same way as increases in the minimum wage—as taxes on employment. One example is the Administration's pending proposal to make employer-paid health insurance mandatory and universal. Whatever the undoubted benefits of the plan,

NOTES
social entropies (par. 49): steadily deteriorating social systems
tenable (par. 50): defensible
a monopoly on (par. 50): exclusive control of
nihilistic (par. 51): A nihilist rejects social and religious morals and values, often believing life is meaningless.
precarious (par. 51): uncertain

a payroll tax is needed to make it work. Another example: In recent years the use of the "wrongful discharge" tort and other legal innovations has swept through the courts of more than half the states, bringing to an end the era of "employment at will," when employees (other than civil servants) without formal contracts—more than three quarters of the work force—could be fired for good reason, bad reason, or no reason at all. Most commentators celebrated the loss of the at-will rule. How could one object to a new legal tenet that prohibited only arbitrary and oppressive behavior by employers?

53   But the costs of the rule are not negligible, only hidden. At-will employment meant that companies could get out of the relationship as easily as employees could. In a world where dismissals are expensive rather than cheap, and involve lawyers and the threat of lawsuits, rational employers must become more fastidious about whom they hire. By raising the costs of ending the relationship, one automatically raises the threshold of entry. The burdens of the rule fall unequally. Worst hit are entry-level applicants who have little or no employment history to show that they would be worth their pay.

54   Many other tax or regulatory schemes, in the words of Professor Walter Williams, of George Mason University, amount to sawing off the bottom rungs of the ladder of economic opportunity. By suppressing job creation and further diminishing legal employment opportunities for young men on the margin of the work force, such schemes amount to an indirect but unequivocal subsidy to crime.

55   The solution to the problem of crime lies in improving the chances of young men. Easier said than done, to be sure. No one has yet proposed a convincing program for checking all the dislocating forces that government assistance can set in motion. One relatively straightforward change would be reform of the educational system. Nothing guarantees prudent behavior like a sense of the future, and with average skills in reading, writing, and math, young people can realistically look forward to constructive employment and the straight life that steady work makes possible.

56   But firearms are nowhere near the root of the problem of violence. As long as people come in unlike sizes, shapes, ages, and temperaments, as long as they diverge in their taste for risk and their willingness and capacity to prey on other people or to defend themselves from predation, and above all as long as some people have little or nothing to lose by spending their lives in crime, dispositions to violence will persist.

57   This is what makes the case for the right to bear arms, not the Second Amendment. It is foolish to let anything ride on hopes for effective gun control. As long as crime pays as well as it does, we will have plenty of it, and honest folk must choose between being victims and defending themselves.

NOTES

tort (par. 52): crime
tenet (par. 52): principle
negligible (par. 53): insignificant
fastidious (par. 53): particular
suppressing (par. 54): curbing
subsidy (par. 54): financial assistance
prudent (par. 55): sensible
diverge (par. 56): differ

Does America Still Exist?

Richard Rodriguez

1   For the children of immigrant parents the knowledge comes easier. America exists everywhere in the city—on billboards, frankly in the smell of French fries and popcorn. It exists in the pace: traffic lights, the assertions of neon, the mysterious bong-bong-bong through the atriums of department stores. America exists as the voice of the crowd, a menacing sound—the high nasal accent of American English.

2   When I was a boy in Sacramento (California, the fifties), people would ask me, "Where you from?" I was born in this country, but I knew the question meant to decipher my darkness, my looks.

3   My mother once instructed me to say, "I am an American of American descent." By the time I was nine or ten, I wanted to say, but dared not reply, "I am an American."

4   Immigrants come to America and, against hostility or mere loneliness, they recreate a homeland in the parlor, tacking up postcards or calendars of some impossible blue—lake or sea or sky. Children of immigrant parents are supposed to perch on a hyphen between two countries. Relatives assume the achievement as much as anyone. Relatives are, in any case, surprised when the child begins losing old ways. One day at the family picnic the boy wanders away from their spiced food and faceless stories to watch other boys play baseball in the distance.

5   There is sorrow in the American memory, guilty sorrow for having left something behind—Portugal, China, Norway. The American story is the story of immigrant children and of their children—children no longer able to speak to grandparents. The memory of exile becomes inarticulate as it passes from generation to generation, along with wedding rings and pocket watches—like some mute stone in a wad of old lace. Europe. Asia. Eden.

6   But, it needs to be said, if this is a country where one stops being Vietnamese or Italian, this is a country where one begins to be an American. America exists as a culture and a grin, a faith and a shrug. It is clasped in a handshake, called by a first name.

7   As much as the country is joined in a common culture, however, Americans are reluctant to celebrate the process of assimilation. We pledge allegiance to diversity. America was born Protestant and bred Puritan, and the notion of

NOTES

atriums (par. 1): open areas
menacing (par. 1): threatening
decipher (par. 2): figure out
a hyphen between two countries (par. 4): for example, Mexican-American
exile (par. 5): separation from one's native country
inarticulate (par. 5): inexpressable
mute (par. 5): silent
Eden (par. 5): paradise
the process of assimilation (par. 7): the process of one culture being absorbed into another
diversity (par. 7): difference
Protestants (par. 7): those religious groups that broke away from the Catholic Church
Puritan (par. 7): an early American religious group that believed, among other things, in predestination; According to this doctrine, God had selected who would go to heaven (the "elect"), and no human action could change this selection. In addition to not knowing whether they were among the elect, believers could not be certain which of their family members and church members had been selected.

community we share is derived from a seventeenth-century faith. Presidents and the pages of ninth-grade civics readers yet proclaim the orthodoxy: We are gathered together—but as individuals, with separate pasts, distinct destinies. Our society is as paradoxical as a Puritan congregation: We stand together, alone.

8   Americans have traditionally defined themselves by what they refused to include. As often, however, Americans have struggled, turned in good conscience at last to assert the great Protestant virtue of tolerance. Despite outbreaks of nativist frenzy, America has remained an immigrant country, open and true to itself.

9   Against pious emblems of rural America—soda fountain, Elks hall, Protestant church, and now shopping mall—stands the cold-hearted city, crowded with races and ambitions, curious laughter, much that is odd. Nevertheless, it is the city that has most truly represented America. In the city, however, the millions of singular lives have had no richer notion of wholeness to describe them than the idea of pluralism.

10   *"Where you from?" the American asks the immigrant child. "Mexico," the boy learns to say.*

11   Mexico, the country of my blood ancestors, offers formal contrast to the American achievement. If the United States was formed by Protestant individualism, Mexico was shaped by a medieval Catholic dream of one world. The Spanish journeyed to Mexico to plunder, and they may have gone, in God's name, with an arrogance peculiar to those who intend to convert. But through the conversion, the Indian converted the Spaniard. A new race was born, the *mestizo*, wedding European to Indian. José Vasconcelos, the Mexican philosopher, has celebrated this New World creation, proclaiming it the "cosmic race."

12   Centuries later, in a San Francisco restaurant, a Mexican-American lawyer of my acquaintance says, in English, over *salade niçoise*, that he does not intend to assimilate into gringo society. His claim is echoed by a chorus of others (Italian-Americans, Greeks, Asians) in this era of ethnic pride. The melting pot has been retired, clanking, into the museum of quaint disgrace, alongside Aunt Jemima and the Katzenjammer Kids. But resistance to assimilation is characteristically American. It only makes clear how inevitable the process of assimilation actually is.

13   For generations, this has been the pattern. Immigrant parents have sent their children to school (simply, they thought) to acquire the "skills" to survive in the city. The child returned home with a voice his parents barely recognized or understood, couldn't trust, and didn't like.

14   In Eastern cities—Philadelphia, New York, Boston, Baltimore—class after class gathered immigrant children to women (usually women) who stood in front of rooms full of children, changing children. So also for me in the 1950s. Irish-Catholic nuns. California. The old story. The hyphen tipped to the right, away from Mexico and toward a confusing but true American identity.

NOTES
derived from (par. 7): comes from
orthodoxy (par. 7): accepted belief
paradoxical (par. 7): seemingly contradictory
pious emblems (par. 9): sacred symbols
pluralism (par. 9): the coexistence of numerous racial, religious, or cultural groups within a society
plunder (par. 11): steal
cosmic (par. 11): Literally, cosmic means affecting the whole world.
salade niçoise (par. 12): a layered salad, originating in Nice, France
gringo (par. 12): scornful term for white Americans
Aunt Jemima and the Katzenjammer Kids (par. 12): These characters reflect racial or ethnic stereotypes (preconceived notions of what a member of a group is like).

15   I speak now in the chromium American accent of my grammar school classmates—Billy Reckers, Mike Bradley, Carol Schmidt, Kathy O'Grady. . . . I believe I became like my classmates, became German, Polish, and (like my teachers) Irish. And because assimilation is always reciprocal, my classmates got something of me. (I mean sad eyes; belief in the Indian Virgin; a taste for sugar skulls on the Feast of the Dead.) In the blending, we became what our parents could never have been, and we carried America one revolution further.

16   "Does America still exist?" Americans have been asking the question for so long that to ask it again only proves our continuous link. But perhaps the question deserves to be asked with urgency—now. Since the black civil rights movement of the 1960s, our tenuous notion of a shared public life has deteriorated notably.

17   The struggle of black men and women did not eradicate racism, but it became the great moment in the life of America's conscience. Water hoses, bulldogs, blood—the images, rendered black, white, rectangular, passed into living rooms.

18   It is hard to look at a photograph of a crowd taken, say, in 1890 or in 1930 and not notice the absence of blacks. (It becomes an impertinence to wonder if America *still* exists.)

19   In the sixties, other groups of Americans learned to champion their rights by analogy to the black civil rights movement. But the heroic vision faded. Dr. Martin Luther King Jr. had spoken with Pauline eloquence of a nation that would unite Christian and Jew, old and young, rich and poor. Within a decade, the struggles of the 1960s were reduced to a bureaucratic competition for little more than pieces of a representational pie. The quest for a portion of power became an end in itself. The metaphor for the American city of the 1970s was a committee: one black, one woman, one person under thirty. . . .

20   If the small town had sinned against America by too neatly defining who could be an American, the city's sin was a romantic secession. One noticed the romanticism in the antiwar movement—certain demonstrators who demonstrated a lack of tact or desire to persuade and seemed content to play secular protestants. One noticed the romanticism in the competition among members of "minority groups" to claim the status of Primary Victim. To Americans unconfident of their common identity, minority standing became a way of asserting individuality. Middle-class Americans—men and women clearly not the primary victims of social oppression—brandished their suffering with exuberance.

21   The dream of a single society probably died with *The Ed Sullivan Show*. The reality of America persists. Teenagers pass through big-city high schools

NOTES

chromium (par. 15): Literally, chromium is a steel gray metal that resists tarnish and corrosion; here, the suggestion is that his classmates shared the same accent despite their different backgrounds.

reciprocal (par. 15): mutually experienced

tenuous (par. 16): flimsy

eradicate (par. 17): eliminate

it becomes an impertinence (par. 18): it becomes irrelevent

analogy (par. 19): comparison

Pauline (par. 19): referring to Paul, author of several books of the New Testament

romantic (par. 20): *Romantic* and *romanticism* are words that refer to imaginative but usually unrealistic ideas.

secession (par. 20): separation

secular (par. 20): nonreligious

brandished (par. 20): displayed

exuberance (par. 20): enthusiasm

banded in racial groups, their collars turned up to a uniform shrug. But then they graduate to jobs at the phone company or in banks, where they end up working alongside people unlike themselves. Typists and tellers walk out together at lunchtime.

22   It is easier for us as Americans to believe the obvious fact of our separateness—easier to imagine the black and white Americas prophesied by the Kerner report (broken glass, street fires)—than to recognize the reality of a city street at lunchtime. Americans are wedded by proximity to a common culture. The panhandler at one corner is related to the pamphleteer at the next who is related to the banker who is kin to the Chinese old man wearing an MIT sweatshirt. In any true national history, Thomas Jefferson begets Martin Luther King Jr. who begets the Gray Panthers. It is because we lack a vision of ourselves entire—the city street is crowded and we are each preoccupied with finding our own way home—that we lack an appropriate hymn.

23   Under my window now passes a little white girl softly rehearsing to herself a Motown obbligato.

NOTES

prophesied (par. 22): predicted

Kerner report (par. 22): the common name for *Supplemental Studies for the National Advisory Commission on Civil Disorders* (1968)

proximity (par. 22): closeness

panhandler (par. 22): beggar

MIT (par. 22): Massachusetts Institute of Technology

begets (par. 22): fathers

Gray Panthers (par. 22): name given to older Americans who, in the 1960s and 1970s, spoke out for the rights of the elderly

Motown obbligato (par. 23): Motown is a record company known for promoting African-American musicians. An obbligato is an essential part of a musical arrangement.

Textbook
Chapters

Introduction

Karen Arms and Pamela S. Camp,
from *Biology*

Harcourt Brace, 1995, pages 1–13

Introduction

O B J E C T I V E S

When you have studied this chapter, you should be able to:

1. Define the following terms and use them in context: organism, evolution, natural selection, selective pressure, adaptation.

2. List three steps in the scientific method, and apply them to investigating a sample scientific problem.
3. List eight characteristics of living things.

P eople have always been interested in the living things around them. They had to be: all food, clothing, and fuel came from plants and animals and so did dangers such as poisons, predation, and disease. Eventually, the study of living things moved from the realm of survival skills to scholarship and became the discipline of natural history.

Then in 1858 two British naturalists put forward an idea that shook the human view of the living world. The two were Charles Darwin and Alfred Russel Wallace, and the idea was how humans and other living things evolve. No longer could humans regard other forms of life as merely neighbors on Earth. They are, in fact, our kin. All **organisms**—the individual animals, plants, fungi, algae, protozoa, and bacteria on Earth—are related. Slice them thin and examine them with a microscope, put them in a test tube and analyze their chemistry, feed them sugar and track how they use it for energy, and you find that all organisms are remarkably similar.

The task of biology is to study this unity of living organisms, describe their immense diversity, outline the history of life on Earth from ancient to modern forms, and learn more about organisms, including ourselves. How are all organisms alike? How do they differ? How do they work, what do they do, how are they made? How do they affect their physical surroundings, the other organisms around them, and human life?

Now is an exciting time for biologists. New techniques, developed in the last 20 years, are shedding fascinating light on questions that have puzzled biologists for decades, and many decisions affecting our future depend upon biological discoveries. Most of the biologists who have ever lived are still alive and reporting the results of their research in thousands of scientific articles every year. No one person can possibly become expert in any but a small segment of this vast body of knowledge. But luckily for students and professional biologists alike, the world of life is unified by a number of concepts and generalizations. It is these general principles that students must master and that professionals must constantly bear in mind.

♦ Organisms evolve by means of natural selection.
♦ Scientific method attempts to determine the causes of natural phenomena.
♦ There is unity in life: all organisms have a common ancestry and hence share many features of their chem

istry, cell structure and function, genetic information systems, and processes of reproduction.
♦ Life is diverse: genetic variation and changing environments result in the evolution of different species of organisms.

1–A   FUNDAMENTAL CONCEPTS OF BIOLOGY

Biology is the branch of science that studies living things: their structure, function, reproduction, and interactions with one another and with their nonliving environment.

It is difficult to define "life" or "living," although we have no trouble seeing that cats and trees are alive, whereas stones and water are not. The usual way of overcoming this problem is to say that living things share a group of characteristics not found in nonliving things. These characteristics of living things are the basic concepts in biology that we shall explore in this book:

1. **Living things are highly ordered.** The chemicals that make up a living organism are much more complex and highly organized than those in nonliving things. An organism maintains a chemical makeup very different from that of its nonliving environment. All organisms contain very similar kinds of chemical building blocks, and they share the same pathways of **metabolism,** the processes by which these building blocks are made and destroyed. This chemical organization is reflected in the overall structure and function of the organism's body.

2. **Living things are organized into units called cells.** A cell is a packet of highly organized living material enclosed by a membrane. Cells are the units of structure, function, and reproduction in organisms. Many small organisms, such as bacteria and amoebas, consist of one cell each. Larger organisms, such as grasses and humans, contain hundreds of millions of cells, each so small that we must use a microscope to see them (Figure 1–2). Each cell is a biochemical factory that shows all the features of life. The reproduction of all organisms involves divisions of cells, forming new cells.

3. **Living things use energy from their environments.** Most organisms depend, directly or indirectly, on energy from the sun. Green plants use the sun's energy to make food, which supports the plants themselves. It is also used by all organisms that eat plants and eventually by those that eat the plant-eaters. Organisms use the energy they take in to maintain and increase the high degree of orderliness of their bodies, to grow, and to reproduce.

4. **Living organisms respond to stimuli.** Most animals respond rapidly to environmental changes by making some sort of movement—exploring, running away, or

even rolling into a ball. Plants respond more slowly but still actively: stems and leaves bend toward light, and roots grow downward. The capacity to respond to environmental stimuli is universal among living things.

5. **Living things develop.** Everything changes with time, but living organisms change in particularly complex ways called development. A nonliving crystal grows by addition of identical or similar units, but a plant or animal develops new structures, such as leaves or teeth, that often differ chemically and structurally from the cells that produced them.

6. **Living things reproduce themselves.** New cells arise only from the division of other cells. New organisms arise only from the reproduction of other, similar, organisms.

7. **Living things contain genetic information.** An organism's genetic material—its chromosomes and genes—contains information specifying the possible range of the organism's development, structure, function, and response to its environment. An organism passes on genetic information to its offspring, and this is why offspring are similar to their parents. Genetic information does vary somewhat, though, so parents and offspring are usually similar but not identical.

8. **Organisms change their environments.** Since life evolved, living things have altered Earth from a planet where modern organisms could not have survived to the planet teeming with life that we know today. For instance, green plants produce the oxygen in the air we breathe, which we need to survive. Because of human numbers and technology, our own species now affects the environment more dramatically and permanently than do other organisms. Some believe that we are actually reversing billions of years of evolution and turning Earth back into a planet unable to support most forms of life.

9. **Living things evolve and are adapted to their environments.** Today's organisms have arisen by evolution, the descent and modification of organisms from more ancient forms of life. Evolution proceeds in such a way that living things and their components are well suited to their ways of life. Fish, earthworms, and frogs are all so constructed that we can predict roughly how they live merely by examining them. The adaptation of organisms to their environments is one result of evolution.

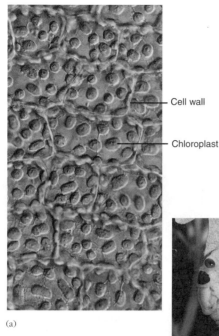

Cell wall

Chloroplast

(a)

(b)

(c)

(d)

FIGURE 1–2   Characteristics of living things. (a) Organisms are composed of cells, usually too small to be seen with the naked eye. The green chloroplasts in these moss cells make food. (b,c,d) Living things develop. This cicada is undergoing its final molt from a nymph with tiny wingpads to an adult with two pairs of large, transparent wings. The crumpled wings expand and straighten as air is pumped into them. The wings and the rest of the external skeleton must then dry and harden before the cicada can fly.   (a, Biophoto Associates)

An organism's environment invariably includes other organisms. Living things adapt to life with other organisms in many ways, evolving ways to escape some, exploit others, and avoid or overcome competition for resources. Many organisms live in intimate long-term **symbioses** (singular: **symbiosis**) with members of other species (Figure 1–3). The partners in a symbiotic relationship supply each other with resources such as food, shelter, or transport.

1–B   EVOLUTION AND NATURAL SELECTION

A living organism is the product of interactions between its genetic information and its environment. This interaction is the basis for the most important generalization in biology, that organisms evolve by means of natural selection.

  Evolution is the origin of organisms by descent and modification from more ancient forms of life. For instance, human beings evolved from now-extinct animals that looked something like apes, and this happened through accumulation of changes from generation to generation. In more

FIGURE 1–3   Symbiosis. This tomato clownfish lives symbiotically with a sea anemone in a Solomon Islands coral reef. The anemone's stinging tentacles protect both animals from predators. However, butterfly fish are immune to the stings and will eat the anemone if a clownfish is not present to drive them away. (Carl Roessler/Animals Animals)

modern terms, we can say that **evolution** is the process by which the members of a population of organisms come to differ genetically from their ancestors.

Like many other great ideas in science, evolution makes sense of many observations of the natural world. Soon after Charles Darwin proposed how organisms evolved, his friend and champion, Thomas Huxley, remarked, "How extremely stupid not to have thought of that!"

The mechanism of evolution was deduced from three familiar observations:

1. Organisms are variable. Even the most closely related individuals differ in some respects.

2. Some of the differences among organisms are inherited. Inherited variations are caused by differences in genetic material. Because organisms inherit their genes from their parents, parents and offspring tend to resemble each other more closely than do more distant relatives, whose genetic material is less similar.

3. More organisms are produced than live to grow up and reproduce. Fish and insects may produce hundreds of eggs, oak trees thousands of acorns, but only a few of these survive to reproduce in their turn.

Some inherited variations are bound to affect the chances that an individual will live to reproduce. Individuals with some genetic variations will therefore produce more offspring (which inherit this genetic material). This is **natural selection,** the production of more offspring by individuals with some genes than with others. Natural selection produces **evolution,** which we can define in yet another, more rigorous way: a change in the proportions of different genes from one generation of a population to the next.

To take an example of natural selection producing evolution, the length and thickness of an animal's hair is largely determined by its genes. A very cold winter may kill many individuals with short, sparse hair. Individuals with longer, thicker fur are more likely to survive the winter and reproduce in the following spring. Because more animals with thicker fur breed and pass on the genetic material that dictates the growth of thick hair, a larger proportion of individuals in the next generation of the population will have genes for thick fur. ▇▇▇▇▇▇ The genetic makeup of the population has changed somewhat from one generation to the next, and that is evolution. The agent of natural selection in this case is low temperature, which acts as a **selective pressure** against those individuals with short, sparse hair.

The result of natural selection is that populations undergo **adaptation,** a process of accumulating changes appropriate to their environments, over the course of many generations. The selective pressures acting on a population "select" those genetic characteristics that are adapted, or

well suited, to the environment. For instance, through selection, populations living in cold areas evolve so as to become better adapted to withstand the cold.

When we say that selection causes organisms to become adapted to their environments, we should note that "environment" in this context is a catchall word meaning much more than merely whether an organism lives in a forest rather than a desert and whether it can obtain enough food. Environment includes all the external factors that act throughout the organism's life and affect the number of offspring it produces.

Let us, for example, consider a frog. Whether it successfully meets the pressure of its environment depends on the speed and normality of its embryonic development, whether bacteria penetrate the jelly coat of the egg and destroy it during development, whether as a tadpole it can find enough food and avoid being eaten by a predator, whether the pond in which it lives as a tadpole dries up before it becomes a frog, and whether as a small frog it avoids death by disease or predators (Figure 1–5).

To make things more complicated, environmental pressures are frequently contradictory. For instance, a hot summer may benefit our frog because frog embryos develop faster at higher temperatures, but it also increases the chance that the tadpole's pond will dry up before it is ready to live on land. And environmental pressures often change. The frog must have characteristics that allow it to withstand both the heat of summer and the cold of winter. It should sit still to be safe from some predators and move quickly to escape from others; and so forth. So the frog's genetic makeup is a compromise brought about by selection for a number of opposing characteristics.

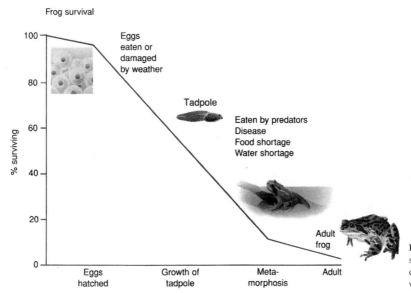

FIGURE 1–5 Frog survival. This graph shows the percentage of frogs surviving to each stage of the life cycle. Few eggs develop into tadpoles that live to reproduce.

Adaptations

We have just defined adaptation as the process by which populations become better suited to their environments as a result of natural selection. Biologists also use the word in a second way. An **adaptation** is any genetically determined characteristic that has been selected for and that occurs in a large part of the population because it increases an individual's chance of reproducing successfully. Note that this may include the capacity to change depending on environmental conditions, as with the ability to learn. Much of biology involves the study of the adaptations of organisms.

Adaptations may be broadly classed as anatomical, physiological, or behavioral. **Anatomical** adaptations involve the organism's physical structure. For instance, a penguin's flippers and webbed feet are anatomical adaptations that permit it to swim. An organism's **physiology** is all of the internal workings of its body: the biochemistry of its cells and the processes that allow it to digest food, exchange gases, excrete wastes, reproduce, move, and sense and respond to the outside world. An example of physiological adaptation is the ability of a camel to walk for days through the desert, where most other organisms would die of dehydration. An example of an impressive **be-**

havioral adaptation is the ability of some birds called bee eaters to catch bees and manipulate them with their beaks and feet so as to eat them without being stung.

Energy and Natural Selection

Living things must take in and use energy to maintain their bodies, to grow, to obtain more energy, and to reproduce. The evolutionarily successful individual is one that leaves descendants, bearing its genetic information, in future generations of the population. Therefore, natural selection favors those individuals that can channel the most energy into producing offspring. The use of energy in other activities such as feeding, fighting, or growing is selectively advantageous only insofar as these activities result in the organism's producing more offspring.

Each individual has an "energy income," all of the energy that it acquires during its lifetime. It also has an "energy budget," its allotment of different amounts of energy to various activities. The most evolutionarily successful organisms are those most effective at converting energy to offspring.

This does not mean that organisms use all their energy directly to produce offspring. For example, suppose that a tree converts some of its energy into growing a large root system. The energy thus spent cannot be used to produce offspring. Its large root system may enable the tree to obtain a lot of water and minerals from the soil and so to produce more leaves, another diversion of energy away from the production of offspring. However, its many leaves may enable the tree to make more food than it would have otherwise and so allow it to recoup some of its previous energy expenditure by producing more offspring in the end.

Thus organisms make energy investments that may ultimately yield energy gains that can be reinvested in the production of offspring. Sometimes these investments will turn out to be selectively disadvantageous because they postpone production of offspring. If the organism meets an early death, it will never get a chance to reproduce. So any item in an organism's energy budget must have the potential to confer an ultimate reproductive gain that makes it worth taking the risks of diverting energy away from the immediate production of offspring.

1–C SCIENTIFIC METHOD

The hallmark of sciences, such as biology, chemistry, and physics, is the **scientific method,** a logical way of answering questions about cause and effect. Similar reasoning is used by business people, athletes, and each of us in everyday life. We do not need specialized training or knowledge to decide whether conclusions are justified from the data presented. We can ask for further tests if someone makes a claim that does not appear to be well supported by evidence, and we can agree or disagree with predictions based on such claims. We can improve the way we do these things ourselves if we first understand how scientists arrive at conclusions about the natural world through the same kind of process.

In principle, the scientific method has three main steps (although in practice scientists work in many different ways). The first and most important step is to collect **observations,** not only by sight, but perhaps using other senses too (hearing, smell, taste, and touch). Scientists often use instruments to extend human senses or to detect things our senses cannot. Examples are microscopes, radar, voltmeters, and oscilloscopes.   Second, the sci-

entist thinks of several alternative **hypotheses** (singular: **hypothesis**), proposed answers to questions about what has been observed. The third step is **experimentation,** performing tests designed to show that one or more of the hypotheses is more or less likely to be incorrect. As a result of these experiments, the scientist should be able to draw some conclusions about *why* the original observed events occur. Let us see how this works in practice.

Observations and Hypotheses

Scientists usually start with observations that stimulate questions. Some years ago, one of your authors was part of a group of biologists discussing the clusters of butterflies that seemed to be everywhere that June (Figure 1–9).

"Today," said one, "I saw about 20 yellow sulfur butterflies by a stream and some black swallowtail butterflies on a manure heap. What are they doing?"

"It's called 'puddling behavior,'" replied another. "You find puddling butterflies in places such as the edges of drying puddles, or sand bars. I don't think anyone knows what they are doing. Another odd thing is that in many species only the males puddle."

These observations led us to ask what the butterflies were doing and why. To answer these questions, we had to think of some hypotheses that would account for the observations. That evening, the hypotheses came thick and fast from our armchair scientists.

"An article I read suggested it was a method of population control. Coming together permits the males to count each other. A newcomer can see if there is likely to be enough land for him to set up a territory in the area. Puddling saves them having to fight over territories."

"That sounds wrong to me," replied one of the company. "How can a butterfly figure out the density of males in the area from a group like that? Besides, swallowtails do fight for territories—I've seen them."

"I think it is more likely they're feeding," another contributed. "It was called 'puddling' in the first place because the butterflies often seem to be sucking something up from the ground with their probosces [tongues]."

"I wonder if they are after nitrogen? In our lab we've shown that butterfly caterpillars grow faster if you feed them extra nitrogen, and there is lots of nitrogen in a manure pile."

"But not in sand," came the objection. "And if they are after nitrogen, you'd expect females to puddle, not males. Extra nitrogen in the female's eggs might be useful to the caterpillars when they hatch."

"It sounds to me," chipped in another, "as if they're after salts—perhaps salts containing sodium. All the puddling places contain quite a lot of salts: manure piles have salts from urine, and puddles have salts at the edges, left behind by evaporation of water. Lots of animals that feed on plants are short of sodium because most plants contain so little of it. We put out salt blocks for cows and horses and end up attracting deer and rabbits as well. Perhaps male butterflies need more sodium than females do."

We could test these alternative hypotheses only by doing experiments. Some hypotheses are no use because they cannot be tested. For instance, the hypothesis "puddling butterflies count each other" is probably untestable because it is hard to imagine an experiment that could show us whether or not another animal has counted its neighbors. Even a testable hypothesis usually cannot be tested directly. We must first develop a testable **prediction** from it. From

FIGURE 1–9 Sulfur butterflies puddling on a sandbank. (Keith Brown)

the hypothesis that butterflies suck up sodium when they puddle, we predicted that if we put out trays containing sodium, butterflies would puddle on them. The hypothesis that butterflies suck up nitrogen generated the prediction that butterflies would puddle on trays of amino acids, molecules that contain nitrogen. These predictions can be tested, and, in this case, both can be tested at the same time, in the same experiment.

Experiments

We must design experiments so that their results are as clear-cut as possible. For this reason, experiments have to include **control treatments** as well as **experimental treatments.** The two differ only by the factor(s) being investigated. For instance, to test our hypotheses, we had to show that butterflies would puddle on an experimental tray containing amino acids or one containing sodium but would not puddle on control trays that were identical except that they did not contain the amino acids or sodium.

Suppose we put out three trays—one containing sodium, another containing amino acids, and a control tray containing something butterflies are most unlikely to eat, such as plain sand or sand and water. We would predict that if butterflies are attracted to puddle on sodium, they would come to puddle on the sodium tray but not on the other two. If they are attracted to amino acids, they would puddle only on that tray. If they are attracted to both, they would puddle on both of these but not on the control tray, and if they are attracted to neither, they would not puddle on the trays at all. Note that there are many other possible reasons for the last result. Butterflies might not come because they never see the trays, or because they avoid trays or the human watchers nearby, or for any number of other reasons. If no butterflies came to puddle on our trays, we would learn nothing.

So that our experiment would not fail for lack of butterflies, we put our trays on a sandbank by a lake where tiger swallowtail butterflies often puddled in large numbers. We filled the trays with clean sand for the butterflies to stand on, and in each tray we pinned a dead male tiger swallowtail as a decoy, because we thought butterflies might be attracted to puddling places by seeing other butterflies there. We put out ten trays of sand and poured the same volume of solution (substances dissolved in water) into each one (Figure 1–10). Then we sat nearby, with binoculars, notebooks, and watches, to see what would happen (Figure 1–11).

Soon dozens of tiger swallowtails were hovering over the trays. Whenever a butterfly landed on a tray, it stuck its proboscis into the sand. At times, as many as 30 butterflies were on a tray together. Most spent a few seconds on several trays, but they puddled (which we defined as staying for more than 15 seconds) on only a few trays: all those

(a)

(b)

FIGURE 1–10   The puddling experiment. (a) Observers watching puddling trays. (b) Butterflies visiting the trays. In the middle of each tray is pinned a dead butterfly to serve as a decoy.   (Paul Feeny)

containing sodium in any form, and those containing amino acids (see Figure 1–10).

We were satisfied that these results were accurate because we had taken another precaution: the people recording the butterflies' visits did not know which tray contained which solution. Making an experiment "blind" in this way is important. Psychologists have shown that, even in a carefully controlled experiment, experimenters tend to find the results they want to find. This is also why scientists think up as many hypotheses as possible to explain their observations. It is easy to bend the facts to fit your only hypothesis without even realizing it.

Those who favored the hypothesis that butterflies puddle on sodium were disappointed that they also came to amino acids. But prejudice can sometimes be useful, even in science! Not only were we disappointed by the results, we were inclined to think they were wrong. Back we went

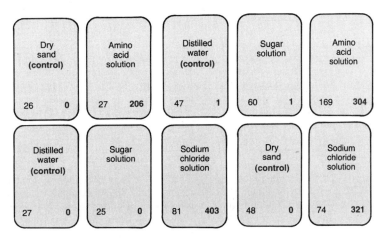

FIGURE 1–11 Arrangement of trays on one day of the puddling experiment. Each tray contained the same volume of sand. Each of eight trays also contained 1.5 liters of water or solution. Different solutions were placed in different trays on subsequent days. (Sugar was tested because swallowtail butterflies eat sugar-filled nectar from flowers, and therefore we wondered if they might be attracted to puddle on sugar.) The black number on each tray shows the number of "sampling" visits (lasting less than 15 seconds) by butterflies. Colored numbers show the number of butterfly-minutes spent puddling on the tray in visits lasting more than 15 seconds. The numbers make it obvious that butterflies puddled on the trays containing sodium and those containing amino acids but not on any of the other trays.

to our bottle of amino acids. We now made an observation that we should have made before doing the experiment: the label said, "Prepared in sodium citrate." According to popular myth, scientists are calm and objective, but we were very excited as a technician analyzed our amino acids: they were chock full of sodium! There followed frantic phone calls and special deliveries to obtain amino acids free from sodium. At last came a suspenseful experiment, which showed that butterflies did not puddle on our new, sodium-free amino acids.

We had now conducted a well-controlled scientific experiment. What conclusions could we draw? Had we proved the hypothesis that butterflies puddle because it permits them to obtain sodium? No. We had not even shown that the butterflies actually drank the sodium solution. All we had shown was that male tiger swallowtail butterflies would puddle on sand containing sodium salts but not on sand containing various other solutions. Many more hypotheses and experiments were needed if we were to learn more.

Limitations of Experiments

One peculiarity of the scientific method is that a hypothesis can never formally be proved but can only be disproved. A correct hypothesis leads to predictions that are borne out by experiments, but an incorrect hypothesis may also produce correct predictions (predictions that are right, but for the wrong reason). Therefore, if the results of an experiment agree with the prediction, we are still not sure that the hypothesis is correct. For instance, the hypothesis that butterflies puddle because they need sodium is not proven by the experimental finding that butterflies puddle on sodium. They might puddle because wherever there is sodium in nature there is also nitrogen or something else they need. We have not even disproved the hypothesis that puddling is a means for the butterflies to "count" each other. They might puddle on sodium merely as a convenient rendezvous (although the fact that the butterflies appear to feed when they puddle makes this hypothesis unlikely). The more alternative hypotheses we disprove or cast doubt on, however, the greater the likelihood that the hypothesis that remains is correct.

Scientists also hesitate to accept the results of an experiment until it has been repeated. Repeating an experiment guards against two kinds of errors. The first is **human error** (a polite term for mistakes). We might have inadvertently switched the solutions, written results in the wrong column of our data notebook, or alarmed the butterflies. Even in this simple experiment, the possibilities are endless. Second, any experiment is subject to **sampling error,** error due to using a relatively small number of subjects. Our experiment sampled only a few dozen butterflies on six days. These butterflies might not have been representative of all tiger swallowtails. We could be more confident of our results if we were to repeat the experiment, using more butterflies (that is, a larger sample) and following the same procedure. How many butterflies do we need? The more the better, but we could not test all the butterflies in the world. In practice, we can use statistical tests to tell how "sure" we are of our results from a given sample.

In fact, variations on our puddling experiments have now been repeated by many different people with a variety of animals. There is now a large body of evidence showing that many animals are nearly always short of sodium—which is vital to the working of every nerve and muscle in the body. As a result, animals from moths to elephants and humans have behavior patterns that provide them with this mineral.

Historically, salt has been a valuable commodity in the trade of human populations unable to obtain salt from the sea. Soldiers in the army of ancient Rome received an allowance of salt called a *salarium*. Later the payment was changed to money to buy salt—hence our word "salary" and the expression "not worth his salt." In New Guinea to this day mountain villages with mineral springs evaporate the water to produce "salt," which can be traded for large quantities of food or clay pots.

A hypothesis supported by many different lines of evidence from repeated experiments is generally regarded as a **theory,** and after even further testing it comes to be generally accepted. An interesting example is the "theory of evolution." A hundred years ago, it would have been accurate to describe as a theory, supported by several lines of evidence, the idea that the organisms on Earth have arisen by evolution. Today, the evidence for evolution is overwhelming. We shall see in this book that we can actually observe evolution happening around us. Evolution is no longer merely a theory.

Correlation Studies

Many scientific questions cannot be studied by the type of experiments we used to study puddling behavior, for practical or ethical reasons. For example, it would be unethical to test a vaccine against AIDS by injecting intact HIV (human immunodeficiency virus) into vaccinated and unvaccinated people. Geologists who study Earth's crust, or paleontologists who study dinosaur fossils, work with events that occurred millions of years ago: it is too late for experiments. We also cannot study long-term changes in Earth's climate by doing experiments because we have no control planet and because the experiment is too big to do.

To test their hypotheses, scientists in such fields depend on **correlations,** reliable associations between two events. We may observe many occasions on which one event al-

ways accompanies another. Also, we may find that if one of these increases, the other increases (or decreases) in a predictable way. If we can explain why this might be so, we may propose the hypothesis that one causes the other. Since we cannot test this hypothesis by experiment, we test it by subjecting it to more observations of as many kinds as possible. The trouble with correlation studies is that events may be linked even when one does not cause the other, and observation is less conclusive than experiment as a way to show causality.

The Ozone Layer For instance, the ozone layer in the atmosphere reduces the amount of ultraviolet radiation that reaches Earth. Ultraviolet radiation damages the genetic material found in all organisms, causing skin cancer in humans and actually killing some smaller organisms. Ozone forms in the upper atmosphere when intense ultraviolet light from the sun acts on oxygen, converting some of it into ozone. Once formed, the ozone itself is a good absorber of ultraviolet radiation and keeps much of it from reaching Earth's surface.

In the early 1980s researchers discovered a hole in the ozone layer in the atmosphere over Antarctica. Nowadays, the ozone layer is monitored by weather balloons and NASA's Upper Atmosphere Research Satellite. Samples of air in various parts of the atmosphere are also collected by the high-flying ER-2, a converted U-2 spy plane.

Scientists studying atmospheric gases had already found that ozone can be destroyed by chemicals containing chlorine, in the presence of sunlight. They hypothesized that holes in the ozone layer form wherever the right kinds of particles are present in large numbers together with chlorine-containing compounds such as **chlorofluorocarbons (CFCs),** pollutants found everywhere in the atmosphere.

CFCs are artificial chemicals that were widely used for producing foam rubber, for cleaning electrical components, and for refrigeration. They have long been used in the production of aerosol sprays. CFCs are ideal aerosol propellants because they do not react chemically with whatever is being sprayed. But this same lack of chemical reactivity means that they are not broken down in the air but slowly make their way to the upper atmosphere. Scientists predicted that as industry and consumers released more and more stable chlorine compounds into the air, destruction of the ozone layer would accelerate.

This prediction was borne out by observation. The concentration of chlorine compounds in the atmosphere increased, and holes in the ozone layer grew larger and more numerous (Figure 1–12). Governments were convinced by the correlation evidence and negotiated international treaties to reduce the output of ozone-destroying chemicals. Industry has responded by cutting the production of CFCs and allied chemicals even more rapidly than mandated by law. The rate of chlorine accumulation in the atmosphere has slowed.

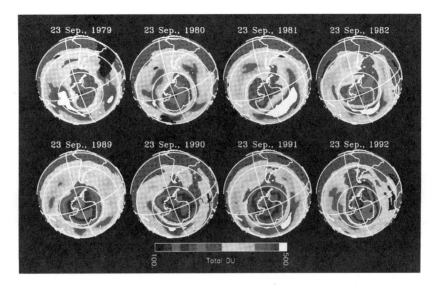

FIGURE 1–12 Ozone depletion: computer views of ozone concentration near the South Pole (where the white lines cross toward the bottom of each view). By 1992, the blue area of low ozone levels increased to more than twice the area of the United States and was 15% greater than in 1991. In 1989, the first area of extreme depletion (purple) appeared. By 1992, it had approximately doubled in size. Ozone concentration is expressed in Dobson Units (DU). The U.S. *Nimbus* satellite has measured ozone with a spectrometer since 1978. In 1991, the task was taken over by a similar instrument on the Russian *Meteor-3* satellite. (NASA)

The test of the hypothesis about ozone destruction that most scientists would consider conclusive is yet to come in the form of yet another correlation. As production of volatile chlorine compounds declines, we should reach the point where their level in the atmosphere will decline. Since ozone will still be formed, we would predict that the ozone level in the atmosphere will increase and holes in the ozone layer become smaller and less numerous.

1–D IT'S A FACT?

"It's a scientific fact" is often presented as the clincher to an argument. Most scientists, however, would argue that any scientific finding is open to question (Figure 1–13). The

FIGURE 1–13 When is a fact not a fact? Nineteenth-century doctors were taught that men and women breathed differently: men used their diaphragms (the sheet of muscle below the rib cage) to expand their chests, whereas women raised the ribs near the top of the chest. Finally, a woman doctor, Clelia Duel Mosher, found that women breathed in this way because their clothes were so tight that the diaphragm could not move far enough to pull air into the lungs. Some women even had their lower ribs removed surgically so that they could lace their waists more tightly. (Bettman Archives)

doubts and uncertainties inherent in scientific method make it impossible to be 100% sure that a scientific discovery is "right."

"Frogs breed in the spring" and "spiders have eight legs" look like facts at first glance, but they are really predictions about what will happen in the future, based on past experience. "This is a table" may also seem like a fact, but it is really a statement resulting from an agreement: all have agreed to call that sort of object a table.

"Facts" are also less sure than they seem because they depend on our faith in our senses. Suppose several people look at two photographs, one of a table and one of an object floating in a lake. Everyone may agree that the first photo clearly shows a table. When they look at the second one, however, some may say, "That is a Loch Ness monster," but the others may disagree. When technology, in the form of a camera, microscope, or oscilloscope, intervenes between our senses and an object, as it often must in scientific research, the problem of interpreting what we see or hear or smell becomes even more difficult. Thus, a "fact" is really a piece of information that we believe in strongly or that seems highly likely to be repeated without change.

The history of science abounds with dogmas that turned out to be wrong, although for a time they were widely accepted. Indeed, many statements in this book will undoubtedly prove untrue in the future. This is one reason why the cautious person or society will not place too much faith or invest too heavily in a new scientific discovery until it has been well tested.

Although scientific findings are less reliable than most people realize, scientists do believe that their methods discover useful information, and that careful study increases the probability that science's generalizations about nature come close to reality. Public support for science rests on the belief that a better understanding of the natural world increases our ability to promote human well-being.

1–E HUMANS AND ENVIRONMENT

Nowadays, a practical interest in biology is often prompted by environmental concerns. For instance, we seek to feed everyone on Earth. We learn that planting trees can make our houses and cities cooler in summer and save on air-conditioning bills.

Our environmental problems stem from the human population explosion. We live in extraordinary times, witnessing an event that has never happened before and will never happen again: the tripling of Earth's human population in less than a century, from fewer than 2 billion people in 1900 to more than 6 billion by 2000. This can never happen again because Earth cannot produce the resources to support triple the present human population.

Like all other living things, we depend on other organisms: to produce the food we eat and the oxygen we breathe, to destroy our wastes and purify the water we drink. As we drive other organisms from more and more of the globe, we imperil our own survival. As we enter the

twenty-first century, our species faces one of our most important evolutionary milestones. If humans are to survive, we must change our behavior from a species that destroys its environment to one that does not.

SUMMARY

Biology is the science that studies living things, using scientific method. Biological research has produced some fundamental concepts of biology.

1. All living things consist of one or more cells. Cells take energy from their environments and use it to maintain a high degree of chemical and structural order and for activities such as maintenance, response to stimuli, growth, development, and reproduction to produce more cells and individuals.
2. Living things contain information in the form of their genetic material. This information dictates how organisms develop, survive, and reproduce, and determines the characteristics they can pass on to their offspring.
3. Organisms change their environments both in the short term and throughout the history of life on Earth.
4. Living things evolve, adapting to their environments and giving rise to new types of organisms.
5. The chief agent of evolution is natural selection, the phenomenon by which individuals with certain genetic traits are more likely to survive and reproduce, thereby increasing the proportion of their own genetic information in future generations of the population. Natural selection ensures that those individuals most effective in converting energy to offspring will be evolutionarily successful. This ensures that a population of organisms becomes well adapted to its environment.
6. Scientific knowledge is developed by subjecting problems to the scientific method. First, scientists make observations. Then they formulate alternative hypotheses that might explain the observations, and they test the hypotheses by experiments designed to disprove one or more of the hypotheses and therefore to strengthen the evidence for those that remain. When biological questions cannot be studied by direct experimentation, they are studied by searching for correlations that may reveal cause and effect.
7. Scientific discoveries and theories are useful, but they are always open to question. Time and again in the history of science, accepted dogmas have turned out to be wrong, and even today scientists are busy discarding or remodeling some of the "facts" presented in this book.
8. Human life depends on the activities of millions of organisms that share Earth with us. Rapid growth of the human population in the twentieth century threatens many of these life support systems and the future of the human species.

Questions for Discussion

1. After every hard rain you find dead earthworms lying on the sidewalk. What experiments would you perform to show the cause of death?
2. Many characteristics of life can be found in some nonliving things. Can you think of examples of these?
3. What might you expect was the selective pressure that resulted in each of the following adaptations?
   an elephant's trunk
   the scent of honeysuckle
   a leopard's spots
   the bark of a tree
   human language
4. Some people believe that the world will never run out of resources because research and technology will find replacements for depleted natural resources. Do you agree? Why?
5. If we imagine the evolution of the human species toward a sustainable society, we encounter a theoretical problem. In general, the people who reproduce most rapidly today are those who are poor, with the least education, and therefore often with the most environmentally destructive agriculture and little concern for environmental problems. Are these, therefore, the most evolutionarily successful people? If so, how can we imagine that humanity will evolve toward an environmentally responsible society with a low rate of reproduction?
6. Scientists often say that science is neither good nor bad; only the use of science, by scientists or by society, has moral consequences. For example, the discovery that the atom could be split was merely a scientific discovery. It was the decision to use this knowledge to build an atom bomb that produced the moral dilemma of whether it was ever right to use such a weapon. Do you think that in practice scientists must take, and society should force them to take, more moral responsibility for the consequences of their research? Is it always possible to foresee that a particular area of research will eventually have consequences?

Suggested Readings

Arms, K. *Environmental Science,* 2d ed. Philadelphia: Saunders College Publishing, 1994. An introductory textbook on the environment.

Arms, K., P. Feeny and R. C. Lederhouse. "Sodium: stimulus for puddling behavior by tiger swallowtail butterflies, *Papilio glaucus.*" *Science* 185:372, 1974. The puddling experiments described in this chapter.

Ehrlich, P. R., and A. H. Ehrlich. *The Population Explosion.* New York: Simon and Schuster, 1990. The environmental and human disasters caused by explosive growth of the human population.

Feshbach, M., and A. Friendly. *Ecocide in the USSR: Health and Nature under Siege.* New York: Basic Books, 1992. The amazing story of land rendered uninhabitable and health destroyed by decades of agricultural and industrial pollution in the former Soviet Union.

Mayr, E. *The Growth of Biological Thought.* Boston: Belknap Press of Harvard University Press, 1982. A historical perspective from an eminent evolutionary geneticist.

Roszak, T. *Where the Wasteland Ends.* Garden City, N.Y.: Doubleday, 1973. Critique of modern science by a man who believes science dominates western society and causes much of its malaise.

The Presidency in Crisis

Policies of the Nixon, Ford, and Carter Administrations 1968–1980

Joseph R. Conlin, from
The American Past: A Survey of American History

Harcourt Brace, 1993, pages 806–823

THE PRESIDENCY IN CRISIS

POLICIES OF THE NIXON, FORD, AND CARTER ADMINISTRATIONS 1968 - 1980

The heroes of Greek myth were constantly pursuing Proteus, the herdsman of the seas, for he could foresee the future and, once captured, he was obligated to reveal what he knew. But Proteus was rarely caught—he also possessed the curious power to assume the shape of any creature or thing, easily wriggling out of a captor's grasp.

Richard Milhous Nixon, so his critics said, was never captured because he was never in his own shape. John F. Kennedy, who ran against him for the presidency in 1960, said that Dick Nixon had assumed so many shapes that he had forgotten who he was and what he stood for. Liberals called him "Tricky Dicky." At several turns in his career, his Republican partisans felt constrained to assure Americans that the "Old Nixon" was no more; it was a "New Nixon" who needed their votes.

But the "Real Nixon," like the real Proteus, remained elusive and enigmatic to the end. Senator Barry Goldwater said that Richard M. Nixon was "the most complete loner I've ever known."

THE NIXON PRESIDENCY

Nixon will always be a compelling figure. He lacked the personal qualities the pundits said were keys to success in late-twentieth-century politics: physical attractiveness, grace, wit, a camera presence, the aura of "a nice guy." Nixon was shy and furtive in manner. His discomfort and defensiveness in front of a crowd often came off as insincerity.

The liberals' hatred for him had the intensity of a diabolical possession, but those who hated the liberals did not love Nixon. Dwight D. Eisenhower came within a hair of dumping him as vice-presidential nominee in 1952 and considered doing so again in 1956. In 1960, Ike humiliated Nixon by saying he was unable to recall a single instance in which Nixon contributed to a presidential decision. The right-wing Republicans whom Nixon served well for more than two decades accepted him without quite trusting him.

Richard Nixon clawed his way from a lower-middle-class background in southern California to the top of the heap through hard work and the tenacious bite of a bulldog. Although he overstated it in his autobiographical *Six Crises*, he overcame tremendous obstacles and repeated humiliation. If the self-made Horatio Alger boy is an American hero, Nixon should be ensconced in a pantheon for, unlike the Alger heroes, Nixon was all pluck and little luck. Whatever else may be said of Richard Nixon, it must be noted that he earned everything he ever got.

Political Savvy

As president, Nixon took little interest in domestic matters, believing that "the country could run itself domestically without a president." He left important decisions and directives to two young White House aides, H. R. Haldeman and John Ehrlichman. Brassy where their boss was secretive, Haldeman and Erlichman insulated Nixon from Congress and even his own cabinet

as effectively as Sherman Adams had done for Ike. But they were themselves arrogant, unpopular with almost everyone. They did nothing to shore up political support for the Nixon administration. They would have few friends when the tides of fortune turned against them.

Nixon left politicking to Vice-President Spiro T. Agnew, a former governor of Maryland who had been named to the ticket to attract blue-collar and white ethnic voters who were drawn to George Wallace. Agnew was an energetic campaigner and, once elected, cheerleader. He delighted conservatives by flailing student antiwar protestors, permissive educators who tolerated their disruptive activities, liberal Supreme Court justices, and the national news media. Agnew was fond of tongue-twisting alliteration, and his partisan audiences loved it. His masterpiece was "nattering nabobs of negativism," that is, journalists.

Agnew's liberal-baiting provided Nixon with a superb smokescreen for, despite his many denunciations of big-spending liberal government, the president was not interested in dismantling the New Deal or even the Great Society. His only major modification of the liberal welfare state he inherited was "the New Federalism," a policy of turning federal tax monies over to the states to spend on social programs.

On other fronts, Nixon might have been a middle-of-the-road Democrat. He sponsored a scheme for welfare reform, the Family Assistance Plan, that was to provide a flat annual payment to poor families in return for the agreement by heads of household to register with employment agencies. (It failed in Congress.) When, in 1971, inflation threatened his reelection campaign, Nixon slapped on wage and price controls, a Republican anathema for half a century.

And yet, the conservative yelping was muted. Quite shrewdly, Nixon understood that the grass-roots conservatives he called the "Silent Majority" had been repelled far less by liberal economic policy than by the myriad non-economic causes that liberals had come to emphasize by the 1970s: what many whites perceived as kid-gloves treatment of blacks, the often gamey demands of feminists and advocates of "gay rights," the antiwar movement's shrill antipatriotism, and the decisions of the Warren Court that emphasized the rights of accused criminals and seemed to hobble police in enforcing the law.

Reshaping the Supreme Court

Thanks to a mistake by Lyndon Johnson in the waning days of his administration, Nixon was able to move immediately to reshape the Supreme Court. Elderly Chief Justice Earl Warren (an old Nixon nemesis) had offered to retire while Johnson was still president so that L.B.J.

could name another liberal activist in his place. Johnson picked an old Texas crony already on the Court, Abe Fortas, who was immediately revealed to have accepted payments for public appearances that were, at best, of dubious propriety. Johnson had to back down and Warren retired only after Nixon was sworn in.

Nixon's choice to replace him was Warren Burger of Minnesota. Burger was conservative but, as an advocate of judicial restraint rather than antiliberal activism, he was somewhat disappointing to the right-wing of the Republican party. When Fortas himself left the Court in 1970, Nixon tried to mollify the right-wingers by naming Clement Haynsworth of South Carolina to the Court. However, Haynsworth had several pro-segregation decisions in his portfolio, and Senate Democrats rejected him.

An angry Nixon then blundered badly. Insisting that the South must have a seat on the Court, he hurriedly named a mediocrity from Florida whose mere knowledge of the law was problematical. When he too was rejected by the Senate, the president had to return to a friend of Burger from Minnesota, Harry A. Blackmun. Nixon's two additional appointments, Lewis F. Powell and William H. Rehnquist (later Chief Justice) were more conservative in the eyes of the "Silent Majority."

Just as Nixon left the basic outlines of the welfare state intact, the Burger Court merely moderated Warren Court rulings. On the domestic front, Nixon seemed to achieve just what he wanted, an equilibrium enabling him to concentrate on what he believed to be the modern president's chief responsibility and his own ticket into the history books: foreign relations.

NIXON'S VIETNAM

No foreign problem was so pressing as the ongoing war in Vietnam. Nixon knew well that Lyndon Johnson's political career had been prematurely snuffed out by the agonizing, endless conflict. "The damned fool" Johnson had, in the words of a protest song of the era, mired himself "hip deep in the Big Muddy," and been helpless to do anything but to tell the nation to "push on." Nixon wanted out of the war. But how to turn the trick?

Vietnamization

Nixon had been vice president when Eisenhower freed the nation from another quagmire in Korea. But Ike's course of action in 1953 was not available in 1969. Eisenhower had threatened the Chinese and North Ko-

reans with nuclear weapons; that was not an option in the era of the nuclear balance of terror. Ike had settled the Korean Conflict on the basis of an independent South Korea with American troops on the scene to ensure security. In 1969, the Viet Cong and North Vietnamese insisted that they would not conclude hostilities as long as there were American troops in South Vietnam. Finally, Eisenhower had not had to deal with a militant antiwar movement at home.

Nixon's scheme was of necessity more subtle. First, to neutralize the antiwar movement, Nixon set out to reduce the sickening casualty lists that weekly provided the protesters with new recruits. In July 1969, he promulgated the Nixon Doctrine, stating that while the United States would "participate in the defense and development of allies and friends," Americans would no longer "undertake all the defense of the free nations of the world."

In Vietnam, the Nixon Doctrine translated as the "Vietnamization" of the war. The large but unreliable A.R.V.N. was thoroughly retrained to replace American boys on the bloody front lines. As South Vietnamese units were deemed ready for combat, American troops came home. At about the same speed that L.B.J. had escalated the American presence, Nixon de-escalated it. From a high of 541,000 American soldiers in South Vietnam when Nixon took office, the American force declined to 335,000 in 1970 and 24,000 in 1972.

Nixon had returned the American ground war to where it had been in 1964 and, so it seemed at first, he had reduced the militant antiwar movement to a hard core of pacifists and New Left "anti-imperialists" whom Agnew denounced as traitors and Nixon as "bums." Democrats in Congress who had defended Johnson's war demanded that Nixon make more serious efforts to negotiate an end to it. But the president replied, not implausibly, that a truculent North Vietnam, and not he, was the major obstacle to peace.

Expanding the War

Politically, Nixon could not afford simply to pull out of Vietnam. He was beholden for his election to his own hard core of "Hawks" who believed that Johnson had failed in Vietnam because he had not been "tough" enough. Nixon reassured such supporters: "We will not be humiliated. We will not be defeated." Much as he and his chief foreign policy advisor, Henry A. Kissinger,

wanted the war ended, they had to salvage the independence of South Vietnam in order to save face.

Consequently, all the while he reduced the American presence in Vietnam, Nixon attempted to bludgeon the enemy into meaningful negotiations by expanding the scope of the war. In the spring of 1969, Nixon sent Air Force bombers over neutral Cambodia to destroy sanctuaries where about 50,000 North Vietnamese troops rested up after battles. For a year, the American people knew nothing of these attacks. Then, in 1970, Nixon sent ground forces into Cambodia, an attack that could not be concealed.

The result was a thunderous uproar. Critics condemned the president for attacking a neutral nation. Several hundred university presidents closed their campuses for fear of student violence, and events at two colleges proved their wisdom in doing so. At Kent State University in Ohio, members of the National Guard, many of whom had joined to avoid being drafted and sent to Southeast Asia, opened fire on demonstrators. Four persons were killed and eleven wounded. Ten days later, two students at Jackson State College in Mississippi were killed by police.

Congress reacted to the widening of the war by repealing the Tonkin Gulf Resolution which gave the president authority to fight it. Nixon responded that the repeal was immaterial. As Commander-in-chief, he said, he had the right to take whatever military action he believed necessary. Nonetheless, when the war was further expanded into Laos in February 1971, A.R.V.N. troops carried the burden of the fighting.

Falling Dominos

Vietnamization did not work. Without American troops by their side, the A.R.V.N. was humiliated in Laos. The Communist Pathet Lao grew in strength until 1975 when it seized control of the country. Tens of thousands of refugees who feared Communist rule fled.

In Cambodia, the consequences of expanding the war were far worse. Many young Cambodians were so angered by American bombing that they flocked to join the Khmer Rouge, once scarcely large enough to stage a soccer game. The Khmer Rouge increased in size from a mere 3,000 in 1970 to 30,000 in just a few years. In 1976, the head of the force, Pol Pot, came to power and created one of the most criminal regimes the world has ever known. In three years, his fanatical followers murdered as many as 3 million of their own people out of a population of 7.2 million! If Hitler's campaign of genocide against the Jews of Nazi-occupied Europe was proportional to Pol Pot's, the toll in the Nazi death camps would not have been 6 million, but something on the order of 150 million.

Eisenhower's Asian "dominos" had fallen, but not because the United States had been weak in the face of a military threat. They toppled because the United States had escalated and expanded a war that, in 1963, had been little more than a brawl. In the process, Southeast Asian moderates and neutrals like Cambodia's Prince Sihanouk were undercut. By the mid-1970s, North Vietnam was dominated by militarists and Cambodia by a monster. Laos was in the hands of a once tiny Communist movement.

Finis

In South Vietnam, the fighting dragged on until the fall of 1972 when, after suffering twelve days of earth-shaking bombing, the North Vietnamese finally faced up to the fact that the war was a stalemate. Foreign Minister Le Duc Tho met with Kissinger and arranged a cease-fire. The Paris Accords they signed went into effect in January 1973. The treaty required the United States to withdraw all its troops from Vietnam within 60 days while the North Vietnamese released all prisoners of war. Until free elections were held, North Vietnamese troops could remain in the country.

South Vietnamese president Nguyen Van Thieu regarded the settlement as a sell-out. It enabled Nixon to save face while Thieu was faced with a massive enemy force within South Vietnamese borders. For two years, the country simmered. Then, in April 1975, the A.R.V.N. collapsed and the North Vietnamese army attacked a virtually undefended Saigon. A short time later, North and South Vietnam were united and Saigon was rather unattractively renamed Ho Chi Minh City.

Ironically, Cambodia's nightmare was brought to an end only when the North Vietnamese invaded the country and overthrew Pol Pot. Rather more remarkable, as late as 1990 the United States insisted that Pol Pot was the legitimate ruler of Cambodia and, in 1991, engineered a settlement in which the Khmer Rouge shared in the government of the nation.

Bottom Line

The long war ravaged a once prosperous corner of the world. Once an exporter of rice, Vietnam remained short of food through the 1980s. About a million A.R.V.N. soldiers lost their lives, the Viet Cong and North Vietnamese about the same number. Estimates of civilian dead ran as high as 3.5 million. About 5.2 million acres of jungle and farmland were ruined by defoliation. American bombing also devastated hundreds of cities, towns, bridges, and highways. The Air Force dropped more bombs on Vietnam than in all of Europe during World War II.

The vengefulness of the victors caused a massive flight of refugees. About 10 percent of the people of Southeast Asia fled their homelands after the war. Some spent everything they owned to bribe venal North Vietnamese officials to let them go. Others piled into leaky boats and cast off into open waters, untold numbers to die. To the credit of the United States, some 600,000 Vietnamese, Laotians, Cambodians, and ethnic minorities (whom every government in Southeast Asia bullied) were admitted as immigrants.

The war cost the United States something like $150 billion, more than any other American war except World War II. Some 2.7 million American men and women served in the conflict; 57,000 of them were killed and 300,000 were wounded. Many men were disabled for life. Some lost limbs; others were poisoned by Agent Orange, the toxic defoliant the army used to clear jungle. Yet others were addicted to drugs or alcohol. Mental disturbances and violent crime were alarmingly common among Vietnam veterans.

And yet, for ten years, Vietnam veterans were ignored, shunned, even discriminated against. Politicians, not only liberals who had opposed the war but the superpatriotic Hawks who had wanted the troops to fight on indefinitely, neglected to vote money for government programs to help them. Only in 1982, almost a decade after the war ended, was a monument to the soldiers erected in Washington, D.C. Not until 1991, after the stunning success of the American military in Iraq, did the then president George Bush feel that the "Vietnam Syndrome" had been put to rest.

NIXON–KISSINGER FOREIGN POLICY

Nixon called the Vietnam war a "sideshow." Henry A. Kissinger said that it was a mere "footnote" to history. Both men wanted to bring the conflict to an end so that they could bring about what, quite rightly, they regarded as a revolution in world diplomacy, a complete reordering of relations among the world's great powers.

The Long Crusade

It is impossible to say just how much of the Nixon-Kissinger foreign policy was Nixon's and how much was Kissinger's, and apportioning credit is not very important. The fact was that both men envisioned a new relationship among the great powers that flew in the face of American assumptions since the dawn of the Cold War.

That is, for more than twenty years before the Nixon presidency, virtually all American policy-makers and shapers of public opinion had described the world as divided into two inevitably hostile camps: the United States and its allies, most importantly Western Europe and Japan; and the Soviet Union and its client states, particularly the gigantic People's Republic of China. Few so eagerly looked forward to a showdown between the two camps as John Foster Dulles had done, but diplomats and politicians who favored *détente*—a relaxation of tensions—had to phrase their views very carefully or have their courage and patriotism questioned.

The pre-presidential Richard M. Nixon had consistently played on the theme of inevitable superpower hostility and the disloyalty of those who were "soft on

KISSINGER ON THE COLD WAR

"The superpowers often behave like two heavily armed blind men feeling their way around a room, each believing himself in mortal peril from the other whom he assumes to have perfect vision. . . . Each tends to ascribe to the other side a consistency, foresight and coherence that its own experience belies. Of course, over time even two blind men can do enormous damage to each other, not to speak of the room."

Henry A. Kissinger,
The White House Years (1979)

Communism." But at some point during Nixon's eight years as a private citizen, he ceased to believe in this rhetoric. Privately, Nixon came to two important conclusions quite at odds with the great anti-Communist crusade.

Premises of Détente

First, Nixon concluded that the nuclear balance of power made a superpower showdown unthinkable. Therefore, to continue to incite high tension between the Soviets and Americans was to waste resources while indefinitely running the risk of accidental world war.

Second, Nixon recognized that the old bipolar view of geopolitics on which the Cold War was predicated was nonsense. Japan, once a docile American client, was now one of the world's economic powers. The nations of Western Europe, groping toward unity, were openly trying to define an independent economic, political, and military role for themselves. The People's Republic of China, if ever subservient to the Soviet Union, was no longer so. Reports reached the West of Sino-Soviet battles on their 2,000-mile-long border.

Nixon thought of himself as a hard-headed realist. He meant to win his place in history by effecting a diplomatic revolution in which the great powers dealt with one another not as Hatfields and McCoys, but as "interested parties" rationally making deals for the benefit of each, and to ensure peace. In 1971, he said, "it will be a safer world and a better world, if we have a strong and healthy United States, Europe, Soviet Union, China, Japan—each balancing the other, not playing one against the other, an even balance."

Nixon's views were influenced and reinforced by Henry Kissinger. A witty, urbane, brilliant, and cheerfully conceited refugee from Naziism, Kissinger never quite lost his German accent nor his taste for *Realpolitik*, the amoral, opportunistic approach to diplomacy of one of his historical idols, Count Otto von Bismarck. Kissinger believed that the leaders of the Soviet Union and China were as little concerned with ideology and crusades as he and Nixon were, and only needed encouragement to launch a new era. His calculation was dramatically confirmed in 1971 at a time when the Vietnam War was raging and, officially, the ripest of denunciations were flying among Chinese, Russians, and Americans.

Rapprochement with China

In 1971, an American table-tennis team on a tour of Japan was startled to receive an invitation from the People's Republic of China to play a series of exhibition games there before they returned home. Sports writers noted wryly that the Chinese had picked a game in which they would trounce the Americans (they did), but diplomats recognized the implications of the apparently trivial event. For more than 20 years, the United States and China had had no open contact with one another, the leaders of both nations ritually denouncing the other as mortal enemies.

Kissinger virtually commanded the ping-pong players to go to China and shortly thereafter opened talks with Chinese diplomats. He flew secretly to Beijing where he arranged for a good-will tour by Nixon himself in February 1972. Only then was the amazing news announced: the lifelong scourge of Red China would tour the Forbidden City and Great Wall and sit down with chopsticks at a Mandarin banquet with Mao Zedong and Zhou Enlai, drinking toasts to eternal Sino-American amity with fiery Chinese spirits.

Nixon's meeting with Mao was ceremonial; the Chairman was senile and fading. However, discussions with Zhou, who had long advocated better relations with the West and his proteges, Hua Guofeng (who was to succeed Mao in 1976) and Deng Xiaoping, who had done time in prison for advocating "capitalistic" reforms of China's moribund economy, reassured Nixon that he had calculated correctly.

Almost overnight, Sino-American relations warmed. The United States dropped its opposition to China's demand for a seat in the United Nations and established a legation in Beijing. (In 1979, the two countries established full diplomatic relations.)

Chinese students were invited to study in American universities and China opened its doors to American tourists, who came by the tens of thousands. American industrialists involved in everything from oil exploration to the bottling of soft drinks flew to China, anxious to sell American technology and consumer goods in the market that had long symbolized the traveling salesman's ultimate "territory."

Détente with the Soviet Union

China did not turn out to be much of a customer. The Chinese population was huge, but the country was poor and in economic chaos; there was neither money nor goods with which to pay for the expensive high-technology exports in which alone, by the 1970s, American industry was still supreme. Nor were the new leaders of China interested in resuming the status of a colonial market or in embracing wide-open political institutions. Their principal motive in courting American friendship

was diplomatic, to win some edge of security in their conflict with the Soviet Union. They were "playing the America card."

That was all right with the realistic Nixon and Kissinger. They were "playing the China card," putting the fear of a closer Sino-American relationship into the Soviets, who represented a genuine threat to American security. Their gambit worked. In June 1972, just months after his China trip, Nixon flew to the Soviet Union and signed a preliminary agreement in the opening series of Strategic Arms Limitation Talks (SALT), the first significant step toward a slowdown of the arms race since the Kennedy administration.

At home, the photos of Nixon clinking champagne glasses with Mao and hugging Brezhnev bewildered his conservative supporters and flummoxed his liberal critics. In fact, as Nixon knew, undoubtedly savoring it, only a Republican with an impeccable Cold-Warrior past could have accomplished what he did. Had a liberal Democratic president shared a Peking duck with Mao Zedong, Nixon himself would have held the noose at the demonstrations outside the White House.

Shuttle Diplomacy

Nixon was grateful to Kissinger and, in 1973, named him Secretary of State. Well into 1974, Kissinger's diplomatic successes piled up. His greatest triumph came in the Middle East after the Yom Kippur War of 1973, in which Egypt and Syria attacked Israel and, for the first time in the long Arab–Israeli conflict, inflicted terrible casualties and fought the Israelis to a draw.

Knowing that the Israelis were not inclined to accept less than victory and fearing what a prolonged war in the oil-rich Middle East would mean for the United States, Kissinger shuttled seemingly without sleep among Damascus, Cairo, and Tel Aviv, carrying proposal and counterproposal for a settlement. Unlike Dulles, who also had represented American interests on the fly, Kissinger was a brilliant diplomat. He ended the war, and the terms he prevailed on all the warring powers to accept actually increased American influence in the region. He won the gratitude and friendship of Egyptian President Anwar Sadat, while not alienating Israel.

After 1974, however, Kissinger lost his magic touch, in part because of revived world tensions that were not his fault. Soviet Premier Leonid Brezhnev may have wanted to reduce the chance of direct conflict between Russia and the United States. However, he continued to aid guerrilla movements in Africa and Latin America. Cuba's Fidel Castro, with a large army to keep in trim, exported advisors and combat troops to several countries, most notably to Angola in southwestern Africa.

But Nixon and Kissinger were also willing, even anxious to fight the Cold War by proxy in the Third World, competing with the Soviets for spheres of influence. While right-wing Republicans opposed to *détente* stepped up their attacks on Kissinger, he was actually pursuing their kind of confrontational policies in strife-torn countries like Angola.

The most damaging mark on Kissinger's record as the diplomat-in-chief of a democratic country came in 1974. It was revealed that, the previous year, he had been aware of and may have instigated and aided militarists in Chile who overthrew and murdered the president, Salvador Allende. Allende had been a bungler but he was Chile's democratically elected head and his American-backed successor, Agostín Pinochet, instituted a barbaric and brutal regime marked by torture and murder of opponents.

WATERGATE AND GERALD FORD

By 1974, when news of the Pinochet connection broke in the United States, Kissinger was no longer serving Richard Nixon. The crisis of the presidency that had begun when Lyndon Johnson was repudiated took on a new dimension of gravity when Nixon was forced to resign in disgrace. The debacle had its beginnings in the election campaign of 1972 in which, thanks to a transformation of the Democratic party, victory was in Nixon's hip pocket from the start.

Redefining Liberalism
Between 1968 and 1972, activist middle-class liberals won control of several key Democratic party committees and remade party machinery according to their ideals. They enacted new procedures and standards for selecting convention delegates that penalized old party stalwarts: the labor unions, the big city machines, those Southern "good old boys" who had not already gone Republican, and other political pros. The McGovern reforms (named for the liberal, antiwar Senator from South Dakota) guaranteed representation of women and minority groups at party conventions largely on the basis of their sex and ethnic origins.

The Election of 1972
As an immediate result of the reforms, the Democratic delegates who gathered in Miami in the summer of 1972 formed the youngest convention in political history, counted more women and members of minorities among the delegates than any other, and was strongly antiwar. They nominated Senator McGovern to head their ticket and adopted a platform calling for a negotiated end to the Southeast Asian war (then Vietnamized but still raging), and supporting the demands of some women's

organizations that the decision as to whether or not a fetus should be aborted belonged to the pregnant woman herself, and no other person or institution.

A sincere and decent man who was deeply grieved by the war, McGovern tried to distance himself from some extremes of his party, particularly "gay rights" advocates who, McGovern understood, were not likely to win the affection of working-class people who traditionally voted Democratic. He emphasized peace in Vietnam and tax reform that would benefit middle- and lower-income people, and his integrity compared well with Nixon's longstanding reputation for deviousness.

But virtually no labor unions supported him and many political pros sat on their hands. The Republicans, by way of contrast, ran an effective campaign. They depicted McGovern as a bumbling and indecisive radical. When McGovern first defended his running mate, Senator Thomas Eagleton, who had undergone psychiatric treatment several years earlier, and then forced Eagleton to drop out, his race was doomed.

Nixon won 60.8 percent of the popular vote and carried every state but Massachusetts and the District of Columbia. In only eight years, he had reversed the Republican humiliation of 1964. He had had a lot of help from the Democrats but his achievement was nonetheless remarkable. However, Nixon's days of glorious triumph were, like Lyndon Johnson's in 1964, to be few.

Covering up a Burglary
On June 17, 1972, early in the presidential campaign, Washington police had arrested five men who were trying to plant electronic eavesdropping devices in Democratic party headquarters in a Washington apartment and office complex called the Watergate. Three of the suspects were on the payroll of the Committee to Reelect the President (an unwisely chosen name inasmuch as it abbreviated as CREEP), and McGovern tried to exploit the incident as part of his integrity campaign. But the ploy fizzled when Nixon and his campaign manager, Attorney General John Mitchell, denied any knowledge of the incident and denounced the burglars as common criminals.

In fact, Nixon knew nothing about the break-in in advance, but he soon learned that the burglars had acted on orders from his own aides. He never considered reporting or disciplining his men. Instead, almost nonchalantly, he instructed his staff to find money to hush up the men in jail. However, two of them, James E. McCord and Howard Hunt refused to take the fall and informed Judge John Sirica that they had taken orders from highly-placed Nixon administration officials.

Rumors began to fly. Two reporters for the *Washington Post*, Robert Woodward and Carl Bernstein, made contact with an anonymous informant who fed them information. A special Senate investigating committee

HOW THEY LIVED

THE TYPICAL AMERICAN OF THE 1980s: A STATISTICAL PORTRAIT

The statistical American of the year 1980 was a Caucasian female, a little more than 30 years old, married to her first husband, with one child and about to have another. She was a shade over 5 feet 4 inches tall and weighed 134 pounds. Statisticians are not sure of the color of her hair and eyes, but they were probably on the brownish side. Statisticians are sure that she had tried marijuana when she was younger, but no longer used it in the 1980s (although some of her friends still did). She did not smoke cigarettes, but at least had tried them in the past; she still drank, just this side of moderately.

The statistical American adult female of the 1980s considered herself middle class, and had attended college but had not necessarily graduated. She was likely to work outside the home, but economic conditions during the first half of the decade made her opportunities uncertain. Her household income was about $20,000 a year; she and her husband were watching their budget closely, which they were not accustomed to doing. It is a toss-up whether or not she voted in 1984 (or at all during the 1970s). She was decreasingly interested in feminism as the 1980s progressed and the failure of the ERA faded into memory. She was marginally more likely to be registered as a Democrat than as a Republican, but she was more likely to have voted for Ronald Reagan in 1984 than in 1980.

More than half of the statistical American's female friends were married. Most of her friends who have been divorced have married again within three years. The statistical American of the 1980s attached no stigma to divorce, and experienced only a slight sense of unease with people who lived with members of the opposite sex without benefit of marriage. But she found it difficult to agree that homosexuality is nothing more than an "alternate lifestyle" on a moral parity with heterosexuality. She was both amused and repelled by the culture of the "gay" communities about which she read, but by 1985 was not so indulgent as she had been because of the quantum leap in the spread of deadly AIDS.

She almost certainly had sex with her husband before they married, and almost as likely with at least one other man. There is a fair chance that she had a brief fling since marriage, probably during a "trial separation."

The statistical American was more likely to be Protestant than Catholic. However, she was more likely to be Catholic than a member of any other *individual* denomination. If a Catholic, she practiced birth control, most likely using the pill, in defiance of Church directives. Moreover, Catholic or Protestant, she attended church services far less frequently than had her mother.

The statistical American was in excellent health; she saw a dentist and a doctor more than once a year, and paid a little less than half of the cost of health care (state and federal government picked up about the same, private industry and philanthropy the rest). She had a life expectancy of almost 78 years, and would outlive her husband by eight years, with the prospects that her dotage would be economically trying.

The statistical American lived in a state with a population of about 3 million people—Colorado, Iowa, Oklahoma, Connecticut—and in a city of about 100,000 people—Roanoke, Virginia; Reno, Nevada; Durham, North Carolina.

Or perhaps, she lived at the population center of the United States, which in 1980 was west of the Mississippi River for the first time in American history. It was located "one mile west of the De Soto City Hall, Jefferson County, Missouri." An equal number of people in the continental United States lived east of that point as west, as many north of it as south.

As the question about her state and city of residence indicates, the statistical American is a somewhat absurd contrivance, distilled out of the majorities, means, and medians of the United States Census Bureau; the responses to surveys taken by a number of public-opinion experts; and, simply, the probabilities of the educated guess.

The virtue of the United States remains rooted in its diversity of people as well as of resources and in the survival of those people's right to change their minds as many times as they wish. And, as far as matters of public policy are concerned, to form majorities and effect their wishes. For a nation that has reached its third century, that is not so bad an accomplishment. In the star-crossed history of the human race, it has not been done in many other places.

headed by Sam Ervin of North Carolina picked away at the tangle from yet another direction, slowly tracing not only the Watergate break-in and cover-up but other illegal acts to the White House itself.

The Imperial Presidency

Each month that passed, dramatic insights into the inner workings of the Nixon presidency were revealed. On Nixon's own orders, an "enemies list" had been compiled. On it were journalists, politicians, intellectuals, and even movie stars who had made statements criticizing Nixon. One Donald Segretti was put in charge of a "dirty tricks" campaign, planting half-truths, rumors, and lies to discredit critics of the administration. G. Gordon Liddy, who was involved in the Watergate break-in, had proposed fantastic schemes involving yachts and prostitutes to entrap "enemies." The "dirty tricks" campaign grew so foul that not even J. Edgar Hoover, the none too squeamish head of the F.B.I., would touch it.

Watergate, it turned out, had been just one of several "surreptitious entries" sponsored by the administration. Nixon's aides also engineered the burglary of a Los Angeles psychiatrist's office to secure information about a Defense Department employee who had published confidential information about the prosecution of the war in Vietnam.

Observers spoke of an "Imperial Presidency." Nixon and his advisors had become so arrogant in their possession of power that they believed they were above the law. Indeed, several years later, Nixon himself was to tell an interviewer on television, "When the president does it, that means it is not illegal."

If imperial in their pretensions, however, "all the president's men" were singularly lacking in a sense of nobility. One by one, Nixon aides abandoned ship, each convinced that he was being set up as the sole fall-guy for his colleagues. Each deserter named others and described their roles in the cover-up and dirty-tricks campaign. A snarl of half-truths and lies descended on the president himself.

In the midst of the scandal, Vice President Spiro Agnew pleaded no-contest to income-tax evasion and charges that he had accepted bribes when he was governor of Maryland. Agnew was forced to resign from the vice-presidency in October 1973. He was replaced under the terms of the Twenty-Fifth Amendment by Congressman Gerald Ford of Michigan.

Resignation

Then came Nixon's turn. He had kept tape recordings of conversations in his Oval Office that clearly implicated him in the Watergate cover-up (and revealed him as having a rather foul mouth: the transcripts of the tapes were peppered with "expletive deleted"). After long fights in the courts, the president was ordered to surrender the tapes to investigators.

Why Nixon did not destroy the incriminating recordings early in the Watergate crisis remains a mystery. It was suggested that greed—the money that the electronic documents would bring after he left the presidency—accounts for his fatal blunder. Others saw the preservation of the tapes as another manifestation of Nixon's imperial megalomania. He could not conceive of the fact that a court could order the president of the United States to abide by laws that applied to mere citizens.

After the House of Representatives Judiciary Committee recommended impeaching Nixon, he threw in the towel. On August 9, 1974, on national television, he resigned the presidency and flew to his home in San Clemente, California.

Richard Nixon forces a smile as he departs Washington after his resignation.

A Ford, Not a Lincoln

Gerald Ford's career had not been distinguished. Holding a safe seat in the House from Michigan, he had risen to be minority leader on the basis of seniority and dutifully toeing the Republican party line. His sole ambition when events made him first vice president and then president, was to be Speaker of the House, but the Republicans never came close to winning a majority of Representatives.

Ford was not a particularly intelligent man. Lyndon Johnson once told reporters that Gerry Ford's trouble was that he had played center on the University of Michigan football team without a helmet. Others quipped that he could not walk and chew gum at the same time. Newspaper photographers fairly laid in wait to ridicule him by snapping shots of him bumping his head on door frames, tumbling down the slopes of the Rockies on everything but his skis, slicing golf balls into crowds of spectators.

And yet his simplicity and forthrightness were a relief after Nixon's squirming and deception. He told the American people that fate had given them "a Ford, not a Lincoln," and he had no pretensions. Democrats howled "deal" when Ford pardoned Nixon of all crimes he may have committed, but Ford's explanation, that the American people needed to put Watergate behind them, was plausible and in character. Two very nearly

Gerald Ford appointed Nelson Rockefeller as his vice president.

The United States was by far the biggest user of non-renewable sources of energy. In 1973, while comprising about 6 percent of the world's population, Americans consumed fully 33 percent of the world's annual production of oil. Much of it was burned to less than basic ends. Americans overheated and overcooled their offices and houses. They pumped gasoline into a dizzying variety of purely recreational vehicles, some of which brought the roar of the freeway to the wilderness and devastated fragile land. Their worship of the wasteful private automobile meant that few taxes were spent on public mass transit systems. They packaged their consumer goods in throw-away containers of glass, metal, paper, and petroleum-based plastics; supermarkets wrapped lemons individually in transparent plastic and fast-food cheeseburgers were cradled in plastic foam caskets that were discarded within seconds of being handed over the counter. The bill of indictment went on but, resisting criticism and satire alike, American consumption increased.

OPEC and the Energy Crisis

About 61 percent of the oil that Americans consumed in the 1970s was produced at home, and large reserves remained under native ground. But the nation also imported huge quantities of crude, and in October 1973, Americans discovered just how little control they had over the 39 percent of their oil that came from abroad.

In that month, the Organization of Petroleum Exporting Countries (OPEC) temporarily halted oil shipments and announced the first of a series of big jumps in the price of their product. One of their justifications was that the irresponsible consumption habits of the ad-

successful attempts to assassinate him by deranged women in California helped to win sympathy for the first president who had not been elected to any national office.

Despite his unusual route to the White House, Gerald Ford had no intention of being a caretaker president. But it was Ford's misfortune, as it had been Tyler's, to face serious problems without the confidence and support of an important segment of his party. The Republican party's right-wing, led by former California governor, Ronald Reagan, did not like *détente* nor Nixon's, now Ford's refusal to launch a frontal attack on government regulation and the liberal welfare state.

Running on Half-Empty

The most serious of the woes that faced Ford struck at a reflexive assumption of twentieth-century American life: that cheap energy was available in unlimited quantities to fuel the economy and support the freewheeling lifestyle of the middle class.

By the mid-1970s, 90 percent of the American economy was generated by the burning of fossil fuels: coal, natural gas, and petroleum. Fossil fuels are nonrenewable sources of energy. Unlike food crops, lumber, and water—or, for that matter, a horse and a pair of sturdy legs—they cannot be called on again once they have been used. The supply of them is finite. While experts disagreed about the extent of the world's reserves of coal, gas, and oil, no one challenged the obvious fact that one day they would be no more.

CONSTITUTIONAL CONTRADICTION?

Gerald Ford was appointed to the vice presidency under the provisions of the Twenty-fifth Amendment, ratified in 1967, which stipulates that "whenever there is a vacancy in the office of the Vice President, the President shall nominate a Vice President. . . ." When he succeeded to the presidency, he appointed Nelson A. Rockefeller to the vice presidency. Neither the president nor the vice president held office by virtue of election. However, as some constitutional experts were quick to point out, Article II, Section 1 of the Constitution provides that the president and vice president are to "be elected."

In fact, the contradiction was always there, if never put to the test. The U.S. Constitution and laws hold that the Secretary of State and the Speaker of the House were next in line to the presidency after the vice president. A case could be made that the Speaker was elected, but not the Secretary of State.

The lines at a Los Angeles gas station stretched for blocks during the gasoline shortage in 1979.

vanced Western nations, particularly the United States, jeopardized their future.

OPEC leaders reasoned that if the oil-exporting nations continued to supply oil cheaply, consuming nations would continue to burn it profligately, thus hastening the day the wells ran dry. On that day, if the oil-exporting nations had not laid the basis for another kind of economy, they would be destitute. Particularly in the oil-rich Middle East, there were few alternative resources to support fast-growing populations. Therefore, by raising prices, the OPEC nations would earn capital with which to build for a future without oil, while simultaneously encouraging the consuming nations to conserve, thus lengthening the era when oil would be available.

From a geopolitical perspective, there was much to be said for the argument, but ordinary Americans (and the people of other consumer nations) rarely thought geopolitically. They were stunned when they had to wait in long lines in order to pay unprecedented prices for gasoline. In some big cities and Hawaii, gasoline for private cars was not to be had for weeks.

The price of gasoline never climbed to Japanese or European levels, but it was shock enough for people who were accustomed to buying "two dollars' worth" to discover that $2 bought a little more than enough to drive

home. Moreover, the prices of goods that required oil in their production climbed too. Inflation, already a problem under Nixon, worsened from 9 percent a year when Ford became president to 12 percent.

Whip Inflation Now!

Opposed to wage and price controls such as Nixon had employed, Ford launched a campaign called WIN!, for "Whip Inflation Now!" He urged Americans to slow down inflation by refusing to buy exorbitantly priced goods and by ceasing to demand higher wages from their employers. The campaign was ridiculed from the start, and within a few weeks Ford quietly retired the WIN! button that he had been wearing on his lapel. He had seen few others in his travels about the country and began to feel like a man in a funny hat.

Instead, Ford tightened the money supply in order to slow down the economy, which resulted in the most serious recession since 1937, with unemployment climbing to 9 percent. Ford was stymied by the same vicious circle that caught up his predecessor and successor: slowing inflation meant throwing people out of work; fighting unemployment meant inflation; trying to steer a middle course meant "stagflation," mild recession plus inflation.

Image Problems

As a congressman, Ford had been a hawk on Vietnam. When the North Vietnamese launched their attack on Saigon early in 1975, his first impulse was to intervene with American troops. Congress refused to respond and Henry Kissinger, who had stayed on as Secretary of State, talked him out of presidential action. Ford tried to display his determination to exercise American armed might in May 1975, when Cambodian Communists seized an American ship, the *Mayaguez*. Ford ordered in the marines, who successfully rescued the captives. But in order to have 39 seamen returned to their homes, 38 marines died.

Kissinger savored the reports that the president hung breathlessly on his every word, but such stories only further enraged the Kissinger-hating right-wing of the Republican party and made it easier for the Democrats to mock Ford as being not bright enough to handle his job.

Early in 1976, polls showed Ford losing to most of the likely Democratic candidates. Capitalizing on them, Ronald Reagan, the sweetheart of the right-wing Republicans, launched a well-financed campaign to replace him as the party's candidate. Using his control of party organization, Ford beat Reagan at the convention but the travails of his two years in office took their toll. He could not overcome the image that he was the most accidental of presidents, never elected to national office. His full pardon of Nixon came back to haunt him and, in November, he lost narrowly to a most unlikely Democratic candidate, James Earl Carter of Georgia, who called himself Jimmy. The Democrats were back, but the decline in the prestige of the presidency continued.

QUIET CRISIS

Since Eisenhower, every president had been identified closely with Congress, the arena of national politics. The day of the governor candidate seemed to be in the past. Then Jimmy Carter came out of nowhere to win the Democratic nomination in 1976. His political career consisted of one term in the Georgia assembly and one term as governor.

Indeed, it was Carter's lack of association with the federal government that helped him win the nomination and, by a slim margin, the presidency. Without a real animus for Gerald Ford, many Americans were attracted to the idea of an "outsider," which is how Carter presented himself. "Hello, my name is Jimmy Carter and I'm running for president," he told thousands of people face to face in his softly musical Georgia accent. Once he started winning primaries, the media did the rest.

CLEANUP

In 1912 the Chicago Sanitation Department cleared the streets of the carcasses of 10,000 dead horses. In 1968 the Chicago Police Department cleared the streets of 24,500 carcasses of dead automobiles.

When television commentators said that there was a bandwagon rolling, voters dutifully responded by jumping on it.

Inauguration Day, when Carter and his wife, Rosalyn, walked the length of Pennsylvania Avenue, was very nearly the last entirely satisfactory day of the Carter presidency. Whether the perspective of time will attribute his failure as chief executive to his unsuitability to the office or the massiveness of the problems he faced, it is difficult to imagine future historians looking at the Carter era any differently than it is now remembered, dolefully.

The Panama Treaty

Carter had his successes, especially in foreign relations. Among his achievements was defusing an explosive situation in Central America where Panamanians and others had long protested American sovereignty over the Panama Canal Zone. The narrow strip of U.S. territory bisected the small republic and seemed to be an intolerable insult in an age when nationalist sensibilities in small countries were as touchy as boils.

American diplomats saw no need to hold on to the Canal Zone in the face of Panamanian protests. The United States would be able to occupy the Canal within hours in the case of an international crisis. After several false starts at working out a treaty under Johnson and Nixon, in 1978 the Senate narrowly ratified an agreement with Panama to guarantee the permanent neutrality of the canal itself while gradually transferring sovereignty over it to Panama, culminating on December 31, 1999.

JIMMY CARTER AND THE SEGREGATIONISTS

Future president Jimmy Carter had an unusual record for a white Southerner of his age on the segregation issue. In the 1950s, as a successful businessman in Plains, Georgia, he had been asked to join the anti-black White Citizens' Councils, whose membership fee was only $5. Carter replied, "I've got $5 but I'd flush it down the toilet before I'd give it to you."

By signing the treaty, Carter muted Latin American denunciations of "*yanqui imperialismo.*" Nevertheless, right-wing politicians, led by Ronald Reagan, who had begun to campaign for the presidency as soon as Carter was inaugurated, denounced the treaty. In the tradition of Joseph McCarthy, Reagan called it yet another retreat from national pride and greatness by a weak president.

Peacemaking

Carter's greatest achievement was to save the rapprochement between Israel and Egypt that began to take shape in November 1977, when Egyptian President Anwar Sadat, risking the enmity of the entire Arab world, addressed the Israeli Knesset, or parliament, calling for a permanent peace in the Middle East. Rather than cooperate with Sadat, Israeli prime minister Menachem Begin, a former terrorist, seemed to sabotage Sadat's peacemaking efforts by refusing to make concessions commensurate with the Egyptian president's high-stakes gamble.

In 1978, Carter brought Sadat and Begin to Camp David, the presidential retreat in the Maryland woods outside Washington. There, Sadat grew so angry with Begin's refusal to compromise that he actually packed his suitcases. Although Carter was unable to persuade Begin to agree that the West Bank of the Jordan River, which Israel had occupied in 1967, must eventually be returned to Arab rule, he did bring the two men together. In March 1979, Israel and Egypt signed a treaty.

In the United States, the political effect of this dramatic diplomatic turn was to swing American sympathies in the dispute in the direction of Sadat. Begin was unpopular even among American Jews, who traditionally were staunch supporters of Israel. Jewish contributions to Israeli causes dropped sharply. Carter himself betrayed impatience and annoyance with the Begin government and sympathy for the Palestinian refugees. Carter deserved the Nobel Peace Prize for pulling off the Camp David Accords.

The End of Détente

The Nobel Committee may have snubbed him because, while Carter advanced the cause of peace in the Middle East, he abandoned the policy of *détente* that Nixon, Kissinger, and Ford had nurtured. Like Nixon, Carter virtually ignored his first Secretary of State, a professional diplomat, Cyrus Vance, and depended on a White House advisor, Zbigniew Brzezinski, for advice.

Unlike the flexible and opportunistic Kissinger, Brzezinski was an anti-Soviet ideologue. Himself a Polish refugee from Communism, Brzezinski's distrust of the Soviet Union blinded him to opportunities to improve

MINORITY PRESIDENTS

When Jimmy Carter won the forty-eighth presidential election by just a hair under 50 percent of the popular vote, it was the sixteenth time the victor had the support of less than half the voters:

President	Year	Percent
John Quincy Adams	1824	30.5
James K. Polk	1844	49.6
Zachary Taylor	1848	47.4
James Buchanan	1856	45.3
Abraham Lincoln	1860	39.8
Rutherford B. Hayes	1876	48.0
James A. Garfield	1880	48.5
Grover Cleveland	1884	48.5
Benjamin Harrison	1888	47.9
Grover Cleveland	1892	46.1
Woodrow Wilson	1912	41.9
Woodrow Wilson	1916	49.4
Harry S Truman	1948	49.5
John F. Kennedy	1960	49.9
Richard M. Nixon	1968	43.4
Jimmy Carter	1976	50.0

Lincoln would surely not have won the election of 1864 by an absolute majority (or at all) had the Southern states not been in rebellion. Three victorious candidates had fewer popular votes than their defeated opponents: John Quincy Adams in 1824, Rutherford B. Hayes in 1876, and Benjamin Harrison in 1888. In the three-way race in 1992, Arkansas Governor Bill Clinton won a substantial electoral vote victory with only 43 percent of the popular vote.

relations between the nuclear superpowers, or even prompted him to sabotage Soviet overtures. Moreover, whereas Kissinger had been a charmer, Brzezinski was tactless and crude in a world in which protocol and manners can be as important as substance. The foreign ministers of several of America's allies discreetly informed the State Department that they would not deal with him under any circumstances.

But Carter was as obsessively hostile to the Soviet Union as Brzezinski and pre-Nixon policy-makers. He denounced the Soviet Union for trampling on human rights while neglecting to mention the far more brutal policies of American allies such as Iran, Chile, and several Central American states.

In March 1977, Carter interrupted and set back the Strategic Arms Limitation Talks with completely new proposals. Eventually, a new SALT-II treaty was negotiated and signed, but Carter withdrew it from Senate consideration in December 1979 when the Soviet Union invaded Afghanistan to prop up a client government in December 1979. By the end of Carter's term of office, *détente* was dead.

*Anwar Sadat, Jimmy Carter, and Menachem Begin shake hands following the signing of the
Camp David Accords in 1978.*

. . . Plus c'est la même chose

Inflation reached new heights under Carter, almost 20
percent during 1980. By the end of the year, $1 was
worth only 15 cents in 1940 values. That is, on the
average, it took $1 in 1980 to purchase what in 1940
cost 15 cents. The dollar had suffered fully half of this
loss during the 1970s.

Carter could not be faulted for the energy crisis. After
the crunch of 1974, Americans had become energy conscious, replacing their big "gas guzzlers" with more efficient smaller cars. Even this sensible turn contributed
to the nation's economic malaise, however. American
automobile manufacturers had repeatedly refused to develop small energy-efficient cars. For a while in the
1960s, after the success of the Germans' Volkswagen
"Beetle," Ford, General Motors, and Chrysler had made
compact cars. But within a few years, "compacts" had
miraculously grown to be nearly as large as the tradi-

tional "full-sized car." Now, in the crunch of the 1970s,
American auto makers had nothing with which to compete with a flood of Japanese imports: Toyotas, Datsuns,
Hondas, and myriad others. The autmobile buyer's dollars sailed abroad across the Pacific.

Even then, by 1979, oil consumption was higher than
ever, and an even higher proportion of it was being
imported than in 1976. American oil refiners actually
cut back on domestic production, which led many people to wonder if the crisis was genuine or was just a cover
while the industry reaped windfall profits—which it did.
As prices soared, all the refiners reported dividends of
unprecedented size.

The price of electricity also rose, by 200 percent and
more, because so much of it was generated by burning
fossil fuels. The utility companies called for the construction of more nuclear power plants in anticipation of even
higher rate increases. But Americans had become ap-
prehensive about nuclear energy as an alternative to

fossil fuels following an accident and near catastrophe at the Three Mile Island nuclear plant near Harrisburg, Pennsylvania; the release, at about the same time, of *The China Syndrome*, a film that portrayed a similar accident; the discovery that a California reactor that was about to open was crisscrossed with flaws, and built astride a major earthquake fault; and the tremendous costs needed to build safe nuclear power plants.

Embarrassment and Drift

Carter was repeatedly embarrassed by his aides and family, and himself had a talent for foolery. Genuinely suspicious of the Washington Establishment, he surrounded himself with cronies from Georgia who did not quite understand the etiquettes and rituals of the capital. Banker Bert Lance, whom Carter wanted as Budget Director, was identified with petty but unacceptable loan scams. Carter's ambassador to the United Nations, former civil rights activist, Andrew Young, met secretly with leaders of the Palestine Liberation Organization (P.L.O.), an anti-Israel terrorist organization that the United States did not recognize. Carter had to fire him.

The national press, stimulated by its role in uncovering the Watergate scandal to constant muckraking, leaped on every trivial incident—a Carter aide tipsy in a cocktail lounge; the president's "down-home" brother Billy's outrageous opinions—to embarrass the president.

The deeply religious Carter himself frankly but disingenuously told an interviewer for *Playboy* magazine, "I've looked on a lot of women with lust. I've committed adultery in my heart many times," and tittering journalists did not allow him to forget it. In 1980, when Carter's career was on the line, his mother told a reporter, "Sometimes when I look at all my children, I say to myself, 'Lillian, you should have stayed a virgin.' "

A much more serious handicap was the Carter administration's lack of direction. "Carter believes fifty things," one of his advisers said, "but no one thing. He holds explicit, thorough positions on every issue under the sun, but he has no large view of relations between them." In this, Carter was not unlike most Americans. He had the "engineer" mentality that is often described as the American way of thinking: as it arises, face each specific problem and work out a specific solution.

Such pragmatism had worked for Franklin D. Roosevelt. It did not work for Jimmy Carter. With him at the helm, pragmatic government resembled a ship without a rudder, drifting aimlessly. Carter was sensitive to what he called a "national malaise" but only embarrassed himself when he tried to address the amorphous problem. He called 130 prominent men and women from every sector of American life to Washington and, having heard from them, was able to announce only that there was "a crisis of the American spirit"—right back where he started from.

For Further Reading

James Gilbert, *Another Chance: America Since 1945* (1984) provides a general overview of this period; Godfrey Hodgson, *America in Our Time* (1976) deals with the first part of it. However, we are too close to the 1970s to expect too dependable a narrative history of the decade. Many contemporary historians were themselves participants and partisans during these years. Many of the major players are still around trying to shape their posterity.

Many have written memoirs, perhaps as much for monstrous advances from publishers as for self-justification. These accounts can, nevertheless, be useful and are, in any case, valuable sources. See *The Memoirs of Richard Nixon* (1978); George McGovern, *Grassroots* (1977); *A Time to Heal: The Autobiography of Gerald Ford* (1979); Henry A. Kissinger, *White House Years* (1979) and *Years of Upheaval* (1982); Jimmy Carter, *Keeping Faith* (1982); and Rosalynn Carter, *First Lady from Plains* (1984). A fascinating study of Nixon written before his fall is Garry Wills, *Nixon Agonistes* (1970). On Kissinger, see Robert Morris, *Uncertain Greatness: Henry Kissinger and American Foreign Policy* (1977).

Carl Bernstein and Robert Woodward, *All the Presi-*

dent's Men (1974) is by the two reporters for the *Washington Post* that doggedly investigated the Watergate affair and helped bring about Nixon's fall. Perhaps the most insightful analysis of what happened is Arthur M. Schlesinger Jr., *The Imperial Presidency* (1973). See also T. H. White, *Breach of Faith* (1975); Leon Jaworski, *The Right and the Power* (1976); and Sam Ervin, *The Whole Truth: The Watergate Conspiracy* (1980).

On national politics and policy during the 1970s, see David Broder, *The Party's Over* (1972); Samuel Lubell, *The Hidden Crisis in American Politics* (1970); A. J. Reichley, *Conservatives in an Age of Change: The Nixon and Ford Administrations* (1981); Theodore H. White, *The Making of a President 1972* (1973). See Henry Kissinger's memoirs above for foreign policy, and on specific issues: R. L. Garthoff, *Detente and Confrontation* (1985); A. E. Goodman, *The Lost Peace: America's Search for a Negotiated Settlement of the Vietnam War* (1978); on Central America, R. A. Pastor, *Condemned to Repetition* (1987); W. B. Quandt, *Decade of Decision: American Foreign Policy Toward the Arab-Israeli Conflict* (1978); and G. Sick, *All Fall Down: America's Tragic Encounter with Iran* (1985).

"Social Responsibility and Business Ethics"

Louis E. Boone and
David L. Kurtz
from *Contemporary Business*,
Seventh edition

Harcourt Brace, 1994, pages 96–131

4

Social Responsibility and Business Ethics

Learning Goals

1. Explain the concepts of social responsibility and business ethics.
2. Describe the relationship between self-regulation and government regulation.
3. Explain how government regulates business.
4. Discuss the impact of deregulation.
5. Understand how social performance can be evaluated.
6. Outline business's responsibilities to the general public.
7. Identify business's responsibilities to customers.
8. Describe business's responsibilities to employees.
9. Explain business's responsibilities to investors and the financial community.

SENDING JOBS OVERSEAS

Cigna Corporation recently bought an empty factory in this small town and hired 120 locals to process medical claims. Across town, another company hired 40 workers to maintain its worldwide circulation files on computer terminals. In a nearby city, a sparkling $300 million international financial center is taking shape; heavyweight firms such as Arthur Andersen, Deutsche Bank, and General Electric have already rented office space. Says one office manager, "This, to me, is a great growth industry."

The only dark side to this glowing picture: these scenes are taking place in Ireland, not the United States. In fact, American companies have laid off U.S. workers in order to open back-office operations here, in a country where people speak English, computer links offer instant access to American networks, and wages are cheaper. In the 1970s and 1980s, many blue-collar workers lost their jobs to overseas competitors. Today, some labor leaders worry that a similar migration could occur for data processing and other service occupations. Sunil Tagare, vice president of Kessler Marketing Intelligence, predicts that the United States is "going to lose a lot of white-collar jobs."

Other popular "back office" locations are Barbados, Jamaica, the Philippines, and Singapore. But Ireland is one of the leading sites, and not by chance: during the last decade, Ireland invested $3.5 billion to upgrade its telecommunications network, making it much easier for foreign branches to hook up to their home offices. A low tax rate also helps. The biggest attraction, however, is the labor. Ireland has lots of well-educated young people (the country's average age is 28). In this nation with chronic unemployment, when people find a job, they stay. Notes American Edward Superson, who manages the Irish benefit payments office for Massachusetts Mutual Life Insurance Co., "I'll never have any turnover. Nobody is going to leave."

Such economies have drawn many companies to open overseas offices. Wright Investors Service, a Connecticut-based investment manager and database publisher, employs Irish financial analysts at salaries that are less than half what a new M.B.A. grad might make in the United States. American software companies such as Lotus Development Corp., Microsoft, and Ashton-Tate have opened foreign offices where lower paid computer programmers craft software. India's information technology industry has grown 59 percent annually since 1985, and current Indian software exports total about $10 to $15 million each year.

Some observers see the spread of such industries as contributing to a better world in which economies will be more equally developed. Others just see the trend as putting U.S. workers out of a job. Still others think the whole idea of wooing data processing functions may be shortsighted. Scotland, for instance, focuses on luring manufacturing jobs rather than data entry functions. Robert Crawford, North American director of the Locate in Scotland program, notes that new technologies, like electronic scanning of printed material, could make many data entry jobs obsolete: "If you think this will create lots of jobs, you better be careful, because you'll lose them."

Does a company have the right to cut U.S. jobs in order to cut costs? On the other hand, does it have the right to overlook workers in other countries who may need the jobs just as badly as Americans do? Where should it draw the line between making a profit and fulfilling its responsibilities to society? What do you think?[1]

CHAPTER OVERVIEW

Most of us would agree that business should be ethical and socially responsible. As you can see from the opening example, many business decisions can involve making decisions about what a company "owes" to society. We define **social responsibility** as management's consideration of the social and economic effects of its decision making.

Why should a company worry about being socially responsible? Because it does not operate in isolation. In fact, we can think of a business as a set of relationships involving its suppliers, distributors, customers, employees, and other firms—all of the people who are somehow affected by that company's operations, as shown in Figure 4.1. Ultimately, every company interacts with national systems in communications, transportation, education, and health care, as well as global systems of trade agreements, monetary exchanges, factor costs, and environmental restraints.

This means that social and ethical problems, at both national and international levels, affect every company. Many important social issues, such as drug abuse, alcohol abuse, ethnic and gender discrimination, and pollution,

social responsibility
Management philosophy that highlights the social and economic effects of managerial decisions.

Figure 4.1   Extended View of a Business Organization

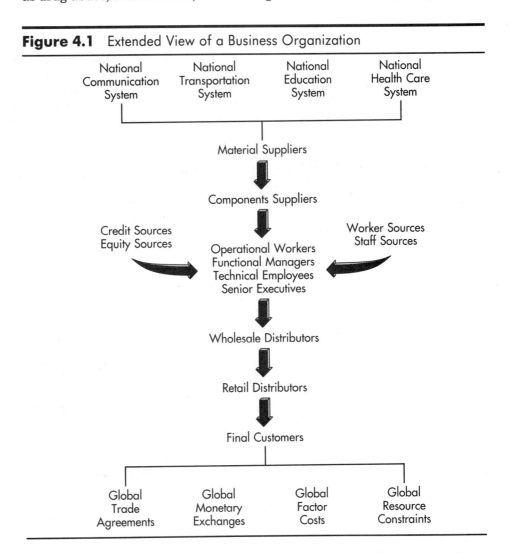

can impact any of these relationships. For instance, social problems affect the quality of a firm's most valuable asset: its work force. Drug abuse and alcoholism can make workers less healthy; discrimination against minorities may restrict the educational opportunities that minority workers receive. This can lead to big financial problems for business. The largest supply expense for General Motors in one year, for instance, is not the purchase of steel or engines, but the purchase of health care coverage for its employees. The biggest problem for many American bioengineering firms is not competition from foreign companies, but the shortage of qualified technical staff.[2] Thus, any steps that a firm can take to resolve social problems can help its employees—and improve its bottom line. Perhaps Jim Casey, founder of United Parcel Service (UPS), said it best nearly 50 years ago: "Are we working for money alone? If so, there is no surer way not to get it."[3]

business ethics
Standards of business conduct and moral values.

In addition to dealing with broad social issues, businesspeople may be required to resolve specific ethical questions. **Business ethics** deals with the right and wrong actions that arise in any work environment. Sometimes a conflict exists between an ideal decision and one that is practical under certain conditions, but it is nonetheless important for companies to evaluate their ethical responsibilities in decision making. A recent study found that 227 out of 300 American and foreign firms had developed written codes of ethics.[4]

Many firms find ethics training to be valuable. Currently about 44 percent of companies provide some type of ethics "training." Usually these programs focus on managers and decision making. Some firms have set up internal groups to identify and resolve long-term issues of economic, social, and environmental issues. While it is difficult to measure precisely the costs and paybacks of such programs, Clorox's long-term planning for social issues is estimated to have saved the company more than $100 million.[5]

SELF-REGULATION OR GOVERNMENT REGULATION?

Corporations frequently have problems regulating themselves. Look at food labels. When consumers became concerned about the amount of fat and cholesterol in their food, many food companies started advertising their products with magic words such as "light," "low-cholesterol," or "low-fat." Some made health-related claims for their products that were without any scientific basis. Things have gotten so confusing that the government—in the form of the Food and Drug Administration (FDA)—finally had to step in. The government issued strict guidelines to food companies about what they could—and could not—put on their labels.

The price of government intervention can be high. One firm, New Jersey–based Great Foods of America spent three years and $10 million building public recognition for its brand name, Heart Beat. The FDA, claiming that the name implied the products were healthier than the competition's, told Great Foods to scrap the trademark.[6]

The Current Status of Social Responsibility and Ethics in U.S. Industry

A recent survey of 1,082 corporate directors and officers, business school deans, and members of Congress found that 94 percent of them believe American business has an ethics problem.[7]

Top-level executives are the source of ethical decision making. It is important for employees to know that ethics and social responsibility are a priority for the firm. Suggestions for achieving an ethical corporate culture include:[8]

- Develop a written code of ethics.

- Establish a "whistle blowing," or reporting, procedure for internal problem solving.

- Involve all employees in identifying ethical issues.

- Include ethical decision making in employees' performance appraisals.

- Publicize executive priorities and efforts related to social issues.

HOW GOVERNMENT REGULATES BUSINESS

Government regulates competition and competitors as well as specific business practices. In the following sections we will look at how government regulation influences contemporary business.

Regulations Affecting Competition

Effective and ongoing competition is the cornerstone of the private enterprise economy. The *laissez-faire* ("hands off") doctrine in effect during the United States' first hundred years was ideal for promoting the rapid growth of the nation geographically, politically, and economically.

But as the country matured, too much economic power became concentrated in too few companies. This led to monopolies in certain basic industries. Mergers further concentrated economic power and caused problems that led to government intervention.

regulated industry
Industry in which competition is either limited or eliminated, and government monitoring substitutes for the market controls.

Approaches to Regulating Competition   When government regulation of competition and other commercial activity came about in the late 1800s, it took two broad forms: the regulation of industry and the enactment of statutes concerning competition. In a **regulated industry,** competition is either limited or eliminated, and close government control is substituted for free competition. Examples of regulated industries are found in public utilities and other industries closely tied to the public interest, where competition would be wasteful or excessive. For example, only one electrical power company can serve a given market. The large capital investment required to construct a pipeline or electric transmission line or to build and operate a nuclear power plant makes this type of regulation appropriate. But the lack of competition can sometimes cause deterioration in services and performance.

Statutes affecting competition and various commercial practices exist at both the state and federal levels. The first effort by the federal government to regulate competition was the Sherman Antitrust Act of 1890. This act, which is very broad, prohibits every contract or conspiracy in restraint of trade. It also declares illegal any action that monopolizes or attempts to monopolize any part of commerce.

tying contract
Agreement that requires a person who wishes to be the exclusive dealer for a product to carry other products of the manufacturer.

interlocking directorate
Situation involving identical or overlapping boards of directors for competitive companies.

consent order
Order under which a firm agrees voluntarily to cease alleged inappropriate conduct.

Additional Competitive Legislation   Another major federal law is the Clayton Act of 1914, which forbids such trade restraints as tying contracts, interlocking directorates, and certain anticompetitive stock acquisitions. A **tying contract** requires a company that wishes to be the exclusive dealer for a manufacturer's products to carry other products of the manufacturer in inventory. The legality of a tying contract is based on whether it restricts competitors from major markets. In an **interlocking directorate,** competitive companies have identical or overlapping boards of directors. Under the Clayton Act, the purchase of stock in another company is also forbidden if it lessens competition.

The Clayton Act is enforced by the antitrust division of the U.S. Department of Justice. Violators are subject not only to criminal fines or imprisonment but also to civil damage suits by competitors or other parties. In some cases, the government allows the accused firm to enter into a **consent order,** under which it agrees voluntarily to cease the conduct the government alleges is inappropriate. The Celler-Kefauver Antimerger Act (1950) amends the Clayton Act to include major asset purchases that decrease competition in an industry.

The Regulation of Specific Business Practices

Government also regulates specific business practices. Table 4.1 shows how selected federal laws impact different aspects of American business.

The Federal Trade Commission Act of 1914 banned unfair competitive practices and set up the Federal Trade Commission (FTC) to administer various statutes applicable to business. The powers and investigative capacities of the FTC have grown rapidly over the years; today it is the major regulatory and enforcement agency in the area of competitive practices. The FTC can sue violators or enter into consent orders with those that agree to cease the questionable practices. The FTC Improvement Act of 1980 gave Congress 90 days to veto any FTC ruling with which it disagrees.

Table 4.1 How Selected Laws Impact Contemporary Business

Name of Law	Area of Impact
Computer Software Copyright Act	Computers and information systems
Environmental Policy Act	Environmental protection
Equal Credit Opportunity Act	Financial management
Equal Pay Act	Human resource management
Federal Reserve Act	Banking
Foreign Corrupt Practices Act	International management
Occupational Safety and Health Act	Production & operations management
Robinson-Patman Act	Pricing
Securities Act	Securities markets
Sherman Antitrust Act	Competitive prices
Small Business Act	Small business
Taft-Hartley Act	Labor-management relations
Tax Reform Act of 1986	Accounting
Uniform Commercial Code	Business transactions
Uniform Partnership Act	Business ownership form

Selected Legislation   Many of the specific business practices regulated by government are covered elsewhere in this text. But there are additional laws with which businesspeople should be familiar. These include:

- The Pure Food and Drug Act (1906) prohibits the adulteration and misbranding of foods and drugs. This act was strengthened by the Food, Drug and Cosmetic Act of 1938 and by the Kefauver-Harris drug amendments of 1962. The latter resulted from the uproar over deformed babies whose handicaps resulted from their mothers taking the drug thalidomide during pregnancy.

A Chemical Waste Management ENRAC® team collects samples of contaminated soil and sludge at the Bog Creek Farm Superfund site in New Jersey. The Environmental Protection Agency is responsible for managing the clean-up of hazardous waste from sites receiving Superfund money and hires companies like Chemical Waste Management for on-site treatment and disposal. The EPA also drafts enviromental regulations that affect business and enforces environmental laws.

- The Robinson-Patman Act (1936) outlaws price discrimination that is not based on cost differences or that injures competition.

- The Wheeler-Lea Act (1938) amends the Federal Trade Commission Act to further outlaw unfair or deceptive acts or practices in business. This act gives the Federal Trade Commission jurisdiction over false or misleading advertising.

- The Fair Packaging and Labeling Act (1967) requires that certain kinds of information, including product identification, name and address of the producer or distributor, and quality information, be disclosed on packages or labels.

- The National Environmental Policy Act (1970) established the Environmental Protection Agency (EPA) and gave it the authority to deal with various types of pollution and those organizations causing pollution.

- The Fair Debt Collections Practices Act (1978) prohibits debt collecting agencies from using harassing, deceptive, and unfair collection practices. The act—which exempts "in house" debt collection organizations such as banks, retailers, and attorneys—provides a maximum $1,000 civil penalty for violations. Specific prohibitions include threats of violence, obscene language, and misrepresentation of consumers' legal rights.

- The Children's Television Act of 1990 requires broadcasters to demonstrate that they are serving the educational and informational needs of children through their programming. The bill also limits the amount of advertising during children's programs. The act is intended to promote the educational potential of television.[9]

The Effects of Deregulation on the Business Environment

deregulation
Elimination of legal restraints on competition.

Deregulation, the movement toward eliminating legal restraints on competition in various industries, has the potential to significantly reshape the legal environment for business. The trend started with the Airline Deregulation Act, which encouraged competition among airlines by allowing them to set their own rates and to add or subtract routes based on their profitability.

The Staggers Rail Act of 1980 altered the Interstate Commerce Commission's power to regulate rail traffic. The law gave rail lines greater freedom to set rates for their freight hauling operations, to sign long-term contracts with freight shippers, and to eliminate unprofitable routes. The federal government also has loosened its grip on the trucking industry, enabling it to adjust its rates to meet market demand and to create new kinds of trucking services.

Deregulation can have a substantial impact on businesses. For example, the Airline Deregulation Act has led to the merger or acquisition of several airlines. Because airlines are now free to select their routes, many have pulled out of smaller markets. As a result, commuter airlines have grown significantly. Commuter airlines such as Britt, Hensen, and Horizon now serve as passenger feeders to major airlines operating out of major airports.

Business Challenges: Ethics and Social Responsibility

FOOD FIGHT

Here's a quiz for everyone who eats food:

1. The term "light" in a food label means that the food inside:
   a. glows
   b. ranges in color from white to tasteful beige
   c. is good for you
   d. means absolutely nothing

2. If a food label says its contents contain "no cholesterol," you can assume that it has no:
   a. taste
   b. sugar
   c. fat
   d. you can't assume anything

   The answer to both questions is *d*. However, if you thought it was *c*, you're not alone. This is a common mistake that a lot of firms are only too happy to exploit.

   For years food companies have dished up highly creative labels that trumpet the healthfulness of their products. This has led to an interesting situation in which taco chips sport "no cholesterol" labels, potato chip packages boast that they're "low in sodium," and boxes of cookies assure us that they are "high in fiber." Some products— Kellogg's Heartwise cereal and Great Foods of America's Heart Beat corn oil—even imply through their names that they're healthier than the competition.

   All this concern about fatty foods does reflect a genuine health problem: High cholesterol levels in the blood can put us at higher risk for two major killers, heart disease and strokes. Studies show that we are more concerned than ever before about our intake

Critics of deregulation often point out the negative effects of the trend. Some say deregulation may lead to higher prices as competitors are eliminated. Others suggest safety may be sacrificed in the name of competition. All of the above are legitimate concerns.

HOW CAN WE EVALUATE SOCIAL PERFORMANCE?

Historically, a company's social performance has been measured by its contribution to the U.S. economy and the employment opportunities it provided. Items such as wage payments were often used to evaluate social performance. While profit and employment are still important, today a firm's social performance is measured by many factors. These include providing equal employment opportunities; respecting the cultural diversity of its employees; responding to environmental concerns; providing a safe, healthy workplace; and producing safe, high-quality products.

A business is also judged by its interactions with the community. Many corporations highlight charitable contributions and community service in their

of cholesterol, fat, and sodium. But do businesses have the right to exploit people's health worries?

No, says the Food and Drug Administration (FDA), the federal agency that is responsible for monitoring the quality of what we put in our mouths. "The public is confused," says Alan Levy, head of consumer research at the FDA's Center for Food Safety and Applied Nutrition. Agency studies show that 40 percent of consumers think that foods labeled "cholesterol-free" are also low in fat. But the depressing truth is that a food may be totally free of cholesterol (found in animal fat)—but loaded with other forms of fat that could be just as bad for you.

The FDA and the Department of Agriculture are cooking up new legal definitions for such popular and misused terms as "natural," "light," and "cholesterol free." The FDA will also issue standards for average serving sizes in 159 categories of food. (Up to now, companies that wanted to proclaim lower calorie or cholesterol counts simply listed smaller serving sizes in their labels). One of the first words to go was "fresh," scattered with cheerful abandon on everything from orange juice to pasta sauce. Already, food giants such as Procter & Gamble, Unilever, Nestlé, and Kraft have wiped the "fresh" claim from products that failed to meet FDA guidelines. Campbell Soup Company, however, can keep its "Prego Spaghetti Sauce Made with Fresh Mushrooms" label; the FDA visited Campbell's Texas plant and found that, yes, the sauce is made with fresh mushrooms.

Some food companies are getting heated about this issue. The margarine industry claims its stuff is healthier than butter and that proposed new rules about disclosing fat content would wipe out its big selling point. "Butter doesn't have to do this," complains Joseph Morris of the National Association of Margarine Manufacturers. Consumer groups, however, laud the FDA's tough new stance. Notes Sharon Lindan, associate director for legal affairs at the Center for Science in the Public Interest, "Consumers are buying products that they think will reduce the risk of heart disease, but which are, in fact, high in fat."

annual reports to demonstrate that they are socially responsible. In addition to its annual report, General Mills publishes *Corporate Citizenship Report,* which focuses on the annual accomplishments of the General Mills Foundation, including donations of money, volunteer work by current employees and retirees, and investment in not-for-profit ventures.[10]

Many Japanese firms, sensitive to their image with the U.S. public, have stepped up their contributions to American charities. At home they also encourage Japanese employees to participate in social service programs that allow them to take paid leave to do volunteer work. A manager at Omron Tateishi Electronics Company notes that social performance—"to be benevolent in the community"—is becoming a more important factor in a firm's image. He comments, "It is becoming a rule in the market that a benevolent company is the company that can make money."[11]

Conducting a Social Audit

social audit
Internal examination of a firm's social responsibility programs.

Some firms measure social performance with a **social audit,** a formal procedure that identifies and evaluates all company activities relating to social

issues such as employment practices, environmental protection, conservation, and philanthropy. The social audit informs management on what the company is doing and how well it is doing. Based on this information, management may take steps to revise current programs or develop new ones.

Many firms are now developing other ways to assess social responsibility. General Motors, for example, publishes an annual Public Interest Report that outlines the corporation's socially oriented initiatives. GM sponsors research into solar-powered vehicles, awards engineering scholarships to college students, buys its parts from minority-owned suppliers when possible, and funds educational shows on public television.[12]

External Evaluations of Social Responsibility

Outside groups may conduct their own evaluations of business. Various environmental, church, and public-interest groups have created standards of corporate performance.

These evaluations are available to the general public. The Council on Economic Priorities produces publications such as *The Better World Investment Guide,* which rates 100 different firms according to their track records on various social issues (including environmental impact, nuclear weapons contracts, community outreach, and advancement of women and minorities). The Council recommends investing (or not investing!) in these firms based on their social performance.[13]

Other Signs of Social Responsibility

Many firms find that consumers "evaluate" their social performance financially—by either buying (or not buying) their goods and services. Visa and

MasterCard, for instance, have introduced "affinity cards" that donate a percentage of the cardholder's bill to a particular conservation group. MCI woos new customers with the promise of donating 5 percent of their monthly telephone bills to any of four major environmental groups; one of these groups, the Nature Conservancy, earned over $150,000 from the MCI program in its first year.[14]

Public opinion can be powerful. For instance, the Ontario (Canada) Trappers Association recently filed for bankruptcy. The Association, which brokered about 75 percent of the raw fur sold in Ontario, saw its profits plummet following protests from animal rights activists. Both the Canadian and Ontario governments, responding to community pressure from animal rights groups, refused to bail out the failing organization.[15]

BUSINESS'S SOCIAL RESPONSIBILITY

Just what does business owe to society? A company, after all, must make money in order to survive in the marketplace. If it goes bankrupt, many people could suffer, including employees, customers, and their families. What happens when, in order to stay in business, a company does things which could be considered harmful?

The social responsibilities of business can be classified according to its relationships to the general public, customers, employees, business associates, and investors and the financial community. (Keep in mind that these relationships often stretch beyond national boundaries.) We will look at each of these categories in the rest of the chapter.

RESPONSIBILITIES TO THE GENERAL PUBLIC

The responsibilities of business to the general public include: dealing with public health issues, protecting the environment, and developing the quality of the work force.

Public Health Issues

Smoking   Smoking has many documented health risks: 96 percent of people who die from lung cancer are smokers, and smoking is one of the three top risk factors involved in heart disease and stroke.[16] The message is getting through to many Americans; fewer than 30 percent of us smoke today (down from a high of 42 percent in 1967).

To tobacco companies, however, this good news is actually bad news, and they are fighting back in several ways. For one, they are targeting products to specific market segments, such as the "Joe Camel" campaign aimed at young male puffers. They are also concentrating on overseas markets where they meet less government resistance. U.S. companies spend millions of dollars annually to court Asia's $90-billion-a-year cigarette market, and their market share is growing. Foreign governments have often been reluctant to interfere because tax revenues from American brand sales are so profitable. But, as Judith Mackay, head of Hong Kong's Council on Smoking and Health, points

Good beer keeps its head.
You should too.

This Memorial Day, remember. Think when you drink. *Miller*

This Miller beer ad promotes responsible drinking. Through ad campaigns encouraging moderation and designated drivers, Miller and other major brewers are working to increase public awareness of the hazards of drinking too much and decrease public acceptance of drunkenness.

out, "Any government that thinks it is making money from taxing cigarettes has not paused to consider the cost in mortality [death], hospital care, and lost productivity."[17]

Alcohol Abuse   Companies involved in selling alcoholic beverages face similar ethical questions. Alcohol abuse is a great social problem in the United States. Motor vehicle accidents are a major killer, and many serious crashes are caused by drunk drivers. Almost 400,000 people are being treated for alcoholism in treatment centers across the country.[18] Alcohol abuse has also been linked to serious diseases such as cirrhosis of the liver. Some brewers have tried to counter these arguments by sponsoring advertising campaigns that promote moderation: "Know when to say when," and, "Think when you drink." However, public opposition to alcohol advertising is steadily growing. Many consumers view both alcohol and tobacco advertising as socially irresponsible.[19]

AIDS   AIDS represents a different type of challenge to business; while no one accuses industry of causing AIDS, firms must nonetheless deal with its consequences. AIDS (acquired immunodeficiency syndrome) is a fatal disease that breaks down the body's ability to defend itself against illness and infection. What is especially dangerous about AIDS is the long time (typically five years) between someone's first exposure to the AIDS virus and actual development of the disease. While people during this period may not show any symptoms of AIDS and probably don't even know they have it, they are still carriers who can give the disease to someone else. It is this large pool of unknown carriers that accounts for the rapid spread of the disease. In 1982 only 838 cases of AIDS were reported; by the end of 1991, nearly 200,000 cases had been reported.[20]

The rapid spread of AIDS means that companies will increasingly find themselves educating their employees about it and dealing with employees who have the deadly disease. Health care for AIDS patients can be incredibly expensive, and small companies could have trouble paying health care coverage. Do companies have the right to test potential employees for the AIDS virus? Some people feel this violates the rights of job applicants. Others feel that firms have a responsibility not to place AIDS patients in jobs where they could possibly infect members of the general public. These are difficult questions in which a business must balance the rights of individuals against the rights of society in general.

Protecting the Environment

ecology
Study of the relationship between living things and their environment.

Ecology and environmental issues continue to become more important to the public. **Ecology**—the study of the relationships between living things and their environment—is now a legal as well as a societal issue for managers to consider.

We all accept the idea that we should maintain an ecologically sound environment, but achieving this goal requires tradeoffs that we are not always willing to make. Although we worry about oil spills from supertankers, we insist on being able to buy all the gasoline we want, and at reasonable prices. Coal-burning boilers, once converted to oil-burning furnaces in order to cut air pollution, are being used again because coal is relatively plentiful in the United States. Obviously, ecological goals are important. However, it is essential that we coordinate these goals with other societal and economic objectives. There may not be quick or easy answers.

maquiladoras
Plants located along the U.S.–Mexico border.

pollution
Tainting or destroying of a natural environment.

Pollution   People living in the 33 counties along the Rio Grande River between the United States and Mexico have significantly higher rates of liver and gall bladder cancer. The rate of hepatitis between Brownsville and El Paso, Texas, is six times higher than the U.S. average. Children born along the U.S.–Mexico border are more likely to have birth defects.

What's going on? Many American companies have built manufacturing and assembly plants in northern Mexico, where wages are lower, workers are plentiful, and pollution laws are less strict. Almost 2,000 such plants, called **maquiladoras,** now employ about half a million people. These plants pump $3.5 billion annually into Mexico's economy and give Mexican citizens steady jobs. But the plants bring something else: pollution.

Pollution—tainting or destroying a natural environment—is the major ecological problem today. Health care workers suspect that the higher rates of disease along the border result from industrial wastes being released into rivers, pumped into the air, and scattered in open dump sites.

The problems don't stop at the border, since pollutants dumped in Mexican rivers often end up in the United States. Toxic wastes in the Tijuana River flow north to empty into the Pacific Ocean near San Diego. Almost three miles of shoreline have been closed, and local officials estimate the closed beach has cost the area more than $100 million a year in lost tourism. At least 12 wells in Arizona have been closed due to contamination from Mexican underground water. More than 100 million gallons of raw sewage, including heavy metals and pesticides, are dumped into the Rio Grande River each day; the river's fish contain dangerously high levels of copper and mercury.

Some companies, such as Union Carbide, regulate themselves and have been praised for treating both their employees and the environment responsibly. Why don't more of the maquiladoras do the same? The answer is simple: money. Under a binational agreement, maquiladoras are supposed to ship hazardous wastes back to the United States for disposal and to notify the EPA (Environmental Protection Agency). But shipping a single 55-gallon drum of hazardous waste can cost anywhere from $150 to $1,000. As a result, many maquiladoras dispose of their waste more cheaply—and illegally. Mexico cannot afford to spend much on enforcing environmental laws, and in fact the Mexican government, eager to encourage industrialization, may be willing to overlook some abuses. The U.S. government may have to step in to force all the maquiladoras to comply with U.S.-style pollution standards. In the meantime, says one physician, "This is a public-health disaster waiting to happen."[21]

This situation highlights two crucial questions that society faces: Are the benefits of cleaning up pollution worth the costs? And, are we willing to pay now for a better environment in the future?

The Greenhouse Effect and Acid Rain   When we burn fossil fuels such as coal and oil for energy, carbon dioxide and sulfur enter our atmosphere. Both of these chemicals cause environmental problems.

greenhouse effect
Situation where carbon dioxide traps heat in the earth's atmosphere.

The extra carbon dioxide collects in the atmosphere and traps heat, leading to the so-called **greenhouse effect** which keeps the earth's temperature warm enough to support life. However, during this century the amount of carbon dioxide in the atmosphere has soared; we are burning more fossil fuels than ever before. Many scientists fear that this could result in global warming, with disastrous results.

acid rain
Rain containing sulfuric acid resulting from the burning of fossil fuels.

Meanwhile, the sulfur from fossil fuels combines with water vapor in the air to form sulfuric acid. The rain that results is called **acid rain.** Acid rain kills fish and trees, and can pollute the groundwater from which we get our drinking water. In the northeastern United States, rain and snow are now about 100 times more acid than normal. Acid rain is also dangerous because wind can carry the sulfur all over the world. Sulfur from factories in the United States is damaging Canadian forests, and pollution from London smokestacks is destroying the forests and lakes of Sweden. Since the "polluter" and the "polluted" may be far apart, it has been difficult to get countries to agree on what should be done. The Clean Air Act revisions of 1990 are a first step toward resolving this serious environmental threat.[22]

The Vanishing Rain Forests   We are destroying forests in more direct ways, too; more than 1.5 acres of tropical rain forest are being destroyed each second. Many of these trees are cut down for firewood, while others are cut down to clear land for farming. (Sadly, the soil is so poor in tropical areas that it is soon worn out, and people continually cut down more rain forest in order to cultivate new land.) The destruction of the rain forest is a tremendous environmental threat because this area of the world is so rich in plant and animal life. At our present rate of destruction, many tropical plants will become extinct before we even discover them. This would be a huge loss. Consider that our entire food

The Body Shop and Ben and Jerry's Homemade are a few of the 55 original members of Businesses for Social Responsibility (BSR). The advocacy group was organized to promote the philosophy that businesses can be profitable as well as sensitive to the environment, to workers, and to society. Other members include Stride Rite shoes, Reebok International, Lotus Development, and Esprit. Their concerns include jobs in the inner city, improved management—worker relations to increase productivity, and tougher environmental legislation.

supply is based primarily on only 20 kinds of plants, and that many of our most important medicines come from plants. Losing such a large proportion of the world's forest would deprive us of many potential new foods and medicines.[23]

The Recycling Solution   Every time we throw away a plastic box, a newspaper, or a glass bottle, we are adding to the world's trash problem. Garbage just never seems to die; it stays intact in landfills for years, and we're running out of places to put it.

recycling
Reprocessing of used materials for reuse.

An important solution is **recycling**—reprocessing used materials so they can be reused. Recycling could provide much of the raw material we need for manufacturing, but we need to do a lot more of it. McDonald's, for instance, has scrapped its old polystyrene containers and now wraps its hamburgers in paper. The fast-food chain is also testing 42 ways that it hopes will reduce its garbage by 80 percent, such as reusable lids for salad containers and pump-style dispensers for ketchup and mustard. H.J. Heinz spent $8 million over three years to develop a squeezable, recyclable ketchup bottle. Procter & Gamble is trying to persuade consumers to go for refills rather than new containers. After customers use up P&G's Downy fabric softener in its large plastic bottle, they can buy concentrate in a small carton that will fill the old bottle when mixed with water. The refill cuts waste by 75 percent and is about 40 cents cheaper than buying a new plastic jug.[24]

While most plastics recycling efforts have focused on containers, some plastics manufacturers are starting to recycle as well. General Electric is testing a program to reclaim the plastic computer housings it sells to Digital Equipment Corp., melt and mix the plastic with 48 percent new plastic, and produce roof panels. The panels have been installed on two McDonald's restaurants in Chicago. McDonald's has committed to spending $100 million each year on recycled plastics for building and remodeling its U.S. restaurants.[25]

green marketing
Marketing strategy that promotes an environmentally safe product.

Just What Is Green Anyway?   Many companies find that protecting the environment helps sell their products. This has spurred the rise of **green marketing**—marketing products as environmentally sound. The problem is that the definition of what's best for the environment can change.

Take the diaper debate. Disposable diapers are convenient but can pile up in landfills. However, it's not clear that reusable cloth diapers are any better. One study found that washing reusable diapers used up to 9,620 gallons of water per child each year; if you use a diaper service, the delivery trucks pollute the air.

Responding to consumers' environmental concerns, Mobil introduced a biodegradable version of its Hefty plastic trash bags—and proudly advertised the fact. But the bags biodegrade only if exposed to open air and sunlight, and over 90 percent of them end up buried in landfills without light and oxygen. The Environmental Defense Fund boycotted the bags, and several states sued Mobil for misleading advertising.

Part of the problem is that there are few legal guidelines. Says Mary Gade, director of the Illinois Environmental Protection Agency, "So many claims are unsubstantiated, misleading, and confusing." A group of 1,000 major corporations has asked the Federal Trade Commission to issue guidelines on environmental advertising. The Environmental Protection Agency is developing standard definitions for the terms *recyclable* and *recycled content*. In the meantime, businesses must be aware that green marketing can be risky. Says David Marshall, vice president for marketing and sales at Mobil, "The biggest thing we've learned in this whole environmental issue is that today's answer may not be tomorrow's. Companies have to be quick on their feet."[26]

Conserving and Developing Energy Sources   We can divide the complex topic of energy into its short-term and long-term issues. In the short run, the

conservation
Preservation of declining energy resources.

problem is one of **conservation**—preserving our declining energy resources. We've seen that burning fossil fuels damages the environment. In any case, our supplies of these fuels are limited and will eventually run out.

Scientists estimate, for instance, that 75 percent of the electricity produced in the United States and Canada is wasted through the use of inefficient appliances. Developing and using more efficient motors, lights, and refrigerators—to name just a few items—could save a lot of energy and reduce pollution.[27]

In addition to conserving current energy sources, we need to develop long-term solutions involving alternative energy sources. Nuclear power, wind, sun, synthetic fuels, and even garbage and other waste products have all been suggested as substitutes for fossil fuels.

California, for instance, is phasing in new emission standards for cars; the goal is that all new cars sold by 2003 will produce no more than one-fifth the pollution spewed by today's automobiles. These strict new guidelines are driving car makers to find alternatives to gasoline; batteries, methanol, and natural gas are some of the candidates. Chrysler will soon start building cars that can run on either gasoline or methanol. GM plans to start selling its first mass-produced electric car around 1995. Automakers are researching even more experimental ideas, such as vehicles powered by fuel cells that use a chemical reaction to produce electricity from methanol, natural gas, or hydrogen.[28]

Developing the Quality of the Work Force

In the past, a nation's wealth has often been thought to consist of its money, production equipment, or natural resources. A country's true wealth, however, lies in its people. An educated, skilled work force is the most valuable asset we can have. It is becoming increasingly clear that in order to remain competitive, American business must assume more responsibility for developing the quality of its work force.

A report from the Hudson Institute, a not-for-profit research organization, identifies several major challenges for American business.[29] These include:

- **Boosting service workers' productivity.** While productivity in the manufacturing sector has risen, productivity in service industries has not. This is crucial to the country's competitiveness since services account for a much larger share of the economy. The Hudson Institute report recommends that more service industries should operate more like manufacturing businesses and be regulated by competition, and that businesses should invest in technologies that could boost productivity.

- **Maintaining an aging work force.** In general, America's work force is aging while the economy and rapidly changing technologies demand increasing flexibility from workers. In many firms worker retraining is limited to managers and technical specialists. Businesses must encourage all employees to continually "reinvest" in their own education to avoid becoming obsolete.

- **Reconciling the often conflicting needs of workers' families with their careers.** In 1960 only 11 percent of women with children under the age of six worked outside the home; today 52 percent do. The United States has become a society in which everyone is expected to work, but for the most part business has not adjusted to this change. Companies must support programs that allow male and female employees to meet the needs of both employers and families. These could include parental leave and better day care.

- **Integrating minorities fully into the economy.** Some minority workers lack access to the educational, job training, and employment assistance opportunities available to other Americans. Private employers are often effective providers of cost-effective, technology-based training programs. Educational systems developed at the work site could play a key role in giving minority workers a "second chance."

- **Improving the education and skills of all workers.** A century ago, no one thought factory workers needed to go to high school. Relatively few people went to college, and few jobs required degrees.

  Between now and 2000, however, most new jobs will require a college education. Many professions will demand 10 years of study beyond high school, and even the least skilled jobs will require a certain level of reading, computing, and thinking. Business must encourage students to stay in school, continue their education, and develop their skills.

RESPONSIBILITIES TO CUSTOMERS

consumerism
Public demand for business to consider consumer wants and needs in making its decisions.

Consumer demands are another social responsibility issue facing business. **Consumerism**—the demand that business give proper consideration to consumer wants and needs in making its decisions—is a major social and economic movement. Ralph Nader is a leading force in this trend.

Since the emergence of consumerism a few decades ago, consumer groups have sprung up throughout the country. Some concentrate on an isolated situation, such as rate hikes by a local public utility, while others attack broader issues. The net effect has been passage of numerous consumer protection laws. There is little doubt that more such laws will be passed in the years ahead which will have a big impact on business.

President Kennedy's Statement of Consumer Rights

President John F. Kennedy presented an excellent description of the consumer's rights in a 1962 speech to Congress. He outlined four specific points:

1. Consumers have the right to be safe.

2. Consumers have the right to be informed.

3. Consumers have the right to choose.

4. Consumers have the right to be heard.

Much of the post-1962 consumer legislation is based on these statements. In fact, many companies go to considerable effort to ensure that consumer complaints receive a full hearing. Ford Motor Company, for example, set up a consumer appeals board to resolve service complaints.

RESPONSIBILITIES TO EMPLOYEES

Businesses are finding that workers—and communities—increasingly look to them to handle a number of needs such as child care. Business's responsibilities to its employees are far ranging. Issues include family leave, equal employment opportunity, sexual harassment, sexism, and comparable worth.

Family Leave

When Wendie Ulku decided to adopt a child from Colombia, her employer helped. Control Data Corporation in Minneapolis helped defray the costs of her six-week stay in Colombia and gave her another six weeks to stay home with the baby. Says Wendie, "I was able to get on a plane and leave knowing my job was secure."

As the number of families with two wage earners increases, conflicts between employees' responsibilities at home and at work may clash. Some employees may care for elderly parents or relatives, while others find themselves juggling child care or other family crises with the demands of their jobs. **Family leave**—giving employees a leave of absence from work in order to deal with family matters—has become an important issue for many workers.

family leave
Giving employees a leave of absence from work in order to deal with family matters.

Some employers worry that a leave of absence could disrupt the firm's operations. However, a survey by the Families and Work Institute found that 91 percent of the firms who granted family leave did not find it to be a problem; most reported no rise in administrative or training expenses.[30]

Ensuring Equal Employment Opportunity

Equal Employment Opportunity Commission (EEOC)
Federal commission created to increase job opportunities for women and minorities and help eliminate job discrimination.

The Civil Rights Act (1964) ruled that discriminatory practices are illegal, and Title VII of the act prohibits discrimination in employment. The **Equal Employment Opportunity Commission (EEOC)** was created to increase job opportunities for women and minorities and to help end job discrimination based on race, color, religion, sex, or national origin in any personnel action. Minorities defined by the EEOC include African Americans (not of Hispanic origin), Hispanics, Asians or Pacific Islanders, and Native Americans or Alaskan Natives.

The goals of the EEOC have been strengthened by passage of the Equal Pay Act (1963), the Age Discrimination in Employment Act (1967), the Equal Employment Opportunity Act (1972), the Pregnancy Discrimination Act (1978), and numerous executive orders.

More recently, the Civil Rights Act of 1991 has given female, minority, and disabled employees more power to fight discrimination. Proponents also hope the new law will resolve cases more quickly. Complaints about job discrimination must still be filed with the EEOC or fair-employment agencies

in most states. However, federal and state agencies are often backlogged, and it may take the EEOC eight months to process a case. With the new law, employees who feel they've been discriminated against can request a "right to sue" letter from the EEOC and go to court without waiting for the agency's verdict.

Many of America's 36 million handicapped citizens fight discrimination every day: Only one-third of disabled people who can work actually hold jobs. The 1991 Civil Rights Act and the Americans with Disabilities Act make it easier to challenge such potentially discriminatory practices as requiring physical endurance tests for job applicants. Section 503 of the Vocational Rehabilitation Act (1973) requires all firms having U.S. government contracts of $2,500 or more to establish programs that promote career advancement for disabled workers and to provide physical access for them.[31]

Vietnam Veterans   The Vietnam Era Veterans Readjustment Assistance Act (1974) provides similar requirements for employers with federal government contracts of $10,000 or more. Such employers are required to protect the employment of disabled veterans as well as able-bodied Vietnam era veterans by recruiting and promoting qualified veterans. In addition, these firms are required to list job openings with local and state employment services.

Affirmative Action Programs   The EEOC helps an employer set up an **affirmative action program** to increase job opportunities for women, minorities, and other protected categories. Such programs include analyzing the present work force and setting specific hiring and promotion goals, with target dates, in areas where women, minorities, and others are underutilized. Penalties for violations can also be imposed.

affirmative action program
Program set up by businesses to increase opportunities for women and minorities.

Removing Employment Barriers for Women   Until the mid-1960s, the classified advertisement sections of almost every U.S. newspaper contained two categories: "Jobs-Male" and "Jobs-Female." Equal employment opportunity laws eliminated these sex-based distinctions. The laws also prohibit use of job specifications that limit employment to men. Employers are not allowed to exclude women applicants unless the firm can prove the job requires physical skills the women do not have.

A second result was a change in job titles. When the U.S. Department of Labor revised its five-pound *Dictionary of Occupational Titles,* many of the sexist job titles in its 15,000 entries vanished. Gone are such terms as *fireman, mailman,* and *housewife;* replacing them are *fire fighter, mail carrier,* and *homemaker.*

Multicultural Diversity

The second-grade teacher thought it was a straightforward question for the class: "There are four blackbirds sitting in a tree. You take a slingshot and shoot one of them. How many are left?"

"Three," says a seven-year-old European. "Four minus one leaves three."

"Zero," answers a seven-year-old African. "If you shoot one bird, the others will fly away."

Who is right? Both and neither, depending on how you look at it. These two second-graders approached the question from different cultural points of view. For the first one the problem represented a hypothetical situation, an abstract question that dealt with numbers. For the second child, the birds formed a social group, and their behavior could be predicted.

Like the American classroom, the American workplace is changing. By the year 2000 women will make up about 47 percent of all workers, while minorities and immigrants will hold 26 percent of all jobs. By the end of the decade white males will account for only 32 percent of those entering the work force. The rich cultural variety that makes up American life as we know it is called **multicultural diversity.** Diversity has always been part of American culture, as new immigrants enter and become part of U.S. society. The challenge for U.S. business is to learn how to manage this diversity creatively, to benefit from the different viewpoints, experiences, and talents of the various cultures in our society.

Dealing with a culturally diverse work force means understanding what motivates employees and how they function best. Says consultant Iris Randall, "When you're working in a corporation, if you're going to empower someone different from you in order to get the best out of them, you've got to look at and understand their behavior."

The answers may differ for different cultural groups. The Personal Profile System shown in   developed by Performax Systems International, has identified four styles of behavior. People with D, or dominant behavior,

multicultural diversity
Racial and cultural blend within a society.

Business Challenges: Valuing Diversity

IS JAPANESE MANAGEMENT BETTER?

Nationwide, more than 350,000 Americans now work for Japanese companies, and that number could double by the end of the decade. A lot has been written—some of it in this textbook—about the differences between Japanese and American business practices, and how some of these differences may give Japan a competitive edge. But what about Japanese management? Is life for American employees better or worse under their new Asian managers?

The answer is: It depends. While many Japanese firms have been successful in applying their manufacturing techniques in the United States, Japanese management philosophy has proven harder to transplant.

Many communities appreciate the money, ideas, and business practices of the Japanese newcomers. "Without the Japanese we'd be a Rust Belt," says an American sales manager at one Japanese-owned firm, Setex, in Troy, Ohio. An American supervisor at another factory praises the safety checks at Setex: "It's a well-run plant." (He toured the Setex factory and borrowed several ideas for his own company.)

On the other hand, some American workers have taken their Japanese bosses to court, charging breach of employment or discrimination. "The vast majority [of these suits] stem from complaints by white-collar managers over the way they were treated and managed," says John Gillespie, a Japanese-American relations specialist at Clarke Consulting Group.

Americans, who come from many different backgrounds, adapt readily to the idea that a culturally diverse work force offers advantages. This is a foreign concept in Japan.

John Rehfeld, the American president of Japanese-owned Seiko Instruments USA, notes that the Japanese draw sharp distinctions between "insiders" and "outsiders." The concept of insider begins with the family and extends to the school, the company, and the country, leading to a strong "old boy" network in each firm. Many Japanese companies will not hire outsiders (employees from other firms) for any positions beyond entry level. Most disturbing for Americans, a non-Japanese is always an outsider, no matter how long he or she may have worked for the company. Says an American supervisor of his bosses at Japanese-owned Ikeda Interior Systems (Ohio), "They really don't want your input. They don't bring you into the decision-making process, just implementation."

Under Japanese management, female employees are outsiders with a capital *O*. Rehfeld notes that in Japan, "attitudes and institutions overwhelmingly work against the effective use of women professionals. . . I've often seen very competent women who have graduated from the top universities do little more than serve tea. Most of the 'career moves' I've seen women make are to graduate slowly from tea servers to note takers to administrative assistants." To make things worse, Japanese tradition forbids a senior executive from having a woman report directly to him; this means an entire level of management is off-limits to women. If a woman with children tries to find work, she'll find it very difficult: There are no day-care centers or baby-sitting services, and working mothers are frowned upon. Some women feel that Japanese managers bring these attitudes with them to American companies.

Gillespie believes that the Japanese have found it difficult to figure out which management models to adopt in supervising people from other cultures. This issue, he says, is "perhaps the most urgent challenge facing Japanese multinationals in the 1990s."

says Randall, "make decisions rapidly. They're interested in results, the bottom line." While some people from all cultural backgrounds fall into this category, most often it seems to include people with a Euro-American heritage, particularly white males.

The second behavior style is I, for influencers. "African-Americans, Hispanics and women in general exhibit more I behavior," believes Randall. "These types are very verbal. They are good at influencing and persuading. They are the cheerleaders: 'I can, you can, we can make a difference.'"

C stands for the cautious style, often seen among Asians: "They are taught not to shoot from the hip, not to be confrontational, always to think before they speak, to make sure they are right."

Finally, S, or steady behavior, refers to workers who are reliable and "hang in there. They are good team players and have no trouble recognizing the person in charge, whereas D-behavior types all act as if they are the boss." Randall feels many Native Americans exhibit S behavior.

Of course, it is important to avoid stereotypes; not all members of these cultural groups will show these particular behaviors. However, developing a better understanding of people's cultures and behaviors will help business people manage culturally diverse staffs more effectively. Says Terry Simmons, a consultant in corporate human resources,

> If 30 percent of your workers are minorities and if almost half are women, we're talking about the vast majority of your workers. If these folks do not feel they are really part of the team, don't feel they really can get to the top, don't feel their ideas are cherished and valued, then a couple of things happen. One is they'll leave and go to an organization where they are valued. Or they leave mentally and motivationally but stay on and just aren't as productive as they could be.

LINCOLN SAVINGS BANK

➤ Paul Nolan is a white, male business executive. As director of corporate training for the Lincoln Savings Bank in New York, he admits that he's always been a classic D type. However, he has been through several multicultural training sessions and believes he is a better manager because of it.

> Even now, when I speak in front of all white males, I'm very structured, very aggressive. But if I had the same discussion before a partly, say, Chinese group, I'd ask open-ended questions, such as "Tell me what you think about this" instead of "This is what I think."

Before the diversity seminars, he often started classes by saying what he thought and then expected the students to challenge him. The Asians on his staff, in particular, would just sit silently. Paul now poses his questions differently, and listens for answers differently:

> It used to be that I always knew the question I was going to ask and what I wanted in terms of a response. But I found that by structuring the classes that way I could be alienating some participants. Latinos, for instance, respond to a style that's a little less structured. I still like structure and I still want to get a certain answer, but now I also want to know why people think the way they do. I've learned to view problem solving in new ways because of the different perspectives other cultures bring to it.

Paul's new approach has brought results: "The participation rate among the minorities on staff has risen dramatically. It almost matches that of the other employees." ◄

Respecting employees' cultural differences is a vital part of management in the 1990s. Says Terry Simmons, "Teams that work together are the more effective teams. That ought to go directly to your bottom line." R. Roosevelt Thomas, Jr., executive director of the American Institute for Managing Diversity at Atlanta's Morehouse College, sums it up: "This is no longer a question of common decency. It is a question of business survival."[32]

Eliminating Discrimination against Older Workers

In the past, many large firms required employees to retire at age 65. The arbitrary choice of 65 as the retirement age appears to have been based on tradition. It was first proposed by nineteenth-century German leader Otto von Bismarck. Also, 65 was named as the eligibility age for benefits when the Social Security Act was passed in 1935. As a result, many private pension plans incorporated 65 as the age for retirement.

Mandatory retirement ages were criticized for years as being unfair to older workers. After all, Galileo, Sigmund Freud, and Thomas Edison made some of their most notable contributions to society when they were past age 60. Mandatory retirement also seems unrealistic, given the general maturing of the American work force that will occur in the next 10 years. Between now and 2000, the number of Americans aged 35 to 44 will grow by almost 16 percent, while the number of Americans between 45 and 54 will jump by 46 percent.[33]

The passage of the Age Discrimination in Employment Act prohibited employers from using age as a basis for employment decisions (hiring, promotions, or separations). The original law was designed to protect workers aged 40 to 65, but in 1986 the law was amended to apply to all persons aged 40 and older.

Sexual Harassment

When a law professor accused Supreme Court Justice nominee Clarence Thomas of sexually harassing her, the resulting hearings focused the country's attention on this issue more than ever before. In one poll 38 percent of women said a supervisor had sexually harassed them on the job.

sexual harassment
Inappropriate actions of a sexual nature.

Sexual harassment refers to inappropriate actions of a sexual nature. Legally, there are two categories of sexual harassment: (1) unwelcome advances and requests for sexual favors that affect promotions and raises; and (2) a "hostile" work environment in which an employee feels hassled or degraded because of unwelcome flirting, lewd comments, or obscene jokes. The courts have ruled that allowing sexual materials, such as pinup calendars and pornographic magazines, at the workplace can create a "hostile" atmosphere that interferes with an employee's ability to do the job.

The Civil Rights Act of 1991 has given more employees the ability to fight sexual harassment. For the first time, women (and men) will be able to win damages for intentional sexual harassment. The law also allows judges to force the losing party to pay the fees of the winner's expert witnesses, an often crucial—but expensive—component of winning a complex harassment case.

Maximum verdicts, however, are controlled by a sliding scale: from $50,000 for companies with 15 to 100 workers, to $300,000 for firms with more than 500 employees.

Even with the new law, however, battling sexual harassment in the courts can be a painful, lengthy process. Lori Sabin sued her former employer because he hassled her on the job; when she insisted that he leave her alone, he gave her a poor evaluation. Witnesses backed Lori up, but even with a strong case, her settlement totaled less than $40,000. And while the company eventually fired the harasser, Sabin had to leave a job she liked for a lower-paid position that she found less interesting. "I'm not unhappy that I sued," she says, "but it doesn't feel like much of a victory."

"With or without a civil rights bill, it's unlikely that people will race to court with complaints that will expose them to criticism and ridicule," notes Philadelphia lawyer Nancy Ezold. "For most people it still won't be worth it."

The new law does make it more important for employers to resolve sexual harassment problems in-house, avoiding lawsuits if possible. Many firms have established anti-harassment policies and employee-education programs. Effective harassment prevention programs include (1) issuing a specific policy prohibiting sexual harassment, (2) developing a complaint procedure employees can follow, (3) creating a work atmosphere that encourages sexually harassed staffers to come forward, and (4) investigating and resolving complaints immediately, and taking disciplinary action against harassers.[34]

Sexism

sexism
Discrimination against either sex, primarily occurring against women.

Sexual harassment is often part of a much bigger problem: **sexism,** or discrimination against women. A study of 94 large corporations found that while women account for 37 percent of the employees, only 17 percent of them are in management positions—and a scant 3 percent of top executives are women. Despite the publicity given to women who enter traditionally "male" fields such as medicine and law, Figure 4.2 shows that the leading occupations for American women today are not that different from the top "female" jobs of 1940.

Some examples of sexism are blatant: a woman being paid less than a male colleague to perform the same job; a male employee being promoted over a female with more experience. Other instances are more subtle: The only female in a work group may not be introduced to a client, or doesn't get a work assignment when a manager passes them out. Such subtle snubs are known as *microinequities*. Microinequities may be deliberate or accidental. A woman may not even be aware of them at first, but over time they can significantly impact opportunities for women at a company.

A report by the U.S. Labor Department notes that many women's routes to corporate success are blocked by a *glass ceiling* of microinequities and more blatant discrimination. In fact, says Labor Secretary Lynn Martin, "The glass ceiling is much lower than we expected." The report gives several reasons. For one, many corporate jobs rely on recruitment by word of mouth and networking; this tends to exclude women and minorities. Women often have less access to training and development programs. Managers' stereotypes can make things worse: at many of the firms studied, male managers often assumed that a woman with children would not be interested in transfers or

Figure 4.2 The Work That Women Do

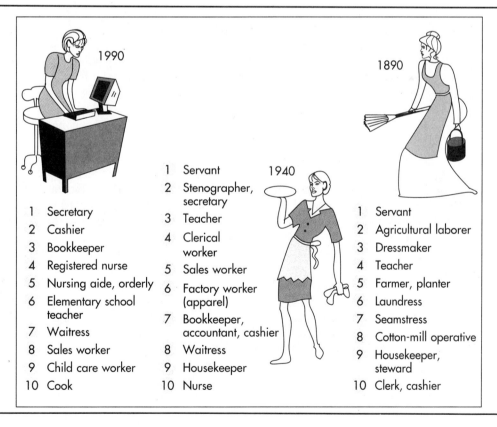

promotions that required longer hours. Executive search firms compound the problem by focusing on white males.

Both male and female professionals believe the best way to improve the situation is for women to continue advancing in their professions. As more women do move into management, they are earning praise for their innovative, motivational management styles.

FLAGSHIP EXPRESS AND THINGS REMEMBERED

➤ Judith Rogala, CEO of Michigan air-freight company, Flagship Express, finds that "the more information people have, the more inspired they are to do good work." In her first month as CEO, Judith set up meetings with employees and their families and established a 24-hour hotline for suggestions and complaints. She never locks her desk drawer, and encourages staffers to read the reports on her desk.

Nadia Ali, southwest district manager for Things Remembered, a gift and engraving store, brought new ideas to her position as well. Nadia found that while half of the customers in her region spoke Spanish, previous managers had tended to hire only English-speaking salespeople. "You don't get the potential out of the business unless you're attuned to your customers," says Nadia. Within 30 days she made conversational Spanish a hiring guideline for new employees and arranged for current employees to take free Spanish lessons. "Corporate [headquarters] had just never thought of it," she notes. Under Nadia's management, district sales have risen 13 percent and fewer employees are leaving. While the company's average turnover rate is 30 percent, in Nadia's region it's only 7 percent.[35] ◄

The Male-Female Wage Gap

American women still earn only 72 cents for every dollar that men earn. This inequity results from two causes. First, women earn less than men in almost every field, even in professions traditionally dominated by females such as nursing and secretarial work. This situation is shown in Figure 4.3. The second reason for the male-female wage gap deals with the concept of comparable worth.

comparable worth
Equal pay for jobs requiring similar levels of education, training, and skills.

Comparable worth means that people should receive equal pay for jobs that require similar levels of education, training, and skills. Comparable worth can be difficult to assess; how do we compare the relative skills involved in totally different jobs? Some measurement systems award employees "points" based on the degree of problem solving, knowledge, and accountability required in a job. For instance, nursing (a predominantly female field) and accounting (a mostly male profession) received similar ratings, but nurses' salaries average only two-thirds of what accountants bring home.

In general, comparable worth has been difficult to prove in court. Workers' salaries are often based on economic factors; jobs for which there is higher demand generally pay more. The court of appeals in the state of Washington allowed an employer to base its pay scale on market rates, even though this resulted in different pay scales for many male and female employees. However, several state governments have adopted comparable-worth systems for their employees.[36] In fact, when Minnesota passed a comparable-worth law, 9,000 of its 29,000 state employees received pay raises!

Figure 4.3   The Gender Wage Gap

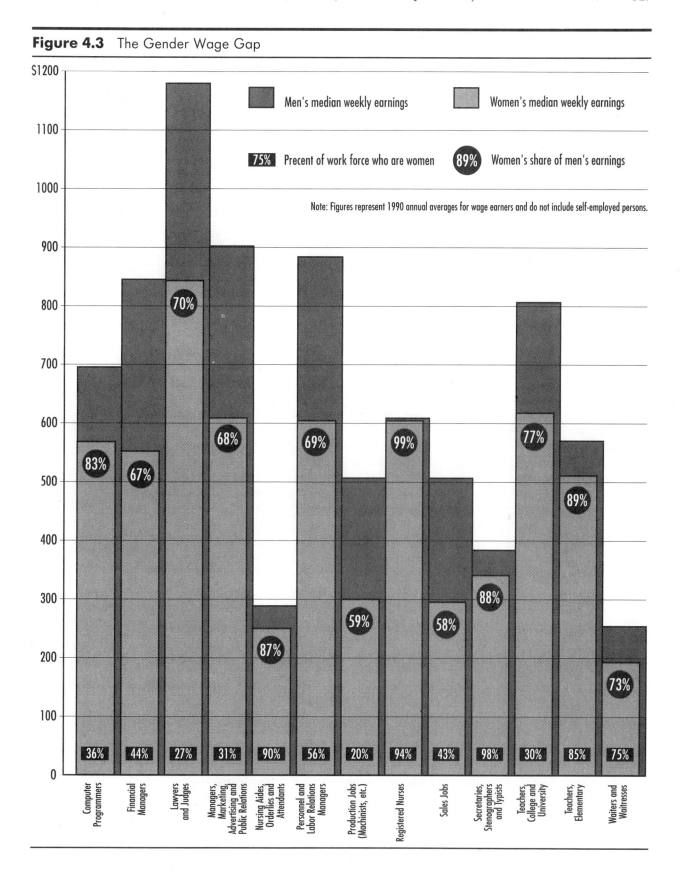

RESPONSIBILITIES TO INVESTORS AND THE FINANCIAL COMMUNITY

There is probably no place where the public expects a higher level of business ethics than in the arena of financial transactions. Just because a business practice is legal doesn't mean that it is also ethical. When it comes to business's responsibilities to investors and the financial community, the public expects behavior that is both legal and ethical.

We will discuss several issues related to business's responsibilities in this area, including honest securities trading, responsible investing, and paying executives a fair salary. As we will see, ethical business behavior is not just something that sounds good on paper. When business does not meet its social responsibilities, it can hurt hundreds or even thousands of people.

Fair Trading

When Michael Irelan was hired to run a new bond trading operation at Boatmen's National Bank in St. Louis, he thought he had it made. Boatmen's wanted to become a bigger player in the Treasury securities market, and Michael was excited about the opportunity.

Four months later Michael was out of a job, having racked up $400,000 in losses on what had seemed a routine, low-risk trade. Unfortunately for him, his first big trade ran up against a "squeeze" in the bond market: a new issue of Treasury notes was in strong demand, but in such limited supply that anyone who bought was forced to pay unusually high prices.

Government investigators found that loose trading practices at Salomon Brothers, a respected financial firm, had allowed the firm to grab more than 90 percent of the Treasury notes during an auction. (The law prohibits any one company from buying more than 35 percent.) Other companies around the country were also hurt by the squeeze. When a Chicago trader called Salomon to complain, a Salomon manager told him, "Our attorneys determined that we are not doing anything wrong."

The government disagreed. Congress began the nation's first public hearings into illegal bond bidding practices. The government accused regulators of having close ties with powerful firms such as Salomon Brothers, and announced plans to overhaul the $2.2-trillion government securities market to prevent similar abuses in the future. Several top executives at Salomon were fired. In an unusual move, the firm announced that it would not award them severance pay or foot the bill for any future legal expenses. Publicity from the bond trading scandal is hitting Salomon where it hurts: its client list. Recently the British government canceled plans for Salomon to act as London's key U.S. underwriter on a $7 billion sale of British Telecommunications shares.

Meanwhile, people around the country are still dealing with the aftermath of Salomon's shady trades. It's estimated that traders and investors lost more than $100 million from the squeeze. Many small trading firms were closed to cut back on operations; some have gone bankrupt. Hickey Securities Inc., a longtime Salomon customer in Chicago, has laid off more than half of its bond traders. In one year, "Our profits are down, we're losing investors, and assets [under management] have gone down from $100 million to $30 million," says president Robert Hickey. Another investment firm lost more than half of its clients in the weeks following the squeeze. Large trading firms in New York and Chicago were flooded with resumes from desperate bond traders who lost their jobs as a result of Salomon's actions.

Like many other people whose lives were affected by Salomon's squeeze, Michael Irelan was astonished by the firm's actions. It is even more difficult for him because he thought he was a personal friend of several Salomon managers who played a key role in the scandal: "My first reaction was shock. I thought I knew them. They seemed like high-quality people. Until the auction, I never had any reason to question their integrity."[37]

Salomon Brothers is not the only financial firm to be accused of unfair trading practices. During the late 1980s several major Wall Street brokers engaged in *insider trading,* in which they made huge profits from trades based on "inside" information. In one sense, of course, all financial firms trade on inside information, since they routinely use rumors and informal data to make business decisions. However, most of this information is available to those who want to find it. Traders such as Ivan Boesky and Michael Milken made millions of dollars by exploiting information to which only they had access. (For more on Michael Milken, see Chapter 5.)

Responsible Investing

If unfair trading practices can hurt hundreds of people, irresponsible investments can hurt millions. By the early 1990s failure rates of banks and savings and loan institutions (S&Ls) were the highest they've been since the 1930s depression. All too often, the reason was too many high-risk investments. The banks used their deposits to finance real estate developers, Third World governments, and corporate leveraged buyouts. When these parties could not repay the loans, the banks went under.

So far the federal government has covered all depositors' losses at failed banks and S&Ls. However, this has meant passing out billions of dollars, and the government agencies that cover the debts are running out of money. Ultimately taxpayers will end up paying for these unwise investments. We will explore the banking crisis in more detail in Chapter 20.

How Much Should Top Executives Earn?

We expect that as workers get promoted, their pay will increase. However, business executives in America are a breed apart; the average CEO (chief executive officer) of a U.S. company earns $2.4 million a year. Executives' pay has risen out of proportion to the rest of the economy. In 1960 the ratio of a CEO's income to that of an average worker was 12 to 1; today, it is 93 to 1![38]

Does a higher income for an executive reflect better performance in his or her company? Not always. A recent study found that while better performance does translate into higher CEO pay, there are other factors involved which make less sense. CEOs working in the New York City area earn an average of 27 percent more than their colleagues in other areas—even in similarly expensive locations like San Francisco and Los Angeles. The number of long-term incentive plans in which the CEO participates (such as stock options) also makes a big difference; on average a top executive's pay increases 28 percent for each incentive plan.

On the other hand, does poor business performance lower executives' pay? The study concluded that there is some relationship between company losses and CEO pay, but not much. If a company's earnings per share drop by 20 percent, CEO pay is still likely to *rise* by 7.6 percent. If earnings go down a whopping 30 percent, CEOs still get a respectable raise of 6.1 percent. It takes more than a 71 percent drop in earnings before CEO compensation actually declines.[39]

BEN & JERRY'S

► Do these statistics make sense? Ben Cohen and Jerry Greenfield do not think so. The two school buddies teamed up in 1977 to start their own business, Ben & Jerry's Homemade, Inc., which today sells more than $100 million of ice cream each year. At Ben & Jerry's Vermont headquarters with 375 employees, there is a 7-to-1 salary ratio that limits top salaries to seven times that earned by the lowest-paid workers.

"We believe that business can be profitable and improve the quality of life for people at the same time," says Cohen. Agrees Greenfield, "Business has an opportunity and a responsibility to be more than just a money-making machine."

What is more, 7.5 percent of the company's yearly pretax profits go to the Ben and Jerry's Foundation, which donates the money to charities. Marketing involves sponsoring peace, music, and art. An ongoing program called the Giraffe Project recognizes people, nominated by their communities, who have been willing to "stick their necks out" to support social causes. One percent of the profits on the company's Peace Pop, an ice cream bar on a stick, go to raise funds for peace. The company also purchases nuts harvested from rapidly disappearing tropical rain forests to make Rainforest Crunch ice cream, and buys brownies made by homeless people to flavor Chocolate Fudge Brownie ice cream and Brownie Bars.

Both Ben and Jerry are excited about the firm's latest initiative: opening a Ben & Jerry's in the Soviet republic of Karelia. Says Jerry, "The whole idea is not to have it be a profit-making venture, but to use the profits from the scoop shop there to help fund cultural exchanges."[40] ◄

SUMMARY OF LEARNING GOALS

1. EXPLAIN THE CONCEPT OF SOCIAL RESPONSIBILITY AS AN ACCEPTED BUSINESS POLICY.
    Social responsibility refers to management's consideration of the social as well as the economic effects of its decisions. It is accepted policy in contemporary business affairs. Business ethics refers to a business person's standards of conduct and moral values. It involves the right and wrong actions that arise in any work environment, as well as a knowledge of the framework within which the decision must be made. Some firms spell out their ethical parameters in formal codes of conduct. Other organizations allow managers to explore the ethical dimensions of decision making through workshops and seminars.

2. DESCRIBE THE RELATIONSHIP BETWEEN SELF-REGULATION AND GOVERNMENT REGULATION.
    History shows that when business fails to respond to social or ethical issues, government may step in. Therefore, self-regulation is in the best interest of the business community.

3. EXPLAIN HOW GOVERNMENT REGULATES BUSINESS.
    Government regulates competition and competitors as well as specific
    business practices. Government regulation of competition became neces-
    sary in the late 1800s, when mergers and monopolies began to cause
    problems in certain industries. This regulation took two broad forms:
    regulation of industry and enactment of laws concerning competition. The
    first act regulating competition was the Sherman Antitrust Act of 1890.
    Since then, other laws have been drafted to further regulate this area.
    Specific business practices are also regulated by government. The law
    affects nearly all facets of business, including forms of business owner-
    ship, small business, human resource management, labor-management
    relations, marketing, production and operations management, computers
    and information systems, accounting, banking, financial management,
    securities markets, international management, business transactions,
    competitive practices, and the environment.

4. DISCUSS THE IMPACT OF DEREGULATION.
    Deregulation, or the elimination of legal restraints on competition, began
    with the Airline Deregulation Act of 1978. Since then, the railroad,
    trucking, banking, and other industries have also experienced deregula-
    tion. This trend has had a significant impact on both the legal and
    economic setting for business. In the air travel industry, for example, it
    has led to the consolidation of many major carriers, as well as the growth
    of commuter lines designed to serve small markets.

5. UNDERSTAND HOW SOCIAL PERFORMANCE CAN BE EVALU-
    ATED.
    Social performance was traditionally measured by such factors as the
    firm's contribution to national output and employment opportunities.
    Today social performance is measured on a broader basis. While no
    generally accepted format has emerged, many companies and industries
    have developed their own measures of social responsibility such as social
    audits. In addition, outside groups may evaluate firms on their social
    performance. The social responsibilities of business can be classified
    according to its relationships to the general public, customers, employees,
    business associates, and investors and the financial community. These
    relationships often stretch beyond national boundaries.

6. OUTLINE BUSINESS'S RESPONSIBILITIES TO THE GENERAL
    PUBLIC.
    The responsibilities of business to the general public include: dealing with
    public health issues, protecting the environment, and developing the
    quality of the work force. Public health issues include smoking, alcohol
    abuse, and educating employees about AIDS. Businesses should also take
    steps to reduce their impact on the environment (working to minimize
    pollution, acid rain, the greenhouse effect, and the destruction of tropical
    rain forests; supporting recycling; and conserving and developing our
    energy resources). Companies must remain alert to changes in environ-
    mental regulations, since the laws can change quickly. It is also important
    to business to develop the quality of its work force, since a well-educated,
    skilled work force is a country's most valuable asset.

7. IDENTIFY BUSINESS'S RESPONSIBILITIES TO CUSTOMERS.
Business's most readily identifiable responsibilities are related to its customers. These responsibilities have been heightened by the consumerism movement, which originated in the 1960s. Most industry and legislative response to this movement has followed John F. Kennedy's statement of consumer rights. These consumer rights were that of safety, to be informed, to choose, and to be heard.

8. DESCRIBE BUSINESS'S RESPONSIBILITIES TO EMPLOYEES.
Relations with employees are some of the most significant social responsibility and ethical issues facing contemporary business. Issues include family leave, equal employment opportunity, sexual harassment, sexism, the male-female wage gap, and managing a culturally diverse work force.

9. EXPLAIN BUSINESS'S RESPONSIBILITIES TO INVESTORS AND THE FINANCIAL COMMUNITY.
There has been considerable publicity in recent years about business's social and ethical responsibilities to investors and the financial community. Important topics include honest securities trading, responsible investing, and paying executives a fair salary.

KEY TERMS

social responsibility 98
business ethics 99
regulated industry 100
tying contract 101
interlocking directorate 101
consent order 101
deregulation 103
social audit 105
ecology 109

maquiladoras 109
pollution 109
greenhouse effect 110
acid rain 110
recycling 111
green marketing 112
conservation 113
consumerism 114
family leave 115

Equal Employment Opportunity Commission (EEOC) 115
affirmative action program 116
multicultural diversity 117
sexual harassment 120
sexism 121
comparable worth 123

REVIEW QUESTIONS

1. What is meant by the terms *social responsibility* and *business ethics?* Cite an example of each. Discuss the current status of social responsibility and business ethics in U.S. industry.
2. Is self-regulation a deterrent to government regulation in matters of social responsibility and business ethics? Why or why not?
3. How does government regulate both competitive and specific business practices? Describe specific regulations with which businesspeople should be familiar.
4. What is meant by deregulation? What are its advantages and disadvantages?

5. Explain the need for internal and external social performance measures in business. What standards can be used for these purposes?
6. What are business's responsibilities to the general public? Cite specific examples.
7. What basic consumer rights were suggested by President Kennedy? How have these suggestions improved the contemporary business environment?
8. What is meant by multicultural diversity? How can the work behavior of different cultural groups be classified?
9. Distinguish between sexual harassment and sexism. Cite examples of each. How can these problems be avoided?
10. What are a firm's responsibilities to its investors and the financial community? Discuss the current issues in this aspect of social responsibility.

DISCUSSION QUESTIONS

1. Speaking to Seattle University's Albers School of Business, President George Bush told the students, "I don't have to tell you the image that many Americans, and many in the press, have of business students. Instead of recognizing that you're learning to help make our economy run better, they've painted a picture of a generation only concerned about quick and easy money. I know that's not true." How can business students prove George Bush is correct, that they are socially responsible and interested in more than just money? Discuss.

2. Respected economist Milton Friedman believes that social responsibility is not really the concern of American business. He says, "There is one and only one social responsibility of business—to use its resources and engage in activities designed to increase its profits so long as it stays within the rules of the game, which is to say, engages in open and free competition, without deception or fraud."[41] Other business scholars argue that companies have the obligation to become involved in social responsibility issues such as those discussed in this chapter. What is your opinion? What arguments do you feel either support or disprove Friedman's position? Explain your answer.

3. Suppose that you own a small company with 12 employees. One of them tells you in confidence that he has just found out he has AIDS. You know that health care for AIDS patients can be disastrously high, and this could drastically raise the health insurance premiums that your other employees must pay. What are your responsibilities to this employee? To the rest of your staff? Explain.

4. Describe the major societal and ethical issues facing the following:
    a. Automobile manufacturers
    b. Real estate developers
    c. Detergent manufacturers

  d. Drug companies selling products used to treat AIDS
  e. Managers of stockbrokerage firms

5. Top CEOs average less than half of what the New York Mets pay outfielder Bobby Bonilla. Are CEOs overpaid? Underpaid? What factors should determine what a person gets paid?

Glossary of Important Literary Terms

action: the events that take place in a story. "Action" covers everything that happens in a story, from a character's thoughts to his or her interactions with other characters. The arrangement of the action is called plot.

allusion: a reference to a person, place, event, literary work, etc. Writers generally use allusions to make their own meaning clearer or to prove a point. For example, Auden, in "Musée des Beaux Arts," makes an allusion to the painting "Landscape with the Fall of Icarus" in order to support his point.

ambiguity: a word, line, event, etc., that can be interpreted in more than one way. The title of Faulkner's story, "A Rose for Emily," can be interpreted in different ways and is thus ambiguous.

analogy: a comparison in which one thing is compared to another in order to clarify meaning or defend a point. In "Death and Justice," Koch makes an analogy between the death penalty and treatments for cancer. His point is that the death penalty may seem harsh as, say, chemotherapy is harsh, but both are necessary to correct problems.

climax: in a story or play, the point at which major change occurs in a character or in the action. This change affects the remainder of the story or play.

conflict: in literature, a struggle between forces: character against character; character against nature; character against society; or character against internal forces. In Brush's "Birthday Party," the conflict is between characters; in Piercy's "Barbie Doll," the main character is in conflict with the expectations of the society in which she lives.

connotation: the meaning associated with a word that goes beyond a dictionary definition. The words "woman," "lady," and "dame" all literally refer to a female, but they have different connotations.

denotation: the dictionary definition of a word.

foil: a character who stands in direct contrast to another character. Through this contrast, the qualities of both characters are easier to see. In Mason's "Shiloh," Leroy and Norma Jean are foils to each other.

foreshadowing: a hint of something that will follow. In O'Connor's "Revelation," Mary Grace's angry looks at Mrs. Turpin foreshadow the violence that occurs later.

genre: "kind" or "type"; some genres of literature are poetry, fiction, and essay.

hyperbole: an exaggeration used for emphasis. Hyperboles are common in everyday speech, such as "I have a million things to do."

image: a mental picture or an association created by a word or group of words. In Thurber's "The Catbird Seat," it is said that Mr. Martin "squirmed slightly." The word "squirmed" reminds us of a worm. In one sense, Mr. Martin is a "worm."

imagery: a group of related images. There are many images of decay in Faulkner's "A Rose for Emily." Thus one speaks of the "decay imagery" in the story.

irony: a conflict between what seems to be and what is, or between what should be and what is. Three types of irony are verbal, situational, and dramatic. Verbal irony is created when one says the opposite of what one means. Situational irony is created when something happens that is the opposite of what one would expect to happen. Dramatic irony is created when the reader knows more than a character knows. In Piercy's "Barbie Doll," the statement is made, "To every woman a happy ending," an example of verbal irony. (The ending has not been happy.) Situational irony is seen in Robinson's "Richard Cory." The character Richard Cory seems to have everything, yet he kills himself. An example of dramatic irony is seen in Porter's "He," in which the reader understands more about Mrs. Whipple's feelings than she does.

metaphor: a literary comparison. Metaphor involves calling one thing another: "he was a lion in battle." In this example, "he" is called a "lion"; however, the comparison is between the qualities of this person and the qualities of a lion. We think of such qualities as courage, strength, determination; thus the person was strong and brave in battle and stuck with the fight. A metaphor may be considered in terms of its two parts, the vehicle and tenor. The vehicle is the concrete image that is presented to the reader; the tenor is the idea or concept that is represented by the vehicle. In Hughes' "Mother to Son," the concrete image presented is that of a stairway (the vehicle); the stairway represents life (the tenor).

motivation: why a character behaves a certain way. In some stories, character motivation is the central issue. In Brush's "Birthday Party," the central question is "Why does the husband behave the way he does?"

narrative: the name given to a piece of writing that tells a story; the word also refers to the story itself.

narrator: the person telling a story. A narrator who is involved in the action of the story should be treated as a character, and his or her attitudes and traits should be examined.

personification: a literary device in which human characteristics are given to a thing or an animal. In Kennedy's "In a Prominent Bar in Secaucus One Day," time is personified: "When time takes you out for a spin in his car, . . ."

plot: the structure of the events of a story. The writer may arrange the events in the order that they occurred (as in "The Lottery"), or the writer may move back and forth in time (as in "A Rose for Emily"). The reader should distinguish between plot and theme.

point of view: the vantage point from which a story is told. A story may be told from a first-person point of view in which someone who is personally involved in the story tells it (as in "I Stand Here Ironing"). A story may be told from third-person point of view. This point of view may be *objective*, in which case the reader is given only those events that are observable ("The Lottery"); or *limited*, in which case the reader is allowed into the mind of one central character ("He"); or *omniscient*, in which case the reader is allowed into the minds of all or several of the characters.

satire: a form of writing that ridicules or makes fun of some situation, person, or human weakness. Some satiric writing only gently ridicules its subject; other satiric writing is harsh or bitter. Satire frequently uses verbal irony. See Auden's "The Unknown Citizen" for an example of satire.

setting: the time and place of the action of a story. "Time" may be as specific as a particular hour of a particular day, or it may be as vague as, say, the nineteenth century or "sometime in the fifties." "Place" may be as specific as a particular room in a house or a particular house in a town, or it may be as vague as the United States or "somewhere in the West." In some pieces, setting plays a more important role than in others. Setting in "The Lottery" and "A Rose for Emily" is very important in shaping the meaning of the story. In other pieces, such as "The Catbird Seat" and "I Stand Here Ironing," setting is relatively unimportant in shaping the meaning of the story. The reader should consider the effects of setting on such things as character, action, and tone.

simile: a literary comparison using "like" or "as." Thus "He was like a lion in battle" is considered a simile, whereas "He was a lion in battle" is considered a metaphor. The function of a simile, as with a metaphor, is to explain something by comparing it to something else. The reader's job is to see what is being said about something through the use of simile. See Hughes' "Harlem," a poem developed chiefly through the use of similes.

symbol: something that represents something else. Like a metaphor, a symbol involves a comparison: what is used as a symbol has something in common with the thing it represents. Thus a lamb may be a symbol for human qualities such as meekness, since lambs are generally meek creatures. Characters in a piece of writing may be symbols or may be considered symbolic of certain human qualities or conditions. An elderly character such as Old Man Warner in "The Lottery," for example, is a symbol for all people who resist change. (Usually elderly people are more resistant to change.) Action also may be symbolic. In "Shiloh," Norma Jean is concerned with improving her body through exercise; this is symbolic of her desire to be emotionally and intellectually stronger.

theme: the main idea or the "point" of a poem, short story, play, etc. A piece of literature may have more than one theme, or the theme may be seen differently by different readers. With some pieces of literature, one can make a neat statement of theme; with other more complex pieces, it is better to talk about the main issues or question raised, since the meaning is likely, as Flannery O'Connor notes, to "go on expanding for the reader the more he thinks about it." Theme should be distinguished from plot. In "The Lottery," for example, the plot consists of townspeople gathering together and holding a lottery. The theme, however is not about lotteries or what happens in them. The theme is a statement about people in general or about human nature.

thesis: the main idea or the point that the writer is arguing. The term *thesis* may be applied to any type of writing but is always used to describe the main idea of essays.

tone: an expression of the writer's attitude. In speech, our attitudes are frequently shown by our "tone of voice"; in writing, tone is shown by such features as description of people, places, and events. Some words that describe tone in writing are "approving," "cheerful," "sarcastic," "angry," and "bitter." The tone of "Dulce et Decorum Est" could be described as "bitter," reflecting the poet's resentment toward those who glorify war.

Credits

Photo

Part Openers
Ralph Fasanell, *The Great Strike—Lawrence 1912*, 1978, 65 x 118, Oil on canvas.

Part I: Poetry
(Page 16) Patrimoine Des Musées Royaux Des Beaux-Arts, Bruxelles
(Page 23) Leah McCraney

Part II: Fiction
(Page 127) © John McGinn/Photo Options

Part III: Essays
(Page 179) Leah McCraney

Part IV: Textbook Chapters

"Introduction," from *Biology*, Fifth Edition by Karen Arms and Pamela S. Camp

Figure 1-2a	Biophoto Associates
Figure 1-2b	Pam and Bill Camp
Figure 1-2c	Pam and Bill Camp
Figure 1-2d	Pam and Bill Camp
Figure 1-3	© Carl Roessler/Animals Animals
Figure 1-9	© Keith Brown
Figure 1-10a	© Paul Feeney
Figure 1-10b	© Paul Feeney
Figure 1-12	NASA
Figure 1-13	Bettmann Archives

"The Presidency in Crisis," from *The American Past: A Survey of American History*, by Joseph R. Conlin

5	UPI/Bettmann
6	UPI/Bettmann Newsphotos
7	UPI/Bettmann Newsphotos
8	Wide World Photos

"Social Responsibility and Business Ethics," from *Contemporary Business*, Seventh Edition, by Louis E. Boone and David L. Kurtz

9	Courtesy of Chemical Waste Management, Inc.
10	© Miller Brewing Company
11	© Dudley Reed/Onyx

Literary

Woody Allen, "The Kugelmass Episode" from *Side Effects* by Woody Allen. Copyright © 1977 by Woody Allen. Reprinted by permission of Random House, Inc.

Excerpts from Karen Arms and Pamela S. Camp, *Biology*, Fourth Edition. Copyright © 1995 by Saunders College Publishing. Reproduced by permission of the publisher.

W. H. Auden, "Musée des Beaux Arts," and "The Unknown Citizen" from *W. H. Auden: Collected Poems*, edited by Edward Mendelson. Copyright © 1976 by Edward Mendelson, William Meredith, and Monroe K. Spears, Executors of the Estate of W. H. Auden. Reprinted by permission of Random House, Inc.

Ronald Bailey, "Seven Doomsday Myths About the Environment" from *The Futurist* 29, Jan/Feb 1995, pp. 14–18. Reprinted by permission of *The Futurist*, World Future Society, Bethesda, Maryland.

Kristine Batey, "Lot's Wife." Copyright © 1978 by *Jam To Day*. Reprinted by permission.

Excerpts from Louis E. Boone and David L. Kurtz, *Contemporary Business*, Seventh Edition. Copyright © 1993 by The Dryden Press. Reprinted by permission of the publisher.

Ray Bradbury, "The Veldt" from *The Saturday Evening Post*. Copyright © 1950, renewed 1978 by Ray Bradbury. Reprinted by permission of Don Congdon Associates, Inc.

Lester Brown, Christopher Flavin and Sandra Postel, "A Planet in Jeopardy" from *The Futurist*, May/June 1992, pp. 10–14. Reprinted by permission from *The Futurist*, World Future Society, Bethesda, Maryland.

Katharine Brush, "Birthday Party" from *The New Yorker*, March 16, 1946. Reprinted by permission of The New Yorker.

Stephen Chapman, "The Prisoner's Dilemma" from *The New Republic*, March 8, 1980. Reprinted by permission.

Joseph R. Conlin, "The Presidency in Crisis" from *The American Past: A Survey of American History*, Fourth Edition, copyright © 1993 by Harcourt Brace & Company, reprinted by permission of the publisher.

Rita Dove, "Daystar" from *Thomas and Beulah*, Carnegie-Mellon University Press, © 1986 by Rita Dove. Reprinted by permission of the author.

Andre Dubus, "Fat Girl" from *Adultery & Other Choices* by Andre Dubus. Copyright © 1977 by Andre Dubus. Reprinted by permission of David R. Godine, Publisher.

Stanley Eitzen, "Violent Crime: Myths, Facts, and Solutions" from *Vital Speeches of the Day*, 61, May 15, 1995, pp. 469–72. Reprinted by permission of Vital Speeches of the Day.

William Faulkner, "A Rose for Emily" from *The Collected Stories of William Faulkner* by William Faulkner. Copyright © 1930 and renewed 1958 by William Faulkner. Reprinted by permission of Random House, Inc.

Marc Feigen Fasteau, "Friendships among Men" in The Male Machine, 1974, pp. 6–19. Reprinted by permission of The McGraw-Hill Companies.

Figure, "The Work That Women Do," adapted from "P. S., How Much Further Do Women Have to Go?" in *Fortune*, September 23. Copyright © 1991 Time Inc. All rights reserved. Reprinted by permission. Illustration by Allison Seiffer. Reprinted by permission of Allison Seiffer.

Carlos Flores, "Smeltertown," first published in *Rio Grande Review*. Copyright © 1987 by and reprinted by permission of Carlos Flores.

Robert Frost, "Mending Wall" and "The Road Not Taken" from *The Poetry of Robert Frost*, edited by Edward Connery Lathem. Copyright © 1916, 1930 by Holt, Rinehart & Winston, renewed 1944, 1958 by Robert Frost. Reprinted by permission of Henry Holt & Company, Inc. (NY).

Excerpt from "Genesis 19:12–26" in The New English Bible. Copyright © 1961 Oxford University Press.

Nikki Giovanni, "Once a Lady Told Me" from *The Women and the Men*. Copyright © 1970, 74, 75 by Nikki Giovanni. By permission of William Morrow & Company, Inc.

Dick Gregory, "Shame" from *Nigger: An Autobiography* by Dick Gregory. Copyright © 1964 by Dick Gregory Enterprises, Inc. Used by permission of Dutton Signet, a division of Penguin Books USA, Inc.

Robert Hayden, "Those Winter Sundays" from *Angle of Ascent: New and Selected Poems* by Robert Hayden. Copyright © 1966 by Robert Hayden. Reprinted by permission of Liveright Publishing Corporation.

Index